Peter Snoad psn

28, 52, 76, 103,

= Check: Randy's speech — jammed the system?
"impossible lto

Draft lottery — regular draft —
level is play → fair — ~~fixed~~
add to Forward's speech re "bias" in the
draft

confirm?

162

RESISTER

RESISTER

A Story of Protest and Prison
during the Vietnam War

Bruce Dancis

Cornell University Press
Ithaca and London

Acknowledgment is made for permission to reprint lyrics from the
following songs: "Blowin' in the Wind" by Bob Dylan, Copyright © 1962
by Warner Bros. Inc.; renewed 1990 by Special Rider Music; "It's Alright
Ma (I'm Only Bleeding)" by Bob Dylan, Copyright © 1965 by Warner
Bros. Inc.; renewed 1993 by Special Rider Music, and "Tombstone Blues"
by Bob Dylan, Copyright © 1965 by Warner Bros. Inc.; renewed 1993 by
Special Rider Music.

First published 2014 by Cornell University Press

Printed in the United States of America

Library of Congress Cataloging-in-Publication Data
Dancis, Bruce, author.
   Resister: a story of protest and prison during the Vietnam
War / Bruce Dancis.
      pages cm
   Includes bibliographical references and index.
   ISBN 978-0-8014-5242-0 (cloth: alk. paper)
   1. Dancis, Bruce. 2. Vietnam War, 1961–1975—Draft resisters—United
States—Biography. 3. Draft resisters—United States—Biography.
4. Political prisoners—United States—Biography. 5. Vietnam War,
1961–1975—Protest movements—United States. I. Title.
   DS559.8.D7D36   2014
   959.704′38—dc23   2013021199

Cornell University Press strives to use environmentally responsible
suppliers and materials to the fullest extent possible in the publishing
of its books. Such materials include vegetable-based, low-VOC inks
and acid-free papers that are recycled, totally chlorine-free, or partly
composed of nonwood fibers. For further information, visit our website
at www.cornellpress.cornell.edu.

Cloth printing   10 9 8 7 6 5 4 3 2 1

Contents

PART THREE: FEDERAL PRISON

PART FOUR: EPILOGUE

RESISTER

Introduction

On December 14, 1966, at the age of eighteen, I stood before a crowd of three hundred people at Cornell University, read a statement denouncing the war in Vietnam and the draft, and tore my draft card into four pieces. I then walked over to a nearby mailbox and sent my statement and the four pieces of my card to my draft board in the Bronx, New York, informing the Selective Service System I would not fight in Vietnam and would no longer cooperate with the draft in any shape or form. I expected to be arrested on the spot.

I was one of the twenty-seven million American men who came of draft age during the Vietnam War. I was also one of the twenty-five million American men who did not fight in that war. But unlike most of those in my age group who did not go to Vietnam, I made a stand against the war and the draft that was public, dramatic, and irrevocable. I became part of a tiny minority of young men—an estimated three thousand—who went to federal prison instead.

It is generally recognized today, as it was then, that avoiding combat in what became the most unpopular war in our country's history was an attainable goal for everyone, except perhaps for those who were either too poor or too poorly educated to find an alternative. The Selective Service System provided many means of staying out of the war.

Joining the Reserves or the National Guard was one way to avoid going to Vietnam, but it often helped to be well connected politically to get into either. (Unlike the recent wars in Iraq and Afghanistan, most members of the Reserves during the Vietnam War remained in the United States.) Deferments for marriage, fatherhood, and economic hardship provided exemption from military service for many, while millions attending colleges, graduate schools, divinity schools, or professional schools received student deferments. Even those without deferments were often able to manipulate the draft system by failing their physical examinations, feigning homosexuality, or just making nuisances of themselves.

Conscientious objector status, which allowed those who held religious objections to participating in war to perform alternative service in lieu of joining the military, was also available to some. Moving to Canada was another possibility, as obtaining "landed immigrant status" in that country eliminated the prospect of being extradited back to the United States. Some draft-eligible men simply failed to register for the draft or ignored their induction orders, their files and cases lost in the bureaucratic mess of the Selective Service System.

It wasn't just war opponents who didn't want to fight in Vietnam. The list of pro-war politicians of the appropriate age who avoided going to Vietnam is lengthy. It includes President George W. Bush (student deferment and Texas Air National Guard), Vice President Dick Cheney (five student and marriage deferments), presidential candidate Mitt Romney (student and ministerial deferments), Speaker of the House Newt Gingrich (student and marital deferments), political adviser Karl Rove (student deferment), radio talk show host Rush Limbaugh (4-F because of a pilonidal cyst), and Fox News host Bill O'Reilly (student deferment).

Although political-satirist-turned-U.S.-senator Al Franken and others have used the derogatory term "chicken hawks" to describe the hypocrisy of these gung-ho types who artfully avoided fighting in a war they wholeheartedly endorsed, I disagree with impugning their courage—even though many pro-war politicians have slandered the honor of those of us who refused to kill. I believed then, and still do today, that no American should have fought in Vietnam.

I chose none of those alternatives to the draft, and became a draft resister. (Some have inaccurately called men like me "draft dodgers," instead of draft resisters. While many of my contemporaries avoided or dodged the draft through deferments and exemptions, I rejected a student deferment and openly defied the Selective Service System.) A few months after destroying my draft card, I began organizing other young men to do the same. Before my nineteenth birthday I had become a leader in the largest movement against the draft in the history of the United States since the Civil War.

During the Vietnam era, only about three thousand men—out of the twenty-five million men who did not serve in Vietnam—were sentenced to prison terms for draft offenses. Those three thousand included nonpolitical draft offenders and members of religious groups like the Jehovah's Witnesses. A much smaller group was the political, or intentional, draft resisters like me—those who openly tied our opposition to the war in Vietnam to refusing deferments, taking such provocative actions as destroying or turning in our draft cards, or refusing induction. Since some judges suspended the sentences of resisters or allowed convicted offenders to go free after serving a minimal amount of time in local jails, only a small group of draft resisters actually spent time in federal prisons.

I was prosecuted by the United States government for willfully destroying my Selective Service certificate. I also refused induction into the military, but I was not prosecuted for that federal offense. I was tried and convicted in a federal court and given an indeterminate sentence of up to six years in prison. In a country that does not recognize political prisoners, I, like other draft re-sisters, was placed within the general inmate population in a federal prison—in my case, a prison in Ashland, Kentucky. After more than nineteen months of incarceration, in late December 1970 I received a parole.

In addition to organizing resistance to the draft, I was part of the radical student movement at Cornell University as a member, president, and cochair-man of the campus chapter of Students for a Democratic Society (SDS), the leading New Left organization of the 1960s. By the 1968–69 academic year, the Cornell chapter had become one of the largest and most active in SDS. My activities landed me on the FBI's Security Index, Agitator Index, and (I'm not making this up) Rabble Rouser Index.

In this book I look back at what happened during those turbulent years and the circumstances leading to my involvement in the social movements of the era. Like many other young people coming of age in the 1960s, I reacted to developments in the unstable world in which I was growing up.

As a high school student, I was driven to repulsion and anger over the violence inflicted upon civil rights workers and demonstrators in the South, leading me to take my first, tentative steps as an activist in support of civil rights. To this day, my personal heroes are the courageous people who risked their lives in the American South to right the wrongs left by centuries of rac-ism and discrimination. They taught me about the necessity of putting your own body on the line when confronting evil.

As I got older, my horror and fury over the American bombs and napalm raining down on the people of Vietnam affected me deeply, as did the ever-growing number of young Americans killed and wounded in the war.

We have all heard the story of a Vietnam veteran returning home in uni-form, only to be spat upon by an antiwar demonstrator. I never witnessed or read any plausible account of such an occurrence. In his book *The Spit-ting Image: Myth, Memory, and the Legacy of Vietnam*, the sociologist Jerry Lembcke debunks the myth of the "spat-upon veteran" and finds its ori-gins in an effort by the Nixon administration to undermine support for the antiwar movement. That doesn't mean it never happened, but such an action would have been contrary to what most of us in the antiwar movement believed. We weren't anti-GI; we were anti–U.S. policy. We wanted to save the lives of American soldiers—and Vietnamese soldiers and civilians—by ending the war and the bloodshed. It should never be forgotten that as the war dragged on, more and more Vietnam veterans joined the ranks of the antiwar movement.

It may be a surprise to readers, coming from an organizer of the first mass draft card burning during the war in Vietnam, that I never supported burning the American flag. Setting the flag on fire struck me as counterproductive. The sight of the stars and stripes going up in flames invariably garnered the most press attention at any antiwar march or rally—particularly from photographers—and enabled the media to ignore the message we were trying to communicate. I always suspected that many flag burners were agent provocateurs.

In contrast, I found few people who had the same kind of protective feeling over a draft card. If anything, draft cards were increasingly seen by young men as symbols of oppression. Yes, burning a draft card was a provocative action, but it made a statement that was quite different from burning the flag.

My experiences raised questions, then and now. Did the illegal actions of the draft resistance movement help build the movement seeking an end to the war in Vietnam? And did that antiwar movement contribute to the eventual ending of the war, or at least in constraining the efforts of the Johnson, Nixon, and Ford administrations to wage it?

This memoir also presents a brief account of my growing up in a secular Jewish home in New York City during the 1950s and early '60s, and encountering racism and anti-Semitism in the heart of the Bronx. I will examine the impact of my home life and the milieu of socialist cooperatives and progressive summer camps on my participation in the civil rights and antiwar movements.

Do We Need Another Book on the '60s?

I first began to reflect on those years in the early 1970s, when I wrote some essays and gave guest lectures on the New Left in a friend's class at the University of California, Santa Cruz. I was also involved in political movements during the '70s and '80s that tried to learn from our past mistakes.

But I gradually began to think less about the '60s, largely because I felt my life's work should not revolve around the activities I was involved in when I was seventeen to twenty-two years old. I also did not want to continually reference what I did on December 14, 1966, and the ramifications of that action on the rest of my life.

I turned toward pursuing a career and raising a family. My studies as an undergraduate at the University of California, Santa Cruz, and as a PhD candidate in American history at Stanford University in the 1970s carried me further back in time than the 1960s. After leaving graduate school with a master's degree but without finishing my doctoral dissertation, I became a journalist. I eventually switched my focus to entertainment—writing, with a political and social edge, about rock and reggae music and movies. In addition to working as a freelance writer, I became the entertainment editor at the *Daily Californian*, the *San Francisco Bay Guardian*, and the *Oakland Tribune*, and the managing editor of *Mother Jones* magazine before spending eighteen years at the *Sacramento Bee*, sixteen of them as the newspaper's arts and entertainment editor.

My desire to return to writing about the Vietnam War and draft resistance came about during the 2004 presidential campaign, in part out of my dismay over Democratic candidate John Kerry's downplaying of his important involvement in Vietnam Veterans against the War. But I was dissuaded from doing so by the *Bee*'s executive editor, Rick Rodriguez. Rick felt that as an editor and member of the *Bee*'s management, I should not be expressing my personal opinions about the presidential race, and I accepted his decision.

I also had a family to nurture. My life as a husband and father and stepfather for four children brought me greater responsibilities, along with irreplaceable love and joy. But I did not have the time to embark on a project as all-consuming as researching and writing a book.

By late 2008, much of this had changed. My kids were all grown up. With the state of newspapers and the fortunes of print journalists declining rapidly, I took a buyout from the *Sacramento Bee*. While I remained a journalist, writing a weekly column on DVDs that was distributed by two newspaper syndicates, I had the freedom to take on other projects. My wife, Karen Dean-Dancis, strongly encouraged me to write a memoir about my days as a draft resister.

As I began to look into the matter, I discovered that very little had been written by either scholars or Vietnam-era draft resisters about the experiences of resisters in federal prisons. David Miller, a Catholic pacifist and the first man to burn his draft card after such actions were made illegal by Congress, devotes a chapter of his memoir to his time in federal prisons in Allenwood and Lewisburg, Pennsylvania.

More pertinent to my own experience is the activism of David Harris, perhaps the second-most-prominent draft resister of the era (after heavyweight boxing champ Muhammad Ali) and the author of several books on the war in Vietnam, draft resistance, and prison. Like me, he was a student radical (at Stanford) before becoming an antiwar and draft resistance organizer.

Yet one size does not fit all when it comes to draft resisters—and David Harris is quite tall, while I'm a little guy. He is from the West Coast, and I grew up in New York. He remained a believer in nonviolence and the tactic of draft card turn-ins longer than I did. He was antagonistic to SDS in Northern California, while I was active in the organization in upstate New York and nationally. He went to prison in the Southwest, and I was imprisoned in Kentucky. He was married to Joan Baez, the most famous female folksinger in the world, and I wasn't (though my wife Karen does have a beautiful singing voice). Our experiences were dissimilar, and we have different stories to tell.

The same goes for many of the histories of SDS, which tend to emphasize the twists and turns of policies emanating from the organization's National Office in Chicago. Yet SDS, more than most groups on the left, was decentralized and often dysfunctional as a national organization. When an SDS national convention or one of the quarterly National Council meetings adopted a program, many local chapters didn't follow through on them. The history of SDS is actually the story of hundreds of different chapters, yet little has been written from the perspective of these local chapters—with the exception of Columbia University SDS, whose members generated massive national attention in the spring of 1968 by occupying campus buildings, holding a student strike, and suffering significant injuries at the hands of the New York Police Department.

From November 1965 through May 1969 my life was intertwined with the Cornell chapter of SDS. In addition to opposing the war in Vietnam and the draft, we conducted vigorous campaigns around Cornell's institutional support for South African apartheid and the university's role in the creation of an overcrowded housing market in Ithaca, New York. I was deeply involved in the events of the spring of 1969 at Cornell, which attracted national attention when black students fighting to build a black studies center seized the campus student union, armed themselves in self-defense after an attack, and gained the support of thousands of white students, led by SDS. The Cornell chapter remained an effective organization during 1968 and the first five months of 1969, while the national organization and many local chapters were being consumed in factional conflicts. In some important ways, the history of Cornell SDS challenges, or at least adds some nuance to, the conventional narrative about the breakup of SDS.

Are There Lessons to Be Learned?

I am not presumptuous enough to believe that the story of my activism and resistance, and its successes and failures, will impart valuable lessons for young people who are today bringing a new commitment to organizing and direct action. For one thing, American society has changed significantly in forty years, and today's challenges differ in many ways from the battles we fought in the '60s. I also believe that having a "presentist" agenda might distort any account of what took place back in those days.

On the other hand, I would be pleased if today's young activists, who have both inspired me and caused me some consternation, learned something useful from this account. At the least, younger readers will find out about organizing in a period before the advent of cell phones, text messages, and the Internet, let alone answering machines, personal computers, and overnight mail.

This book inevitably reflects the evolution of my political beliefs over the nearly five decades that have elapsed since these events took place. While my core values have remained consistent over that long period, changing times and circumstances demand that I adapt to them—including taking a new and critical look at the past. To remain locked into the same viewpoint and ideology I had in the late 1960s might demonstrate steadfastness, but it would also suggest the absence of any new ideas and the ossification of old ones. My attitude toward what I and others did forty years ago has itself changed over the years, and will probably continue to evolve as long as I am able to think.

If I communicate anything in these pages, I hope to convey the youthfulness, audacity, and spirit of those times. While the age of eighteen is not too young to die, or too young to resist the efforts of those who would send young men off to kill and die, at that age I was ill prepared for the task of leading a national antidraft campaign. My fellow resisters and I lacked the organizational skills and financial resources needed to nonviolently combat the awesome might of the U.S. government. Although we received some useful advice and financial and moral support from our elders in the movement and veterans of previous struggles, we were essentially winging it.

But with our youth came a boldness bordering on (and sometimes crossing into) arrogance. If we found no road map showing us how to build an antiwar and antidraft movement, we were also unaware of fearful lessons to be learned. The times demanded action, and worrying about their consequences became secondary. For some, this attitude led toward a recklessness that obscured or negated our purpose and goals. But for others, and I would include myself here, it enabled us to take risks that sharpened the struggle and increased the seriousness of the movement.

Without losing sight of the anguish, disappointment, and confinement that many of us endured in the struggle to end the war, we also had a lot of fun. We were part of a counterculture—its activist left wing, to be sure—that was rebelling not only against our government's foreign policy but also against the values we were expected to gratefully inherit from our parents.

We were objecting to war, poverty, and racism, but also to greed, prudery, uptightness, and decorum.

To college professors expecting submissiveness and fawning appreciation, we offered challenges to both their authority and ideology. In opposition to buttoned-down, crew-cutted bureaucrats, we men preferred T-shirts, jeans, and long hair, while young women rejected makeup and double standards and began to challenge the expectation that they would lead subservient lives to men. While it may be a cliché, it's also true that to a dour and humorless elite drunk on power, we countered with nature's own marijuana and rebellious rock 'n' roll.

And in the face of the largest display of state-sponsored violence in the history of the world, we promoted love and peace, and rebellion, too—laughing, shouting, and struggling all the way.

A General Note on Sources

This is a work of memory and reflection, offering my personal remembrances and opinions about some of the events and personalities of the '60s. But I was trained as a historian and have included references and citations whenever I believe they may prove useful to readers.

My FBI file and Federal Bureau of Prisons file, obtained through the Freedom of Information Act, helped me reconstruct many of the events and actions of those days. The thousands of pages I received were both repetitious and heavily censored—the FBI file, in particular, often included pages in which many or most of the words were blacked out. There were obvious gaps in both files, as well as frequent misinformation. However, if I wanted to know the date of the first Cornell SDS meeting I attended, my FBI file supplied the information—thanks to an undercover agent or informer.

In addition to back issues of the *New York Times,* the *Cornell Daily Sun,* and other publications, the articles, leaflets, memos, movement publications, and letters saved and collected by my friends Felix (formerly Larry) Kramer and Alan Snitow have been very useful. Felix's collection is now housed in the Division of Rare and Manuscript Collections within the Kroch Library in the Cornell University Library, as are the collected papers of former Cornell president James Perkins, radical Catholic priest Daniel Berrigan, and the East Harlem Project sponsored by Cornell United Religious Works. All were helpful in telling this story.

Part One

THE MAKING OF A
DRAFT RESISTER

Chapter One

Boy from the Bronx

SPOTLIGHT: FIRST NIGHT IN FEDERAL PRISON, MAY 29, 1969

"Hey man, where you from?"

It was about midnight during my first night in the federal prison in Ashland, Kentucky, an hour after lights out. An inmate I didn't know was talking to me over the short wall separating our beds.

"I'm from the Bronx, in New York City," I replied. But the other inmate wasn't really interested in my background or my birthplace.

"Hey, let's go to the shitter and fool around," he said while stretching his arm over the wall to touch my head. I may have been the new guy in prison, but it wasn't hard to figure out that he wanted to have sex in a bathroom stall.

I brushed his hand away and told him to fuck off.

He persisted: "Come on, man. If you don't do it with me, some big nigger's gonna get you."

I again said I wasn't interested, that I had a fiancée (yes, that was quite a non sequitur, but I was improvising), and told him to leave me alone. After a couple of minutes, he stopped bothering me. I eventually fell asleep.

I was five feet, seven inches tall and weighed 135 pounds when I entered the (euphemistically named) Federal Youth Center in Ashland, Kentucky, a medium security prison of about five hundred inmates, almost all under thirty years of age. I wasn't bad looking. I had been aware from the first time I seriously thought about resisting the draft that prison offered considerable danger to my physical safety.

Back in the summer of 1966, when I was organizing tenants in East Harlem, I discussed going to prison with a friend, Bob Rivera, who was on the staff of the East Harlem Tenants Council. Bob was very sympathetic with my antiwar and antidraft position but expressed considerable concern about the harm that could befall me in prison.

Even though I was in relatively good shape, I wasn't very big, and it had been years since I had thrown a punch in anger or self-defense. Bob urged me to start lifting weights and take classes in self-defense, but I never found the time.

In his excellent *In the Service of Their Country: War Resisters in Prison*—one of the best books I've read about the experiences of Vietnam-era draft resisters in prison—psychoanalyst Dr. Willard Gaylin discussed why and how resisters were often targeted by sexual predators. Many were smaller and thinner than the average prisoner, had less experience with physical violence and self-defense, and were regarded as easy targets. Even when a resister was able to fight off or avoid sexual attack, "the terror was there the whole time," as one of his subjects told Gaylin.

I knew before I entered prison that I might be subject to sexual pressure. I was ready to fight if I had to. I made it through the first night in Ashland unscathed. But what about tomorrow?

I was a long way from the Bronx.

A Very Large Neighborhood

My maternal grandfather Harry Schachner used to joke about an old crony who visited him at his new apartment in the Bronx near the end of World War II. Harry, Grandma Esther, and Aunt Eleanor had followed my parents and brother (I wasn't around yet) from Brooklyn to the Bronx, moving to a housing development in the east Bronx known as Parkchester. More than forty-two thousand people resided there, in fifty-one redbrick apartment buildings standing six, seven, and twelve stories high. Spread over 129 acres, Parkchester was the largest apartment complex in the country when it opened in 1940.

Harry, who had been one of the founding members of the Socialist Party of America at the turn of the twentieth century, had invited an old comrade—let's call him Morris—to ride the subway up to the Bronx to check out the family's new digs. Morris took one look at Parkchester's immaculate streets and sidewalks, its freshly cut grass, central oval filled with trees and fountains, playgrounds teeming with kids and stores packed with shoppers, and nearly burst into tears.

"Socialism," Morris intoned with awe, admiration, and joy, "has come in our time."

As laughable as that may sound today (and as narrow a view of "socialism" as it entailed), in the 1940s and '50s outsiders often viewed Parkchester, a for-profit enterprise built and operated by the Metropolitan Life Insurance Company, as an oasis for ordinary folks in the middle of the Bronx. In 1941, the *Christian Science Monitor* called it "Middletown on the Subway." In the same year the *New Republic* praised Parkchester's "carefully selected families of mechanics and truck drivers, or merchants, or minor executives of any nationality or religion."

I was born on May 14, 1948, and raised in this city within a city. And while I had a happy and healthy childhood, Parkchester is where I first learned about anti-Semitism and racial prejudice. It's also where I discovered that a gap existed between what my parents espoused and some of the life choices they made. This was all the more surprising because of their backgrounds as socialists and integrationists.

My parents met in the Young People's Socialist League (YPSL), the youth group of the Socialist Party, in the late 1920s. My mother followed closely in her father's political footsteps, becoming a street-corner orator for the Socialist Party and YPSL while only thirteen years old. All of five feet tall, she would get plopped on top of a box or milk carton by her comrades and start speaking. Whether she was in Union Square or on a sidewalk in their Brooklyn neighborhood, she would always attract crowds of onlookers.

My dad came to socialism without any parental influences, as his father had died when my dad was only five, and his mother was not interested in politics. He joined the socialist movement when he attended New York's City College at night, while holding a full-time day job.

My folks had already known each other for five years in 1933 when they married. My dad had just been elected national secretary of YPSL, and they moved to Chicago, where the Socialist Party's national office was located. A protégé of perennial Socialist presidential candidate Norman Thomas, my father became a member of the party's executive committee and a leader of its pacifist wing. He was also a member of the War Resisters League (WRL) and a conscientious objector during World War II. Dad remained an active socialist-pacifist until 1948, when he left both the Socialist Party and the WRL. He had come to the conclusion that nonviolence could not be effective in resisting ruthless dictators like Adolf Hitler and Joseph Stalin, and that the Socialist Party had lost its relevance.

By the time I was born, the Cold War was raging and anticommunism had become as central to my parents' political views as their critique of capitalism. Their perspective was not only based on Stalin's creation of an authoritarian dictatorship in the Soviet Union. They also had direct experience fighting with American communists, particularly during the early 1930s when the international Communist movement viewed liberals, progressives, and democratic socialists like my parents as "social fascists"—that is, as enemies who were as harmful as capitalists to the true cause of working people.

Years later, when I talked to my mother about her radical past, among her most vivid memories were of communists trying to break up socialist meetings at Brooklyn College in the early '30s, and of the American Communist Party's support for the Hitler-Stalin Pact in 1939. In my father's case, he had been a speaker at a YPSL rally in 1933 at New York's Union Square protesting the rise of fascism in Europe when he and others were heckled by communists who demanded their own speaker. For both of them, working with American communists or communist front groups on any issue or cause was political anathema. Early on, they tried to teach me about the differences between democratic socialism and authoritarian communism.

By the late 1940s they had both turned their attention to raising their family, working (my father as an economist for the New York State Department of Labor and, later, the State Insurance Department, my mother as a social studies teacher at Junior High School 127 and Theodore Roosevelt High School in the Bronx) and organizing for their trade unions (the American Federation of State, County and Municipal Employees and the United Federation of Teachers, respectively).

My mother's involvement in the teachers union provided me with one of my earliest memories of a successful struggle. I watched with pride as she led her fellow teachers at my junior high school in a strike for union recognition. I contributed to the effort by going to school during the strike—as the union advised—and harassing and disrupting the efforts of the scabs who were trying to maintain order.

Although my older brother Doug and I were surrounded by Jewish culture throughout our childhoods, religion was another matter. My mother was a militant atheist. According to family legend, when my grandmother insisted that my uncle Monroe have a bar mitzvah, my mother and grandfather boycotted the service. My father was an agnostic. But my parents wanted their children to have some sort of moral education. So they joined the Ethical Culture Society, a national organization of freethinkers and secular humanists, and sent my brother and me to the society's Sunday school. I spent every Sunday for a decade attending classes about the different religions of the world, the Golden Rule, and leading an ethically and socially responsible life.

Learning about Anti-Semitism

But in the context of Parkchester, which was made up largely of Italians, Irish, and Jews, we were unequivocally Jewish. We Parkchesterites may have all lived in similar apartments in our identical-looking buildings, but there was little melting going on in this urban pot. Most of the Catholic kids went to the local parochial schools, and the Jewish kids went to the local public schools, as did the few Protestant children in the neighborhood.

As for my parents, they were no better at crossing this divide than I was. Our family knew all the Jewish families in our apartment building on East Tremont Avenue, and virtually none of the Catholics. I was a friendly and gregarious kid, and I tended to smile at everybody. But I was puzzled why none of the members of the Irish Catholic family living in the apartment next door to us—neither the parents nor their three older children—ever returned my smiles or hellos when we'd meet in the hallway or the elevator. When I asked my parents about this, they explained that our neighbors did not seem to like Jewish people.

I was only about six at the time and hadn't yet learned about anti-Semitism or the Holocaust, so my parents had to gently clue me in. They also explained that things were getting better in our neighborhood, as my brother, six years older than I was, had to endure taunts of "Christ killer" from Catholic children when he was my age.

Athletically inclined kids like me all played together in the relative harmony of the Parkchester Little League. But in those days of largely unstructured play without parental involvement, the Jewish and Catholic kids were veritable strangers when we encountered each other at local playgrounds. For the most part, we stuck with our own groups and tried to avoid direct contact with the others. The only controversy I remember is when my friends and I entered a basketball tournament, and an opposing team changed our name on the sign-up sheet from the Bengals to the "Koshers."

Apartheid in the Bronx

Parkchester's management could not be blamed for the community's failure to provide a setting for a new era of brotherhood among Jews and Gentiles. But when it came to matters of race, Parkchester and its Met Life owners were guilty of operating an American-style system of apartheid.

For the first twenty-two years of Parkchester's existence (and the first fourteen years of my life), Parkchester excluded black and Puerto Rican families. The only people of color one would ever see in Parkchester were the building custodians and the cleaning women who came into the neighborhood to work for individual families.

My folks were not racists. They were members of the NAACP and contributed money to other civil rights groups like the National Urban League. They treated the black custodian who worked in our building with kindness and respect. They taught me to be against racial prejudice, and through my attendance at the Ethical Culture Sunday school gave me a broader outlook on the goodness and diversity of humanity.

Even the long Sunday drives from our apartment in the Bronx to Central Park West in Manhattan, where the Ethical Culture Society was located, made me more aware of poverty and prejudice. My dad always drove on First and Second Avenues, through East Harlem, before heading over to the West Side of Manhattan. The slum housing of East Harlem ended around Ninety-Sixth Street, where the neighborhood was almost miraculously transformed from dilapidated tenements to luxury apartments, and the inhabitants changed from black and Puerto Rican to white.

Each week gave me a graphic education about the existence of two groups of people—one rich, the other poor; one dark-skinned, the other light-skinned—in our nation of plenty. I wasn't yet a teenager, but I knew in my heart that any society that allowed such poverty and misery to exist while some people lived in luxury was failing. I didn't know much about capitalism and socialism, but I was gaining an understanding of right and wrong.

As a kid I was always calling out my neighborhood friends (all white) whenever they used a racial slur or stereotype. By the time I was a teenager and became more conscious of Parkchester's segregated status, I began asking my parents about the matter. Their explanation was unsatisfactory: they professed their opposition to Met Life's policies and said they wished Parkchester were integrated. But they were not willing to leave a neighborhood that was clean and safe, charged reasonable rents, and was served by good public schools.

Controversy surrounding Met Life's discriminatory policy had been around for years. In 1943, when the company opened its Stuyvesant Town apartment complex in lower Manhattan, its whites-only policy—already in effect in Parkchester—was protested by civil rights advocates. A decade later, protests arose in Parkchester when a group named the Parkchester Committee to End Discrimination in Housing staged a sit-in at Met Life's corporate offices in Manhattan to protest the pending eviction of a black family that had sublet a Parkchester apartment from a sympathetic white family. The protesters were all arrested, as were supporters of the black family when New York police forcefully evicted them the next day. Throughout, Met Life maintained it had no discriminatory policy against any minority groups, even though not a single black or Puerto Rican family had ever been able to rent an apartment in Parkchester.

Eventually, pressure from civil rights groups compelled Met Life to change its policy and begin renting to a small number of minorities. It wasn't until 1968, when New York City's Commission on Human Rights charged Met Life with "deliberate, intentional and systematic" exclusion of blacks and Puerto Ricans from each of its three large properties—Parkchester, Stuyvesant Town, and Peter Cooper Village—that the company began renting to minorities on a much more equitable basis.[1]

Yet my parents never became involved in any public criticism of Met Life. The reason now seems obvious: many of the groups in my parents' political orbit viewed the protesters against Met Life's policies in the 1950s as either communists or "fellow travelers" (communist sympathizers). According to historian Cheryl Lynn Greenberg, the Jewish Labor Committee, the NAACP, the American Jewish Congress, the National Urban League, and the Workmen's Circle—organizations in which my parents were either members or contributors—"all refused to join an effort to integrate housing in Parkchester, because it was spearheaded by, in the JLC's words, a 'Cominform apologist.'"

I don't fault my parents for opposing the evils of communism as practiced in the USSR, Eastern Europe, and China. Early on, they and their fellow socialists recognized that the Bolsheviks had created a police state that murdered dissenters or sent them to the gulags, conducted vicious campaigns against Russia's Jewish population, allied itself (however temporarily) with Hitler, and had turned Eastern Europe into a sea of oppressed satellite nations. Yet their anticommunism also gave my parents and their socialist friends an excuse for inaction in the face of racial discrimination.

When I was a kid, I didn't know anything about this political subtext to my parents' unwillingness to confront Parkchester's prejudicial policies. I also didn't understand the insidiousness of housing segregation in New York—even if one wanted to live in an integrated, middle-class neighborhood, few existed in the 1950s or '60s.

The rise of the civil rights movement in the late '50s and early '60s provided an education about racism and prejudice for me and other young white people. I was a preteen when I first learned about the brave African American college students sitting in at segregated lunch counters in the South. I watched in horror as news reports showed Freedom Riders being beaten by mobs of

---

1. Met Life also owned the much smaller Riverton apartment complex in Harlem, which did rent to minorities and was known as the company's "black property."

angry southern whites when they tried to desegregate interstate bus lines and public accommodations.

Shortly before my fourteenth birthday, in 1962, I went to the movie *Judgment at Nuremberg*. It was the first time I saw footage of the Nazi concentration camps—the death ovens, the piles of dead, naked bodies dumped in large holes in the ground, the emaciated, barely living survivors. I was horrified, of course, by the human suffering, but what also came through was the guilt and complicity of the German people. To me, there was a parallel between the Nazis' barbaric treatment of Jews and the oppression of black people by segregationists in the American South. If the Nuremberg trials taught me anything, it was that decent people had a moral and social responsibility to resist evil. In America in the early 1960s, the faces of that evil were the politicians and policemen trying to maintain segregation.

By 1963, after I watched TV coverage of police in Birmingham, Alabama, turning their dogs and high-pressure hoses on nonviolent protesters—many of them high school kids like me—I had to get involved.

March on Washington

My first action, at fifteen, was taking part in the March on Washington for Jobs and Freedom on August 28, 1963. This was the historic civil rights demonstration that brought more than a quarter of a million people to the nation's capital. I took the train to Washington, D.C., with my aunt Eleanor, a labor mediator and activist.

Once we arrived in Washington and began the long walk from Union Station to the Lincoln Memorial, I was immediately struck by the sheer number of people around us and how cordial everyone was to each other. Perhaps my youthful naïveté was coloring my observations, but it seemed as if the black folks looked proud to be taking part in the protest and pleased that so many whites had joined them. As for the whites, who made up between a quarter and a third of the marchers, they looked the way I felt—happy that other whites had joined the demonstration and honored to be part of such an important event.

The crowd was so enormous—filling the entire area around the reflecting pool between the Lincoln Memorial and the Washington Monument and spreading beneath the nearby trees and over the streets and fields—we never got close enough to the steps of the memorial to see any of the speakers. But we were able to hear the many speakers and entertainers over loudspeakers. Still, it was hard to focus. The singing of Bob Dylan, Joan Baez, and Peter, Paul and Mary and the speeches of civil rights notables like John Lewis of

SNCC (Student Nonviolent Coordinating Committee), Roy Wilkins of the NAACP, and Walter Reuther of the United Auto Workers flew right by me in the sultry heat.

By the time Dr. Martin Luther King Jr., one of the last speakers, was introduced, Eleanor and I had already started our long walk back to the train station. But when he began to talk, we stopped to listen, and I'm glad we did. Although we didn't know at the time that Dr. King's "I Have a Dream" speech would be viewed as one of the greatest orations in American history, we were moved by the power of his rhetoric and the beauty of his vision.

I don't remember much about the train ride back to New York, except that my fellow marchers all seemed pleased with what had taken place, even if many were exhausted from all the walking and standing around in the oppressive Washington heat. We all knew we had just made history.

Civil Rights and Bronx Science

When I returned from Washington and started my junior year at the Bronx High School of Science, I began wearing a civil rights button with an equal sign. This led immediately to an angry clash with Arnold Canell, my very conservative high school English teacher, over its display on my shirt. An excellent teacher, Canell was a cantankerous sort who continually challenged me—not just over civil rights, but on atomic testing, labor unions, the presidential candidacy of Barry Goldwater, and other issues as well. I had to be prepared every day for argument and debate, as I never knew when he would choose to start or provoke a verbal battle with me. More than any teacher I've had, Canell forced me to educate myself so I could represent my position with knowledge and clarity. I owe much to this reactionary teacher for making me a more effective radical, as well as introducing me to some great literature.

Later in high school I joined other Bronx Science students, including my girlfriend, Bonnie Neilan, the student-body president, in a citywide boycott of public schools to protest de facto segregation and inequality in our educational system. I was also a member of Youth for Ethical Action, a project of the Ethical Culture Society, which worked with Friends of SNCC to raise money for the civil rights movement.

In the spring of 1964, SNCC issued a call for "Freedom Summer," where they planned to bring hundreds of white and black college students to the South to help with voter registration and other civil rights organizing. This was the summer in which three civil rights workers—James Chaney, a black Mississippian, and Mickey Schwerner and Andy Goodman, two Jewish guys from New York—were abducted and murdered by the KKK, with the complicity of the local police. Their disappearance in the beginning of the summer drew national attention to the case. The discovery of their bodies at summer's end shed new light on the horrors of Mississippi and gave America three new martyrs to the cause of civil rights.

When I first heard about the plans for Freedom Summer, I wanted to go. My parents wisely talked me out of it. Looking back, it's hard to imagine how a sixteen-year-old New Yorker could have made much of a contribution to the movement in Mississippi.

Yet as much as I still turned to my parents for guidance on matters of politics and conscience, our living in Parkchester forced me to see what I viewed as hypocrisy on the part of two people I had admired unequivocally. I always respected my parents for their humanistic values and the decency with which they treated other people. If they had taught me anything, it was to have a social conscience and to stand up for my beliefs.

But for the first time I had become aware of the disjuncture between what my parents believed and what they did about it.

SPOTLIGHT: FREEDOM RUNNER, MARCH 14–16, 1965

To paraphrase Dr. King, running across the Pulaski Skyway with an unlit torch in my hand was my first real stride toward freedom. It may have been an odd, even strange, way to take part in the civil rights movement, but it was the most serious thing I had yet done in my life.

It was March 14, 1965, and the unlit torch symbolized that the light of freedom had gone out in Selma, Alabama. A week earlier, in the culmination of a series of confrontations between civil rights advocates and local police, Sheriff Jim Clark and his deputies had attacked a group of nonviolent marchers who were attempting to walk across the Edmund Pettus Bridge on their way from Selma to the state capital of Montgomery to demand the right to vote. The shocking images of deputies clubbing, trampling, and teargassing peaceful demonstrators were broadcast around the world and focused attention on the violent means southern whites were still willing to use to suppress the freedom movement. The brutal beating of the marchers sparked protests around the country.

In New York, civil rights groups quickly organized a protest march in Harlem that drew more than fifteen thousand demonstrators. But members of the Harlem chapter of CORE (Congress of Racial

Equality), led by Gladys Harrington, wanted to do more. Along with Ethel George, the head of an antipoverty and anti–juvenile delinquency group in Harlem known as the Adult Volunteer Service Corps, they decided to organize a Freedom Run to carry their protest over the outrages in Selma to the White House.

The idea was for a team of runners, accompanied by three station wagons bearing large signs reading "Freedom Run, New York to Washington, D.C., in Support of the Right to Vote and March in Alabama," to carry the unlit torch over the 230-mile journey along old U.S. Route 1 and deliver it to President Lyndon Johnson.

I was a senior at Bronx Science when I learned about the planned Freedom Run from my friend Eddie Neale. A freshman at Columbia University, Eddie had been my predecessor as cocaptain of the high school track and cross-country team. Bright and poised, with a reserved demeanor that masked his devilish sense of humor, Eddie was one of a tiny group of African American students attending Science in those years.

Although Eddie and I often talked about racism and the civil rights movement, neither of us had done much. But when he learned about the pending Freedom Run, he suggested we both take part in it. We went down to the CORE office in Harlem and signed up for the run, which was scheduled to embark the following evening. Unfortunately, Eddie ended up not being able to go, as he felt he couldn't afford to miss too many classes at Columbia. I, on the other hand, was cruising through my senior year in high school with few cares about my academic performance. My parents reluctantly agreed to let me go.

When I showed up Sunday night on the New York side of the George Washington Bridge, where the runners were gathering, I discovered I was the only white person taking part. And with Eddie not participating, I knew no one among the seventeen other runners and three or four chaperones. But I quickly became friendly with another guy my age, Tony Spencer, who was Gladys Harrington's nephew.

The media was on hand to record our departure at around 9:45 p.m. Two former Olympic gold medalists, John Woodruff and Andy Stanfield, carried the torch in the opening legs across the bridge. Then the rest of us took over.

The plan was for our group of eighteen to run a relay, with each of us running a mile or two while carrying the unlit torch, then handing off the torch to the next runner. Runners would rest in the station wagons between our stints. We tried to run either on the sidewalk or the shoulder, but sometimes the condition of the road required us to run on the street next to the curb. Our crowded station wagons drove slowly nearby, squeezed to the right side of the lane.

I took my first turn in New Jersey shortly after we crossed the George Washington Bridge. Despite the cold and rain, and my wearing only a pair of sweatpants and a new "Freedom Now" sweatshirt, the flush of excitement provided all the warmth I needed during my first two-mile stretch.

But as others in our group took their turns, a problem immediately emerged: even if the spirit was willing, spirit alone could not make a person capable of running for several miles without stopping. It quickly became apparent that among our group, I was the only experienced runner. Fortunately, Tony and one other guy were in good enough shape to run for a mile or two when their turns came. But the others, many of whom were cigarette smokers, couldn't last more than a few hundred yards at a time, despite their good intentions; four ended up dropping out.

Yet the added burden was not a problem. It might have been cold and wet outside, and tightly packed inside our station wagons, but it felt good to stretch out over a mile or two of easy running.

We must have been a strange sight for local police: three station wagons filled with black people (and one white teenager), driving very slowly on the side of Route 1, then stopping to change runners and pass the torch. But for the most part the cops didn't bother us, probably because we quickly left their jurisdiction.

A problem arose as we approached the Pulaski Skyway late Sunday night or in the wee hours of Monday. The skyway, which opened in 1932, is a massive bridge of steel and concrete that rises to 135 feet as it crosses the Hackensack and Passaic Rivers and the New Jersey Meadowlands, connecting Jersey City and Newark. The structure is three and a half miles long, but when the connecting ramps on both sides are added, it stretches out to about five miles.

A cop told our lead car that no stopping was permitted on the skyway, which had neither a sidewalk nor a shoulder on the right. This meant we would not be allowed to pass the torch among our runners. But as long and steep as the skyway may have been, it didn't seem that daunting to me, and I told Gladys I was sure I could run the entire distance by myself. I was used to doing training runs of up to twelve miles.

By this time, the cold rain had turned into snow flurries, and I was shivering as I started the long climb up the eastern side of the skyway. My gaze was straight ahead, and I never looked down to see the water

and ground below. Two of our wagons drove ahead to the end of the
skyway, while one stayed with me, accompanied by a police car. I'm
not sure what the cops were worried about—did they think we would
stage a sit-in on the skyway in the middle of the night?

Maybe I was being carried along by the emotions of the cause, but
the steep climb wasn't all that tiring, and the road soon leveled out for
the main section of the span. By the time I began the long descent
on the Newark side of the bridge, I was almost floating along, taking
long, easy strides. When I reached the end of the skyway, I took my
seat in the car with a great sense of accomplishment.

The rest of the Freedom Run was uneventful. We didn't stir up a lot
of emotions—either positive or negative—as we ran through towns
and cities in New Jersey, Pennsylvania, Delaware, and Maryland.
Someplace outside Philadelphia, a guy yelled "nigger lover" at me. But
we received more applause and honking horns than abuse from the
people we passed.

On Monday night, President Johnson addressed a joint session of
Congress and a national TV audience about the Selma crisis and his
pending voting rights legislation. Johnson referred to the outrages of
Selma as "a turning point in man's unending search for freedom" and
stated that "it is not just Negroes, but really it's all of us, who must
overcome the crippling legacy of bigotry and injustice." He memora-
bly ended his address by saying, "And we shall overcome."

We listened to Johnson's address in our station wagons. While
everyone in my car was pleased to hear the president of the United
States speak so strongly in support of civil rights and voting rights
legislation, no one seemed elated. Too many unfulfilled promises by
politicians had been made in the past, and suspicion remained over
Johnson's commitment to the cause.

Our caravan reached Washington, D.C., late Tuesday afternoon,
March 16. We were met at the southwest gate of the White House by
Clifford Alexander, deputy special assistant to the president and one of
the few blacks among Johnson's aides, and liberal New York congressman William Fitts Ryan. Tony handed the unlit torch to Alexander
and urged him to ask President Johnson to light it and keep the flame
of liberty and freedom burning. Ethel gave Alexander a statement, addressed to Johnson, explaining the purpose and goals of our action.

We were all weary, achy, and wet, but pleased to have finished
what we set out to do. We spent the night as guests of Morgan State
University, a historically black college in Baltimore. Our drive home
Wednesday morning passed quickly—it's a lot faster to ride from

Washington to New York on highways and turnpikes than plodding along on foot.

The Freedom Run had a profound effect on me. No longer was I just making small, mostly verbal, gestures in support of civil rights. To be sure, participating in the Freedom Run was a limited commitment, and not a very dangerous one at that. It was still worlds away from the day-to-day struggles of SNCC organizers in the South. Yet it allowed me to feel the sense of solidarity one gets when acting with others for a common purpose.

Most important, participating in the Freedom Run set me on a path of activism that grew more intense and more serious over the next four years.

Chapter Two

Socialism in Two Summer Communities

While my grandfather's buddy was way off the mark in describing Parkchester as the fulfillment of his "socialist" dream, I actually spent more than two months of every year while I was growing up living in a summer community organized by real socialists.

The Three Arrows Cooperative Society was founded in 1936 by members of the Socialist Party and YPSL. Their goal was to create a summer community based on cooperative principles. The founders sold enough shares to raise $22,500 to purchase 125 acres in Putnam Valley, New York, a rural area in Putnam County only a few miles north of the Westchester County line and the tiny town of Shrub Oak and about fifty miles north of New York City. The parcel of land came with a farmhouse, a barn, and a lake. A prospectus from January 1937 promised "a sanctuary from which the profit system is completely barred." The community's first brochure announced "A Country Home in a Cooperative Colony at Proletarian Prices."

As legend has it, the name "Three Arrows" was adopted out of admiration for the Austrian Socialists who had battled Hitler's fascists in the early 1930s. It was said that the arrows stood for the three wings of the socialist movement: The party, the trade unions, and the cooperatives. Subsequent research has shown that the insignia was first used by German socialists in 1932, who felt they needed their own insignia to rally supporters to fight the Nazis' swastika. It was also the symbol of the Popular Front government of France in the mid-1930s. Over the years, various other meanings have been given to the symbol: the three main principles of the Socialist Party (unity, activism, and discipline); the three pillars of the socialist movement (the party, the unions, and workers' sports clubs); the three enemies of socialism (variously capitalism, fascism, and reaction, and Nazism, communism, and monarchism), and three ways the socialist movement works for a better society (education, agitation, and solidarity). Perhaps it isn't surprising, a friend from Three Arrows once joked, that socialists can't even agree about their own symbols.

All the land at Three Arrows, which remains a thriving community today, is owned cooperatively, but members built and own their houses. In the early years, short money (the Great Depression) and short supplies (World War II) made housing construction impossible for most, so members lived either in the main house or in tents and other makeshift constructions. Once World War II ended, prosperity returned (for most); many of the early members became more affluent, and a construction boom started. That's when my dad and a Shrub Oak carpenter built our small, two-bedroom summer house. Early on, it was decided that the cooperative should not grow larger than seventy-five sites (or houses).

My folks were not among the small cadre of founding fathers and mothers, but by 1941 they were already active members. My dad served multiple terms as the cooperative's president from 1954 through 1959. Throughout its history but especially in its formative years, Three Arrows was built by the cooperative labor of its membership—roads, a water system (including a well, a reservoir, pumps, a filtration plant, and piping), a dock on the lake, a social hall named after Norman Thomas, a co-op store, tennis courts, a softball field, a day camp for kids, and much more. As my father wrote in a twenty-fifth-anniversary reflection on Three Arrows' early years, "In seven years after we came into being, we were a solvent, going concern with greater assets than liabilities, not only in matters of dollars and cents, but in those intangible values that do not lend themselves to monetary measurements."

Culture and Politics

Those intangible values included establishing a vibrant cultural and political life in the community. Every summertime weekend featured both a "schmooze" (a talk on a topic of current political or social interest by a guest speaker or a member, followed by a lively discussion) and a night of entertainment (songs, sketches, culminating in a full-length, Broadway-style Labor Day show) provided by talented and not-so-talented members. During the week, there would be folk dancing, poetry readings, book and play discussion groups, sewing circles, Yiddish classes, crafts, and a lot more. And that was just for the grown-ups.

A highlight of every summer from 1937 until 1967, a year before his death, was the annual visit by Norman Thomas. Many Three Arrows members knew Thomas well, having worked with him within the Socialist Party and on his campaigns for president. (Thomas headed the Socialist ticket in 1928, 1932, 1936, 1940, 1944, and 1948.) When visiting Three Arrows, he would deliver two talks—one in the afternoon to the assembled day campers, the other in the evening to the adults. Even as time went on and fewer and fewer cooperative members retained their Socialist Party affiliation, Thomas remained a hero and inspiration.

During its first several decades, Three Arrows was remarkably homogeneous—its members were overwhelmingly Jewish New Yorkers who had been involved in the socialist or trade union movements. As far as I know, there were no communists in Three Arrows—they would not have survived a vote for membership, given the hatred that still existed in the late '30s, '40s, and '50s between socialists and communists. And there were no minority members in the first generation—due more, perhaps, to the largely white milieu of the Socialist Party and its allied fraternal organizations like the Workmen's Circle than to racial prejudice on the part of the membership. An African American family rented a home in Three Arrows for several summers in the early 1950s and sent their kids to our day camp, but they never joined the cooperative. (It wasn't until my generation, the second generation, grew up and began to intermarry that Three Arrows had its first minority members.)

The cultural and political homogeneity of the place did not mean that Three Arrows avoided strife. Monthly membership meetings were infamously rough, frequently featuring old friends yelling at each other as they debated the most mundane matters. Even though the political leanings of most members were becoming less and less radical as the '40s melted into the '50s and beyond, those who had come to political maturity in the midst of sectarian debates never lost their sectarian combativeness.

There was little turnover in membership at Three Arrows during my childhood, which meant that virtually everyone knew everyone else quite well. There weren't many large families among the members (the Fromowitzes still hold the record, with five children), but there were a lot of us kids. Our day camp peaked at about 150 children and teens in the mid-1950s, divided into various age groups. My "group"—that's what we called them—of about twenty baby boomers born in 1947, '48, and '49 was one of the largest and about evenly divided between boys and girls. Many of us remain members of Three Arrows to this day, so I have a fairly large cohort of friends I've known since as long as I can remember.

The joy of escaping from the hot streets of New York City to what we called "the country" was vividly expressed by Robert Melnick, a professor of landscape architecture at the University of Oregon, and one of my closest

Three Arrows friends since childhood. "As a city boy," he wrote, "I underwent a dramatic transformation each summer, as I left my friends and streets and hard-edged playgrounds the day after school ended in June, only to discover and rediscover the woods and stone walls, and worn paths through the forest that I could traverse at night without a flashlight."

Robert didn't mention the mosquito bites and poison ivy rashes that were the result of walking through those woods at night, but even with their presence I had a great time at Three Arrows throughout my youth. I got to swim, row boats, paddle canoes, make crafts, sing, hike, sleep out under the stars, perform in plays and, most important, play softball, Wiffle ball, and punchball almost every day and evening.

Three Arrows provided me with friendship, heritage, community, and freedom. Surprisingly, given the socialist origins of the cooperative and the erstwhile radical politics of most of its members, the political atmosphere in Three Arrows was far from didactic or doctrinaire. Whether because of greater personal affluence, more family responsibilities, the decline of the Socialist Party, the Cold War, or McCarthyism, by the 1950s most of our parents were less radical than they had been in their young socialist days.

Still, it was impossible not to be affected politically as a youth in Three Arrows. I grew up seeing my parents and my friends' parents take part in cooperative labor and direct, participatory democracy. I was imbued with the shared community values about the rights of unions and the wrongs of prejudice, sang songs from the labor movement, and listened to older brothers and sisters talk about their new experiences on the picket lines and protests of the emerging civil rights and "ban the bomb" movements. Three Arrows' influence on what I became and who I am is incalculable.

SPOTLIGHT: AN EARLY ANTIWAR RALLY, JUNE 8, 1965

The pickets numbered only around a hundred, but their hatred was magnified by their angry faces, angry signs reading "Kill the Commies," and angry chants of "Red, Red, Red." I encountered these right-wing counterdemonstrators—as well as Norman Thomas one more time—just before my high school graduation. Having missed the SDS-sponsored, Washington, D.C., rally against the war in Vietnam two months earlier, I eagerly attended an antiwar rally in New York's Madison Square Garden in early June, sponsored by the National Committee for a Sane Nuclear Policy.

My opposition to U.S. policy in Vietnam began to crystallize, as it did for many others, in February 1965 when President Johnson ordered the bombing of North Vietnam and approved a huge increase in the number of U.S. troops to be sent to South Vietnam. By supporting the South Vietnamese government, we were backing, in the name of freedom, one military dictatorship after another, regimes that brutally suppressed all opposition. Like others, I watched with horror and amazement as TV news footage showed Buddhist monks burning themselves to death in protests against their government.

Given my family background, I distrusted the communist government of North Vietnam, led by Ho Chi Minh. But I had already learned enough about the history of Vietnam to know that Ho had been the leader of a communist-nationalist coalition that had resisted, in succession, French colonialists, Japanese occupiers during World War II, and then the French again after the Japanese were defeated. I also knew the South Vietnamese government had violated the Geneva Accords of 1954 by refusing to hold promised national elections. Former President Dwight Eisenhower wrote that had elections been held throughout Vietnam at the end of the fighting between the French and the Viet Minh, Ho Chi Minh would probably have won 80 percent of the vote.

In 1960, the National Liberation Front (crudely referred to by the U.S. military and the media as the Viet Cong) was formed as a coalition of opposition forces, and the civil war began. The NLF was aligned with North Vietnam against the South Vietnamese government and the United States.

By 1965 the United States and South Vietnamese were conducting the war with apparent disregard for its impact on the civilian population of the South. Just two days before the Madison Square Garden rally, I read a report in the *New York Times* on the consequences of U.S. air strikes on an area in South Vietnam where NLF troops had been operating: "Many Vietnamese—one estimate was as high as 500—were killed by the strikes. The American contention is that they were Viet Cong soldiers. But three out of four patients seeking treatment in a Vietnamese hospital afterward for burns from napalm, or jellied gasoline, were village women."

Unlike the SDS event, which included youthful speakers and had a more radical tone, the New York rally featured the elder opposition. In his speech, Norman Thomas challenged the United States' self-appointed role as the world's policeman. He was joined onstage by professor Hans Morgenthau, pediatrician Dr. Benjamin Spock, Coretta King (the wife of Dr. Martin Luther King Jr.), folksinger Joan Baez, veteran civil rights activist Bayard Rustin, and Senator Wayne Morse, a Democrat from Oregon.

Morse had been one of only two U.S. senators to oppose the Gulf of Tonkin Resolution, the August 1964 measure that passed the Senate following an alleged attack (later proved to have been bogus) by North Vietnamese torpedo boats on a U.S. Navy destroyer. The resolution gave President Johnson the power to "take all necessary measures to repel any armed attacks against the forces of the United States and to prevent further aggression." In his speech, Morse argued that the Johnson administration was concealing the truth about the war from the American people and that the brutal tactics of our government in Vietnam were turning millions of Asians into communists.

The crowd, an inspiring seventeen or eighteen thousand on a weekday night, was also older than at the earlier SDS rally. But I was there with a friend from Bronx Science, and we saw plenty of other college- and high school–age students in attendance.

My father, the former pacifist, was not pleased that I had attended the rally. Dad's opposition to communism was so deep he could not see the problem with the United States backing one South Vietnamese dictatorship or military junta after another—as long as they were fighting the North Vietnamese and the NLF. Still, Dad just as strongly believed I had the right to make my own decisions about politics.

The rally showed me I was part of a growing movement of opposition to U.S. policy in Vietnam. I took special note of a prescient line in Senator Morse's speech, in which he predicted that President Johnson and the U.S. armed forces "will continue to widen and expand this war unless the American people rise up to stop them."

Buck's Rock, Breeding Ground for Teenage Radicals and Counterculturalists

A few years earlier, just as the recently elected president John F. Kennedy was promising a New Frontier for America, in 1961 I had gotten the chance to explore some new territory for myself. When I turned thirteen, my parents agreed with me that I had outgrown the offerings of the Three Arrows day camp, and they were now affluent enough and generous enough to send me to a summer camp geared for teenagers.

Buck's Rock Work Camp in New Milford, Connecticut, was a sleepover summer camp founded in the 1940s by two Montessori-trained Austrian educators, Ernst and Ilsa Bulova, who had fled to the United States to escape the Nazis.

Drawing its thirteen-to-fifteen-year-old clientele from the New York metropolitan area, Buck's Rock offered city and suburban teens a rural experience with its animal farm and vegetable gardens where a camper could actually earn money for his or her labor. (One encounter with a group of pigs whose sty I had been assigned to clean concluded my own farmwork experience.) The camp was best known for its large array of performing and visual arts and crafts programs, as well as sports. There was even a camper-run radio station and a construction crew that built a new structure every summer.

The Bulovas operated Buck's Rock on the principle that teenagers should be able to choose their own activities and schedules, except for meals, bedtimes, and those activities that had to take place at set times.

I attended Buck's Rock for five summers, from 1961 to 1965—three as a camper, followed by a year as a CIT (counselor-in-training) and another summer, between high school graduation and the start of college, as a junior counselor and lifeguard.

Like many privately owned summer camps catering to New Yorkers, Buck's Rock was largely Jewish. It also attracted politically progressive and culturally rebellious campers and counselors. The folk music revival was in its heyday during the early '60s, and at Buck's Rock this meant we received a healthy dose of traditional Americana music, bluegrass, Delta blues, and contemporary protest songs. Well-known folk and blues musicians like Dave Van Ronk and the Reverend Gary Davis made the trip to Connecticut to meet campers, lead workshops, and perform; in earlier years, Pete Seeger had been a visitor to Buck's Rock.

I can't overstate the importance of topical folk songs to my political development. Songs from the civil rights movement played a significant role in rallying activists and maintaining morale, and I was inspired by "Keep Your Eyes on the Prize," "Oh Freedom," "We Shall Not Be Moved," "If You Miss Me at the Back of the Bus," "We Shall Overcome," "We Shall Never Turn Back," and other freedom songs. Although nothing could come close to experiencing the risks and dangers faced every day by civil rights organizers in the South, singing those songs made me feel that I was voicing my own solidarity with the struggle.

The early protest songs of Bob Dylan—"Blowin' in the Wind," "A Hard Rain's a-Gonna Fall," "Only a Pawn in Their Game," "With God on Our Side," "The Times They Are a-Changin'," and "The Lonesome Death of Hattie Carroll"—were also very influential. They articulated my own feelings with eloquence far beyond my scope and provoked me to think about American history and society in new ways. In particular, it was impossible not to be moved by "Blowin' in the Wind," with its demand for individuals to take personal responsibility—"How many times can a man turn his head/And pretend that he just doesn't see?"

One other political song that came out in early 1965 had a profound effect on me—Phil Ochs's "I Ain't Marching Anymore." As Dylan was making his musical transition from folk to rock and the lyrical transition from overtly political material to more introspective, stream-of-consciousness words, Ochs became the leading light of the topical song movement. "I Ain't Marching Anymore" chronicled the legacy of America's wars and openly discussed resistance to the draft.[1]

Happy Traum, Folksinger and Activist

Taking over as Buck's Rock folk music counselor in 1964 was a highly regarded musician, Happy Traum, who later became the editor of the magazine *Sing Out!* and remains a performer and teacher today. As a member of the New World Singers with Gil Turner and Bob Cohen, Happy recorded the first versions of Dylan's "Blowin' in the Wind" and "Don't Think Twice, It's All Right." Dylan also wrote the liner notes for the group's 1963 Atlantic Records album.

I was already playing the jug in a jug band organized by older campers and younger counselors, which we called, tongue in cheek, the New Milford Ramblers and Studebakers, when Happy got me singing. He invited me to join an ensemble he organized to perform folk songs and songs of the civil rights movement at Buck's Rock and other summer camps in Connecticut and New York.

We spent a lot of time, especially in 1965, talking about civil rights, the ban-the-bomb movement, and the escalation of the war in Vietnam. I was especially interested in Happy's account of being arrested several years earlier for refusing to take cover in an air raid drill. (In the late '50s and early '60s, Americans were ordered to "take cover" in absurd civil defense measures that gave us all the false expectation we would survive a nuclear attack by simply crawling under our school desks or staying inside.) For his act of civil disobedience, Happy spent thirty days on Hart Island, which then was the site of a workhouse and prison for New York City.

By 1964, my ears were also opening to the sounds of the Beatles, the Rolling Stones, and the British Invasion, to Dylan's new music, particularly

---

1. One surprising sidelight was my father's reaction to another of Ochs's songs, the satirical "Draft Dodger Rag," which humorously listed the numerous ways in which young men were avoiding the draft. Even though he was no longer a pacifist, Dad believed in the right of conscientious objection to war and continued to serve as a draft counselor for the Central Committee for Conscientious Objectors. To him, Ochs's song devalued and mocked this principle, as CO's often had to combat the view that they were dodging the draft rather than taking a moral stand against war. Like many of his generation, Dad never "got" the mordant sense of humor that so many young people possessed in the '60s.

his 1965 albums *Bringing It All Back Home* and *Highway 61 Revisited,* and to folk-rock bands like the Byrds. The Beatles' second movie, the irreverent and antiauthoritarian *"Help!"* came out in August '65, only a few months after the album cover for their *Yesterday and Today* was censored by their record label—it featured the Fab Four covered with blood, hunks of raw meat, and broken baby dolls; John Lennon said it was "as relevant as Vietnam."

Meanwhile, the Stones' "(I Can't Get No) Satisfaction," the band's first significant attempt at social commentary and its first number-one hit in America, dominated the airwaves during the summer of '65—including on the transistor radios of Buck's Rock campers and counselors.

Although direct political indoctrination of campers would have been counter to the Bulovas' intentions in enabling teenagers to learn to think for themselves and make their own decisions, there was one area in which Ernst allowed his progressive perspective to come through. Every August 6 was commemorated as Hiroshima Night, where a film, a performance, or a talk about nuclear war was presented. Campers were not required to attend, but I always did. Learning about the decimation of the civilian populations of Hiroshima and Nagasaki, and the effects of radiation poisoning on those who survived the initial bombings, made a big impression on me.

I also learned a lot from my fellow campers. When I was fifteen, in the summer of 1963, I bunked with three other boys my age. Our little aluminum shack became the center for continual, though not hostile, political debate. David Fine took the liberal capitalist side, while I argued from a socialist perspective and Andy Polon from a Marxist-communist viewpoint. Our debates might not have been profound, but they forced me to defend and articulate my beliefs—and sometimes change them.

David McReynolds, Nonviolence, and the Draft

Buck's Rock also occasionally invited peace and civil rights activists to meet with and talk to campers. One of these guests had a significant impact on my life and political development.

David McReynolds of the War Resisters League was soft-spoken yet forceful, articulate and fearless. He spent a week at Buck's Rock during the summer of 1965 conducting workshops on nonviolence and other issues, and I soaked up as much as I could. That Dave was also a democratic socialist made his message even more appealing to me.

Dave's main point was that nonviolence provided a humane yet potentially revolutionary means to fight against social injustice. He believed the civil rights movement's creative use of civil disobedience to attack segregation could be developed by the fledgling antiwar movement to generate opposition to the war in Vietnam. He also talked about an individual's responsibility to confront evil rather than sitting idly by and bemoaning it from the sidelines.

I was already leaning in a pacifist direction, as I had been learning about the creative use of nonviolent resistance by Gandhi in India, by Danes against their German invaders during World War II, and by the civil rights movement. Dave solidified my beliefs.

Most significantly, he provoked me to start thinking about what I would do concerning the draft. I had just turned seventeen, so my date to register for the draft was nearly a year away. Still, I recognized that at some time in the not too distant future I would have to make my own decision about the draft. I already knew that joining the army and fighting in Vietnam was out of the question. But what about my other choices? Could I accept the 2-S student deferment I would be eligible for by attending Cornell University, where I would be a freshman in a few months? Was applying for conscientious objector (CO) status a reasonable alternative? My father was encouraging me to move in that direction.

There was one other alternative—not registering at all with Selective Service. This didn't mean ignoring my eighteenth-birthday obligation to register and hoping I would get lost in the bureaucracy, but rather informing my draft board that I would not register with an organization I so profoundly opposed.

As the summer of '65 ended, I knew I had many months to consider all these possibilities before making my choice. But from then on, as it would be for so many in my generation, deciding what to do about the draft became the central issue of my life.

Part Two

THE MOVEMENT AGAINST THE WAR, THE DRAFT, AND UNIVERSITY COMPLICITY

Chapter Three

First Year at Cornell:

Runs, Pledges, and Sit-Ins

I may have held rapidly emerging radical views and sported longer-than-mainstream Beatlesque hair when I arrived at Cornell University in September 1965, but during my first year I engaged in the usual collegiate pursuits. I went out for and made a sports team (the freshman cross-country team), joined the Folk Music Club, bemoaned the three-to-one male-female ratio among undergraduates, rushed a fraternity, ate hero sandwiches at midnight, and struggled to wake up for 8 and 9 a.m. classes.

Cornell in September 1965 stood on the cusp of change, but wasn't quite there yet. An Ivy League university with thirteen thousand students in the isolated small city of Ithaca, New York (a six-hour drive from New York City in those days), Cornell was a schizy place. Part of it was Ivy League, with its lush and august quads and seriously competitive Arts and Engineering schools. But it also resembled a Big 10 university in its rah-rah spirit, powerful fraternity and sorority system (an estimated 80 percent of male undergraduates rushed fraternities), and academic divisions that were run by Cornell but were also part of the New York State University system, including the schools of Agriculture, Home Economics (now Human Ecology), Veterinary Medicine, and my own Industrial and Labor Relations (ILR).

Unlike the Arts and Engineering colleges, which drew students from across the United States and internationally, the ILR school attracted students like me—predominantly New Yorkers with good SAT scores but high school grades that wouldn't have gotten us into Arts or Engineering. Perhaps some of my fellow ILR students really wanted to become mediators, arbitrators, human resources technocrats, and corporate personnel managers, but most of us just wanted to go to Cornell.

I hadn't given much thought as to what kind of career I wanted to pursue, but if pressed I would have said I wanted to become a labor lawyer. I could see myself defending workers and unions from transgressive employers, and the ILR school seemed like a good place to begin.

Cornell had been known, historically, as a rather apolitical university. To be sure, small groups on the left had been around for decades. In 1958, students staged a large protest that turned into a riot against administration rules concerning student conduct—including a ban on female students attending parties or even visiting off-campus apartments unless they were chaperoned. (The May '58 demonstrations were immortalized by a participant, Richard Farina, in his novel *Been Down So Long It Looks Like Up to Me.*) Some of these rules lasted until the mid and late 1960s, when, I'm proud to say, student radicals helped abolish them.

Although the university made a sincere commitment in the late '60s to expand the enrollment of African Americans and other minorities, in the fall of 1965 both the student body and faculty remained almost all white.

I attended the fall term's opening meeting of the Ad Hoc Committee to End the War in Vietnam, the group whose members had engaged the previous spring in an acrimonious debate on campus with a pro-war guest speaker, Ambassador Averill Harriman, and led a student sit-in at the university president's annual review of Cornell ROTC. But I wasn't too impressed. The organization seemed like a debating society in which members took vehement, antagonistic positions on different approaches—from emphasizing education and outreach to calling for large demonstrations demanding immediate withdrawal of all U.S. troops in Vietnam to engaging in civil disobedience—none of which seemed mutually exclusive to me. I also disliked the group's pretentious name.

Rock Music Gets Serious

Mostly, I was spending my time on other things. Within one week in late October and early November, I attended live concerts at Cornell by the Rolling Stones and Bob Dylan—two-thirds of the Holy Trinity (with the Beatles) of modern and meaningful rock music. In a now-you-see-them-now-you-don't thirty-minute set, the Stones displayed their usual hard-rocking style, with their best new songs, like "Satisfaction," communicating a youthful anger with society. For me, the highlight of their short set was when Mick Jagger introduced the band's new single, "Get Off of My Cloud," by saying "We're singing this song so they don't drop the bomb over Vietnam."

As for Dylan, he performed an hour solo, accompanying himself on acoustic guitar and harmonica, followed by ninety minutes of electric rock with a backup group soon to be known as The Band. Although my political friends and I bemoaned Dylan's decision to leave behind the protest music of his past, abandon his role as an active supporter of the civil rights movement, and avoid any direct comments on the war in Vietnam, we were also aware that his new songs were in their own ways radical indictments of capitalism and American society. Dylan may have stopped writing what he called "finger-pointing songs" and rejected the role of a movement leader, but his newer material challenged obedience to authority, the cult of commercialism, and sexual repression. How else could one interpret "It's Alright Ma (I'm Only Bleeding)," which featured such memorable lines as "Money doesn't talk, it swears," or the reference in "Tombstone Blues" to Jack the Ripper sitting "at the head of the chamber of commerce."

I was also excited by Dylan's turn from acoustic music to loud rock 'n' roll. The musical times were a-changin' too, and rock seemed like the music of the future. Even some older beatniks got into the act when the Fugs (originally the Village Fugs), a group led by poet-provocateurs Ed Sanders and Tuli Kupferberg, released their first two albums in 1965 and '66. Combining elements of the Dadaists, Beat jazz-poetry, civil rights movement songs, anarchism, pacifism, sexual liberation, satire, profanity, and antiwar politics, the Fugs pushed the boundaries of what was acceptable and brought both outrage and an outrageous sense of humor to rock music. Featuring songs such as "Slum Goddess," "Nothing" (a nihilist-anarchist anthem), "I Couldn't Get High," "Boobs a Lot" (a riff on male objectification of women's bodies), and "Kill for Peace," the Fugs became regulars on my personal playlist.

(Although the Beatles never made it to Cornell on their subsequent 1966 U.S. concert tour—which would be their last live appearances in this country—they certainly attracted my enthusiastic support for the antiwar attitude they expressed at U.S. press conferences. All four members said "we don't like war," and John Lennon answered a direct question about their attitude toward the war in Vietnam by saying "We think of it every day. We don't like it. We don't agree with it. We think it's wrong." Unfortunately, their strong antiwar position was somewhat obscured by the even greater controversy that erupted over John's offhand comment that the Beatles were "more popular than Jesus.")

Cross-country training took up most of my free time. We had an excellent freshman team, winning most of our meets. I was far from the best runner on the team, but I was good enough—about fifth or sixth—to be a part of the seven-man traveling team that competed in meets held at other colleges and cities. I even got to race against a future Olympic gold medalist, Yale's Frank

Shorter. But my season, and my intercollegiate athletic career, ended prematurely when I suffered a minor back injury in a dual meet against Harvard.

Although I didn't stand out on the cross-country team for my running ability, I did attract the attention of other athletes by getting into a loud locker-room argument over Vietnam with a very large and accomplished shot-putter and hammer thrower named Tom Gage. A graduate student, Gage was the Cornell record holder in both weight events, former captain of the track and field team, and later a member of the 1972 U.S. Olympic team. He seemed to get all of his information about the war from *U.S. News & World Report,* a weekly newsmagazine that was even more conservative than its competitors, *Time* and *Newsweek.* When I heard Gage spouting off about something I knew wasn't the case, I walked over to him and started arguing.

I don't know if onlookers were more shocked by the discrepancy in our size—he was about six foot two and must have weighed over 230 pounds, while I was half a foot shorter and a hundred pounds lighter—or the temerity of a freshman picking an argument with one of Cornell's most celebrated athletes, but it caused a stir.

Even before I got injured, I found myself torn between the time needed for training and competing—several hours every afternoon plus meets on Saturdays—and my desire to take an active part in the antiwar movement. I was disappointed that I had to miss an antiwar rally in Buffalo in mid-October because of a cross-country meet.

What wasn't tearing at me was a commitment to my academic studies. I began college with the same sort of indifference to schoolwork I had in high school—I would do well enough to get by, but never extended myself in a pursuit of excellence. I can't blame my classes or instructors for this, either. Among my teachers during my freshman year were two leftist professors—Doug Dowd and Bill Friedland—who were excellent lecturers, as well as a really smart grad student teaching Introduction to English. I had some less-than-scintillating classes, to be sure—a dull macroeconomics lecture class at 8 a.m., a snoozer on "Formal Organizations"—but the fault lay largely with me.

Two events in early November 1965 affected me profoundly. On November 1, a Baltimore Quaker named Norman Morrison burned himself to death in front of the Pentagon to protest the suffering and loss of life caused by the war in Vietnam. A week later, a Catholic pacifist named Roger LaPorte similarly immolated himself in front of the United Nations. Although both actions were shocking and disturbing, and I had no desire to copy them, they served as personal challenges: If these men, like the Buddhist monks in South Vietnam, were willing to take their own lives in an effort to end the war, what are you willing to do?

Organizing Cornell SDS, Attracting the FBI's Attention

Also in November, I became part of a small group of Cornell students, led by Tom Bell, who started a chapter of Students for a Democratic Society.[1] Although SDS had been around since the beginning of the '60s, first as the youth group of the League for Industrial Democracy, I had heard of it largely because of its role in organizing the first mass demonstration against the war back in April 1965. That action had almost overnight transformed SDS into the leading antiwar group in the country.

Tom, a former football player at Wesleyan University and now a Cornell grad student, exemplified what was new about the New Left. He and his wife, Ann, who grew up in an affluent suburb of Buffalo, didn't have left-wing family backgrounds but had developed a type of grassroots American radicalism. They were unencumbered by the sectarian disputes of the past and were eagerly and openly seeking answers to questions about American foreign policy and domestic issues and what to do about them. They did not have a prefabricated political line to fall back on. Tom's openness to new ideas and his natural charisma were compelling, and he became a good friend and a major influence on my political development.

As someone who was both pro–civil rights and antiwar, I strongly agreed with the multi-issue perspective of SDS. I read SDS's founding document, the Port Huron Statement, which made a lot of sense to me even if developments like the expanded war in Vietnam had rendered it somewhat outdated. Mostly, I was impressed with the organization's commitment to activism.

So, evidently, was the FBI, which sent an agent or informer to Cornell SDS's very first meeting. According to an item in my FBI file, dated November 19, 1965, "Subject was at a Cornell SDS meeting held in the Art Room of Willard Straight Hall on November 17, 1965. He stated at this meeting he would try to set up a literature table downtown or on campus to disseminate anti-draft material."

That is an accurate enough account, but why was the FBI spying on a meeting of Cornell SDS? As a newly registered student organization, SDS had done nothing locally to become the object of a surreptitious government investigation. Nor had the national organization of SDS, other than sponsoring a legal rally against U.S. foreign policy. And why was my participation in the meeting something noteworthy enough to be recorded by an FBI agent or informer? At this point in my life I had done nothing illegal—except perhaps in my thoughts.

---

1. During the previous school year, some students had attempted to form an SDS chapter but abandoned the effort after a few meetings.

It became known years later that the Johnson administration began in April 1965 to pressure FBI director J. Edgar Hoover to investigate SDS and the antiwar movement. In response, Hoover wrote a memo about SDS for the president. "While I realize we may not be able to technically state that [SDS] is an actual communist organization," Hoover wrote, "certainly we do know there are communists in it.... I believe we should intensify through all field offices the instructions to endeavor to penetrate the Students for a Democratic Society so that we will have proper informant coverage similar to what we have in the Ku Klux Klan and the Communist Party itself."

The FBI then began to secretly recruit students to work as undercover agents and infiltrate SDS chapters.

I followed through on my promise to distribute literature on alternatives to the draft. I encountered some hostility passing out our pamphlets and brochures at the SDS table in the lobby of Willard Straight Hall, the Cornell student union commonly known as "the Straight." But the situation was a lot more tense when we took our literature and signs to downtown Ithaca and set up pickets outside the U.S. Navy recruiting station on East State Street.

Given how widespread antiwar sentiment became throughout American society within the next few years, it may be surprising that it was still quite lonely being an antiwar protester in the fall of 1965. When I stood, often alone, outside the navy recruiting office, holding an antiwar sign and passing out leaflets, I never knew what to expect from passersby or from the young men entering and exiting the office. There was occasional encouragement, but the other SDSers and I encountered hostility in many forms— from outraged looks to curses and verbal abuse to aggressive tearing up of our leaflets.

Cornell SDS also initiated a project to educate the campus community about the human cost of the war. We decided to raise funds for medical supplies to aid South Vietnamese civilians, with aid going to areas controlled by the South Vietnamese government and to areas controlled by the National Liberation Front. We were trying to make the point that we were not the enemies of the Vietnamese people and wanted to stop a war that was inflicting such hardships on them.

It was the latter part of our plan that proved most controversial, as supporters of U.S. policy claimed we were giving aid and comfort to the enemy. A *Cornell Daily Sun* headline, "SDS Sends Aid to Cong," fanned the flames, and one conservative columnist at the *Sun* accused us of "treason."

When SDS tried to spread the word about this new program at our table in the student union, our plans were upended by the student-run Scheduling, Coordination and Activities Review Board (SCARB) and the Straight's board of managers, both of which objected to student groups aiding the NLF in any manner. This set off a campus debate over free speech, medical aid, and the right to solicit funds on campus for off-campus purposes (a key issue in the Berkeley Free Speech Movement demonstrations of 1964). Eventually, the executive board of student government overruled the other two bodies and allowed SDS to raise funds for medical aid.

A Young Pacifist's Progress

That fall, I also joined the War Resisters League, the leading pacifist organization in the United States. I already knew David McReynolds from the past summer at Buck's Rock. When I visited the WRL office at 5 Beekman Street in New York City I was greeted almost like a prodigal son. It turned out that many of the WRL staffers and most active members—including Ralph DiGia, Igal Roodenko, and Jim Peck—knew my father from the old days and remembered him fondly even though he had left the organization nearly twenty years earlier.

It was around this time that I began reading *Liberation* magazine, a monthly edited by Dave Dellinger, which had become the leading voice in America for nonviolent direct action. The writings of Dellinger, A. J. Muste, Paul Goodman, Staughton Lynd, and Barbara Deming provided me with theoretical as well as practical justifications for my belief that revolutionary nonviolence need not be the least bit passive.

I got to meet Dave in February 1966 when he came to Cornell to give a lecture on the New Left. After his talk, I introduced myself, and he asked if I was related to Winston Dancis. When I said that Winston was my father, Dave seemed very pleased. He had warm feelings toward my dad, even though the two had disagreed over strategy during World War II. The debate then had been whether pacifists should pursue a legal and nonconfrontational approach, including advocacy and acceptance of conscientious objection (my dad's position) versus those who favored resistance to the draft and going to prison (as did Dellinger, Ralph DiGia, and Bayard Rustin).

As evidence that my new immersion into radical politics had not yet led to a total change in my outlook on life, I took part in the annual January ritual among Cornell freshmen known as fraternity rush. I ended up "pledging" one of the university's Jewish fraternities, Tau Delta Phi, which had the reputation for being among Cornell's most liberal houses and one that had been accepting black members for some time. I also needed a place to live during my upcoming sophomore year, and, as of January 1966, there were few alternatives at Cornell between living in a fraternity and spending another year in the dorms. (At this time, the Collegetown neighborhood of Ithaca was just beginning to swarm with undergraduates seeking independent housing away from the frats or dorms.)

Fortunately, my new brothers in Tau Delt didn't spend much time indoctrinating us pledges in fraternity lore or bothering us with juvenile hazing. They were for the most part a decent bunch of guys. The problem for me was that as the weeks went on, I found I had less and less in common with my fraternity brothers, and every meal or meeting I spent with them meant spending less time with my growing number of friends in SDS and the antiwar movement. After a few months I "de-pledged," or quit. It was a painless decision, though it left me up in the air as to where I would be living the following fall.

The Origins of a Draft Resistance Movement

The FBI continued to monitor Cornell SDS meetings and record my attendance and participation in them throughout the 1965–66 school year. Sometimes the notations were solely that I attended a meeting in such and such a place on such and such a date. Other notes were more explanatory. From April 14, 1966: "DANCIS attended a Cornell SDS meeting in Ives Hall on April 13, 1966. He was one of five members present who stated they would be willing to give talks at Ithaca High School to eleventh and twelfth grade students concerning Selective Service and filing claims as conscientious objectors, or for alternate service."

As that last report indicated, the draft was moving to the center of SDS concerns at Cornell, as it was in other SDS chapters. At the University of Michigan, SDS members led a sit-in at the local draft board in Ann Arbor—which provoked the Michigan draft director to punish the men involved by reclassifying them from 2-S (student deferment) to 1-A (eligible for immediate induction).

Although pacifists and other antiwar activists had been burning their draft cards since 1960, by 1965 such provocative actions, though not numerous, had become a focus of media attention. For the fledgling antiwar movement, draft card burning was just about the most militant action one could take to oppose the war. It was also something that provoked an angry response from conservative members of Congress.

In August 1965, the House passed a bill authored by conservative South Carolina Democrat L. Mendel Rivers to make it a federal offense, punishable by a fine of up to $10,000 and a prison term of up to five years, to "knowingly destroy" or "knowingly mutilate" a draft card. The bill, which was approved by the House Armed Services Committee without public hearings, was passed by the full House on a vote of 393–1. Rivers said the bill would put draft-card-burning antiwar demonstrators "where they belong—behind bars." Rep. William G. Bray, a Republican from Indiana, took the occasion to describe such protesters as "generally filthy beatniks."

A few days later, the U.S. Senate passed a similar bill, sponsored by Strom Thurmond, a Republican (and former ardent segregationist) from South Carolina. President Johnson quickly signed the bill into law.

Rather than having a deterrent effect on antiwar activists, the law provoked a defiant response. At an October 15 antiwar rally in New York, a Catholic pacifist named David Miller became the first man to burn his draft card following the passage of the new law. Less than a month later, five more men, including Dave McReynolds, burned their cards at another New York antiwar rally.

Meanwhile, the SDS National Office was falling behind the growing radicalism of the membership. It put out proposals in favor of members applying for CO status or some sort of alternative service, but did not call for a rejection of student deferments. These proposals, which were eventually called the "Build, Not Burn" program, were later rejected in a national referendum by the membership of SDS.

The Draft Exam: Where Pass or Fail Met Life or Death

But one action of the federal government did succeed in uniting SDS and radicalizing thousands of students. It revealed the strange knack of the powers-that-be during the Vietnam era—from the federal government to university administrations—to make dumb decisions that only provoked stronger, more militant responses from young people.

In this case, it was a decision by Selective Service System director General Lewis Hershey to reinstitute a Korean War practice of giving student deferments only to those with high grades or high scores on a special test. This meant that (1) colleges and universities had to compile class rankings for male students based on grades and make that information available to Selective Service, and (2) if a student's class rank was low, he was ordered to take what was called the Selective Service College Qualification Test.

The reaction to this new policy, at Cornell and around the country, was immediate, loud, and angry. Using grades, in the form of class rankings, as a determinant of whether a student could keep his 2-S deferment—and thus remain in school and avoid getting drafted and having to fight in Vietnam— seemed like an abuse of academic freedom and the antithesis of what an open and honest learning environment should be. Having a university administer such a controversial exam seemed to place that university in complicity with the war effort, as such exams had no academic value on their own.

Demonstrations against both the exam and the prevailing policy in which universities released the class rankings of male students to Selective Service sprang up around the country, usually led by SDS chapters. Though national SDS still lacked a coherent position on the draft, and a proposal that SDS members boycott the exam was rejected in a membership ballot, the National Office did succeed in preparing a nationwide counter-draft exam to be handed out by SDS members at exam sites. The purpose of the alternate exam was to educate students about the war and the draft.

Here are two questions from the SDS counter-exam:

1.   Which of the following American military heroes has, in the past, warned against committing a large number of American troops to a land war on the Asian mainland?: (A) Gen. Douglas MacArthur; (B) Pres. Dwight D. Eisenhower; (C) Gen. Matthew B. Ridgway; (D) Gen. Maxwell Taylor; (E) Gen. James Gavin; (F) Gen. Omar Bradley. [Answer:] All have made such warnings.
2.   The war in South Vietnam is supposed to be part of our policy to contain Communist Chinese aggression. How many Communist Chinese troops are actively engaged in combat in Vietnam?: (A) None; (B) 1,000; (C) 50,000; (D) 100,000; (E) 500,000. [Answer:] (A) none.

At Cornell, we voted to both endorse a boycott of the exam and distribute the counter-draft exam. We also began planning an all-day symposium, "The Draft, the University and the Cold War," to reach out to other students, and we called upon the university administration to respond to our demand that they not sponsor the draft exam.

When Cornell president James Perkins finally replied to us three days before the exam, his response was evasive and unsatisfactory. Perkins called the exam "voluntary" and stated that university facilities were being made available as a convenience to Cornell students. He also said "the examination recognizes the national interest in making possible, for those qualified, the attainment of the highest possible levels of training and education" by taking the decision as to who should receive student deferments out of the hands of local draft boards.

Exam day, on Saturday, May 14, went by quickly and peacefully. I joined other SDS members in passing out our counter-exam at the Cornell testing site. No one reacted hostilely to our presence, and many of the students I saw looked sheepish and embarrassed to be taking the test. The only incident

I heard about involved a student, unaffiliated with SDS, who disrupted the exam by banging on his desk in the testing room and refusing to stop when ordered to by Lowell George, the university proctor (Cornell's top cop). The student was eventually arrested and sentenced to thirty days in jail.

May 14 was also my eighteenth birthday, the time when I had to make my own decision about the draft. Since my birthday fell on a Saturday, when Day Hall, the Cornell administration building where students registered for the draft, was closed, I waited until the following Monday.

I knew I would never join the U.S. military, but I wasn't yet ready to declare my total noncooperation with Selective Service, a decision I believed would have quickly resulted in my being prosecuted and sent to federal prison. I declined to request a student deferment, which I viewed as racially and class biased because it gave college students the opportunity to avoid the draft, an option not available to others who were not able to attend college. But I had not yet given up on the alternative of becoming a conscientious objector. So I went ahead and applied for CO status, though I was still bothered by my decision to essentially postpone matters from coming to a head.

I didn't realize I would be returning to Day Hall the very next day for a different reason.

SPOTLIGHT: TAKING OVER THE UNIVERSITY PRESIDENT'S OFFICE, MAY 17, 1966

The campus cops were just a little too slow to keep up with us. When we ran from the steps of the student union to the administration building, they failed to stop me and six other demonstrators protesting Cornell's complicity with Selective Service from rushing into and sitting down in the office of President Perkins.

I had been attending an antiwar rally on the front steps of the Straight. Along with three hundred or so others, I heard Doug Dowd talk about the need for people to attend demonstrations and begin taking more vigorous actions against U.S. policy in Vietnam. A graduate student, David Green, gave another good speech, calling for us to write our members of Congress about the war and work toward electing peace candidates in congressional elections.

About thirty minutes into the rally, it became Tom Bell's turn to speak, as the president of Cornell SDS. After criticizing the university administration for allowing the Selective Service exam to be given on campus, Tom surprised everyone—including me—by urging the crowd to join him in marching up to Day Hall and sitting in at

Perkins's office. His action was rash and fundamentally undemocratic, as at no time had SDS voted in favor of civil disobedience over this issue. Tom's apparently unplanned, impromptu call for immediate action produced a surge of movement in the direction of the administration building.

It wasn't as if I was blindly following Tom—though I did look up to him as a friend and leader, and trusted him completely. All of us who had been involved in protesting the Selective Service exam and what we saw as Cornell's complicity with it were fed up with the university administration's decision to administer the "pass and go to class, fail and go to Vietnam" exam.

I was one of the first to join Tom as we scrambled into Perkins's office, and five more students succeeded in joining us before the campus cops caught up and locked the door. Within minutes, another fifty demonstrators tried to get into the office as well, but, finding Proctor George and his men barring the door, they decided to sit down in the adjacent hallway. A few hours later, our ranks had expanded to over one hundred demonstrators, including at least one faculty member, Robert Greenblatt, a young assistant professor of mathematics.

It turned out that Perkins and most of the university administrators were out of town. According to the next day's *Cornell Daily Sun*, Perkins was "reportedly extremely upset at the sit-in in his office." We were asked by one of Perkins's aides if we would like to meet with him when he got back to Ithaca, and we made an appointment for the next afternoon.

Since the sit-in had been unplanned, the seven of us in Perkins's office immediately began formulating our demands and writing a statement explaining what we were doing. I wrote the first draft, which stated "We are sitting in the Administration Building: 1) to protest the War in Vietnam, demanding immediate withdrawal of American military personnel; 2) to assert that Cornell University is deeply involved in this war as is the whole society, and 3) to demand that the University refuse to administer the Selective Service College Qualification Test." Later on, when we were able to communicate with our fellow demonstrators sitting in the hallway outside, we added the demands that the university stop computing class ranks, that the university not take the initiative in supplying draft boards with information about students, and that a student-faculty committee be set up to investigate Cornell's involvement in the war in Vietnam.

Late in the afternoon, at around 5:45, the proctor began citing the seven of us to appear before the Undergraduate Judiciary Board or, in Tom's case, since he was a graduate student, the Faculty Committee on Student Conduct. The formal charge was that we "invaded the privacy of the University President's office...engaged in a 'sit-in,' disrupted the normal operating procedures of the office...were illegally trespassing in that office after the normal closing time of 5:00 p.m., refused to leave when requested by a University Official and stayed in the office until 9:35 p.m." Using a divide-and-conquer strategy, the university did not cite any of our one-hundred-plus fellow demonstrators for sitting in just outside the president's office.

The seven of us finally agreed to leave Perkins's office because we felt our point had been made and we wanted to join our brothers and sisters in the corridor in order to remain a unified group. In solidarity with the seven, the other demonstrators demanded that they too receive the same disciplinary charges we faced.

We ended our protest around one o'clock the next morning. Although all we had gained at first was a promise from Perkins that he would meet with us to fully discuss the issues relating to the university and the draft, we soon discovered we had succeeded in moving campus opinion in our direction.

The Sit-In and Campus Attitudes

Over twenty-one hundred students signed a petition we had begun circulating stating that "the use of University facilities for the administration of the Selective Service Qualification Test exceeds the proper function of the University."

The executive board of student government voted 7–1 to ask the university *not* to hold the draft exam on campus; requested that the registrar's office *not* compile male class ranking for draft purposes; asked the U.S. government to withdraw support from the Ky regime in South Vietnam; called for free elections in Vietnam under United Nations auspices; called for an immediate cease-fire in Vietnam and the ultimate withdrawal of U.S. forces; and, finally, asked for a complete reevaluation of Cornell's relationship to the Selective Service System. The executive board also decided to hold a campus-wide referendum on these issues.

But perhaps the biggest surprise was that the Undergraduate Judiciary Board dismissed all the charges against us for the sit-in, largely on the grounds that our actions were justified and protected by the First Amendment, and that we had taken our protest directly to the only official (the university president) who had the power to satisfy our petition.

Our sit-in wasn't an unqualified success. The Faculty Committee on Student Conduct overturned the UJB's decision and convicted us for illegally trespassing in the president's office and refusing the proctor's order that we leave. We seven were each slapped with a "reprimand"—worse than a "warning," but not as severe as "disciplinary probation," suspension, or expulsion—and letters were sent to our parents.

But the reprimand did not have its intended effect on me or my future behavior. Instead of being intimidated or chastened by the ruling, I took my reprimand as a badge of honor.

The referendum's results were somewhat disappointing. The turnout was huge—the *Sun* called the eighty-five hundred votes "astounding"—but Cornell students supported by a 2–1 margin the administration's decision to continue holding the draft exam on campus and rejected the strongest antiwar resolution advocating immediate U.S. withdrawal from Vietnam. But the students did vote in favor of a cease-fire in Vietnam, holding free elections, and denying U.S. support to Ky's regime—all of which represented the first time that the Cornell student body had taken a stance against the war and against official U.S. policy.

The Cornell faculty was also affected by our actions, and also in mixed, even contradictory, ways. Shortly after our sit-in ended, some faculty members circulated a petition approving of "the way in which the President handled this delicate issue." The petition was signed by 480 (out of 1,300) faculty members. The university faculty as a body also met and voted their "strong approval" of the university administration's policy of conducting the draft exam on campus.

On the other hand, the faculty at the College of Arts and Sciences voted by a 2–1 margin not to compile all-male standings for the purposes of the draft—essentially agreeing with the SDS position. And the university faculty, apparently unaware that it was contradicting its vote in support of the administration, went on record opposing the use of academic performance and special examinations as a basis for draft deferments and opposing the use of class standings and grades for draft deferments.

What is clear is that SDS's activities throughout the 1965–66 school year, culminating with our sit-in at President Perkins's office, had stimulated the most vigorous debate on the war and the draft that Cornell had ever seen. In addition to forums, symposiums, and teach-ins on these issues, small debates among students were breaking out all over campus. In one academic year, we had gone from being a tiny group of radicals in lonely opposition to the war to a group that had won the support of thousands of students and faculty members. We might not yet have represented the majority of student and faculty opinion, but we were making great advances in that direction.

We also learned that the fight against the war and the draft was not for the meek. It took our illegal, collective act of civil disobedience to demonstrate the seriousness of the issues at hand, to galvanize student and faculty opinion and move it to the left. Among ourselves, the sense of solidarity and unity we gained while engaging in an audacious action was palpable and transforming.

Our action also came to the attention of the FBI. My FBI file contains a lengthy report on the demonstration outside the student union, as well as the subsequent sit-in, including a list containing the names of the seven of us who got inside the office. It also noted that Tom Bell, Ken Long, and I were members of Cornell SDS. Although the person informing the FBI about all this had his or her name blacked out, the informant was identified as being from the "CU Safety Division." (Both Proctor George and Assistant Proctor Richard Travis were former FBI agents.) My guess is that this reference to the CU Safety Division was also supposed to have been blacked out, but the censor didn't do a good enough job. This raises an obvious question: Why were employees of Cornell University's Safety Division reporting directly to the FBI about antiwar and antidraft activities on campus?

Attending the SDS National Council Meeting

The sit-in couldn't have come at a worse time for my scholastic activities. I had already been shirking my studies in favor of meetings and discussions, and now the prime time for cramming for finals was taken up by attending even more meetings and judicial hearings. I ended up getting poor to mediocre grades for the most part.

Just before school ended, my buddy Peter Agree (the only other freshman in Cornell SDS) and I were elected to represent our chapter at the June National Council meeting of SDS at the University of Michigan in Ann Arbor. Nothing of great importance occurred at the meeting. SDS, at least at the national level, was not willing to advocate that members give up their student deferments or take actions such as noncooperation, refusing induction, or burning draft cards. However, attending my first national SDS meeting left me so impressed with the intelligence and debating skills of veteran SDSers like Steve Max, Jane Adams, Paul Booth, and Cathy Wilkerson that I almost felt out of my league. But I was proud to be part of an organization led by such bright and capable people.

I was also affected by a talk at the National Council by SNCC's Ivanhoe Donaldson, who was there to explain his organization's recent turn toward "black power," why SNCC believed only blacks should organize in black communities, and what this might mean for the future relationship between SNCC and SDS. This had particular relevance for me, as in just one week I would start work on a summer project organizing tenants in New York City's East Harlem.

A Draft Board Surprise

Meanwhile, my draft board in the Bronx made a surprising decision. The board classified me I-A—meaning that I was eligible for immediate induction. When I registered for the draft I declined a student deferment, but I also formally requested the application for conscientious objector status. I was still waiting to receive these CO forms.

I suspect that my draft board's hasty action in classifying me 1-A was in retribution for my participation in antidraft actions at Cornell. It was certainly in line with General Hershey's threat to use reclassification as a weapon against antidraft protesters, as well as the action already taken in Michigan against student demonstrators. In addition, as I noted above, my FBI file shows that someone in the Cornell Safety Division reported my participation in the sit-in to the FBI.

Prior to March 1965, draft boards required those seeking CO status to demonstrate that they were not only opposed to all wars (that is, they could not selectively oppose a particular war, like Vietnam), but also had a long-standing religious basis for their beliefs, as shown by their membership in a pacifist church such as the Quakers or Mennonites. A Supreme Court decision in March '65 changed this somewhat, ruling that a deep-seated, personal "religious" opposition to war was sufficient. However, according to the study by Lawrence M. Baskir and William A. Strauss on the draft and the war in Vietnam, many draft boards failed to implement or comply with this decision and routinely denied CO status to most applicants.

When I finally received the CO questionnaire, I gave it my best shot, answering all the questions—about the use of force, my background, the religious/philosophical basis for my beliefs—as honestly as I could. One of my dad's closest friends, Abe Kaufman, a former executive director of the War Resisters League, served as my draft counselor and advised me about how best to fill out my form. I wrote about the Ethical Culture Society, my father's history as a CO, and my own antiwar activities. I even wrote about my participation in the protests at Cornell to demonstrate the sincerity of my feelings against war. The essential point, or so I thought, came in the section on my attitude toward violence and war. I wrote: "My conscience tells me that to participate in war, in which large numbers of men are indiscriminately slaughtered, would be an immoral act."

Then came a question about the use of force. "I wholeheartedly endorse the use of nonviolent force to affect social change," I wrote. "For myself, it is the most moral and practical way to overcome or resist evil." I did, however, acknowledge that "I can foresee a time when I could possibly commit some act of violence. If someone else were to be ruthlessly attacked, I might react violently to stop or capture the attacker. I would hope that if I ever did so react, it would be as a restraining force and no other."

There was one humorous sidelight to this. While investigating my CO application, the FBI contacted a close family friend, Myron Wisotsky, to ask him about my propensity for violence. Myron told the agent he believed I was sincere in my pacifist beliefs. But when pressed further about my attitude toward the use of force, Myron said that I was certainly willing to take out a shortstop while sliding into second base in order to break up a double play.

I thought I had made a strong case for my CO claim, but I was also beginning to see that CO status had some of the same problems as a student deferment. Although as a pacifist I could sincerely claim to be against all wars, I felt that others who opposed particular wars, like Vietnam, but not all forms of military conflict, were just as worthy as I. The CO form was difficult to fill out, asking for answers to vague and poorly worded questions about religious beliefs, the use of force, and the like. I was a student at an elite college who was being advised by a well-informed draft counselor. How would another young man fare, especially one who lacked my education and sophistication and who did not receive any draft counseling? The system seemed stacked in favor of upper- and middle-class men.

I appeared before my draft board in mid-July, spending about fifteen minutes in the company of three dour, middle-aged white men who didn't even try to conceal their contempt for me and my beliefs. Since I had been advised that local boards in New York were routinely denying CO applications, and the only way to win approval would be through the appeal process, I wasn't surprised that my application was quickly rejected. I then appealed the board's decision, which led to a mandatory FBI investigation.

It would be nearly six months before a final decision was made on my CO status, by which time I had already moved in another direction.

Chapter Four

Tenant Organizing in East Harlem

The changes in the civil rights movement during 1965 and '66 were unsettling for a person like me who wanted to make a greater personal commitment to the movement. By the mid-1960s, the effort to build a racially integrated society had run into major obstacles. Despite a decade of nonviolent bus boycotts, lunch counter sit-ins, mass demonstrations, voter registration drives, and legal and political victories, the unyielding racism of many whites—in both the North and the South—ensured that every positive step to end segregation would be met with hostility, obstruction, and even violence. The persistence of poverty continued to act as a deadweight upon the poor, pulling impoverished people down in a pile of need and despair.

Now some of the leading people in the movement, in particular the activists in SNCC, were expelling whites from their organization, renouncing the principle of nonviolence, and abandoning the goal of integration in favor of what new SNCC chairman Stokely Carmichael called "black power." As historian Clayborne Carson wrote in his *In Struggle: SNCC and the Black Awakening of the 1960s,* "Shattering the fragile alliance of civil rights forces, the black power upsurge challenged the assumptions underlying previous interracial efforts to achieve national civil rights reforms."

It was quite a contrast from 1964's Freedom Summer, when SNCC brought hundreds of white college students to Mississippi to help organize voter registration drives. Being kicked out of SNCC and told to "organize in your own communities" was a bitter blow for many white civil rights activists who had risked their lives for the movement.

But for this eighteen-year-old, the movement to end segregation and poverty and build a just, integrated society remained compelling, even as the war in Vietnam and the draft elicited my attention and protest. As a freshman at Cornell I had heard about a civil rights project, led by Doug Dowd and graduate student Charlie Haynie, in which a group of Cornell students had moved to Fayette County, Tennessee, during the summers of 1964 and 1965 to assist local blacks in attempting to register to vote. I was disappointed to learn that the project would not continue with student volunteers.

Moving to 110th Street

So I decided to take part in a project led by Rev. Paul Gibbons, a United Church of Christ chaplain at Cornell United Religious Works (CURW), which was bringing about forty Cornell students to live and work in East Harlem during the summer of 1966. It was the second year of the project, which was cosponsored by the East Harlem Tenants Council, an antipoverty organization. Some of the students were involved in setting up a day camp for neighborhood children, while others tried to develop food cooperatives. My responsibility, shared with some other project members, was to organize tenants into a cohesive group that could force their landlords into making long-overdue repairs in their apartments and buildings.

The students were divided into four groups, each renting apartments on a single block. My group lived on 110th Street between Park and Lexington Avenues and was led by a veteran of the previous summer's project, Jon Sabin, a friend from Cornell SDS. I shared a fifth-floor walk-up apartment with Jon and Bruce Cohen, while five women and two other guys stayed in two additional apartments on our block.

While I still believed in racial integration, I had great respect for SNCC and took its new policy seriously. If the civil rights workers I most admired were saying that whites were no longer wanted as organizers in the black community, what was I doing? Having signed up for the summer project earlier in the year, I was now questioning the validity of my working in East Harlem at all. I was troubled that nearly all the students, including me, would be leaving East Harlem for the comfort of our homes and university when the summer was over—unlike the older SDSers working in ERAP (Economic Research and Action Projects) who had moved into low-income neighborhoods in northern cities with the goal of building an "interracial movement of the poor." I viewed many of my Cornell compatriots as being insufficiently aware of these issues, and saw in them a do-gooder, paternalistic mentality.

I also had doubts about our cosponsor's new relationship with the Johnson administration. The East Harlem Tenants Council had been founded in 1964 by Ted Velez, a local Puerto Rican activist. It gained status and supporters in the community through its organizing rent strikes against landlords. During the winters of 1964–65 and 1965–66, some of its members had sat in at City Hall to demand action against East Harlem landlords who were failing to provide heat in their apartment buildings.

But, as a sign of its success, in early 1966 the Tenants Council began receiving funding from the federal antipoverty program, which enabled it to increase its staff, expand its community work, and move into larger offices. While I understood the value of federal funding, I worried that this would compromise the militancy of the organization.

It was also clear that East Harlem was quite different from Central Harlem. It was a more diverse community, whose residents included blacks, Puerto Ricans, and whites (mostly Italians, though my own apartment still had a Mezuzah outside the front door, indicating that a Jewish family had lived there in the not-too-distant past). Since I believed the struggle for civil rights needed to be fought beyond the South, I agreed with Rev. Gibbons's viewpoint that "the work of the Tenants Council represents a direct attempt to deal with some of the most acute problems of poverty, ignorance and prejudice in the North."

Confronting Slums and Poverty

I certainly wanted to do something about the terrible living conditions the residents of East Harlem were enduring. Although some of the buildings on 110th Street were in better shape than others, all suffered from their landlords' inattention. Front door locks didn't work, nor were there any buzzers or doorbells to individual apartments. With no front-door security, junkies would often enter the buildings to shoot up—usually on the stair landings between the top floor of the building and the roof.

The hallways were almost unbearable—poorly lit, with graffiti all over the walls, they smelled of urine and garbage. The courtyards, which most of the inside windows faced, were piled high with garbage and broken glass and were teeming with rats. Adding to the debris, it had become something of a sport for residents to try to kill these rats by hurling glass bottles down on them from upstairs apartments. Most often the result was shattered glass, but no dead rat.

Many of the apartments had holes in their wooden floors, plaster falling off walls and ceilings, bathtubs in the middle of kitchens, and unreliable electricity. Refrigerators and stoves were old and always breaking down. I was told that during the winter the heat often didn't work.

The Tenants Council had come into existence to ameliorate these conditions, since the city's Housing Authority was too understaffed, underfunded, and overwhelmed by the condition of New York slum apartments to take needed action. The Tenants Council's strategy was to organize block action committees (BACs) made up of residents of each particular city block. By the time we moved into our apartments on 110th Street, a BAC already existed, and its members were looking forward to our arrival. We found a vibrant and noisy block—the subway ran beneath Lexington Avenue, with a station at our corner, and the New York Central Railroad (now Metro North) ran aboveground on Park Avenue. The tenements were lined up across the street and adjacent to an elementary school and community center.

Although the BAC worked primarily with the Cornellians in setting up and administering the summer day camp, the Tenants Council provided staffers to train and assist us in tenant organizing. Being somewhat familiar with the SNCC style of organizing in the South, and with the Saul Alinsky methodology of community organizing in the North, I recognized that the role of the organizer was to help put people in motion and identify potential local leaders but to avoid assuming leadership ourselves.

The summer of '66 was hotter than usual in New York, befitting a season in which the number-one hit was the Lovin' Spoonful's "Summer in the City." It hit 107 degrees one awful day in late July, and residents—none of whom had air conditioning, though a few might have had fans—spent as much time as possible outside.

During my first weeks on 110th Street, I mostly hung out with my new neighbors. Many residents thought I was Puerto Rican, as I bore a resemblance to two young men, Neftali and Jimmy, who lived on the block. Initially, the most welcoming residents were the people our own age and the kids, who were excited to have all of these friendly college students as camp counselors and neighbors. We would spend hours just talking with residents, answering their questions about why we were there and asking them about their lives, aspirations, and living conditions. I also started smoking for the first time. I found out that it was considered impolite, particularly among Puerto Ricans, to refuse a gift offered in friendship, so I felt I had to accept the cigarettes offered to me.

I became especially friendly with a man in his early twenties named Milton Ayala, who lived in the building next to mine. Milton's apartment, where he lived with his wife, Molly, and baby daughter, was directly across an alley from my bedroom window, and we often talked late into the night while listening to rock 'n' roll on the radio. We had similar tastes in music, and Milton also shared my opposition to the war in Vietnam and a general countercultural attitude.

Milton, who worked in the garment industry, was a natural leader. He was able to hang out with the guys on the front steps of the tenements while also being a good family man. His charisma made him the most popular person on the block, one who moved easily between black residents and Puerto Ricans like himself. Being accepted by Milton opened doors for us all along 110th Street.

In a way, hanging out with Milton and his friends opened up all of East Harlem to me. On some nights we would go for walks in the area. Once, about six of us strolled over to the East River; another walk brought us to the northeast section of Central Park. We never encountered any trouble on these journeys—no gangs or territorial hostility—nor did we cause any problems. I felt no fear, despite being in places I had always been warned to avoid, especially late at night.

Although Milton and other residents of 110th Street did much to further my education and understanding of their community, there was one area in which Jon and I contributed to expanding their view of New York City. During the summer, Central Park hosted a series of free rock concerts. While the parts of the park near East Harlem were familiar to Milton and his pals, they seldom went farther downtown to where the concerts were held. With Jon and me leading the way, Milton and about four others from the block became regular attendees at the park concerts. I don't remember all of the shows, but we saw the Blues Project, the Youngbloods, and Tom Rush at one, and the Animals and Mitch Ryder and the Detroit Wheels at another.

The concerts taught Milton and his friends that the cultural offerings of New York City were not just there for affluent whites. And because of circumstances beyond my control, I also found myself taking a bunch of children from 110th Street on a journey to another, even more exotic location in the city.

SPOTLIGHT: A VISIT TO THE BRONX ZOO, JULY 18, 1966

The *New York Times* did not have to publish a story with the headline "Negro Child Eaten by Alligator in Bronx Zoo—White College Student Blamed—Riots in East Harlem." Nor did the *Daily News* scream "Gator Bait: Harlem Kid, Cornell Student in Zoo Horror—Riots in East Harlem." And I never had to say, "I'm sorry, Mrs. Johnson, but we lost little Dwayne in the Reptile House and he was eaten by an alligator" when we returned to our block on 110th Street after her five-year-old son Dwayne wiggled free of my grasp in the Bronx Zoo's Reptile House.

But we came very close to an unspeakable tragedy—one that would have irrevocably harmed the Cornell project, not to mention race relations in East Harlem, and not to mention Dwayne.

I wasn't supposed to be at the Bronx Zoo at all. I had little training as a counselor or babysitter, nor the desire to obtain such training. My purpose for being on 110th Street was to organize tenants.

I was awakened one Monday morning in July by a teenage camp counselor, one of several 110th Street residents hired by our project, pounding on my apartment door. It turned out that none of the Cornell students who worked at the day camp and arranged the campers' trip to the zoo had yet made it back to East Harlem after spending the weekend away. I was already pissed off that my colleagues had left the neighborhood in the first place. Going away for the weekend was an activity beyond the means of nearly all the residents on the block. It seemed to me that one's commitment to living in East Harlem for the summer did not allow for vacations or other extravagances that would further set us apart from our new neighbors. That my colleagues failed to show up to take kids to the zoo made me even angrier.

The twenty-five children were all lined up on the sidewalk and ready to go, but there was no adult to take them. The only counselors in attendance were four neighborhood teens, two boys and two girls, all around fifteen years of age. Since I was, at eighteen, a grand old adult, and it was known that I was from the Bronx, I was asked to lead the expedition. I reluctantly agreed.

Fortunately, I knew my way around both the New York City subway system and the Bronx Zoo. But such knowledge did not adequately prepare me for safely transporting twenty-five squirmy and excitable children, all ten and younger—about half clinging to me and the other counselors, the other half trying to run free of our constraints—there and back. None of the kids had ever been to the zoo, and few had even had much of a chance to leave our block.

The subway ride, which involved transferring to another line, wasn't easy. A few of the kids neglected to bring money for subway tokens, and the counselors and I were barely able to scrounge up enough money for the round trip. Keeping all the kids together on two rows of subway seats took all of our energy and attention. At least the kids were wearing their camp T-shirts, which helped us locate and identify them. Eventually, we made it to the West Farms subway station in the Bronx and walked several blocks to the zoo.

After our entrance, we walked alongside the African Plains, visited the Monkey House, and played in the Children's Zoo. The kids

screamed *"Mira! Mira!"* with great excitement and delight every time
they saw another exotic creature. So far so good.

Some children had also forgotten their lunches, and none of
the counselors had enough money to purchase any snacks. But the
counselors and other kids shared their food, and we kept everyone
reasonably happy.

Dwayne and the Gators

All was going better than I had expected until our visit to the
Reptile House. I was really looking forward to this exhibit because
I knew its cool and dark confines would provide some relief from
the sultry Bronx afternoon. And, truth be told, I've always had
a love-hate or fascination-fear relationship with members of the
order of Crocodilia. Like other boys, I was enthralled with dino-
saurs while growing up and later transferred my allegiance to their
modern-day representatives—crocodiles, caimans, gharials, and
alligators.

Up to this point in our Bronx Zoo visit, Dwayne and his seven-
year-old half brother Hennie had been among the clingers, having attached themselves to my arms and hands. They were both
sweet little guys, but kind of needy. Even on the block, they always
seemed to be touching or holding on to their camp counselors and
the other Cornell students. After meeting their mother, I could see
why. Mrs. Johnson was a bitter, unhappy person. A single mom on
welfare, she had few prospects and a perpetual scowl on her face.
It seemed as if she repeatedly took out her own frustrations on her
kids. I never saw her smile, but frequently heard her screaming at
her boys.

As soon as we walked into the Reptile House, Dwayne jerked his
hand away from mine and ran off.

If I had to choose the building or exhibit in the Bronx Zoo where
I would *least* like a child to get lost, it would be the Reptile House.
The principal attraction was a large pit, about ten feet below the
main walkway, filled with water, plants, grasses, sand, rocks...and
the resident alligators. I knew it would take only a little climb over a
short wall and then a fall into the pit for Dwayne to become the main
course in a nonscheduled feeding.

Frantic does not begin to describe my state as I alerted the other
counselors about Dwayne's escape. After leaving one teenager in
charge of the other kids, the rest of us fanned out through the Reptile
House in search of our lost boy. As I pushed my way through the

crowd, I kept expecting to hear screams coming from the alligator pit—either Dwayne's or from observers looking on in horror.

But when I got there, everything was quiet. The alligators were either asleep or doing their best imitation of it. Zoo visitors were gazing down on them with a mixture of awe over their size and ferocious appearance and disappointment over their lethargy. And Dwayne was not among either group. I assumed that if he had been eaten or chomped on, I would have heard something.

So I kept looking. After a few minutes, I found Dwayne—not as gator bait, but quietly staring at a twenty-foot-long boa constrictor...through a plate glass window. I was so relieved to find him safe that I didn't even yell at him. I just hugged him. When I asked him why he ran away from me, he just smiled shyly and shrugged his shoulders. I did not let go of Dwayne until we were back on 110th Street.

But I learned a lesson: being a day camp counselor—or more broadly, taking care of underprivileged kids—was a lot more stressful than organizing tenants in dingy, dangerous, rat-infested buildings.

Door-to-Door Organizing

In order to meet more residents and excite their interest in tenant organizing, we conducted a door-to-door survey in the apartment houses on our block. Working with Milton and a representative of the Tenants Council, we wrote and distributed a leaflet that read (in English and Spanish):

> As you have noticed, there are a number of college students living on this block. They will be working with the summer program along with your 110th Street Block Action Committee. For the next few weeks, these students will be visiting you in your home to discuss housing problems. Your full cooperation with the students will help us build a better community. Come to your own Block Action Committee's meetings at the DeWitt Clinton Community Center every Thursday night at 7:30.

With the leaflet as my introduction, I began knocking on apartment doors. We aimed to find out what concerns the residents had about their living conditions, whether they were interested in working with their fellow tenants to try to change those conditions, and which residents had leadership potential.

I discovered such a leader in Mrs. Stevens, a single mother in her late twenties or early thirties with two kids. Of Puerto Rican and African American descent, she was bilingual, very intelligent and articulate, angry as hell about her landlord's unwillingness to make needed repairs in her apartment, unafraid to speak her mind, and, truth be told, a knockout. (Mrs. Stevens was so beautiful I worried that some of the women in the building might be unwilling to let their husbands attend meetings in her apartment.)

Residents in about twenty of the twenty-five apartments in Mrs. Stevens's building were willing to talk to me about housing. Most people met me warily at their front door, but some invited me inside their apartments. After consulting with the Tenants Council, we decided that this combination of widespread interest and the leadership potential of Mrs. Stevens was so promising I should concentrate on this building. I told Mrs. Stevens about the strong interest I had found among the tenants in her building, but explained that we needed someone who lived in the building to take the lead in getting everyone together. She agreed to be that person. We worked together to write a short leaflet describing the awful condition of the apartment building and asked interested tenants to come to a meeting in her apartment.

I had talked to Mrs. Stevens about the importance of her chairing the meeting rather than me, but said I would be there to offer help and encouragement. One of our goals in the first meeting was to get neighbors to begin talking to each other about their shared problems. To our delight, fifteen people showed up. After a few awkward minutes, Mrs. Stevens suggested we go around the room and have each person express his or her concerns. It didn't take much to persuade everyone to talk. Bouncing back and forth between English and Spanish, the residents jumped at the chance to vent their feelings over their mistreatment. Particularly poignant were the fears of many that their small children might be bitten by rats.

After everyone had a chance to speak, the group decided to send a letter to their landlord, asking him to clean up the piles of garbage in the alley and make some long overdue repairs in the apartments. The letter threatened that the residents would withhold future rents and go on a rent strike if he didn't respond quickly.

To my amazement, within two or three days the landlord showed up at the building. He saw me standing on the sidewalk nearby—someone must have told him about my role in organizing the tenants' meeting—and he walked over to me.

"What have I ever done to you?" he asked in an aggrieved manner. I responded that it wasn't personal, and that his tenants were only asking him to make their apartments safer and more livable.

To my additional amazement, by the end of the next week the landlord began to bring in work crews to fix up the building. I'll never know whether the tenants' demands had made a deeper impression on the landlord's conscience or on his wallet.

It was the goal of the Tenants Council to maintain these newly formed tenant committees after the student organizers left East Harlem at the end of the summer. Unfortunately, in most of the organized buildings, including mine, this didn't happen. Perhaps this was because the tenants became acquiescent after the landlord started making some repairs, and failed to remain a cohesive force capable of maintaining their pressure on him. My leaving the neighborhood at the end of August also contributed to this failure. I did not adequately prepare the tenants for a long-term struggle.

East Harlem and the Antiwar Movement

The war in Vietnam also drew some of my attention during the summer. When I heard about plans for an antiwar demonstration on August 6, Hiroshima Day, sponsored by the Fifth Avenue Peace Parade Committee, I wanted to get involved. I came up with the idea of organizing a feeder march from East Harlem to join the main demonstration in midtown.

To my surprise, my proposal was met with considerable hostility from some members of the Cornell group, especially from a respected veteran of the project. He argued that since we were all living in East Harlem as representatives of the Tenants Council, we had no right to involve that organization in an antiwar protest. Echoing the views of the more conservative civil rights groups, which had attacked SNCC and CORE for their opposition to the war on the grounds that such protests diluted the freedom struggle and alienated the movement's friends in the White House and Congress, he accused me of trying to "use" the people of East Harlem for my political ends. He also raised the possibility that our antiwar protest might anger a (hypothetical) East Harlem mother whose son had died while fighting in Vietnam, thus endangering our entire project.

I disagreed with such arguments, particularly since the soldiers who were being drafted and bearing the brunt of the fighting and dying in Vietnam were overwhelmingly poor—like those young men who lived in East Harlem. I refused to back down on holding our march, but in the interest of unity and compromise I agreed to two conditions: we wouldn't leaflet our neighborhood about the antiwar march, relying instead on word of mouth among our friends and acquaintances; and we wouldn't begin our march on the blocks where we lived and worked.

On the morning of Saturday, August 6, 1966, about fifty of us—half from the Cornell project (including Rev. Gibbons), the other half from the neighborhood (including some Tenants Council staffers)—gathered just outside our neighborhood to begin our feeder march. Carrying homemade signs reading "East Harlem against the War" and "End War and Poverty," we

were in great spirits as we marched down Fifth Avenue. We arrived early at
the spot where the speeches were scheduled to take place, at Sixth Avenue and
Forty-Eighth Street, so we decided to walk over to Times Square. We marched
single-file around Times Square several times, drawing the attention of thousands of tourists and cops, before joining the main group of demonstrators—
now twenty thousand strong.

The rally was highlighted by the statements of family members of the Fort
Hood Three, a group of active-duty GIs who had been imprisoned earlier in
the summer after publicly declaring they would refuse to fight in a war they
considered "immoral, illegal, and unjust." I was also moved by a Marine cor-
poral who told the crowd "I will not serve even one more day as a Marine—in
conscience I cannot," and by Lincoln Lynch of CORE, who linked the horrors
of the war with racism at home.

The Difficulties of Organizing

As the summer went on, I began to take a different view as to what I could
accomplish in East Harlem. Some of my thoughts were expressed in a report
I wrote for the project organizers:

> I came here wanting to get in there and organize tenants and hold rent
> strikes. I wanted tangible results. [But] I [now] feel that perhaps my best
> and most important work has been at night in bull sessions with people
> on the streets.... We have shown (or have tried to show) that there is
> another world outside of East Harlem. I believe that this groundwork is
> necessary for a true and meaningful organization to grow on this block.
> The feeling of helplessness and despair and the idea of "what good will
> it do" must be erased.

Essentially, I recognized that organizing in a poverty-stricken community
made up primarily of blacks and Puerto Ricans would face many problems
and take a long time. In the conclusion to my report, I wrote: "[I] hope my
work will pave the way for action in the fall, winter, next summer or whenever
it can and must occur."

Although I generally agreed with Rev. Gibbons's assessment of our
project—"We found ourselves largely accepted, though our reception was less
whole-hearted by many Negroes than by the Puerto Ricans"—I had gained
a much better understanding of Carmichael and SNCC's position. I actively
took part in debates among our Cornell group over the viability of continued
white involvement in projects in minority neighborhoods. I argued that even

if we were all willing to remain in East Harlem and continue our efforts to organize its tenants, black or Puerto Rican organizers could probably achieve better results.

These debates and discussions were taking place throughout the East Harlem project. By the end of the summer, a Puerto Rican friend, Bob Rivera, who was a staff member of the Tenants Council, joked that it would be a sign of progress if the Cornellians became the first whites to be kicked out of East Harlem by the local movement.

Today, I'm less sure. What if I and others from Cornell had remained in East Harlem, deepened our ties to the community, and learned Spanish? Sure, some people might still have resented the intrusion of middle-class whites into their neighborhood. But others would undoubtedly have welcomed our staying there, just as they welcomed us upon our arrival. The East Harlem Tenants Council needed organizers, as there weren't enough local people ready to take on that job. Our presence might have helped break down barriers between the Puerto Ricans, African Americans, and whites in the neighborhood. We might have made a real difference.

I also learned something so obvious that it's a cliché—"You can't judge a book by its cover." I never had much to do with Protestant clergymen before working with Paul Gibbons. I may have admired the black ministers of the civil rights movement, starting with Dr. Martin Luther King Jr., but white ministers? Rev. Gibbons's quiet strength, commitment, openness, and honesty were a revelation to me, once I could see beyond his crew cut and title. I would soon meet and befriend even more Christian ministers in the antiwar movement, but he was the first to challenge my assumptions and open my eyes.

I left East Harlem and returned to Cornell with a new commitment to organizing—but in this case it would be organizing my fellow college students to oppose the war and the draft. I felt badly that Mrs. Stevens's building remained a crumbling six-story walk-up, despite the landlord's improvements. But there was some solace in knowing it was a lot less likely that a baby in the building lying asleep in his or her crib would be bitten by a rat.

Chapter Five

From Protest to Resistance

An un-named anti-draft group was formed at CU [Cornell University] in September, 1966. The purpose of the group was to oppose the Selective Service System by all possible means, both legal and illegal. Dancis was identified as one of the original members.
—An FBI agent's report in October 1966

When I arrived back in Ithaca in September 1966, to begin my sophomore year at Cornell, I was approached by my SDS friend Tom Bell about joining him in organizing a draft resistance union in Ithaca. Over the summer, Tom had decided to drop out of graduate school and become a full-time organizer for SDS in upstate New York (the Niagara region). He had also taken part in a meeting in Des Moines, Iowa, of about fifty people, mostly from SDS, concerning what to do next about the draft. Those assembled debated two strategies—a "big bang" proposal for a mass draft card burning or turn-in of draft cards, versus a more long-range approach of building community-based draft resistance unions. The group decided to pursue the latter, which would be organized locally around the theme of, as Tom put it, "We won't go into the U.S. military, and will encourage others to do the same."

Meanwhile, the SDS national convention, held in Clear Lake, Iowa, failed to produce any programs or strategies about the draft or draft resistance, though it did elect new, more militant national officers, including national secretary Greg Calvert and vice president Carl Davidson.

Early on, when there were only three or four of us in the Cornell group, we were aided by discussions with Mendy Samstein, a veteran SNCC organizer who had been one of the coordinators of the 1964 Mississippi Summer Project. Mendy, who was trying to push the white New Left to "put our bodies on the line" in the same way SNCC members had, was particularly helpful in talking about the day-to-day tasks of organizing.

The organizing strategy Tom favored was to go slow, add members one by one, and try to build a group of men who would stand together in opposition to the draft. We decided to offer draft counseling at Cornell and in downtown Ithaca to provide men with information about all the alternatives—applying for CO status, emigrating to Canada, and so on. Eventually, we would "go public" with our stance and support each other in refusing induction and in whatever legal battles we faced. Within a month or two, and after hours of intense, personal discussions, our numbers had grown to about ten.

Two other important developments took place over the summer while I was in East Harlem. In July and September, meetings of antiwar activists from around the country were held in Cleveland to form the Mobilization Committee ("the Mobe"), which would take a leading role in organizing future mass demonstrations against the war. Two activist professors from Cornell, Doug Dowd and Bob Greenblatt, were among those involved, further tying the Cornell antiwar movement to the national movement.

During the 1966–67 academic year, Doug and his family lived in Bologna, Italy, where Doug, an economic historian and Fulbright scholar, was doing research. In his absence, Bob took his place as Cornell's main connection to the Mobe and as a Cornell faculty member who was in tune with student activists. A Hungarian Jewish refugee as a child during World War II, Bob was an assistant professor of mathematics at Cornell and one of the only faculty members to join us the previous May in the sit-in at President Perkins's office.

In Ithaca, the rise in antiwar activity during the previous spring led to the opening of a new headquarters for printing and disseminating antiwar literature for Cornell, Ithaca, and beyond. Set up the previous year in an extra bedroom in the house of Cornell graduate student Joe Griffith and his wife, Pat, a Fayette County project veteran, the office began with a simple mimeograph machine. A used offset printing press was soon added. The office became the national headquarters of the Inter-University Committee for Debate on Foreign Policy, the organization that developed out of the "Teach-In" movement, and Pat became its field secretary. Soon, the office was pumping out antiwar literature. Equally important, it became a clearinghouse for speakers and a communications center for people and organizations opposed to the war. When the volume of activity and the noise from the printing press grew too busy and loud for the Griffiths' house, a small office was rented just a few blocks from the Cornell campus.

The Office and the Glad Day Press, as the new space was called, expanded its role as a nationwide printer and distributor of antiwar and radical pamphlets, articles, periodicals, and leaflets. It also became the headquarters for just about every left-of-center organization on the Cornell campus and in Ithaca, a hub of energy and lively discussions, a social center, and my new home away from home. Remarkably, the Office ran for years without falling victim to left sectarianism, as each affiliated group shared in the printing and other work. Existing entirely on donations (largely from Cornell faculty) and literature sales, the Office succeeded without ever enacting a formal constitution or legal agreement. As it expanded, a few staffers were paid subsistence wages, but most labor was performed by volunteers.

Having spent the summer working in East Harlem, I had neglected to arrange housing for myself back at Cornell. Fortunately, an SDS friend, Carl Anderson, had some extra space in a Collegetown apartment he was renting with some other students, and they offered it to me.

Cornell SDS's New President

I was elected president of Cornell SDS at the beginning of the fall term. I didn't think I was the ideal person for the position. I was only eighteen years old and politically inexperienced; I felt I lacked the solid background in political ideology, history, Marxism, and economics an SDS leader needed. But the membership apparently thought otherwise, and I was elected without opposition. Evidently, members of our chapter believed my commitment to the cause, (relative) articulateness in expressing the SDS viewpoint, ability to chair a meeting fairly, and willingness to take on the bureaucratic responsibilities that came with the position (like filling out the forms required for us to be recognized as a campus organization or securing information tables in the student union) were sufficient.

Cornell SDS was still a small organization in September 1966, with only about thirty "card-carrying" members (those who actually paid the minimal national dues required to obtain an SDS membership card and receive the organization's weekly newspaper, *New Left Notes*). But there were as many as 250–300 sympathetic students and faculty members, as shown by the participation and support we had built during the previous spring's sit-in. And an even larger group of students was beginning to pay attention to what we were doing.

Shortly after the fall term began we started protesting the involvement of the Cornell Aeronautical Laboratory (CAL) in secret research on chemical-biological warfare. CAL was a think tank and research facility near Buffalo that had been affiliated with Cornell since 1946. CAL had several contracts with the U.S. Army to work on aerial delivery systems for chemical-biological weapons. Cornell SDS charged that such research was incompatible with the university's purpose of contributing to the free development and exchange of ideas.

After a relatively quiet two months, in mid-November I had an unexpected encounter with a representative of the Cornell administration.

SPOTLIGHT: THE BUTTON INCIDENT, NOVEMBER 17, 1966

The campus cop grabbed me from behind and swung me around. He then seized the lapels of my coat and pushed me down about six or seven steps at the front of the student union. As he started to drag me to the police office on campus, I pulled my arm free. A crowd of about twenty people started to gather around us. I told the cop he had no right to grab me. He responded by saying he wanted to talk to me in his office. He then reached for a button I was wearing and pulled it off my coat, leaving the pin part still dangling from my lapel.

It was a fine autumn morning in November 1966, and I had been minding my own business when I was accosted. For this, I, along with a bunch of other SDS members, were called "discourteous," "juvenile," "cowardly," "tasteless," and "indecent," as we had "violated Cornell's standards of decent relations between human beings." A lengthy report on my transgressions appeared in my FBI file.

My crime: along with dozens of other students, I was wearing a pink button that read "I am not yet convinced that the Proctor is a horse's ass." That's what the campus cop, Richard Travis, the assistant proctor, tore off my coat. He didn't get the chance to grab the smaller, light-blue companion button, which read simply "I am convinced."

The university proctor at Cornell, according to an official university document, "is primarily concerned with the investigation of all student misconduct (other than academic fraud) committed both on and off campus." The proctor was, essentially, the top police officer in the campus Safety Division. Since 1952, the proctor's position had been held by a former FBI agent named Lowell T. George. Proctor George was the chief enforcer of university rules and the chief investigator of any breakage of them. He was the prosecutor of students committing acts of civil disobedience, like our sit-in at the president's office, and the narc who busted students for illegal drug use.

Shortly after the fall 1966 semester began, George was involved in disciplining one of our Cornell SDS members, Burton Weiss, for "disrupting" a university-sponsored symposium on drugs. Burton believed that a truth-seeking academic discussion or debate about psychedelic drugs such as LSD or marijuana needed to include at least one defender of drug use. Burton had earlier suggested that the planning committee invite a pro-psychedelics academic researcher, such as former Harvard professors Timothy Leary or Richard Alpert, to appear alongside the critics the symposium planners had enlisted. For standing up in the audience at the beginning of the symposium to criticize the unfair and unbalanced nature of the proceedings, Burton was cited by the proctor and eventually placed on disciplinary probation for two semesters.

Anyone holding the position of top cop on the campus would have incurred the wrath of rebellious and radical students in the mid-1960s, but George didn't help matters with his cold, mean, and humorless demeanor. In *Been Down So Long It Looks Like Up to Me,* Richard Farina's novelistic account of Cornell in the late 1950s, which culminates with a student riot against *in loco parentis* rules and regulations, the author gave Proctor George the *nom de mollusque* of "Proctor Slug."

The idea for the two buttons was not mine. It came from another SDS member, one who had strong feelings about Proctor George. This member had witnessed the hard side of George in the political realm, as had many of us who had encountered the proctor's grim visage from antiwar picket lines and demonstrations. But this student had also been subjected to the wrath of George when, as an underclassman, he was busted for smoking pot.

He asked me, as SDS president, to authorize spending fifty dollars to produce 250 sets of the buttons. I quickly agreed. Selling the buttons for fifty cents a set, we easily made back the money and gave the "profits" to our community antiwar office. Soon, they would become a collector's item.

We had actually been wearing the buttons for nearly a week before the incident took place. I was walking in front of the Straight when a man (Travis) who I knew worked in the proctor's office but whose name I didn't know called me over and asked if my name was "Dancik." I told him it was Dancis. He said he always confused me with Mike Radetsky (another dark-haired, Jewish SDS member from New York City). It was when I started to walk away that Travis came after me.

Travis made the mistake of losing his cool and grabbing me and my button in a very public place—the steps of the Straight—where there were at least twenty-five students sitting around and watching the incident unfold, including a bunch of my friends in SDS and two reporters from the *Sun.* They quickly surrounded Travis and me, preventing him from dragging me farther along the way to the Safety Division office.

An agitated debate then began. Travis said he grabbed my button because he didn't like it. In response, Mike Shaffer, one of the SDSers in the crowd, said, "If I didn't like your tie, would I have the right to rip it off your neck?" Travis then held up his tie and dared anyone to "yank it off." Nobody did.

We continued arguing, and then Travis said if he ever saw me wearing the button again, he would break a more serious law. Someone in the crowd asked him if he was acting in his capacity as a member of the proctor's office, and Travis responded, "No, I'm acting for me." After a little more arguing, he left, repeating his appeal to me to come to his office to talk about it.

I wrote a statement offering my description of what had happened. Fifteen witnesses signed the statement, concurring with what I had described. I also demanded that Travis publicly apologize for his behavior and that the administration censure Travis for his actions and defend the rights of students.

A Brief Briefing

Coincidentally, an already scheduled student briefing with the Cornell administration was slated for that afternoon. Students had been complaining about the high cost of food at university-run dining facilities and were threatening a boycott. The administration thought a public briefing would cool down the controversy. Naturally, a bunch of us from SDS attended in order to ask the administration about the incident with Travis. Naturally, we were wearing our buttons.

Steven Muller, Cornell's vice president for public affairs, began the briefing by reading from a prepared statement. Angering nearly every student in attendance, he said the administration would not participate in any event—including its own briefing—in which our button was displayed. To do so, Muller said, "would be to condone and share in this open breach of fairness and decency."

Muller claimed this decision was reached by the administration prior to my altercation with Travis. He charged that the button "represented a cowardly and inexcusable personal attack, not on an office but on a single individual." He called the button "ugly," "tasteless," "below the belt," "vicious," and "vulgar." And, of course, he said the blame for the meeting being canceled "rests entirely and solely with those who have deliberately chosen to make it impossible for us to proceed."

What a pile of smug bullshit! Judging from the administration's response, you would think my fellow button wearers and I had launched an obscene assault on all that was good and decent at Cornell University, and I had somehow assaulted Travis with my terrible button. To us, and to many students, Proctor George was both a public figure and a symbol of authority, and thus a fair target for satire.

Unfortunately, the Faculty Council chose to side with the administration over the button dispute. It condemned "the series of provocations and incidents of offensive behavior of a small group of students," calling us "discourteous, juvenile and cowardly." The council said nothing about free speech, free expression, and the right to not be assaulted by a police officer for wearing a button, save for stating that it was "convinced that appropriate measures were being taken." An unsigned memo to President Perkins— probably from Vice President for Student Affairs Mark Barlow— informed him that the "Fac. Council...are withholding their 'big bertha' statement for later, in case it is needed when there is a more serious confrontation."

Making matters even more ludicrous, in its two front-page stories on the incident and the canceled briefing, the *Cornell Daily Sun* couldn't quite bring itself to actually print what the button said. Instead, the stories quoted the button as reading "I am not yet convinced that the proctor is (similar to a horse's hindquarters)."

Although the administration officially continued to stand firm in its horror over the button, it did announce the formation of a special committee to investigate the Travis-Dancis altercation, which was now known throughout the campus as "the button incident." The committee was made up of VP Barlow, an associate dean, and a department chairman. Evidently, no students were deemed suitable for the investigative committee.

The overreaction of Muller, the administration, and the Faculty Council to us button wearers, not to mention Travis's flip-out, became the most discussed issue on the Cornell campus, the source of numerous *Sun* editorials, columns, and letters to the editor, and the subject of considerable mockery. One letter writer suggested I be "spanked," and another wrote that Proctor George was really a wonderful guy, but most of the opinions expressed leaned toward our side.

At least student government backed me, as its executive board issued a statement calling for Travis's suspension during the investigation. And they understood—as the administration and Faculty Council did not—that there was a serious issue at stake: "Mr. Travis' behavior displays a complete and total disregard for civil rights and liberties."

After a weekend to assess the situation and no doubt debate the merits of good taste versus reportorial accuracy, the *Sun* decided it could actually print the words "horse's ass" rather than "similar to a horse's hindquarters."

There also were indications that some members of the administration were beginning to recognize their overreaction was making them, not SDS and the button wearers, look ridiculous. The *Sun* quoted an unnamed member of the administration admitting, "Okay, maybe we're in a box, but let's try to keep the lid from being nailed on."

Within a few days, I was called to testify before the investigative committee. So were Travis, four eyewitnesses, and Proctor George—who was neither a witness nor a participant in the incident. Meanwhile, committee members were receiving considerable behind-the-scene lobbying by George. As I found out decades later while examining the James Perkins Papers in the Cornell Library, George—hardly an independent party in any of this—had demanded that the committee back his office as vigorously as possible. He also urged the committee to not use the word "reprimand" in its determination of what should happen to Travis.

"A Complete Whitewash"

Twelve days after the button incident, President Perkins announced that Travis had been "reprimanded" for "his unwise display of temper." But in a nine-paragraph statement, which he said was based on the investigative committee's report, criticism of Travis's actions occupied all of one sentence, and even that sentence said that "Mr. Travis was obviously provoked, but that cannot excuse..." The rest of the statement included a brief recounting of the incident but was largely devoted to criticism of me, the button, and those who were wearing those dastardly pins.

Perkins also stated that "the overwhelming majority of students believe in decent behavior and fair play and will support efforts to ensure such standards of behavior." Trying to drive a wedge between us indecent and foul-playing radicals and the rest of the student body, he said, "These students have my full confidence."

But on what basis was Perkins assessing student opinion? In making such a claim, he contradicted the still-unreleased report by the investigative committee, which criticized student attitudes for not accepting "remorse at the indecencies to which Mr. George had been subjected by these buttons."

The button incident probably would have ended there had the administration not scheduled another open briefing for the following day. This time Vice President Muller did not cancel the briefing, even though a lot of students were again wearing the buttons. But he got awfully ticked off when I rose from my seat to read a reply to Perkins's statement. According to the *Sun,* he even called for Proctor George to "quell" my interruption. However, I concluded my statement before George could quell me.

In response to a question from the audience, Muller said the administration would not release the investigative committee's report, adding with a straight face, "We don't see any purpose in publishing the complete facts." He justified his position by saying that discussing the details of the fact-finding investigation would "just arouse people's emotions."

The FBI, the former employer of both George and Travis, reported on and interpreted the button incident differently. According to a report filed on January 9, 1967, by a special agent working out of the FBI's Albany bureau, it was I, not Travis, who "was reprimanded by university officials," and not for an unwise display of temper, but "for wearing and distributing buttons considered obscene by some university officials."

So what should one conclude from the "button incident"? To me, it showed how out of touch the administration and many faculty members were with students' attitudes toward authority and justice, and what constituted humor and satire. It also showed that in a conflict between decorum and defending the status quo, on one hand, and civil rights and civil liberties (even rude rights and liberties), on the other, our elders would choose the former.

However, within less than six months the university would have longed for such "discourteous," "juvenile," "cowardly," "tasteless," and "indecent" behavior on the part of Cornell's radical students.

As for my judgment of whether or not Proctor George was a horse's ass, I can say, unequivocally, I am convinced.

Thinking about Prison

In the fall of 1966, many of us in Cornell SDS were open to exploring different tactics and strategies to build opposition to President Johnson's war policy. We were willing to join in coalitions with other groups to expand the antiwar movement.

A new group called Students for a Constructive Foreign Policy was formed by liberal student-government types, including Bruce Cohen, one of my roommates in the East Harlem project, to go to the freshman dorms to talk to students about the war. It was the kind of grassroots organizing that I, as SDS president, should have been promoting, but had not. Nevertheless, many SDS members joined SFCFP in going to the dorms.

Also active on campus were the Young Friends, a Quaker-affiliated group that organized a weeklong fast for peace with the support of many of Cornell's chaplains. Although I wasn't too familiar with the Quaker tenet of "witnessing," I decided to take part in the fast. I consumed nothing but water for seven days, spending part of each evening meeting with other fasters to discuss peace and maintain our morale.

At around the same time I also persuaded my apartment mates to join me in a new nationwide protest of Congress's adoption of an increase in federal taxes on telephone bills (from 3 percent to 10 percent) to provide revenue to pay for the war in Vietnam.

Unfortunately, neither the fast, the telephone tax protest, nor any other activity against the war swayed the Johnson administration. By the end of the year, the number of American troops in Vietnam had reached nearly four hundred thousand. Over six thousand U.S. soldiers had already been killed in Vietnam.

Like many others in the antiwar movement, I was growing frustrated with our lack of effectiveness. I felt this even within our draft resistance union. By late November, our ranks were up to about twenty. We were all committed to refusing to fight in Vietnam but remained divided and unclear about what to do next. In part, this reflected our political diversity. While some of us came out of SDS, others were not part of any group. We had Christian pacifists, anarchists (like Matty Goodman, a non-registrant and the son of the radical social critic Paul Goodman), and some who defied ideological categories. Most of the group was still opposed to actions that would almost certainly result in going to prison.

But this attitude started to change after we met with Ralph DiGia of the War Resisters League. Ralph had spent time in federal prison during World War II. Our conversations with him convinced many of us we could survive several years in prison. For me, these discussions helped remove the only thing keeping me from severing my ties with Selective Service—fear of the repercussions.

By the beginning of December, my draft card was (figuratively) burning a hole in my pocket, and I couldn't stand remaining complicit with the system that was integral to perpetuating a war I abhorred. I was also concerned that the momentum of the antiwar movement had stalled. I felt people needed to take stronger, riskier actions both to keep the pressure on the Johnson administration and to increase the seriousness of the movement itself. I hoped my own action would, in a small way, help build a larger and more committed antiwar movement. I was willing to act alone, but hoped that others would be joining me in the not-too-distant future.

That's when I decided to destroy my draft card and cut my ties to the Selective Service System. When I told my fellow draft resistance union members about my decision, some were concerned that I had not sufficiently explored the consequences of such an action. But most recognized that my choice was based on months of deliberation and a clear understanding of what could happen to me. Although none of the others was ready to join me in openly breaking with the draft system, we decided as a group to make a public declaration of our opposition to military service.

For me, the only questions remaining were just what kind of action should I take? And when should I do it?

Having made my decision, I didn't want to wait too long to carry it out. As I talked to my closest friends, Bob Greenblatt suggested an upcoming meeting in which the university faculty was to vote on the proposals offered by a faculty committee on Selective Service. The faculty meeting was scheduled for Wednesday, December 14.

I called my parents to tell them of my intentions, and they urged me to wait until after the upcoming Christmas vacation so we could discuss it further. I said that my mind was made up. My parents undoubtedly knew how determined, and stubborn, I was, but they nevertheless immediately drove up to Ithaca to make one final attempt to dissuade me. I felt bad that I was putting my folks through such stress and worry, but I refused to change my mind. My parents left Ithaca troubled and anguished, but I knew they understood how hard I had thought about this. I hoped they would be proud of me and would stand with me.

It was purely a coincidence that Wednesday, December 14, 1966, began with our antidraft union's statement appearing in the *Cornell Sun*. Signed by twenty-one men, the ad read in large letters: "WE WON'T GO." Beneath that headline, it said, "The undersigned men of draft age will not serve in the U.S. military. We encourage others to do the same." Our statement closed with "People needing help with the draft, and anyone interested in signing this statement, please contact one of the above."

Statements such as ours, which were beginning to appear in campus newspapers around the country, not only represented the first time significant numbers of draft-age men pledged to refuse to fight in Vietnam, but also suggested that we would try to build a larger movement of resistance. At the time, even such public declarations were considered potential targets for federal prosecution or reprisals by Selective Service.

The publication of our statement, coupled with the news that Pat Griffith was accompanying three other antiwar women on an illegal trip to North Vietnam to investigate civilian casualties and other concerns, made December 14 a particularly important date for the Ithaca antiwar movement. Later that day, I would make my own contribution.

SPOTLIGHT: IT'S UP TO HIM, AND YOU, AND ME, DECEMBER 14, 1966

Rebels don't usually "dress up" when they openly defy their government. But as I stood in front of the chemical engineering building at Cornell late in the afternoon on a cool mid-December day, about to make my own, personal declaration of independence and take a step that would affect the rest of my life, I was clad in a blue blazer, tie, and white button-down shirt. I chose to wear such clothes not to pretend I was someone I was not, but in an attempt to avoid being marginalized as a "beatnik" or "hippie."

A crowd of about three hundred people had gathered near the front steps of Olin Hall, where I planned to speak. Most were friends and supporters, who knew why I was there, but a vocal group of hostile engineering students was also present, no doubt curious as to why all these strange people had arrived on their turf. Inside the building, the university faculty was voting to support the proposals of the faculty committee on Selective Service, which perpetuated the existing policies of the Cornell administration. The local media were also in attendance, having been contacted by our draft resistance union.

Earlier in the day, the Albany bureau of the FBI had sent a text marked "Urgent" to FBI director J. Edgar Hoover. After identifying me as a Cornell student, president of the Cornell SDS chapter, and an "active member of anti-draft group," it stated, "Info received from source that subject intended to burn his draft card at Four PM this date prior to meeting of Cornell faculty.... After publicly burning card, subject intended to mail remanents [sic] to his local draft board. Reports of alleged burning have been made on local radio stations and have caused considerable local interest. Bureau will be advised subsequent developments."

Scheduling my action for 4 p.m. made sense logistically, as it would coincide with the faculty meeting. But having to wait until the late afternoon was very difficult, as the hours passed at an agonizingly slow pace. I spent some time going over the statement I intended

Bruce Dancis tears up his draft card in front of Olin Hall
on the Cornell University campus, December 14, 1966. (*Cornell
Daily Sun*; all rights reserved)

to read and then mail to my draft board in the Bronx; I also passed
the time just hanging out with my pal Peter Agree.

I had no second thoughts about my plan. I knew I was about to
take my life into territory I could barely imagine and for which no
map existed, yet I was never consumed by fear. Whatever stress I was
feeling seemed manageable, no worse than the butterflies I used to get
before a track or cross-country race. Then again, I was chain-smoking
unfiltered Lucky Strikes, and Pete remembers me shaking a bit in my
cold, drafty apartment, so perhaps I'm not the best judge as to the
state of my nerves on that day.

To keep my spirits up I listened over and over to recordings of the song "Universal Soldier"—both Buffy Sainte-Marie's original version and Donovan's cover. Nothing better captured my determination to stand up for what I believed in than the song's eloquent plea for people to take personal responsibility.

I was also inspired by the eloquent words of Mario Savio, one of the leaders of Berkeley's Free Speech Movement in 1964 and perhaps the greatest orator to come out of the student New Left. Although I was still in high school and not paying too much attention to the events in Berkeley in December 1964 when Savio spoke, his ringing call for civil disobedience had become legendary in the movement and was widely reprinted. His words, which were also relevant to the draft, moved and encouraged me:

> There's a time when the operation of the machine becomes so odious, makes you so sick at heart, that you can't take part; you can't even passively. And you've got to put your bodies upon the gears and upon the wheels, upon the levers, upon all the apparatus, and you've got to make it stop. And you've got to indicate to the people who run it, the people who own it, that unless you're free, the machine will be prevented from working at all.

A Speech and an Action

When I arrived outside Olin Hall, my supporters had set up a loudspeaker and a microphone. I prefaced my remarks by stating I was acting as an individual and not as a member of any organization I belonged to at Cornell. (Neither Cornell SDS, of which I was president, nor the Ithaca draft resistance group had yet taken official positions in support of draft resistance actions.) I then started reading my statement to Selective Service Local Board No. 26, which explained my decision to refuse a student deferment and summarized the actions I had taken thus far against the war. I said I had not done enough.

The crowd was generally somber and supportive, though some of the engineering students heckled me. One even yelled out, "Three cheers for Dow!"—a reference to the Dow Chemical Company, which had become a frequent target for antiwar protests because it manufactured napalm for use in Vietnam.[1]

---

1. Napalm had become a symbol of the inhumanity of the war in Vietnam. It was a thickening agent often mixed with gasoline to set vegetation on fire. But when napalm came in contact with human flesh, as it often did after being dropped by U.S. planes, it burned.

My speech lacked Sainte-Marie's grace and Savio's imagery, but it accurately expressed what I was feeling:

> The genocide committed by Nazi Germany is condemned by all decent human beings. We say that the German people should have said no to concentration camps, and to the murder of six million Jews. Likewise, we Americans must say no to napalm, to pacification programs, and to the mass murder of the Vietnamese people. I must say no to the draft.
>
> By cooperating with the draft I am forced to work along with an organization that is contrary to any democratic principles. With the draft system, the most basic human right—the right to live—is taken away from a person. Aside from the horribleness of forcing a person to kill, conscription forces a human being to disrupt his life and act at the whim of another human being.
>
> The destruction of the American conscience, the destruction of thousands of people, and the destruction of our universities is being caused by the United States government, its Selective Service System, and by our acquiescence. I cannot aid in that destruction. I must live by the principles that I consider ethical and good. For these reasons I must declare my noncooperation with the Selective Service System and sever all ties with it.
>
> Yours for peace and freedom,
> Bruce Dancis

I then took my draft card out of my pocket, tore it into four pieces, placed it in an envelope that had been stamped and addressed to my draft board, and sealed it. I said a few more words about Vietnam, racism, and the need for change, then walked over to a nearby mailbox and deposited the envelope.

I thought I would immediately be arrested. (From my FBI file, it appears that at least six FBI agents and/or informers witnessed my action.) But according to the *Sun*'s report, a local FBI agent stated it was not the federal government's policy to have the FBI step in when a person mutilated his draft card.

The *Syracuse Post-Standard* quoted a local FBI official as saying, "We are cognizant of the facts and are conducting an investigation.... The facts will be presented to the U.S. attorney who will then decide whether to prosecute." The story also cited a second FBI official who said my action was the first in upstate New York "involving deliberate draft card mutilation, a violation of the Selective Service

Law." (According to Kirkpatrick Sale's *SDS*, I was the first SDS member to publicly destroy his draft card.)

The Syracuse newspaper story, written by staff correspondent Jon Levy, was a strange mixture of dubious and mistaken information. Citing "informed sources in the Cornell administration," Levy wrote that I was "a devout pacifist" [true] who was "being manipulated by other persons within the organization to which he belongs" [utterly ridiculous]. It also claimed that the subject had previously been involved in an incident where a university proctor "told him to remove a button [partially wrong] which he was wearing protesting university food prices" [wrong again].

The story also conveniently listed my home address, which may have enabled some friendly types to send me hate mail. One unsigned note read: "Of all the chicken livered cowards! You didn't dare to destroy your draft card [?], yet you taunt the Proctor. You are a stinking Jew!"

Some of my friends were surprised that I decided to tear up my draft card rather than burn it. One of my reasons was practical: What if I lit a match and the wind blew it out? I didn't want to be nervously fumbling with matches or a cigarette lighter. But more important, since I was seeking a confrontation with the draft system, I felt that by sending my board the actual pieces of my draft card I was making a clear and unambiguous statement: I will no longer obey your laws that support evil and destructive policies.

I knew I was forcing the issue and would undoubtedly go to prison for my actions. But resistance had to start sometime, so why not now? And if it had to start with one person taking a stand and saying no, why shouldn't that person be me?

A College Dropout

So what do you do on the day *after* you've committed a felony that could get you a prison term of five years and a fine of $10,000? You return to class in a halfhearted and ultimately futile attempt to salvage an academic semester that had begun with divided attention and was concluding with total neglect. I had stopped going to my classes during the week prior to tearing up my draft card, and now, over the last weeks of the fall semester (which continued through the end of January 1967), I tried to cram in a semester's worth of work. But even my last-minute attempts to catch up were halfhearted, as my action had taken me to a place where school didn't seem very important.

By the end of January I had decided to take a leave of absence from Cornell to work full time in the antiwar movement. I wanted to devote my attention to the forthcoming Spring Mobilization to End the War in Vietnam, scheduled for both New York City and San Francisco on April 15, 1967. Bob Greenblatt had already taken a leave from his faculty duties to serve as a cochair of the Mobe's steering committee, and he welcomed my participation in building support for what we hoped would be the largest antiwar demonstration in history. I also wanted to keep working with Cornell SDS and with our antidraft union. The Office, where I was already spending a lot of time in lieu of being a serious student, became my full-time workplace when I wasn't in New York with Bob.

Even though schoolwork seemed far removed from where I was going, I nevertheless tried to keep my options open. I took an official leave of absence from the ILR School, retaining the possibility of returning to Cornell in September '67.

This decision did not sit well with my parents, who cut off the monthly stipend they had been sending me for room and board. To them, this was a matter of political principle. They may have loved me, but they did not support my political aims or the aims of the groups I was working with. As my mother put it at the time, "If your movement needs you so much, it should financially support you." Fortunately, by putting together the small savings I had accumulated, a few bucks here and there from the Office and Bob Greenblatt, and my roommates' graciousness in letting me pay less rent, I had enough money to get by.

I now took on a new role, as a nonstudent activist. Within a year or so, more and more Cornell students would either drop out or remain in Ithaca after graduation to work for the movement. It ended up creating a problem for the Cornell administration: what to do about these nonstudents who continued to be involved in campus activities, through SDS and other organizations.

A Radical Romance

The ending of my (formal) education at Cornell coincided with the beginning of something new in my personal life: I fell in love. I had gone out on dates only a few times as a freshman and sophomore and hadn't had a steady relationship since high school. This could be attributed to a combination of my own shyness, the three-to-one male-female ratio among Cornell undergraduates, and the absence of women my own age in the movement, particularly during my freshman year.

But this all changed when I met Jane.[2] A first-year student in Cornell's College of Home Economics (now Human Ecology), Jane had started attending SDS meetings late in 1966. Given what was happening in my life, it would have been hard to get involved with someone who was not politically sympathetic. Jane was extremely bright, had a wonderful sense of humor, and was absolutely gorgeous. The mutual attraction between us was palpable from the start, and we got very close very fast.

As our relationship deepened and became more intimate, Jane and I naturally wanted to spend the night together. But we were confronted with reactionary *in loco parentis* rules at Cornell that discriminated against female students. Undergraduate women were subject to strict curfew regulations; undergraduate men had no such rules to obey. Prior to the 1966–67 academic year, all female undergraduates under the age of twenty-two were required to live either in university dormitories or sorority houses. This rule was slightly amended in September 1966 to permit a quota of 150 senior women to live in off-campus housing. There were no similar regulations affecting male undergraduates.

But there was a strange loophole in the rules: a first-, second-, or third-year female student could "sign out" to spend a weekend at the off-campus residence of a female senior or graduate student. Fortunately for Jane and me, we had two women friends in the movement, Marjorie Holt and Susan Mokotoff, who were seniors sharing an apartment in Collegetown. They offered to provide a cover for Jane—she could sign out to stay with them, but she would actually be at my place.

We were able to use this subterfuge for the rest of the school year. Over the next three years, women's curfews were eliminated. Starting in September 1968, junior women joined senior women in being allowed to live off-campus. About a year later, prodded by first-year student and SDS member Becca Harber, the university abolished curfews for undergraduate women.

I had not been aware that my previously "single" status had been a topic of conversation among friends at Cornell until one weekend morning when I was leaving my apartment on College Avenue. Walking on the other side of the street was Matty Goodman, from our draft-resistance union, along with his girlfriend Epi Epton. When Matty, an irrepressible sort, saw me, he yelled out across the busy street, "Dancis, you still a virgin?" I blushed in embarrassment, but I couldn't totally suppress my smile.

(Tragically, Matty died six months later in a mountain-climbing accident near his family's summer home in New Hampshire. He was only twenty years old.)

2. Jane asked that I not include her last name in this book, and I am honoring her request.

Obscenity and Freedom of the Press

Around the time I decided to drop out of Cornell, the Ithaca district attorney and a university administrator took another action that had the effect of angering and radicalizing a substantial part of the student body.

The *Trojan Horse* was a campus literary magazine. In January 1967, the Ithaca company that regularly printed the magazine decided that a forthcoming article was obscene and refused to print it. The printing company also alerted Ithaca district attorney Richard Thaler about the article.

The *Horse*'s editors, Jim Moody and Greg Heins, turned to the Glad Day Press, where Marjorie Holt (Greg's girlfriend and future wife) was one of the volunteer printers. Marjorie printed the article, the journal of a former Cornell student that included his drug-inspired sexual fantasies and the use of the dangerous word "motherfucker." They then stapled the article into the magazine.

After the *Trojan Horse* went on sale, James Herson, the head administrator of the Cornell Safety Division, directed Proctor George and his men to confiscate copies of the magazine on the grounds that it was obscene. Herson evidently coordinated his action with Thaler, who on the same day obtained and served an injunction on the *Horse*'s editors prohibiting future sales of the magazine.

President Perkins and other top Cornell administrators were in New York City for a board of trustees meeting. Although Perkins intervened to stop Herson from confiscating any more copies of the *Horse,* he couldn't prevent Thaler from pursuing the matter.

Meanwhile, the *Horse*'s editors refused to back down in the face of the injunction. They announced they would attempt to sell the magazine on the steps of the Straight the following day at noon.

A rally at 11:30 a.m. at the Straight started things off. Over two thousand students listened to the *Horse*'s editors, plus several faculty members, denounce literary censorship and the DA's injunction. But Thaler and several of his plainclothes detectives were also on hand. When, at noon, Moody and Heins began selling the magazine, the detectives arrested them and a few other students. The appearance of Thaler and his men on campus broke a hundred-year-old tradition of the local police not getting involved in Cornell campus matters.

As Thaler's men put the arrested students into a car, a large group of students spontaneously surrounded the car to prevent it from being driven away—precisely what had occurred in the Berkeley student revolt of 1964. Unable to leave and facing a crowd of thousands of angry students, Thaler agreed to release the students in the car after they promised to sign a statement admitting their defiance of the injunction. The situation temporarily defused, Thaler and his men quietly left the campus.

By the next day, opposition to censorship was spreading throughout the campus community. Over fifteen hundred students and faculty members signed a statement of complicity in selling the *Horse*. The Inter-Fraternity Council voted to provide bail funds for anyone arrested. SCARB, the student group in charge of the student union, voted 8–0 to defy the DA and his court injunction and permit the sale of the magazine on its premises. John Marcham, the highest-ranking Cornell administrator still in town (Perkins remained in New York), stated that the administration would not interfere with sales.

Thaler, evidently chastened, decided to let the issue drop, a decision rendered moot on January 25, when a state court overturned the injunction and ruled that the magazine was not obscene. A few weeks later, Herson was forced to resign his position at the Cornell Safety Division. Herson's next job? He was hired as Ithaca's deputy chief of police.

The *Trojan Horse* incident was a spontaneous demonstration by students affirming their commitment to free speech and their opposition to censorship. It showed that many students, not just those in and around SDS, were beginning to understand that resistance to illegitimate authority was sometimes necessary. The willingness of Cornell students to challenge authority would again become a major issue on the campus in the not very distant future.

Chapter Six

Draft Cards Are for Burning

I was still, surprisingly, a free man in early February 1967. The federal government didn't seem to be in a big hurry to arrest me for tearing up my draft card, although two FBI agents had come to my apartment to talk to me. I told them, on the advice of my attorney, that I had nothing to say to the FBI.

At my parents' behest and the recommendation of Harrop Freeman, a professor at the Cornell Law School and an antiwar Quaker, I had contacted the New York Civil Liberties Union (the New York state affiliate of the ACLU) about defending me. The NYCLU had represented David Miller and other draft resisters, and I hoped it would take my case once I was indicted. The NYCLU agreed and put me in contact with Faith Seidenberg, a liberal, feminist attorney from Syracuse who often represented the NYCLU in cases originating in upstate New York.

Faith agreed to be my attorney, and for the next two and a half years she provided me with legal counsel that was always caring and intelligent. She understood my approach to civil disobedience and gave me her complete support. She never asked me for a cent in payment for her many hours of work on my case.

Cutting my ties to Selective Service had a liberating effect on me from the start. I later learned that such exhilaration after resisting unjust laws was referred to by civil rights activists as a "freedom high." I felt good about overcoming whatever hesitation I had about resisting the draft, and I was eager to work full time for the movement.

My spirits were also buoyed by some other events. In late December, the SDS National Council meeting in Berkeley had approved the strongest antidraft statement in the organization's history, putting SDS on record as opposing conscription and favoring the building of draft resistance unions, signing "We Won't Go" statements, and encouraging men already in the armed services to oppose the war. I was disappointed the resolution didn't go further by endorsing acts of noncooperation or renouncing student deferments, but I understood that SDS could not mandate its members to place themselves in legal jeopardy. It was clear that SDS was moving "from protest to resistance," in the words of national secretary Greg Calvert.

In January 1967, *New Left Notes* published an article that helped inform our opposition to the draft. Peter Henig, an SDS member in Michigan and researcher for SDS's Radical Education Project, had discovered a Selective Service System document on "Channeling" that had been distributed to local draft boards in 1965. It openly discussed how the draft was used not only to procure men for the armed forces but to "channel manpower." The granting of student deferments was viewed as a means to force young men to continue their education, while the issuing of occupational deferments had the purpose of steering men into certain socially acceptable jobs. The coercive nature of the draft and its apparatus of deferments were starkly explained in the document:

> Throughout his career as a student, the pressure—the threat of loss of deferment—continues. It continues with equal intensity after graduation. His local board requires periodic reports to find out what he is up to. He is impelled to pursue his skill rather than embark upon some less important enterprise and is encouraged to apply his skill in an essential activity in the national interest. The loss of deferred status is the consequence for the individual who acquired the skill and either does not use it or uses it in a non-essential activity.
>
> The psychology of granting wide choice under pressure to take action is the American or indirect way of achieving what is done by direction in foreign countries where choice is not permitted.

From then on, quoting from the "Channeling" document became a regular part of my speeches about the draft.

At around the same time, the Spring Mobilization hired the Reverend James Bevel, one of Dr. Martin Luther King Jr.'s top aides in the Southern Christian Leadership Council (SCLC) and a veteran of civil rights struggles in Birmingham, Selma, and other southern cities, to be the national director of the forthcoming antiwar demonstrations in New York and San Francisco, scheduled for April 15, 1967. Although the Mobe's leaders hoped that Bevel's involvement would attract more African Americans to the antiwar movement and help pave the way for Dr. King to take part in the New York event—King had just begun to speak out publicly against the war—Bevel was himself a gifted orator. His dynamic speaking style combined street-smart lingo with the soaring rhetoric of a black Baptist preacher. A slight man with a shaved head always covered by a skullcap, he was one of the most exciting and compelling public speakers I had ever heard. During civil rights rallies in the South it was Bevel's job to excite and warm up the audience prior to a speech by Dr. King.

I got to know Bevel when I traveled to New York with Bob Greenblatt for Mobe meetings and when I picked him up at the Syracuse airport for a speech at Cornell. He was particularly cordial to me. As a civil rights veteran familiar with civil disobedience, Bevel believed that draft resistance and other forms of nonviolent struggle were needed to end the war. He nicknamed me "Mr. Resister."

Draft resisters were also receiving enthusiastic support from some of our elders in the peace movement, in particular Mobe leader Dave Dellinger, teacher Norma Becker, writer Grace Paley, social theorist Paul Goodman, and the venerable pacifist leader A. J. Muste (shortly before he died in February). We also had the reliable backing of the folks at the War Resisters League, whose encouragement proved very important in the next few months.

"A Call to Burn Draft Cards"

The Ithaca draft resistance union faced a crisis following my action and the appearance of our "We Won't Go" statement in the *Sun*. When the group met to decide how to support me, Tom Bell later wrote, "We found it all too obvious that the only meaningful support from us would be to destroy our draft cards with him....The effect on the group at first was disturbing. While it did raise the level of seriousness, as only an action can, we found no way to be *together* in the action."

In January we opened a Selective Service counseling center in space rented from the Unitarian Church in downtown Ithaca. Our goal was to provide information on alternatives to the draft to men who were not attending Cornell. Although we staffed the center with draft counselors six days a week, we usually spoke to only a few men each day. Within a short amount of time, some in our group wanted to take more vigorous action.

The idea of a mass draft card burning had been kicking around the antiwar movement for several years, though no one had yet attempted to organize such a provocative and illegal action. In February a few of us in the Ithaca group began to seriously discuss the possibility of leading such an action, to coincide with the Spring Mobilization in New York.

At first, we debated how many people we thought we could get to burn their draft cards. I argued that however many men we recruited, we would most likely have the largest draft card burning in history. But others felt there would be more safety in numbers when facing prosecution, and wanted us to set a minimum number for our action to take place. I was persuaded to support that plan. We started at ten thousand, then quickly brought the number down to a seemingly more reasonable five hundred.

Tom had not yet decided whether to participate. He recognized that a mass draft card burning would be the strongest act of resistance against the war and the draft to date. But Tom did not believe draft resisters should go to prison. Instead, he thought resisters should, at the last minute, go underground. His view, which was soon to be shared by many in SDS nationally, was that prison should be avoided because it would remove the most dedicated people from the struggle and possibly cause them considerable harm as well.

Nevertheless, we decided to circulate a pledge to burn draft cards that would only go into effect if five hundred people signed it. Since I had already dropped out of Cornell, I became the full-time organizer for the action.

I wrote the first draft of a "Call to Burn Draft Cards," a statement that was forceful but not eloquent. Another member of our group, Burton Weiss, then wrote a second draft, which was far more poetic than mine. Dated March 2, 1967, it read:

> The armies of the United States have, through conscription, already oppressed or destroyed the lives and consciences of millions of Americans and Vietnamese. We have argued and demonstrated to stop this destruction. We have not succeeded. Murderers do not respond to reason. Powerful resistance is now demanded: radical, illegal, unpleasant, sustained.
>
> In Vietnam the war machine is directed against young and old, soldiers and civilians, without distinction. In our country, the war machine is directed specifically against the young, against blacks more than against whites, but ultimately against all.
>
> Body and soul, we are oppressed in common. Body and soul, we must resist in common. The undersigned believe that we should BEGIN this mass resistance by publically destroying our draft cards at the Spring Mobilization.
>
> We urge all people who have contemplated the act of destroying their draft cards to carry out this act on April 15, with the understanding that this pledge becomes binding only when 500 people have made it.
>
> The climate of anti-war opinion is changing. In the last few months student governments, church groups, and other organizations have

publically expressed understanding and sympathy with the position of individuals who refuse to fight in Vietnam, who resist the draft. We are ready to put ourselves on the line for this position, and we expect that these people will come through with their support.

We are fully aware that our action makes us liable for penalties of up to five years in prison and $10,000 in fines. We believe, however, that the more people who take part in this action the more difficult it will be for the government to prosecute.

Our statement was originally signed by five men, all affiliated with Cornell: graduate student Jan Flora, undergraduates Burton Weiss, Michael Rotkin, and Timothy Larkin, and Robert Nelson, director of the Commons, a coffeehouse and meeting place inside the building housing the campus ministries.

On the bottom of our statement was a place for people to sign: "I pledge to destroy my draft card at the Spring Mobilization in New York City on April 15, 1967 if there are at least 500 people who will take this action at the same time." Signers were asked to return the pledge form to me at the Office in Ithaca.

At first, I didn't think I should sign the call since I no longer had a draft card to burn. But as I began speaking to antiwar groups and SDS chapters about our proposed action, I was met with the question of why I hadn't signed the pledge myself. Even though I had a good, technical explanation—no draft card—I came to believe this was an insignificant reason. So in the subsequent printings of our call, I added my name to the signers.

As its principal organizer, I can state that the April 15, 1967, draft card burning was one of the most poorly organized acts of mass civil disobedience in the history of the antiwar movement. Still short of my nineteenth birthday, I had no experience at organizing a national action. We had virtually no funds for publicity, relying on mailings to SDS chapters, antidraft unions, and a contact list provided by the Inter-University Committee for Debate on Foreign Policy, and my speaking at campuses in New York City and in upstate New York. We also didn't have a lot of time to organize—we began our campaign only six weeks before the Spring Mobilization.

We were so naïve we used the regular U.S. Mail to send out our call and pledge form. We later found out that many of our letters never got through, as thousands of them were returned, with no explanation, after the event.

But our efforts were helped by allies who were more adept at generating publicity and using the media than we were. Paul Goodman wrote a widely circulated letter of support that appeared in a number of publications, including the *New York Review of Books,* and was sent to individuals on various antiwar mailing lists. Dave Dellinger and historian Staughton Lynd wrote and circulated another statement of support. Nat Hentoff used his weekly column in the *Village Voice* to reprint our call, and he quoted me as saying, "Whatever happens on April 15, this is not the end. It's the beginning. If we get 500 now, maybe we can get 2,000 in a few months."

Draft Resisters versus Cornell Bureaucrats

Those of us involved in organizing the draft card burning realized we might be arrested even before the event took place, because simply advocating resistance to the draft could be seen as an illegal act, and a conspiracy as well. But we never expected that the threat of arrest or punishment would come from the Cornell administration and some Cornell students.

Although our campaign was not an official activity of Cornell SDS, many of us in the draft resistance union were also involved with SDS, and the membership agreed to let us solicit pledges at the SDS information table we regularly maintained in the student union lobby. I was concerned that the administration might try to use my nonstudent status as a pretext for not allowing us to set up our table, so I formally stepped down as the president of Cornell SDS. We elected Henry Balser as acting president, though members still considered me the de facto president. (The *Sun* began to refer to me as the "non-titular head" of Cornell SDS.)

Our first two days of soliciting pledges to burn draft cards went off quietly, without incident, as we collected the pledges of twenty students. But then SCARB, the student group that oversaw campus organizations and the student union, decided that our solicitation was in violation of the Selective Service Act of 1948 and prohibited us from continuing. SCARB also ruled, after I had already resigned as Cornell SDS president, that nonstudents could not be officers of any recognized student organization.

At an emergency meeting of SDS, we decided to defy the ban. As I told a *Sun* reporter, "We're risking a $10,000 fine and five years in jail, and I personally couldn't care less about the senseless decisions of some bureaucrat." We had legal arguments in defense of our action: the Supreme Court had not yet ruled on whether the law prohibiting the destruction of draft cards, currently being appealed, was constitutional; solicitation was a form of free speech, and the university had no right to impede it. (We also should have pointed out that just two months earlier, during the *Trojan Horse* affair, SCARB had voted to defy a court injunction and the order of the Ithaca district attorney by permitting sales of the magazine in the student union. Evidently, resistance to some legal rulings was acceptable, but resistance to the draft was not.)

The conflict was not one that we in SDS were seeking. We were not interested in arguing with SCARB or the Cornell administration. Our fight was with the Selective Service System and the policies of the U.S. government.

On March 16, a few hours after we resumed taking pledges to burn draft cards, Proctor George and his men came into the Straight and ordered us to stop. We refused. George then ordered several students to accompany him to his office. They refused. The proctor then issued temporary suspensions for ten students and cited them to appear before the Undergraduate Judiciary Board. Later that day, we held a brief sit-in at the proctor's office.

The confrontation continued the next day, with the proctor arriving at the Straight and again ordering us to stop, while we again refused to obey him. But as crowds of students started gathering in the lobby of the Straight to see what all the fuss was about, something new and unprecedented occurred: spontaneous debates started to break out all around, involving SDS members and our supporters, students who opposed what we were doing and those who were just curious. Many of these arguments were one to one, but some were more dramatic and public, as several of us and some on the other side stood on top of tables in the lobby and addressed the crowd. The debates covered not only the legality of our draft card burning solicitation and whether Cornell had a right to prohibit it, but wider issues concerning the war, the draft, university complicity with the war, and civil disobedience. According to one account, "in passionate language" I addressed the crowd:

> We're saying that we will no longer go along blindly, or go along without doing anything, while our government is committing what we consider to be mass murder in Vietnam. We are willing to risk five years in jail and a fine of $10,000 to stop this murder. We are saying that the university rules and Proctor George are irrelevant to this killing. We cannot be hung up here while people are dying in Vietnam. We feel that this war is wrong. We said we will not fight in it, and we are going to destroy our draft cards because we feel it's wrong....We appeal to you to feel the same way: To say no to this government, and to destroy your draft card...on April 15th.

As the confrontation continued, antiwar faculty members emerged to support us. Some of them tried to place their bodies between the SDS table and the campus cops. In addition to the impromptu debates taking place every day in the Straight's lobby, the faculty also conducted two days of public teach-ins in another part of the Straight, where professors debated the legal and moral issues surrounding our solicitation.

Meanwhile, a group of fifty Cornell graduate students voted to allow any student suspended in conjunction with our solicitation to attend their classes anyway. We received telegrams of support from around the country, including from Dave Dellinger of the Spring Mobilization and Greg Calvert of SDS. We also received support for our right to conduct our draft card burning campaign from the board of CURW, the umbrella organization for the various denominational chaplains at Cornell.

We continued to set up our table in the Straight, but after five days of confrontations Proctor George stopped showing up to cite students. With disciplinary hearings about to begin, President Perkins finally defused the situation by putting the reins on the proctor and establishing a commission to examine the university's interpretation of *in loco parentis* rules governing political conduct on campus.

Eventually, ten of the students suspended by Proctor George received punishment, with Burton Weiss, Henry Balser, and Jill Boskey placed on disciplinary probation, and the other seven (including Marjorie Holt and Sue Mokotoff) receiving reprimands. The administration must not have figured out what to do about me, because as a nonstudent I wasn't subject to the university's legal system, and they didn't want to call in the Ithaca cops, particularly so soon after the *Trojan Horse* incident.

Of course, there was opposition on campus to both our call and our tactics. A petition apologizing to Proctor George for "the inexcusably rude treatment to which he was subject" was signed by about 450 students. And the Faculty Council, while expressing some concerns about the "wisdom" of SCARB's interpretation of campus regulations, criticized the "flagrant violations by some individuals of the University's rules and procedures and their refusal to follow due process."

But those of us involved viewed our action as an overwhelming success. By the time we finished our solicitations, over forty Cornell students had signed the pledge to burn their draft cards—far more than anyone expected. Hundreds, if not thousands, of other students and faculty members had demonstrated their support for our actions. Eventually, an estimated fifteen hundred Cornell students drove to New York City in cars and buses to take part in the Mobilization.

The draft card burning confrontation at Cornell also confirmed some lessons I had learned from the previous year's sit-in at President Perkins's office and from my own act of resistance. Active resistance to an unjust war and university policies that buttressed the war effort were effective in reaching the larger body of students and faculty who were turning against the war. Our actions provided space for others to take less militant, but nevertheless important steps of their own.

Problems with the Mobilization and Dr. King

But as April 15 drew near, two additional developments threatened to adversely affect our plans. The first was from an unexpected source—the Spring Mobilization's steering committee.

Although our call stated that we would hold the draft card burning at the Spring Mobilization in New York, we had never worked out precisely where and when it would take place. Given the confrontation we had been engaged in at Cornell and the support we had received from Mobe cochairs Dave Dellinger, Norma Becker, and our own Bob Greenblatt, as well as James Bevel, we assumed our action would be a part of the march and rally. Some of us even imagined that the burning of draft cards would be conducted from the speaker's platform at the United Nations, where the rally was to be held.

Unknown to us at Cornell, our plans were upsetting some of the groups and individuals who were part of the Mobe's broad antiwar coalition. These included some unions, liberal groups, and reform Democrats who thought our action was too controversial and would detract from the overall impact of the demonstration. Also against us were the Mobe reps of the Communist Party and the Trotskyist Socialist Worker's Party, both of whom opposed draft resistance.

Most seriously, Dr. King, who had agreed to speak at the rally, did not want to be associated with draft card burning. The most well known and respected civil rights leader and a recent recipient of the Nobel Peace Prize, King had recently started to publicly criticize U.S. policy and was receiving much criticism for it (publicly and privately) from other civil rights leaders and the Johnson administration. But he remained opposed to civil disobedience as an antiwar strategy.

Our stance put our allies among the Mobe leadership in a difficult position. They believed in what we were doing and wanted to actively support us, yet they realized our action could upset the delicately balanced coalition they had worked so hard to put together.

With time growing short—it was less than two weeks before April 15—the Mobe's leaders decided to speak to us directly, and they chartered a small plane to fly a half dozen of us from Ithaca to New York City for a high-stakes meeting. Bernard Lafayette of SCLC, representing Dr. King, told us we were threatening the success of the entire Mobilization, and that King might withdraw his participation if we persisted. One of our group made matters even more tense by stupidly and insultingly referring to Dr. King as an "Uncle Tom," which infuriated the usually mild-mannered Lafayette and embarrassed the rest of us. Al Evanoff, a trade union leader, argued that we should postpone our action until the following day—"You can even hold the draft card burning in my backyard," he said—in order to spare the Mobe any embarrassment.

Dave Dellinger and Norma Becker then came up with a compromise: we would still have our draft card burning on April 15, but it would take place in Central Park's Sheep Meadow, the march's assembly point, just before the start of the march. Although we came to no formal agreement during the meeting, after we returned to Ithaca our group decided we had no alternative but to go along with the compromise.

A Well-Timed Indictment

The second development took place shortly after we got back to Ithaca, when I was finally indicted for tearing up my draft card. On April 4 my case was presented to the federal grand jury in Auburn, New York (near Syracuse), by Assistant U.S. Attorney James Shanahan, and an indictment was issued. I was ordered to appear for arraignment in the U.S. District Court in Syracuse on April 10—just five days before our action.

About forty supporters accompanied me from Ithaca to Syracuse for the arraignment, where we were joined by some Syracuse University SDS members. I stood before Judge Edmund Port, with my attorney Faith Seidenberg alongside me, and entered a plea of not guilty. I was released on my own recognizance and in the custody of my attorney without having to post bail, and Faith was given ten days to make motions for dismissal.

I always suspected that the timing of my indictment must have had something to do with the upcoming April 15 draft card burning, but I never had any proof until years later when I obtained parts of my FBI file. Among the documents was a teletype dated March 26, 1967, and marked "urgent." It was from the director of the FBI, J. Edgar Hoover, to the FBI office in Albany: "The department advised today that USA [United States Attorney], NDNY [Northern District New York], was contacted telephonically re subject's card mutilation case. It was agreed during phone conversation that USA would present to FGJ (Federal Grand Jury) on April six next. Department prefers to have presentment made prior to student mobilization planned at New York City April fifteen next. Follow this matter very closely and keep Bureau promptly advised."

Underneath that was a note: "Dancis is head of SDS chapter at Cornell University.... He is a prime mover in the nationwide student mobilization being planned NYC 4/15/67 at which efforts are being made to convince at least 500 students to participate in simultaneous public burning of their draft cards. This matter being handled separately and is being followed closely by a number of field offices."

TELETYPE   URGENT

TO SAC ALBANY (25-12191)

FROM DIRECTOR FBI (25-546234)

BRUCE DAVID DANCIS, SSA, ONE NINE FOUR EIGHT.

THE DEPARTMENT ADVISED TODAY THAT USA, NDNY, WAS CONTACTED
                          MUTILATION
TELEPHONICALLY RE SUBJECT'S CARD WL./... CASE. IT WAS AGREED

DURING PHONE CONVERSATION THAT USA WOULD PRESENT TO FGJ ON

APRIL SIX NEXT. DEPARTMENT PREFERS TO HAVE PRESENTMENT MADE

PRIOR TO STUDENT MOBILIZATION PLANNED AT NEW YORK CITY APRIL

FIFTEEN NEXT. FOLLOW THIS MATTER VERY CLOSELY AND KEEP BUREAU

PROMPTLY ADVISED.

COPY MAILED NEW YORK.   REC 73

1 - NEW YORK

NOTE: Dancis is head of SDS chapter at Cornell University.
We have just completed a CO investigation of him.* He is a
prime mover in the nationwide student mobilization being
planned NYC 4/15/67 at which efforts are being made to
convince at least 500 students to participate in simultaneous
public burning of their draft cards. This matter being
handled separately and is being followed closely by a
number of field offices.   MAR 29 1967

* CO investigation included investigation concerning card
  mutilation by Dancis.

TRD:ghw   FEDERAL BUREAU OF INVESTIGATION
51 APR 3 1967   U. S. DEPARTMENT OF JUSTICE
                                     COMMUNICATION SECTION
                                         MAR 28 1967
  MAIL ROOM ☐ TELETYPE UNIT ☐   TELETYPE

Teletype marked "Urgent" from FBI Director J. Edgar Hoover to
the FBI office in Albany, New York, dated March 28, 1967. The
message states that the U.S. attorney for the Northern District
of New York State had been contacted about bringing the case
of Dancis's draft card destruction before a federal grand jury
prior to the planned April 15, 1967, draft card burning in
Central Park in New York City. (Bruce Dancis FBI file)

Ironically, on the same day I pleaded not guilty in Syracuse, the U.S. Court of Appeals in Boston ruled that the amendment to the Selective Service Act making it illegal to mutilate or destroy draft cards was unconstitutional. The three-judge panel declared that draft card burning was a "symbolic action" that "may be protected speech." Their ruling was in direct conflict with earlier rulings by two other appellate courts that affirmed the constitutionality of the anti-draft-card-burning amendment. Given this conflict, it would be up to the U.S. Supreme Court to make a final determination.

The case involved David O'Brien, a pacifist from Massachusetts who had burned his draft card on the steps of a Boston courthouse in March 1966. He had been convicted and sentenced by a lower court but was free on bail pending his appeal. Unfortunately for O'Brien, the same appeals court upheld his conviction on the grounds that he had violated the Selective Service Act by not having his draft card in his possession.

While I welcomed the Boston appellate court decision, I believed it was unlikely that the U.S. Supreme Court would concur. But the decision, temporary as it may have been, certainly raised our spirits at the right time.

Before I headed to New York to prepare for April 15, I sent out a letter—which we mailed from Syracuse in an attempt to avoid the problems we were having with the Ithaca post office—to all those who had submitted pledges to burn their draft cards. Only 115 people had signed pledges and returned them to us, though I expected others were planning to join us. But it was likely we would not reach our goal of five hundred draft card burners. I announced we would have a meeting in New York City of all signers of the pledge on April 14, the eve of the Mobilization, to discuss how to proceed. I also explained what had transpired between the Mobe's steering committee and our Ithaca group, and reported that we were working out the logistics of staging our action in Central Park's Sheep Meadow. Despite our failure to obtain five hundred pledges, we were still optimistic that a draft card burning could be held.

SPOTLIGHT: SHEEP MEADOW, CENTRAL PARK, NEW YORK CITY, APRIL 15, 1967

It was impossible to separate the throng of photographers, undercover FBI agents, and draft resisters when we began to burn draft cards on a cold, cloudy, and windy April day in New York's Central Park. All of our plans for a dignified and orderly action, with demonstrators standing on a rock formation on the southeastern side of Sheep Meadow and making their own, personal statements about why they had chosen to resist the draft, dissolved in the mass of people crowding around us. Yet the chaos led to a triumph of spontaneity over planning.

The large meadow was also the staging area for the start of the march to the United Nations, where the Spring Mobilization's rally and speeches would take place. Based on the giant crowd already in the Sheep Meadow by 10 a.m.—two hours before the official start of the march and one hour before our planned action—we knew the overall demonstration would be huge. But we didn't yet know how many people would burn their draft cards.

In fact, it wasn't until the previous evening that we were assured the burning would take place at all. The meeting in a large, dingy loft in New York's Free University off Union Square was attended by about 150 men who had either signed the pledge to burn draft cards or were still trying to make a decision about it, plus some female supporters and a few FBI undercover agents.

I opened the meeting by explaining, for those who hadn't received our final communication, that although we had failed to secure five hundred pledges to burn draft cards, many of us wanted to proceed anyway. But before we discussed the issue and took a vote, I introduced three sympathetic attorneys—Aryeh Neier of the ACLU, Ken Cloke of the National Lawyers Guild, and my own lawyer Faith Seidenberg—to answer questions about the legal issues facing potential draft card burners. In hindsight, it was a bad decision to invite the participation of lawyers, as it bogged us down for over an hour of speculative discussion about the federal government's possible responses to our action. But we felt it was necessary that everyone planning to take part understand the risks. Unfortunately, the legal discussion took away the time we might have more beneficially used to share our thoughts and build group solidarity beyond our Cornell gang.

Eventually, we decided that if at least fifty people agreed to burn their draft cards—a number we considered large enough to make this a significant action—we would proceed.

I asked those crammed into the loft, "How many will burn their cards if fifty do it at the same time?" After a tense period of counting votes, I was able to announce that fifty-seven men had decided to burn their cards the next day. We assumed that additional resisters, including some who were unable to attend the Friday night meeting, would join us on Saturday.

The plan was to pass out as a leaflet at Sheep Meadow our "call to burn draft cards" and to give each burner the opportunity to make a brief statement. We also handed out a leaflet to inform others gathering in the Sheep Meadow about our intentions and asking them to join us.

We had recruited a group of older supporters—members of Veterans and Reservists for Peace led by Keith Lampe and Bob Ockene, War Resisters League stalwarts David McReynolds, Ralph DiGia, Karl Bissinger, and Igal Roodenko, writers Grace Paley and Paul Goodman, Mobe leaders Dave Dellinger and Norma Becker, and others—to form a phalanx to keep back the reporters, photographers, supporters, and government agents we expected to show up.

Chaos on the Rocks

It didn't work. The rock formation, which we had hoped to use as a natural platform from which to speak and burn the draft cards, proved impossible to secure. Even before I could begin to make a statement, the horde of onlookers, led by press photographers, collapsed our line of supporters and ended up standing in our midst. With our plan in disarray, we decided to just go ahead and start burning the cards.

Matches and cigarette lighters quickly emerged, and little pieces of paper began to go up in smoke all around us. Burton Weiss used his pipe to ignite his draft card. Someone had brought a coffee can (thank you, Maxwell House!) filled with either paraffin or sand and lighter fluid, which was handed to me. Since I no longer had my own draft card to burn, I held the flaming coffee can aloft and provided a steady flame for others to burn their cards. Soon, dozens and dozens of draft cards were aflame, one setting another afire, as small clusters of resisters and their friends gathered around the area. Some women also took part, holding on to the burning cards of their boyfriends and husbands.

It immediately became apparent, as scores of men came out of the crowd to join us, that many more than fifty-seven people were burning their cards

The *New York Times*'s Douglas Robinson wrote, "Cheers and chants of 'Resist, Resist' went up as small white cards—many of which were passed hand to hand from outside the circle—caught fire. . . . Like the rest of the demonstrators, the card burners were a mixed group. Most were of college age, and included bearded, button-wearing hippies, earnest students in tweed coats and ties, and youths who fitted in neither category."

Bruce Dancis (right foreground, in jacket and tie) holds a
coffee can torch for burning draft cards in Central Park's
Sheep Meadow, April 15, 1967. An estimated 175–185 men took
part in the antiwar protest, the first mass draft card burning
in American history. (Burt Glinn, Magnum Photos; all
rights reserved)

Then, another surprise. Onto the rocks stepped a tall young man,
Gary Rader, wearing the dress uniform of the U.S. Army Special
Forces (the Green Berets). At first, I thought he was a counterdemonstrator. But when Gary took out his own draft card and started
to burn it, I realized he was one of us. I found out later that Gary
was a Special Forces reservist whose antiwar and antidraft views
developed while he was serving on active duty. He soon became
an activist in Chicago, helping to form Chicago Area Draft Resistance (CADRE).

Agents from various federal and local law enforcement bodies
watched the proceedings with considerable interest. According to
Tom Wells's account,

New York Red Squad and FBI agents swarmed around the area
[of the draft card burning] like bees around a hive. At one
point two plainclothesmen edged into the center of the crowd.
One snatched a burning piece of paper from the coffee can and

began to examine it. As the crowd closed in on him, the other ran away. "Go get him," yelled the first agent. The protesters turned to look at the fleeing figure. His partner then sauntered off, the paper in his pocket, a smile on his face.

Although it was impossible to get an accurate count of the number of draft card burners at the Sheep Meadow, we estimated that 175 to 185 men took part in our action.

Once the draft card burning concluded, the march from Central Park to the rally site at the United Nations seemed anticlimactic. But the spirit of the Cornell resisters was buoyant. Marty Jezer, a writer for the pacifist periodical *WIN* and a participant in the draft card burning, gave one account of the march: "The Cornell contingent, numbering in the thousands, was led by its 'We Won't Go' organization and draft card burners under a large banner, 'WE WON'T GO' emblazoned in the school colors. Locked arm and arm they were literally dancing down the street, joyful, defiant, irresistible. 'Hell, No, We Won't Go,' their words vibrated between the sterile buildings on Madison Avenue and echoed up and down the canyon-like side streets."

The march and rally attracted so many people—four hundred thousand, in the Mobe's estimate—it took hours to walk the relatively short distance from Central Park to the United Nations. By 4 p.m., some marchers hadn't even left the park. By the time the Cornell group arrived at the UN, most of the speakers had already finished. (The NYPD estimated the crowd at the UN to be between 100,000 and 125,000, which vastly undercounted the total number of participants in the march and rally.)

So I missed the speeches by Dr. Benjamin Spock, Floyd McKissick of CORE, Dr. King, Rev. Bevel, Dave Dellinger, and others. I felt particularly bad I didn't get to hear Stokely Carmichael of SNCC ally himself and his organization with the draft resistance movement by proclaiming "Hell No, We Won't Go" from the speaker's platform. It might not have been what we had originally hoped for—which was to have resisters burn their draft cards from that platform—but it was good enough.

I went back to my parents' apartment in the Bronx feeling elated. Although we had not succeeded in organizing the five hundred draft card burners we had initially hoped for, our numbers represented, by far, the largest act of civil disobedience against the draft in the history of the war in Vietnam.

Our success, I hoped, would lead to bigger and bigger draft resistance actions in the future. At the very least, we had made draft resistance the cutting edge of the growing movement against the war. We defied the fear that had been keeping so many young men from resisting the draft, and we created a moment in the long history of Americans rebelling against injustice. As Marty Jezer wrote about his own participation in the action, "Not to have burned a draft card April 15th would have been tantamount to living in Boston in 1773 and not to have dumped tea in Boston harbor."

Despite the fears of some in the Mobe, our action did not detract from the overall impact of the march and rally. As our supporter Paul Goodman wrote a month later, "The burners never got lost in the shuffle nor did they hog the publicity."

Indeed, the headline for the *New York Times* story about the day's events balanced the larger march and rally with our action, even if it did undercount the number of demonstrators and gave far too much publicity to a minuscule group of counterprotesters: "100,000 Rally at U.N. against Vietnam War—Many Draft Cards Burned—Eggs Tossed at Parade."

The Spread of Resistance

One other important development occurred on April 15. In San Francisco, sixty thousand antiwar demonstrators were taking part in the West Coast's Spring Mobilization. One of the speakers, former Stanford University student body president David Harris, announced plans for a nationwide draft card turn-in, to take place on October 16.

A month earlier, Harris and his friend Dennis Sweeney had met with two Berkeley activists, Lennie Heller and Steve Hamilton, who were already planning a nationwide action. They even had a name for the new organization that would carry it out: the Resistance. Harris and Sweeney immediately agreed to take part.

Such was the primitive state of communications in the movement at the time that I didn't learn about the formation of "the Resistance" until a month later, when Heller made his first organizing trip to the East Coast. Immediately after our April 15 action, a few of the draft card burners from New York City and I formed a new organization, Draft Denial, to plan additional antidraft actions. A group of our older supporters organized Support-in-Action to provide both moral and active support for the draft card burners when and if we faced prosecution. By the summer of 1967 Draft Denial had become the

New York City chapter of the Resistance, while Support-in-Action changed its name to Resist, an adult draft resistance support group.

The government didn't wait long to begin questioning participants about the draft card burning. Within a week, agents tried to talk to resisters in New York, Ithaca, Chicago, and at Penn State University, and there may have been other instances I didn't hear about. At the advice of our attorneys, I destroyed all of the pledges we had obtained prior to April 15. Tom Bell and I also sent out a letter to draft card burners that advised participants to refuse to speak to the FBI without an attorney being present.

Only one of our draft card burners was arrested in the immediate aftermath of the April 15 action. To no one's surprise, the target of the government was Gary Rader, the Special Forces reservist who had joined us at Sheep Meadow. He was arrested in Chicago on April 19 on charges of violating the Selective Service Act by mutilating his draft card and illegally wearing his military uniform at the demonstration.

Back at Cornell, while some activists were beginning their "sentences" for defying the university, our impact was growing.

The Faculty Committee on Student Affairs voted to suspend the enforcement of SCARB's ruling that we weren't allowed to solicit draft card burning pledges in the student union. Although this didn't save those who had already been punished for their actions, it meant that future draft resistance efforts at Cornell would not face such legalistic opposition.

Our success in generating support from the campus clergy had apparently caused considerable consternation among Cornell administrators. In a memo to President Perkins in late April, the vice president for student affairs, Mark Barlow, bemoaned this support and the "essentially unmanageable situation in Anabel Taylor" (the building on campus with offices for all the chaplains). He warned Perkins, "We need to get [the chaplains] back into making a legitimate impact on all students, not just the lunatic fringe."

Even more significantly, our action had clearly moved people to the left and gave many the strength to take more militant actions themselves. In May, we began circulating another "We Won't Go" statement, the first since twenty-one of us signed our names to one the previous December. The new statement, published in the *Sun* on May 24, read: "We, the undersigned, having concluded that our government is waging a war of aggression in Vietnam, declare that we will not serve in the armed forces so long as the United States is engaged in this or any other unjust and immoral war." (The *Sun* refused to print the concluding sentence, "We encourage others to take this position," on the grounds that such a statement could possibly subject the newspaper to prosecution under federal law.)

The statement was signed by 221 "draft-eligible men"; 170 others, mostly women, were listed as "Those not eligible for the draft who support the above."

The growing antiwar and draft resistance movements were having an impact on the Johnson administration. *New York Times* columnist James Reston reported in early May about debates taking place within the administration on the draft and student deferments. In March, a national commission investigating reform of the Selective Service recommended getting rid of most student deferments. But, according to Reston, this idea was rejected by the administration. "The opposition to the Vietnam war in the universities is already an embarrassment and an irritation to the Administration," Reston wrote. "But there is genuine fear here that abolition of all or most college deferments might lead to *massive defiance* [my emphasis] among undergraduates. One estimate here is that if college students were called like any other nineteen-year-olds, as many as 25 per cent of them might refuse to serve."

Two weeks after the draft card burning, heavyweight boxing champion Muhammad Ali refused induction into the armed forces. Ali, who had become a follower of the Nation of Islam (known as the Black Muslims) and declared, famously, "I ain't got no quarrel with them Viet Cong," had been turned down on his applications to obtain conscientious objector status and, later, a ministerial deferment from the draft. He was then classified 1-A.

A few months later, Ali was tried, convicted, and sentenced to the maximum penalty—five years in jail and a $10,000 fine—and stripped of his heavyweight crown. Although the U.S. Supreme Court four years later unanimously overturned Ali's conviction, at the time the news of his action was electrifying. As David Remnick wrote in his book about the fighter, "Ali's refusal to go to Vietnam touched young people, especially young African-Americans, profoundly."

Early in May, Tom Wicker of the *New York Times* wrote a column about Ali and draft resistance that raised several crucial questions: "What would happen if all young men of draft age took the same position? What, indeed, would happen if only, say, 100,000 young men flatly refused to serve in the armed forces, regardless of their legal position, regardless of the consequences?

"A hundred thousand Muhammad Alis, of course, could be jailed," Wicker wrote. "But if the Johnson Administration had to prosecute 100,000 Americans in order to maintain its authority, its real power to pursue the Vietnamese war or any other policy would be crippled if not destroyed. It would then be faced not with dissent, but with civil disobedience on a scale amounting to revolt."

Chapter Seven

The Summer of Love and Disobedience

The summer of 1967 has been remembered as the "Summer of Love," a season of urban bucolic bliss, especially in the San Francisco Bay Area, celebrating sex, drugs, and rock 'n' roll. The African American residents of Newark, Detroit, and other cities experienced a different kind of summer, one of riots, rebellion, and military occupation. But for me, the summer of 1967 was a short, intense period of antiwar and antidraft organizing, getting sucker punched by a pro-war counterdemonstrator, civil disobedience, and invading the New York Stock Exchange.

Bob Greenblatt was attempting to develop a new strategy for the antiwar movement following the success of the Spring Mobilization and draft card burning. While some antiwar activists were taking part in Vietnam Summer, a nationwide organizing drive to bring the peace movement's message to new communities, Bob began exploring ways in which the Mobilization could expand its role from sponsoring mass marches and rallies to promoting direct action and resistance. Taking as his model the civil disobedience actions of the civil rights movement, as well as the draft resistance confrontations at Cornell, Bob came up with the idea of establishing "Direct Action Teams."

The idea was to recruit groups of ten to twenty dedicated young people—made up primarily of resisters and others willing to commit acts of civil disobedience—to engage in "nonviolent confrontations" in particular communities as a means of building resistance to the war and prodding others to get more involved in the movement. The idea was to send these teams into communities where we could easily fit in (that is, don't send white college students to Harlem or other largely African American neighborhoods) and which were already somewhat amenable to an antiwar message.

Since the participants would all be young, the theory was that it would not take a lot of money to sustain us. Although some in our group had savings or independent sources of income, I didn't. Bob promised to get me fifteen dollars a week, which was inadequate, even though I was living cheaply by staying in my parents' apartment in the Bronx.

Working initially with a group of about eight of us from Cornell, Bob established the Mobilization Direct Action Project (MDAP) and targeted the Flatbush section of Brooklyn, particularly the neighborhood around Brooklyn College. This was a generally liberal area that was thought to be ripe for increased antiwar activity. But none of us had any previous ties to the neighborhood. While a few from our group moved into an apartment in Flatbush, we never took the time to make deep, personal connections with its residents. I decided to split my time between MDAP and working in the new office of the Resistance in Manhattan, where we had begun organizing for the nationwide draft card turn-in slated for October 16.

My first assignment with MDAP was to contact any draft resistance groups in the area. It didn't help that Brooklyn College was already out of session for the summer and the campus was pretty deserted. But I was able to locate a member of a small group called the Brooklyn Anti-Draft Union, and he agreed to help distribute some of our antiwar literature in Flatbush. So did local members of Women's Strike for Peace and the High School Mobilization committee, who were contacted by others in our MDAP group.

Our first public activity in Brooklyn was to hand out antiwar leaflets on street corners and on the Brooklyn College campus. We then decided to set up information tables next to armed services recruiting stations. We hoped to meet young men who were considering enlisting in the military and offer them alternatives, and to spread our antiwar message to passersby.

We were not oblivious to the dangers of our plan. Although antiwar opinion was growing by the summer of '67, taking an antiwar message into neighborhoods and city streets was still a relatively new tactic and carried the risk of provoking hostile responses by pro-war individuals and groups.

To prepare us for any attacks or arrests, we took part in workshops on nonviolent direct action techniques led by Bruce Hartford, a veteran of the Southern Christian Leadership Council. We discussed the do's and don'ts of nonviolent action, role-played to test our response to abusive language and behavior by pro-war forces and the police, and practiced protecting our bodies if physically attacked.

"Attacked on the Streets of Flatbush"

On the morning of Tuesday, July 11, about ten of us set up two peace information tables. I was with a small group at the army recruiting station at Flatbush and Nostrand Avenues, handing out leaflets and sitting at a small card table. A similar group was half a block away at a navy-marines recruiting station. These locations gave us high visibility, as both recruiting stations were across the street from Brooklyn College and next to a subway station, and there was a lot of foot traffic.

For most of the morning, things went about as expected. We were on the receiving end of some heckling, nothing too serious or threatening, and we were congratulated by others walking by. The recruiters themselves didn't talk to us on the few occasions when they stepped outside of their stations to take a look at what was going on. A couple of uniformed policemen stood outside both recruiting stations.

By around 2 p.m., the situation at the navy-marines station had deteriorated, as the number of hecklers had grown and their demeanor was getting angrier. Apparently, the recruiters had recruited their own friends and supporters to come down and give us a hard time. Several of these counterdemonstrators started throwing eggs at our people, but they stopped when the police intervened. With the crowd beginning to grow increasingly menacing, the group sent someone running over to us outside the army recruiting station to ask what to do.

Bob, our leader, was nowhere around; he had left the area earlier in the morning after we set up the tables. As we tried to reach Bob (in those days before cell phones), we decided the other group should take down its table and move to where the rest of us were. Unfortunately, they brought the hostile crowd, now numbering around fifty or sixty, with them.

It was now around 5 p.m. I was passing out leaflets, and two of my Cornell buddies, Alan Snitow and Larry Kramer, were sitting nearby at our table. As the growing mob reached our site, two men confronted Alan and Larry at the table, screaming at them and waving small American flags in their faces. Without warning, one of the men grabbed the table and turned it over, knocking Alan to the ground. As he lay there, another guy came over and kicked him squarely in the face. As I rushed over to Alan, who was bleeding profusely from his nose, I felt a hard blow against my ear. Someone had sucker punched me. I didn't go down, but a small trickle of blood started coming out of my ear, though nothing like the blood flowing from Alan's face.

The police, who had been standing idly by while all this was happening, finally moved in. Four or five uniformed officers were present by now, and they were able to keep the belligerent crowd away from us and called an ambulance for Alan. Finally, Bob arrived on the scene and accompanied Alan to the nearest hospital.

By then it was 6 p.m. The recruiting stations closed down, and the rest of us decided to leave as planned. The police held back the crowd as small groups of us got into cars or, in my case, went underground to the subway station. No one from the mob followed us. When I got back to the Bronx I was no longer bleeding from my ear, though I did have a headache.

When we met the next day to go over what had happened, we decided to call an emergency meeting in the neighborhood to rally support. Alan, meanwhile, was moved to a hospital closer to his parents' home in Westchester County, where he underwent reconstructive surgery on his nose.

We secured the Church of the Evangel, a local church with a sympathetic minister, for our meeting. We handed out in the neighborhood a leaflet with the screaming headlines, "WHAT IS HAPPENING TO AMERICA?!" and "ATTACKED ON THE STREETS OF FLATBUSH!" It offered a brief account of the incident, expressed concern over the "suppression of dissent," and asked those who were concerned to attend.

I was chosen to chair the meeting at the church. But outside of our group, only about twenty Flatbush residents showed up. I was pleasantly surprised that two of the neighborhood people were my aunt Anne and uncle Matty, who lived in Flatbush, but the meeting was a failure. We had wanted to generate a community reaction to the assault, but it was apparent that by moving so quickly we had failed to reach many people. And those who did attend were not inclined to do anything other than offer sympathy.

We should have returned to the recruiting stations to show we could not be intimidated, but we did not. Sometimes, violence succeeds at intimidation.

I was pretty angry with Bob for not being there at the crucial time when the threat of violence against us was escalating. Perhaps he might have been able to defuse the situation; perhaps not. But to me he had failed to provide the leadership we needed in a crisis. To be a leader in the movement, you had to be willing to take the same risks as the people you were leading.

We soon abandoned our Brooklyn campaign, and most of us started working on other antiwar projects. Ed Fields, also from our Cornell group, and I began to work full time for the Resistance. But MDAP wasn't quite over yet.

SPOTLIGHT: A NAVAL BLOCKADE, AUGUST 6, 1967

I was wearing a gruesome death mask and a black shroud when the two New York City cops picked my limp body off the ground, carried me over to their police wagon, and dumped me inside. I had just been arrested, along with eleven others, alongside a U.S. Navy destroyer, charged with disturbing the peace, unlawful assembly, resisting arrest, and (my personal favorite) masquerading in public.

The short story of our demonstration was told by *New York Times* reporter John Kifner: "The United States Navy repulsed a boarding party of a dozen demonstrators against the war in Vietnam yesterday." Even better was the *Daily News* headline: "Peaceniks Take a Walk Off a Plank."

This is a slightly longer version of the saga of the *Newman K. Perry* Twelve:

August 6 is Hiroshima Day, a day when people around the world commemorate the United States' dropping an atomic bomb on the Japanese city of Hiroshima in 1945. More than one hundred thousand people—most of them civilians—died instantly, while tens of thousands died later or became ill from radiation poisoning. Along with the U.S. bombing of Nagasaki, Japan, a few days later, it represents the only use of nuclear weapons in history. Whatever one thinks about the efficacy of using such weapons on civilian populations, or whatever position one takes on the still-debated issues surrounding the Japanese surrender and the end of the Second World War, Hiroshima Day is a time to mourn the human suffering caused by weapons of mass destruction.

Therefore, some of us in the peace movement viewed August 6, 1967, as a particularly inappropriate time for the U.S. Navy to host a visitor's day onboard the USS *Newman K. Perry,* a destroyer just back from the coast of Vietnam. The ship was docked at Pier 90 on the Hudson River at Fiftieth Street. It seemed almost obscene to festively open a warship for kids and families on this day.

Shortly after the incident in Flatbush, some in our MDAP group began working with the Bread and Puppet Theater in preparation for a Hiroshima Day demonstration at the ship. Bread and Puppet, a radical theater group founded in the early '60s by Peter Schumann, had been involved with the peace movement since its first days. The group was also generous in sharing its mask- and costume-making materials and techniques with others.

Since I was spending most of my time at the Resistance office, I wasn't involved very much in the planning of the August 6 demonstration or in making the fantastical-looking papier-mâché death masks and black shrouds under the guidance of the Bread and Puppet folks. Nevertheless, I was there, wearing a mask and shroud, when the protest began.

Around noon, a dozen of us (ten men and two women) who were in costume and prepared to risk arrest marched toward the Fiftieth Street pier from a park a few blocks away; a few of us clanged tiny hand cymbals and rang little bells. We were joined at the pier by a support group of about the same size wearing "civilian" clothes.

We were aware of the existence of an obscure state law that made it illegal for groups of three or more adults to wear masks in public. Specifically, the law, which originated in 1845 when tenant farmers in the Hudson Valley disguised themselves as Indians and attacked their landlords, forbade "an assemblance in public houses or other places of three or more persons disguised by having their faces painted, discolored, colored or concealed." Anticipating that the police might try to get rid of us as soon as we showed up *en masque*, we had already decided to remove the masks to avoid arrest. We were there to protest the war, not the mask law.

Sure enough, when we reached the entrance to the pier the cop in charge told our spokesperson, Rodney Robinson, that we would be arrested if we didn't take off the masks. We complied by turning them around to the back of our heads. The police then moved us to a space they had set up for pickets. We vigiled, clanged, and rang while our supporters marched around us, carrying signs reading "Danger, Ship of Death," "This Ship Is Not a Toy," "Destroyers Destroy People," and "Hiroshima—August 6, 1945 / Vietnam—August 6, 1967."

The *Newman K. Perry* was supposed to open at 1 p.m. Surprisingly, the police let us onto the pier and allowed us to walk slowly toward the ship and get in line behind the other visitors. Meanwhile, the NYPD's "Red Squad" took photographs of all of us.

When we reached the ship's gangplank, one sailor pulled a metal chain across to stop us, and a small group of sailors stood together in a human chain behind it, in case we pierced the destroyer's first line of defense. One of the ship's officers, Commander John A. Smith, then came down to meet us.

"I'm going to deny your visit until general visiting is secured," he said (as reported by Leticia Kent in the *Village Voice*). "In view of your aims stated here"—he had one of our leaflets in his hand—"you appear to be under a misconception as to the mission and general purposes of a destroyer in the United States Navy, and I will be happy to personally escort you after we permit the large group waiting outside to make their tour."

Rod replied that we sought no special privileges and wanted to board the ship with everyone else. The commander ignored him and walked back up the gangplank to the ship. As we stood in front of the gangplank, effectively blocking it, sailors opened up a second gangplank about twenty feet away to allow other visitors to board the ship. Immediately, four of us walked over to the second gangplank and tried to step onto it. This time, a group of sailors linked arms and started pushing hard against the four, who then decided to sit down. I was with the group at the first gangplank, and we sat down as well.

At this time, the police brought the port captain of Pier Ninety over to where we were sitting. They asked him if he wanted us arrested. He declined.

Rod then went over to the policeman in charge to complain about the sailors' pushing and shoving, but he was told the police did not have any jurisdiction on the pier except in the case of protecting life and property. Hearing that, we decided to put our masks back on.

It was then the police's chance to confer, and after a few minutes they began arresting the twelve of us. Most of us went limp (hence the resisting arrest charge) and were either carried or dragged over to an NYPD patrol wagon. As we were being arrested, we heard some boos and taunts from the other visitors. But we also heard a parent replying to his child's questions about us by saying we represented dead Vietnamese.

Despite being under arrest, we were all in buoyant spirits when we arrived at Precinct Sixteen on West Forty-Seventh Street. The ten men were placed in a holding cell, while the two women in our group (Jill Boskey and Ellie Dorsey, both from Cornell) were allowed to wander around. To pass the time, we started singing freedom songs and antiwar songs.

Suddenly, one of our group burst out, quickly joined by the others, with a spirited rendition of the theme song to the TV sitcom *Car 54, Where Are You?* a show about wacky members of the NYPD, while standing in a holding cell in a New York City police station. Maybe because we were neither angry at the cops nor threatening in any way, the police didn't even get mad at us for our irreverent choice of singing material.

After a few hours, we were all taken to the courthouse downtown. We men were moved around a bit—first to a large cell with other prisoners, later to a smaller cell adjacent to the courtroom—before we went before a judge. Our supporters had miraculously come up with enough money to bail out all of us—most for twenty-five dollars. By 10:30 p.m. we had all been released.

The newspaper coverage of our protest was much greater than I had anticipated. Most of the stories ran alongside photos of us wearing our Bread and Puppet costumes. It was getting harder and harder to obtain media coverage of antiwar demonstrations, so our success at generating such coverage was undoubtedly due to the spectacle we had created by wearing the death masks and shrouds. I was sure that had we taken the exact same action while wearing our regular clothes, we would have been ignored by the press.

The wheels of justice rolled quickly for the *Newman K. Perry* Twelve. We had a one-day trial on August 24, in which we were defended as a group by Alan Levine and Burt Neuborne of the NYCLU. (Alan Snitow's parents got him his own attorney.) After throwing out the masquerading, resisting arrest, and disorderly conduct charges, the judge considered only the unlawful assembly charge.

The fast-paced trial was highlighted by Alan Snitow's testimony as a representative of all the defendants, and the judge's angry admonitions to Jill Boskey after Jill kept dropping her knitting needles on the courtroom floor, resulting in one loud clang after another. But then our defense attorneys pulled out a surprise. It turned out that a film crew—I can't remember whether they were from Great Britain or Germany—had been making a documentary about our demonstration. They began with our constructing the masks and sewing the shrouds with the Bread and Puppet Theater and concluded with our getting arrested at Pier Ninety. Our lawyers were allowed to screen some of the most pertinent raw footage in court. They were able to show that, despite our sit-down in front of the *Newman K. Perry*'s entrance gangplank, the navy's opening of a second gangplank allowed other visitors to come and go. In other words, although we tried to walk up the two gangplanks to the ship, the navy outflanked us, pushing us back, and we failed. Hence, we were not an "unlawful assembly."

We were all acquitted.

Hippies and Radicals

There were differences between hippies celebrating their "Summer of Love" and New Leftists and antiwar people like me. Contrast the hippies' "free your head" ethos with the civil rights movement's effort to free black people from segregation and the antiwar movement's fight to free Vietnamese of American bombs.

But by the summer of 1967, some of these differences began to disappear on both a superficial level and more deeply. Among us young radicals, long hair was increasingly common for men. We were smoking pot and "experimenting" with psychedelic drugs like LSD. Sexual freedom, enhanced by the availability of birth control pills, was on the rise. And you couldn't tell us apart from hippies by the way we dressed.

Primarily because of my legal status—I was under indictment and awaiting a trial date for tearing up my draft card—I was more wary than most of my friends about drugs. I assumed that I could be arrested at any time for the April 15 draft card burning and believed the authorities would have loved to bust me for pot possession and smear my cause accordingly.

I adopted a few rules. First, I would never take psychedelics like LSD or "magic mushrooms" that could render me temporarily out of control. I did not want to put myself in a position where I might be arrested while tripping. Second, I would never purchase or carry any pot on me and would be cautious about when and where I smoked. I might enjoy a joint in the quiet confines of a friend's apartment, but I tried to avoid loud and rowdy parties that might attract the police or narcs. I don't think I was being paranoid, just cautious.

As for sexual freedom, I was in a monogamous relationship with Jane. I had many opportunities in the late '60s to sleep with different women, but I didn't. Ever. I may occasionally have had lust in my heart (as Jimmy Carter later put it) for other women, but I kept my pants on.

Jane was also spending the summer in New York City, living in her parents' home and working as a nanny and babysitter. Between her working hours and my uncertain schedule, which included frequent night meetings, we didn't get to see each other more than once a week—usually when she had a day off in the middle of the week and her parents were at work.

She wanted me to meet her folks. I was up for it, as I'm a personable guy and I usually got along well with the parents of my friends. I figured I could charm her parents. Unfortunately, Jane's parents had already decided they didn't like me. They had come to the conclusion that a young man who had dropped out of college and was apparently headed for prison wasn't the best catch for their daughter. They were fearful that I was taking Jane deeper into a world of community organizing and political protest.

After a tense boyfriend-meets-parents dinner at their home, Jane's father offered to drive me to the bus stop, about a mile away. What a nice, friendly gesture, I thought, as we began driving, until he turned to the curb and stopped the car. His previously calm demeanor had disappeared, replaced by fury. He demanded that I stop seeing his daughter and ordered me to have nothing more to do with her.

I was taken aback, but I kept my cool. I replied that Jane was an adult (she had turned eighteen shortly before we got together) and had the right to make her own decisions. We drove the rest of the way to the bus stop in silence.

The conflicts that were arising between many in my generation and our parents were called the "generation gap." The term represented the gulf separating the social and cultural values, as well as the political differences, between our parents and us baby boomers.

Increasingly, my generation's antagonism to our elders and the world they had created was embodied by our rock 'n' roll.

The Beatles continued to lead the way in giving voice to our feelings and aspirations. John Lennon, Paul McCartney, George Harrison, and Ringo Starr were as much a part of the youth movement of the '60s and affected by it personally as they were key influences upon it.

In the Beatles' new album, *Sgt. Pepper's Lonely Hearts Club Band*, released in the United States on June 2, 1967, the use of recreational drugs, a freer attitude toward sexuality, a communal ethos among youth worldwide, and the chasm between the young and the old and the hip and the square were all given new expression. *Sgt. Pepper* spent fifteen weeks at number one on the *Billboard* charts during the summer of '67, and its influence was felt just about everywhere.

While *Sgt. Pepper* was impressing grown-ups as well as young people with its experimentation and novel use of mellotrons, sitars, and the strings, woodwinds, and brass of a classical orchestra, it was just the tip of the musical iceberg. This spectacular season saw the first great rock music festival, Monterey Pop (in mid-June), the crossover success of a grittier style of soul music led by Aretha Franklin and Otis Redding, the national emergence of San Francisco Bay Area bands like the Jefferson Airplane, Grateful Dead, and Country Joe and the Fish, and the incendiary recording debuts of the Doors and the Jimi Hendrix Experience.

It was also the summer in which Arlo Guthrie, Woody Guthrie's twenty-year-old son, debuted "Alice's Restaurant," his lengthy, shaggy dog of an antidraft story, in front of twenty thousand fans at the Newport Folk Festival. He released it, as "Alice's Restaurant Massacre," on a recording in September, filling the entire first side of his folk-rock debut album.

Enter Abbie

If young people were all listening to the same music, few saw the potential connection between hippies and the movement better than Abbie Hoffman. I had first met Abbie some months earlier, when I was organizing for the draft card burning at the Spring Mobilization. Abbie, a former SNCC organizer in Mississippi, was running Liberty House, a "freedom store" in Greenwich Village where he sold crafts made by the Poor People's Corporation in

Mississippi. Although Abbie was not eligible for the draft (he had received a 4-F for bronchial asthma), he was one of the Support-in-Action folks who stood by us when we burned our draft cards.

Given his later fame, it's strange to picture Abbie Hoffman working behind the counter at a retail store. It was a job he didn't hold for long, as he was just beginning his journey from the civil rights movement to countercultural activism on the Lower East Side and East Village. He became a Digger, which was a sort of radicalized hippie. The Diggers, who took their name from a group of utopian revolutionaries in seventeenth-century England, were founded in California by members of the San Francisco Mime Troupe with the purpose of providing free food and clothing for hippies. These West Coast Diggers were hostile toward leftist politics and political action, preferring to work as cultural rebels. They also sought anonymity, which one would hardly associate with Abbie (although the author of his first book, *Revolution for the Hell of It*, was listed as "Free").

Abbie, like those of us in MDAP, was an admirer of the Bread and Puppet Theater. He had concluded, according to his biographer, Jonah Raskin, "that mass media coverage was essential if the movement was to grow. Moreover, if the movement was to capture media attention, it would have to stretch its own provincial boundaries and stage highly visual events that were made for TV." When he saw the Bread and Puppet Theater at antiwar demonstrations dressed in their death masks and black shrouds and carrying large, black coffins, Abbie said, "That was drama, not explanation."

Abbie and his new comrade-in-capers, Jim Fouratt, tried out their new ideas in May 1967 when they formed the Flower Brigade, a small group of hippies and antiwar folks dressed like hippies. The brigade tried to take part in a "Support our Boys in Vietnam" march and rally in New York, a pro-war response to the Spring Mobilization. Carrying flowers, American flags, and signs with "Love" written on them, they gently tried to make the point that the best way to support U.S. soldiers in Vietnam was to bring them home. Their participation culminated in a flurry of punches, kicks, and thrown eggs from some in the march, but the Flower Brigade ended up getting as much media attention as the pro-war demonstrators.

Abbie and Jim continued to experiment with guerrilla theater. They staged a "sweep in" in the East Village complete with brooms, mops, and other cleaning equipment; tried to plant a tree in the middle of crowded St. Mark's Place; held a marijuana "smoke-in" in Tompkins Square Park; and threw soot in the air outside the headquarters of Con Edison, the local power utility.

More seriously, shortly after the Newark riots of mid-July had ended, with the New Jersey National Guard still occupying the black neighborhoods of the city, Abbie and some Digger friends brought food, clothing, and other needed supplies to Tom Hayden and the Newark Community Union Project (NCUP), an SDS offshoot. NCUP then distributed the supplies in their neighborhood. In *Revolution for the Hell of It*, Abbie, no pacifist, remembered this remark: "We brought a lot of canned goods, Tom, so the people can eat them or throw them at the cops."

A few of us were so impressed with Abbie's action that we tried to form a group to respond with aid should additional rebellions break out in the New York–New Jersey area. Abbie, with his usual cheekiness, even suggested a name for our group—the Committee of Concerned Honkies. But we abandoned our efforts after one public meeting descended into a cacophony of dangerous ideas—such as arming ourselves and joining the black rioters or trying to disrupt or delay the police, National Guard, or the army if they were called out to suppress a riot.

I had kept in touch with Abbie throughout the summer and admired his courage, creativity, and sense of humor. When he called me at the Resistance office one day in late August to recruit me for a proposed action, I quickly agreed to take part and offered to try to find other people to join us.

There was one logistical problem—the date Abbie had chosen for his action happened to be the same day as the trial of the *Newman K. Perry* Twelve. We couldn't ditch the trial, obviously, but there was a two-hour break for lunch.

Just enough time to run from the city courts building to the New York Stock Exchange.

SPOTLIGHT: INVADING THE NEW YORK STOCK EXCHANGE, AUGUST 24, 1967

Business stopped on the floor of the New York Stock Exchange, the citadel of American capitalism, when the money began to fall from the sky. But the dollars weren't manna from heaven. They were thrown from the visitor's gallery of the exchange by a raucous group of demonstrators led by Abbie Hoffman.

According to reporter John Kifner's story in the *New York Times*, some of the "hippie" demonstrators "were dressed in their normal studied shabbiness, but others had disguised themselves with haircuts, jackets and ties." I was one of those demonstrators in "disguise," although my mother would have sworn that I hadn't had a haircut in some time. The reason some were wearing the uncustomary uniforms of jackets, ties, and dresses was that a bunch of us were on trial in a nearby courthouse for our protest a few weeks earlier on Hiroshima Day.

Abbie was not yet well known, even in the East Village, as was shown when the underground newspaper the *East Village Other* referred to him as "Abbe" Hoffman in its coverage of the stock exchange demonstration. (The *New York Post* story about the demonstration called him "Abbey.") But he had come to the attention of the administration of New York mayor John Lindsay, a liberal Republican, who appointed Abbie and Jim Fouratt to the city's Youth Board Council.

Abbie needed some troops for his planned action and found some of them among our group of defendants. When our trial reached its lunch recess, we rushed downtown to meet Abbie and others on the Wall Street sidewalk outside the stock exchange. After Abbie and Jim passed out about one hundred dollars in dollar bills, we politely joined the line to the visitors entrance for the third-floor gallery. We were accompanied by a squad of reporters, photographers, and TV cameramen.

In his 1968 book, *Revolution for the Hell of It*, Abbie wrote, "We didn't even bother to call the press," a claim he repeated in his autobiography, *Soon to Be a Major Motion Picture*. That simply wasn't the case. Even then, Abbie was already adept at using the media to publicize his activities.

When we reached the security desk, the guard looked disapprovingly at the long-haired Abbie and Jim. After Jim said that he and the others were members of ESSO, the East Side Service Organization (ESSO was the acronym for the oil company that became Exxon), the guard started giving them a hard time. He warned that no demonstrations of any type would be allowed.

Abbie responded by shouting, with impish incongruity, "You won't let me in because I'm Jewish!"

Flustered, the guard hardly noticed when those of us who were dressed for success casually walked right by. The rest of the demonstrators rushed in behind us.

Armed only with the one-dollar bills given to Abbie by a contributor for use in this action, we started throwing. Some spectators later said we used Monopoly money; not true, it was the real green. And one demonstrator claimed we tossed out $1,000—but what do hippies know about money?

Never having had the experience of hurling money off a high platform, I was surprised by how long it took for our bills to waft down to the floor below. But even more surprised were the stock exchange workers on the receiving end of our largesse.

At first, the brokers, traders, and runners watched in stunned silence. Then some began to cheer.

Others were not as pleased, or at least that's what I inferred from all their yelling and cursing in our direction. Still others were too busy scrambling to pick up the loot as it floated to the ground.

It was all over in a minute. We turned around and raced out and back to the street. Mission accomplished, and no one arrested. The front page of the *New York Post* later that afternoon ran a photograph of a laughing Abbie and a shyly smiling yours truly, in my sports jacket, white shirt, and tie, running out of the visitors gallery.

Some demonstrators stayed around outside the stock exchange to dance in a circle and sing "Free, free" while Abbie started to burn a $5 bill. According to the *Times* report, an angry stock exchange staffer grabbed the fiver out of Abbie's hand, shouted "You're disgusting!" and stomped on it.

The *New York Post*, then a liberal Democratic newspaper before its purchase and transformation into a right-wing rag by Rupert Murdoch, quoted a "camera-toting tourist" saying, "The way I'm throwing money away in New York, I might as well join them."

According to Jonah Raskin's biography of Abbie, which includes the most complete account of the stock exchange demonstration and its origins, Jim Fouratt told a reporter he had gotten the cash from the mother of General William Westmoreland, the top U.S. general in Vietnam, because she "disapproved of her son's military policy in Vietnam."

When reporters asked Abbie what his name was, he said, "I'm Cardinal Spellman," the conservative leader of the New York Roman Catholic archdiocese.

But I missed all that, as we had to race back to the courtroom, where our civil disobedience case was about to resume.

The stock exchange demonstration did not lead to "the death of money," as some of our group hoped. From all appearances, money and its pursuit are both alive and well more than forty-five years later. I can see why some hardworking folks might have viewed us as spoiled kids who cared little about throwing money away.

There were several direct consequences of our action. Less than two months later, the stock exchange erected a bulletproof glass barrier at the visitors gallery to prevent future money tossings.

Through all the coverage the action received in the media, Abbie became a well-known figure in New York and beyond. His involvement shortly thereafter in planning an "exorcism" and "levitation" of the Pentagon—the October 21 demonstration in Washington, D.C.,

Abbie Hoffman and Bruce Dancis (in jacket and tie) run outside the New York Stock Exchange on August 24, 1967, after throwing dollar bills from visitors gallery down onto traders on the exchange floor. (Arty Pomerantz, *New York Post*)

called by the National Mobilization Committee to End the War in Vietnam—brought him even greater national attention.

Shortly after the New York Stock Exchange action, Abbie and Jim were fired from their one-hundred-dollar-a-week positions on Mayor Lindsay's Youth Board Council, apparently for giving the Lindsay administration "a bad image," according to an administration spokesman interviewed by the *East Village Other*.

But our raid on the stock exchange was a nonviolent shot heard 'round the world in the battle against greed. Through humor and guerrilla theater, we reached far more people than we would have using more traditional forms of protest. For a fleeting moment, it showed that there was more to life than the dogged accumulation of wealth and riches.

And it produced an enduring legend and a few laughs along the way.

Black Militancy and Urban Disorders

For the third consecutive summer, riots broke out in black ghettos around the country. The deadliest uprisings took place in July, first in Newark, where twenty-six people were killed, then in Detroit, where forty-three people lost their lives. Both cities were occupied by National Guard troops, with Detroit also bringing in thousands of U.S. Army paratroopers to maintain order.

Even before the riots began, many former civil rights activists had moved in the direction of black nationalism and armed black resistance to white oppression. Malcolm X, who had been assassinated in 1965, was probably more popular than he had ever been while alive.

In May 1967, a relatively new group out of Oakland, California, named the Black Panther Party for Self Defense, shocked the country—and the movement—by appearing at the California state capitol in Sacramento armed with rifles and clad in black leather jackets and black berets. Their action was brilliant guerrilla theater, as well as a protest against a gun-control law that had recently been passed in the state legislature—a law that had been inspired by the Panthers' armed citizen patrols in Oakland.

The Panthers, led by Huey P. Newton and Bobby Seale, had a ten-point, anticapitalist program that broadly addressed the issues of poverty and police brutality in the black community and called for self-determination for black Americans.

The newly elected chairman of SNCC, H. Rap Brown, was soon matching the Panthers' militant rhetoric. In speeches around the country during the long, hot summer, Brown grew more and more inflammatory. In Jackson, Mississippi, he charged that America was "headed toward a race war." Responding to the riots in Detroit, Brown urged his followers, "If America don't come around, we going to burn it down." After being arrested on state and federal charges following a speech in Cambridge, Maryland, Brown told a crowd in Queens, New York, that the summer's urban riots were "dress rehearsals for rebellion."

I heard Brown speak in person at the end of August when he addressed a crowd of three thousand—about 75 percent white—at the Village Theater (later renamed the Fillmore East) in the East Village. This was one of the occasions when Brown uttered one of his most infamous lines, "Violence is as American as cherry pie," and called on white radicals to "help us get some guns or you can do like John Brown and pick up a gun yourself and go out and help us shoot our enemy because you know where he is."

All this left many of us white radicals in a quandary as to how to respond. The urban rebellions represented a spontaneous outpouring of anger by African Americans over police brutality and poverty. To us, the riots revealed how deeply racism was embedded in American society. Although most white radicals and liberals were no longer working in black communities, that didn't mean we no longer cared about racism in our country or the conditions in which so many of our fellow citizens were living.

On the other hand, for someone who still believed in nonviolent resistance, the urban rebellions seemed self-defeating. It was not for me to tell black people what to do, but it seemed clear that burning down the neighborhoods in which people lived—even if white-owned stores and the white-dominated police were the original targets—would most seriously harm the inhabitants of those neighborhoods. The riots expressed rage, but rage wasn't a solution.

Similarly, the rhetoric of the Panthers and Brown, particularly their exaltation of guns and violence, struck me as illusory. Did they really believe that by arming African Americans with handguns, rifles, and Molotov cocktails they could actually match the military might of the police, the National Guard, and the U.S. armed forces? Armed struggle seemed like a recipe for disaster. Unfortunately, at this time many of my white friends in SDS became enthralled with the Panthers' and Brown's "pick up the gun" rhetoric and began to imagine themselves as armed insurgents engaged in a revolutionary struggle.

I was also alarmed by the antiwhite rhetoric. Calling whites "honkies" and dehumanizing cops as "pigs" meant that black revolutionaries had given up all hope of building an interracial society based on freedom, justice, and brotherhood. I had a thick enough skin to not walk away when Brown and others inveighed against whites. Being called a "honky" wasn't the same thing as a white person calling a black person a "nigger," because the oppressor and the oppressed did not live on equal footing, and the n-word had a long history in connection with white violence against blacks.

But I knew that for America to ever become a progressive, multiracial society, many white people would have to change their attitudes toward African Americans. I had seen this starting to happen during the civil rights movement's heyday in the early and mid-'60s, but by the summer of '67 this goal seemed far removed from reality.

Even though I was not enamored with efforts by the New Left and antiwar movement to get involved in electoral politics, the utter failure of the National Conference for New Politics (NCNP) over the Labor Day weekend contributed to my concerns over where black-white relations were heading. The conference was disrupted by black radicals who heckled and interrupted a speech by Dr. King. They demanded, and received, 50 percent of the votes even though they accounted for only about 10 percent of the three thousand or so participants, and pushed through a resolution condemning Israel for waging an "imperialist Zionist war" (the Six-Day War). The conference disbanded after producing less than nothing.

All this left many in the movement feeling hopeless and troubled. As Todd Gitlin, a former president of SDS and a keen observer of the history of the New Left, later wrote, "For the New Left, the summer of love was the summer of desperation." In addition to the urban riots, "the war itself went on, swollen and unrelenting, like an irreversible plague." With respect to blacks and whites working together for progressive change, Gitlin wrote, referring to the NCNP debacle, "Attempts to create political alliances...fell afoul of bombast and purification rituals."

Todd's perspective was reflected at the time by Andrew Kopkind, one of the Left's most observant journalists. In the aftermath of the NCNP, Kopkind wrote: "To be white and a radical in America this summer is to see horror and feel impotence. It is to watch the war grow and know no way to stop it, to understand the black rebellion and find no way to join it, to realize that the politics of a generation has failed and the institutions of reform are bankrupt, and yet to have neither ideology, programs nor the power to reconstruct them."

Planning a Pentagon Demonstration

I shared the frustration over the antiwar movement's seeming inability to affect the Johnson administration's war effort. But I also believed the movement was in the process of getting more serious, which could be seen in the increasing willingness of people to engage in civil disobedience and draft resistance. At the end of August, the organizers of the Spring Mobilization—now calling itself the National Mobilization Committee to End the War in Vietnam—announced plans to "confront the war makers" in Washington, D.C., on October 21–22.

The official announcement, made at a press conference called by the Mobe, stated "We will gather in a massive antiwar presence, and some will take on the most serious responsibility of direct dislocation of the war machine." The goal was to "shut down the Pentagon": "We will fill the hallways and block the entrances. Thousands of people will disrupt the center of the American war machine."

The coalition that made up the Mobe remained diverse. Jerry Rubin, a veteran Berkeley antiwar activist, had been brought in as the project director of the planned action, as James Bevel was ill. But two other people who had not previously worked with the Mobe also gave their support for the protest at the press conference.

Rap Brown, out on bail but confined by the federal courts to New York City, was a surprise attendee. When asked by a reporter whether he planned to bring a gun to the demonstration, Brown responded defiantly, "I may bring a bomb, sucker."

Abbie, a new friend of Rubin's, was also there, announcing plans for an "exorcism to cast out the evil spirits" at the Pentagon and to encircle the giant building in order to "raise the Pentagon three hundred feet in the air."

As an attendee at the press conference, I cringed over Brown's comment and laughed at Abbie's. Bringing the protest to the Pentagon made sense to me, though I knew such an action contained many risks.

Combined with the Resistance's nationwide draft card turn-in scheduled for October 16, it looked like the fall of 1967 would begin a new stage for the antiwar and draft resistance movements. I was determined to play a role in both. But I had yet to figure out where I would be doing this organizing. I could have stayed in New York City, where I was already on the staff of the local Resistance group and in close contact with Mobe leaders like Bob Greenblatt, Dave Dellinger, and Norma Becker. Returning to Ithaca also had considerable appeal, even though I had no desire to resume my studies at Cornell. Jane was going back to Cornell for her sophomore year, and I missed her. As a couple, we had not been broken by her parents' hostility toward me, and we wanted to maintain and strengthen our relationship.

I also felt a commitment to continue building the draft resistance movement in Ithaca. We had made great strides at Cornell during the previous spring, yet I believed we were on the cusp of having an even more significant impact on the university community.

My desire to continue organizing students had been influenced by a debate that was raging within SDS about the proper focus of organizing. I was still paying attention to SDS, even though I was, for a time, somewhat alienated from the organization. My differences with the SDS national leadership over draft resistance and going to jail, and the value of large antiwar demonstrations like the Spring Mobilization, remained as strong as they had been for the past year or so. I felt the national leadership was out of touch with the desires of rank-and-file members, particularly over antiwar organizing. In his history of SDS, Kirk Sale wrote about this disjuncture between local chapters and the National Office during the summer of '67, pointing out that "while the National Council scorned the idea of mass marches, kids in every SDS chapter went out and organized for them."

The Progressive Labor Party, a Maoist organization, had stepped up its efforts to infiltrate and influence SDS chapters.[1] PL began pushing SDS

---

1. In 1965, SDS adopted a policy of "nonexclusion," in which the organization would admit to membership all who stated an agreement with its general principles. While the goal of the new policy was to break with the sectarian past of the Old Left and remnants of McCarthyism, it enabled students affiliated with the Communist Party, Progressive Labor, and various Trotskyist groups to join SDS and try to influence SDS members and policies.

to pursue a "worker-student alliance," which essentially meant students abandoning their campuses and trying to organize industrial workers in factories. This program seemed like the return of crude Marxism-Leninism from the 1930s and a denigration of the important role students were play-ing in the movement. Coupled with PL's lack of interest in either antiwar or antidraft organizing, it made it easy for me to oppose the group.

Partly in response to PL and partly out of a genuine attempt to develop a new type of Marxian class analysis that made sense in late-1960s America, others in SDS began writing about the crucial role of students in the mod-ern economy. The perspective that students were being trained in colleges and universities to become part of a "new working class" of professionals, technocrats, and clerical laborers wasn't a completely new idea. It had been intimated in SDS's early Port Huron Statement, in the writings of sociologist C. Wright Mills, and in European socialist circles. But in the spring of '67, the idea, buttressed by the release of the Selective Service System's "On Man-power Channeling" document, was introduced within SDS. I took note of a speech that SDS national secretary Greg Calvert gave in March, reprinted as a pamphlet later that spring, which presented a strong rationale for organiz-ing students: "We must stop apologizing for being students or for organizing students. Students are in fact a key group in the creation of the productive forces of this super-technological capitalism.... We can see that it was a mistake to assume that the only radical role which students could play would be as organizers of other classes."

At the time, I was much more an activist than a radical scholar or theo-retician. My main interest in the SDS debates was in finding support for the strategic necessity of organizing students. Altogether, considering SNCC's admonition that white radicals should organize in our own communities, my belief that one needed to break free of the chains created by the draft system, and my own skill as an organizer of students, it seemed clear what I should be doing, and where.

Chapter Eight

The Resistance

In September 1967 Judge Port decided to go ahead with my trial for tearing up my draft card. Since the U.S. Supreme Court had yet to rule on the legality of the law forbidding draft card burning and other such acts of paper destruction, we had not expected to be in court so soon. Faith and I had not even discussed our trial strategy or what witnesses we might call.

On the mid-September day I was scheduled to appear in court, supporters from Ithaca, Rochester, and Syracuse gathered outside the federal court building in Syracuse to show their solidarity. Along with Faith, fellow resister Burton Weiss, and a new member of the Cornell community, the radical Catholic priest Daniel Berrigan, I took part in a press conference with the local media.

I had met Father Dan, a Jesuit, a few days earlier at Cornell, where he had just been hired as associate director of Cornell United Religious Works (CURW). Although I knew his reputation as a radical priest who had once defied Cardinal Spellman and been expelled by the Archdiocese of New York, I only then learned of his ardent support for draft resisters and his belief that those not eligible for the draft needed to stand beside us with their own acts of civil disobedience. As I got to know Dan over the next few years, I also learned what a caring, inquisitive, fearless, and irreverently funny man he was. I was amazed that the Cornell administration allowed CURW to hire him, given that top administrators like Mark Barlow had already been warning about the growing radicalism of many of the campus chaplains.

Father Dan had grown up in the Syracuse area, and his brother Jerry and sister-in-law Carol still lived there. At the press conference, he told the assembled media that my trial was a historic day for Syracuse. He took the occasion to announce he would dedicate himself to disrupting the draft system and envisioned going to jail in support of draft resisters like me. "We must fill the jails with people who choose conscience over killing," he said.

Once we entered the courtroom, Judge Port made the surprising decision to grant Faith's motion to postpone my trial until the Supreme Court made its ruling on the draft card destruction law. I was relieved, to be sure, and very pleased to have made a new ally and friend in Father Dan.

Doug Dowd had also returned to Cornell after a year in Italy, and he immediately resumed his antiwar activities along with his teaching. Although Doug had missed the April 15 draft card burning and the conflict at Cornell that preceded it, he arrived back in the United States with a strong commitment to support draft resisters.

Doug and Dan were part of a growing number of men and women above draft age who stood beside us resisters. During the summer a group of radical intellectuals led by Marcus Raskin and Arthur Waskow of the Institute for Policy Studies and Bob Zevin of Columbia University began circulating a document entitled "A Call to Resist Illegitimate Authority." Published in the *New York Review of Books* and the *New Republic* in the early fall with 158 signatures, it proclaimed that soldiers refusing their orders and draft resisters openly breaking the draft laws were taking actions that were "courageous, moral and legally justified." It put the signers on record as encouraging these actions, a statement that itself made them subject to prosecution for "counseling, aiding and abetting" resistance. A year later, over two thousand people had signed the call.

While Doug and Dan may have been at the forefront of Cornell faculty and clergy supporters of draft resistance, they were hardly alone. We were receiving public encouragement and support from campus chaplains of different denominations, including Dave Connor (Catholic), Paul Gibbons (United Church of Christ), Hollis Hayward (Methodist), Richard Gilbert (Unitarian), and Richard Bausman (Baptist). In addition to Doug, we found ardent supporters on the faculty of the ILR School (Jay Schulman, Eqbal Ahmad, and Bill Friedland) and in the departments of English (Doug Archibald, James Matlack, Neil Hertz, Jonathan Bishop) and Mathematics (Lenny Silver, Michael Balch, Paul Olum, and Alex Rosenberg), among others.

There were also Cornell faculty members who were not inclined toward activism but provided the intellectual basis for antiwar and progressive thought. In the Government Department, George McT. Kahin and John Lewis were among the nation's most respected Southeast Asia scholars, and their critical writings about the history of the war in Vietnam and their appearances at antiwar teach-ins were influential. The political scientist Andrew Hacker was always a stalwart supporter of the civil rights movement and free speech. Among Cornell's historians, Walter LaFeber had emerged as a noted critic of American foreign policy, while David B. Davis was a pioneering scholar in American intellectual history and the history of slavery.

The support and the atmosphere provided by these faculty members and clergymen helped sustain me and the other Cornell resisters. Although I may no longer have been a Cornell student, I was always welcomed by antiwar students, faculty, and clergy as a member of the Cornell community.

"Stop the Draft Week"

The Resistance's plan to organize a nationwide draft card turn-in on October 16 was the logical next step for the draft resistance movement following our draft card burning. As the date neared, the Resistance had set up operations in ten states. We hoped that at least one thousand men nationwide would turn in their draft cards. From the beginning, we viewed October 16 as just the first step (or second, if you counted the April 15 draft card burning) in a sustained national effort.

The Resistance strategy was generating a mixed response from SDS. At Cornell, there was complete cooperation, even integration, between both groups, largely because many draft resisters, like me, were also members and leaders of the SDS chapter. This was true at other campuses as well, and "October 16" buttons were worn by some delegates to the SDS national convention during the summer.

But on the West Coast and in Boston, for example, Resistance organizers contacting SDS chapters found a mixture of hostility and lukewarm, perfunctory support. In the San Francisco Bay Area, this conflict would be heightened during the period from October 16 to 21, called "Stop the Draft Week."

Shortly before October 16, the SDS National Council tried to have it both ways. A resolution encouraged all chapters to support those participating in the draft card turn-in. But the resolution also stated, somewhat condescendingly, that while "SDS recognizes the validity of all direct challenges to illegitimate authority, seeing the insufficiency and misdirection of symbolic confrontation-oriented movements, it urges members of 'the Resistance' to involve themselves in local community organizing projects aiming to build a powerful insurgent white base inside the United States."

October 16 saw a variety of Resistance demonstrations and draft card turn-ins around the country. The largest was in San Francisco, where 300 draft cards were brought to the federal building; later that day, more than 120 nonviolent demonstrators were arrested for a sit-in at the Oakland Induction

Center. In Boston, more than 5,000 people attended a rally on the Boston Common before 237 men turned in their draft cards at a ceremony in the historic Arlington Street Church, a home for abolitionists more than a century before. (Later that week, on the eve of the Pentagon demonstration, several of the speakers at the Boston rally and members of Resist, including Rev. William Sloane Coffin Jr. and Dr. Benjamin Spock, traveled to Washington, D.C., to personally deliver those and other draft cards to the Justice Department.) In New York City, after U.S. marshals prevented demonstrators from turning in their cards at the federal courthouse, nearly two hundred cards were placed in envelopes and mailed to the U.S. attorney general's office in Washington.

In Ithaca, our rally began shortly after lunchtime on the steps of the student union, with about five hundred people on hand. I had been chosen to speak on behalf of the Resistance, to explain what we were planning to do and to introduce the other speakers. Epi Epton, the girlfriend of the late Matty Goodman, talked about how Matty, a non-registrant and noncooperator, would have been there with us. Doug Dowd and Father Berrigan spoke of their support and the support of others among the Cornell faculty and clergy.

Two campus ministers, Rev. Paul Gibbons and Father David Connor, announced they would both turn in their own draft cards and renounce their ministerial deferments. (Paul was already thirty-five years old and the married father of three children.)

We then marched from the Cornell campus to the Ithaca draft board, about a mile away. Fourteen men, including English professor James Matlack and three of my closest friends—Larry Kramer, Lew Zipin, and Mike Rotkin (who must have had an extra card, since he had already burned one on April 15)— walked inside the draft board to turn in their cards. They were accompanied by fourteen professors and six ministers who submitted statements of support.

By the time we finished counting nationwide, over twelve hundred men in at least twenty-three states had turned in their draft cards. The numbers weren't overwhelming, but in the six months since April 15 we had grown from 175 or so draft card burners in the Sheep Meadow to more than a thousand.

A few days later I drove down to Washington, D.C., for the Mobilization-sponsored antiwar rally, to be followed by a demonstration and acts of civil disobedience at the headquarters of the U.S. war machine, the Pentagon. I went with a commitment to risk arrest in what I hoped would be a massive outpouring of what we had called for half a year earlier—"powerful resistance—radical, illegal, unpleasant, sustained."

Although we didn't learn the full story until later, events during Stop the Draft Week in the San Francisco Bay Area had produced new splits in the draft resistance movement over the issue of violence. Monday, October 16, was given over to nonviolent activities—the draft card turn-in in San Francisco and a peaceful sit-in at the Oakland Induction Center. But the following day, when three thousand people staged another demonstration at the induction center, they were met by club-wielding cops and suffered injuries and arrests.

This all led to a larger confrontation between police and demonstrators at the induction center on Friday. This time around, more than ten thousand protesters, many wearing helmets and carrying shields, used what became known as "mobile tactics" to engage the police, then pull back and build barricades in the streets out of parked cars and trucks, potted plants, street benches, and parking meters.

For some in SDS and the wider movement, nonviolence had come to be viewed as irrelevant, even wimpy, and fighting in the streets was now seen as a legitimate response to the war, the draft, and police repression.

SPOTLIGHT: CONFRONTATION AT THE PENTAGON, OCTOBER 21, 1967

The defender stood directly in front of me, his arms outstretched to impede my progress. I feinted to the left, and when he went for my fake, I quickly scurried past him on the right. Others on my side immediately followed me through the open space, heading toward our goal.

But this was not a basketball game. The defender was a uniformed MP who had been given the impossible task of keeping antiwar demonstrators from marching down one of the paths that led directly to the Pentagon. Instead of having a basketball in my hand, I was carrying a banner that read "Cornell—We Won't Go." Fortunately, I didn't have to physically engage the MP—I wouldn't have pushed him, since I was committed to nonviolence—but was able to simply outrun him. Once I was through the gap, many others behind me ran past the MP.

I felt a powerful sense of exhilaration as I ran toward the citadel of American military power, my banner flowing in the air. But as I got closer to the massive five-sided building, I could see another group of defenders, as thousands of soldiers and federal marshals had formed a defense perimeter around the Pentagon.

It was the late afternoon. Earlier that day, I had been among about one hundred thousand antiwar demonstrators, including a thousand from Cornell, who had attended a rally near the Lincoln Memorial. Once the speeches by Dr. Spock, SNCC's John Lewis, and others were over, many of us marched across the bridges over the Potomac River to Arlington, Virginia, and headed for the Pentagon.

Despite Rap Brown's rhetoric at the late August press conference announcing the demonstration and Abbie Hoffman's jocular promise to "levitate" the Pentagon, the Mobe organizers hoped for a peaceful demonstration that would be followed by nonviolent civil disobedience. This plan at first alienated some of the liberal groups that were part of the antiwar coalition yet opposed illegal actions. And it initially failed to win over the national leadership of SDS, which viewed this as just one more national demonstration that sapped energy from local organizing.

But about two weeks before October 21, the federal government made a blunder that served to unite the antiwar movement once again. Government representatives meeting with Mobilization organizers threatened to withdraw permits for the legal demonstration at the Lincoln Memorial if the Mobe did not renounce civil disobedience at the Pentagon.

The ultimatum from the Johnson administration had the opposite effect from what was intended. Tom Wells described the reaction of the antiwar movement: "The response was overwhelmingly combative. Many people previously hesitant about joining the protest took the government's threat as an omen of serious political repression and felt the action had to go on for civil liberties reasons alone. SDSers now saw something sufficiently revolutionary in store."

The Demonstrators Meet the Troops

Having failed to deter the Mobe's plans for civil disobedience, the government tried to impede protesters' access to the Pentagon. The authorities blocked roads that led directly to the building, erected wire fences at other possible entrance points, and tried to keep demonstrators away from the mall in front of the building by confining them to a parking lot over a thousand feet away. To repel the demonstrators, the feds amassed a force of more than six thousand U.S. Army troops (with twenty thousand more soldiers on alert), two thousand National Guardsmen, two thousand Washington police, and a large number of U.S. marshals.

But the authorities, outnumbered by the demonstrators, were unwilling at this point to use the troops to keep us penned in the north parking lot. Their hastily constructed wire and wood fences were torn down or cut through by protesters, who quickly advanced toward the steps of the Pentagon. The MP I encountered was one of those trying unsuccessfully to impede our progress.

As I approached the building, the scene was chaotic. Helicopters were flying noisily overhead, while army sharpshooters on the Pentagon's roof (alongside Secretary of Defense Robert McNamara, we learned later) looked down on the crowd below. Several dozen demonstrators, breaking away from the main group, found an unguarded side door to the Pentagon and actually got into the building before being clubbed and arrested.

Thousands of demonstrators were already milling around when I arrived, while others began to engage in a mass sit-in just a few yards from the building itself. The soldiers, many from the Eighty-Second Airborne Division, were standing side by side in a protective ring around the Pentagon. The soldiers stood stoically with their rifles and bayonets, inches away from demonstrators, trying to avoid eye contact with protesters who attempted to talk to them. Some demonstrators even placed flowers in the soldiers' rifle barrels.

As late afternoon passed into evening, our ranks started to thin. Some people had to get back to the buses that had brought them to Washington, while others were simply tired from the day's events or getting cold. But thousands of us remained. As darkness fell, protesters began singing songs—"We Shall Overcome" and the Beatles' "Yellow Submarine" were among the most popular.

Jerry Rubin and a few others tried to incite the crowd to physically battle the troops and marshals. But when Rubin began throwing lit pieces of wood at the marshals, he was quickly stopped by cooler heads among the Mobe leadership, including Doug Dowd.

Instead of fighting the troops, speakers with bullhorns began to address the soldiers directly: "Join us! Our fight is not with you." One of the most effective was Gary Rader, the army reservist who had burned his draft card on April 15. He talked about his experiences in the army, the history of the war in Vietnam, and his decision to turn against the war and join the antiwar movement. As he spoke, one could hear the officers in charge ordering their men to "hold your line."

Greg Calvert of SDS, who had been hanging out with my Cornell friend Tom Bell, was also observing the tense situation. Among SDS national leaders, Greg had been more supportive of draft resistance than others. He even called me, humorously but with affection, "the boy wonder of the Resistance."

Facing the troops, Greg tried to convince them that they had far more in common with their age-group peers demonstrating at the Pentagon than with their superior officers: "You are our brothers. We want you to come home to us. You don't belong to them, the generals, who are going crazy up there in the top part of the Pentagon because we're talking to you."

According to several accounts, at least two soldiers dropped their rifles, took off their helmets, and attempted to walk into the crowd. They were quickly grabbed by their officers and taken away.

In the eerie darkness, demonstrators started to spontaneously burn draft cards. Within minutes, it appeared that several hundred cards had gone up in flames. Bonfires were started from leaflets and pieces of wood fencing.

"Failure to Move"

The siege continued until after midnight, when the marshals began making arrests of demonstrators who were sitting down. Some of the protest leaders with bullhorns urged the crowd to begin leaving the area, claiming victory. Others, like me, decided to proceed with what I had expected to do all day—take part in a sit-in and get arrested.

I had become separated from my Cornell friends by this time, so I joined those sitting on the ground, locking arms with the people on both sides of me. As we sat, the troops were ordered to inch closer to us, their boots pushing and kicking our butts. One by one, marshals came from behind the soldiers to pick us off and take us away. Many people went limp and were clubbed for their passive resistance.

I was lucky. The marshal who arrested me was less violent than some of the others, and I received only a few pokes in the ribs from his baton as he dragged me toward a nearby van.

I was taken to a federal prison camp in nearby Occoquan, Virginia, and placed in a large barracks with hundreds of other demonstrators. I quickly ran into a friend, Greg Heins, one of the Cornell draft card burners. Greg had graduated the previous June and was now living in New York's Lower East Side with his wife, Marjorie Heins (formerly Holt). We spent the rest of the night talking quietly with each other and with some of our fellow demonstrators. Although we had cots to lie down on, I was too keyed up from the events of the day and evening to get any sleep.

The next morning I went before a U.S. commissioner in a make-shift courtroom at Occoquan, charged with "failure to move" when ordered to do so by a U.S. marshal. Having made the point I wanted to, I had no desire to remain locked up or get involved in a long legal case. So, along with most of the others, I pleaded nolo contendere and paid a fine of fifteen dollars.

As soon as I got out of Occoquan, I made my way back to the Pentagon, where demonstrators were still conducting a vigil and staging another sit-in outside the building. I arrived just in time to see the marshals arrest more than two hundred additional protesters. This time I didn't join those sitting in. One arrest seemed like enough civil disobedience for one weekend.

To me, we had achieved our goal of "confronting the war makers." Sure, we never managed to shut down the Pentagon or disrupt its operations. Such an effort would no doubt have been resisted far more violently by the troops and marshals. It also might have been more successful had we scheduled the protest on a weekday, when the building's thousands of staffers would have been added to the mass of bodies. Then again, maybe we were able to recruit so many anti-warriors precisely because this was a weekend action.

Some demonstrators later described the nighttime scene outside the Pentagon as "terrifying." It's not that I was impervious to danger, but I never felt scared. Then again, I wasn't one of the protesters beaten by the marshals. I returned to Ithaca proud to have been among the nearly seven hundred demonstrators arrested—the largest number of people ever arrested at an antiwar demonstration.

A Turning Point for the Movement

The lessons drawn from the major events of October 16–21, 1967—the Resistance's draft card turn-ins, the use of mobile tactics in Oakland, and the confrontation at the Pentagon—were much debated in the movement during the following months.

Most of us who were involved in the Resistance viewed the October 16 turn-in as a successful beginning to what we hoped would be a series of increasingly large draft resistance actions. A second day of nationwide draft card turn-ins was already scheduled for December 4.

The Oakland and Pentagon actions were not directly comparable, as most of the demonstrators at the Pentagon remained nonviolent throughout the long weekend of October 21 and 22. Contrast the appeal to soldiers outside the Pentagon as our "brothers" with the increasingly popular characterization of the Oakland police as a bunch of "pigs."

Yet many New Left militants saw the Stop the Draft Week violence in Oakland and the confrontation at the Pentagon as the beginning of a new phase for the movement. As one demonstrator wrote about the Oakland action: "This week the first crack appeared in the egg that will hatch white revolution in America."

Several weeks later in New York City, a group of demonstrators led by SDS members broke away from peaceful protesters outside the Hilton Hotel, where Secretary of State Dean Rusk was speaking. The SDS contingent and their followers—which included some members of the Resistance—began to pour animal blood and red paint on luxury automobiles, disrupt traffic, overturn garbage cans, and, in some instances, fight back against the police.

The NYPD helped provoke the demonstrators' reaction by forcing them down side streets away from the Hilton. The cops dragged men and women by their hair and clubbed handcuffed protesters who had already been arrested and peaceful demonstrators who were merely in attendance. Yet some members of SDS had arrived at the demonstration wearing helmets and carrying clubs, with the intention of physically resisting any effort by the police to control them.

Activists committed to nonviolence were also escalating their resistance. On October 28, just a week after the Pentagon action, Rev. Phil Berrigan, Dan Berrigan's younger brother and also a Catholic priest, and three others (later known as the Baltimore Four) entered the office in Baltimore where the region's Selective Service files were stored. Once they found the files of men classified 1-A, they poured blood all over them. They were quickly arrested.

I enthusiastically supported Father Phil's action, as it marked both a new tactic of resistance and a new way in which those not eligible for the draft could support draft resisters. But I felt ambivalent about the escalation of violent confrontational activity. I was concerned over the eagerness of some on our side to fight the cops. I was also dubious about what in later years would be called "macho posturing" on the part of middle-class students and other young people who were trying to act tough. Yet I also believed that much of the violence in both Oakland and New York was started by or provoked by the police, and that demonstrators had generally responded to that violence in self-defense.

Perhaps the various wings of the youth movement—the Resistance and SDS, nonviolent draft resisters and those who viewed it as necessary and desirable to build a movement willing to battle the police—could find common ground. That was the perspective of Frank Bardacke, one of the leaders of Oakland's Stop the Draft Week and soon to be one of the defendants in the Oakland Seven conspiracy trial. Bardacke wrote:

> Although most of the Left admired the passion and eloquence of the Resistance leaders, they disapproved of burning and turning in draft cards as an anti-draft tactic. They claimed the Resistance was moving back to a position of apolitical moral witness and they demanded to know what was the political purpose of spending five years in jail.
>
> Never has the Left so thoroughly missed the point. The Resistance made Stop the Draft Week possible. Young men burning their draft cards on Sproul Hall steps changed the political mood of the [University of California at Berkeley] campus. This example and that of the hundreds who turned in their draft cards gave the rest of us courage....
>
> Stop the Draft Week changed the movement...we became a more serious and more radical movement....We did not loot or shoot. But in our own way we said to America that at this moment in history we do not recognize the legitimacy of American political authority....We consider ourselves political outlaws. The American government has the power to force us to submit but we no longer believe that it has the authority to compel us to obey.

The Professor, the Priest, and a Room with No View

When I returned to Ithaca, I had no money and no place to live. The latter was temporarily solved by Larry Kramer. Larry was one of the most upbeat people I knew in the movement. When he got behind something, whether it was organizing for the Resistance or the Pentagon demonstration, no one was more dedicated or creative.

Larry would soon come up with a new, tongue-in-cheek antiwar tactic to raise the cost of the war in Vietnam for American corporations. He encouraged peace-loving people to write antiwar messages on or stuff antiwar literature into the paid-in-advance business reply mail envelopes and postcards used by retailers, publishers, and other corporations.

"Even five million people sending one letter a day would cost the business community over $180 million a year [in] postage, not to mention secretarial time and stationery costs," Larry wrote in an article proposing this plan. And he announced the formation of two new organizations to run this campaign—Deploy Righteous Indignation for Tomorrow (DRIFT) and Business Reply Envelope Antiwar Campaign Hassles (BREACH).

Although no bedrooms were available in the apartment on College Avenue that Larry shared with a few other friends, off the main hallway was a large closet, big enough for a single mattress on the floor while leaving sufficient space to open the door.

Good thing I wasn't claustrophobic. These were not the most luxurious accommodations, but I couldn't beat the rental price of zero. Larry and my other new apartment mates even tried to spice up the space by putting up "wallpaper" in the closet—a combination of leaflets, photographs, posters, and aluminum foil.

Although I found my bedroom closet acceptable as a place to sleep, it wasn't the most desirable place for me to entertain Jane on an overnight visit. Now a sophomore, she was still living in the women's dorms, but we were again able to find some friendly female seniors and graduate students to whose apartments she could sign out. Jane was pretty game about my new digs, and she even managed to spend a few nights there. But for the most part, when we wanted to have some intimate time together we had to borrow a friend's room and bed.

Both my living conditions and financial well-being were improved by some new benefactors—Doug Dowd and his wife, Kay, a staffer in Cornell's architecture school. As Doug and I began to work together on both the Resistance and the Pentagon demonstration, our relationship changed from professor-student to close friends.

Knowing I needed some financial support to continue my work for the movement, Doug and Kay offered to give me a stipend of one hundred dollars a month. Even in 1967–68, that wasn't a lot of money. But it was enough for me to afford to pay fifty dollars a month in rent, and I moved into a just-vacated room in a house in Collegetown, at 315 1/2 Eddy Street (popularly known as "the Half"), with Burton Weiss, Mike Rotkin, and Karen Frost (Mike's girlfriend and future wife), and soon, Lew Zipin. My new room had most recently housed Jill Boskey, one of the *Newman K. Perry* Twelve, who had just graduated from Cornell. From Jill I obtained another roommate, one who didn't pay any rent at all—her dog All Right.

It was around this time that Doug and I became partners on speaking tours, bringing our antiwar, antidraft message to colleges and communities throughout New York and neighboring states. Over many long hours, Doug would drive, in his old but reliable Peugeot convertible with an Italian bumper sticker containing a peace symbol and the words "*Fate l'amore non la guerra*" (Make love, not war), and we would talk.

Or to be more accurate, Doug would talk and I would listen. It was during our long rides together where I first witnessed Doug's great skill as a raconteur. While he may have been long-winded, his stories were never boring. And he was funny as hell.

During those rides and over the years, I have heard many a tale from Doug—and I believed most of them. There were stories from his youth, about his wayward Irish father, dutiful Jewish mother, and a beloved aunt who consorted with—and married—gamblers, and growing up poor in Depression-era San Francisco. Then there were tales from the 1940s, '50s, and early '60s, about flying air rescue planes in the Pacific during World War II, managing Henry Wallace's 1948 campaign for president on the University of California–Berkeley campus, fighting McCarthyism at Cornell, and working on voter registration with black farmers in southern Tennessee as part of the civil rights movement.

There was lighter stuff as well, such as stories about Doug's tap dancing at the 1939–40 World's Fair on Treasure Island in San Francisco Bay, landing the title role in Eugene O'Neill's *The Emperor Jones* in a community theater production, and his lack of skill on the basketball court, despite his six-foot-three height.

Doug and I established a close relationship that would grow and endure over the next forty-plus years. It was a unique relationship from the start. Though Doug was a friend, a comrade, a mentor, and a major supporter (politically, personally, and financially), he wasn't a father figure for me. I already had a dad who performed his fatherly role with love and affection.

On some of these weekend trips Doug and I would be joined by Dan Berrigan. Father Dan had quickly become a good friend. He reached out to radical students and activists, having us over to his small apartment for dinner (where I ate, for the first time, a hamburger with an egg in the middle of it) and visiting our houses and apartments. When Dan ate dinner with us at the Half, he doubled over with laughter when Lew's very intelligent parakeet, Nuba, flew onto his shoulder and began repeating the words Lew had so carefully taught him: "Fuck you, little birdie!"

In his memoir *Blues for America*, Doug described how the three of us worked together on these speaking trips: "Dan would begin, mesmerizing the audience with his eloquence, humor, and wisdom. I would follow, with a somewhat professorial analysis of what we were doing in Vietnam and why we should get the hell out of there; and Bruce would end up with an organizing pitch."

In our long car rides together, we would usually talk about politics and people. But on one occasion, when I must have been feeling particularly nervy, I asked the Jesuit priest, "Dan, do you really believe in all that God stuff?" Father Dan paused, and then replied with a laugh, "Sort of." He then began telling, as he often did, an allegorical story. This one was about growing up on a farm near Syracuse. When one of the family's horses died, Dan's father gave him the chore of digging a large hole and burying the animal.

After procrastinating for a while and then making a poor effort at hole digging, Dan (with some help from his brothers) dragged the dead horse over to
the hole and dumped its body in it. He then covered it up with dirt—barely.
As he walked away, he started feeling guilty about the inadequate hole he
had dug for the large animal. Then, all of a sudden, the dead horse let out a
huge, loud fart. Dan let me draw the appropriate conclusion that God works
in mysterious ways.

A few days after we returned to Ithaca, Dan paid me back for my imperti-
nence. Without my knowledge or approval, he entered my name as a reader of
scripture for an upcoming Sunday ecumenical service at Cornell's venerable
Sage Chapel—a building I had never entered before. To make it more difficult for me to back out, he placed my name in the service's printed program.
I don't remember the biblical passages he chose for me—the Bible and I have
never been on close terms—but they were appropriately about peace and
understanding. Not wanting to displease Dan, I went through with it. Dan
was making the point, to both the audience at Sage Chapel and to me, that
even notorious radicals were a beloved part of the university community. The
service was broadcast live on the campus radio station, and Larry taped my
reading to torment me with it later on.

It was all, as they say, an education. I learned a lot from Doug and Dan
about public speaking. Doug was analytical and historical, giving his audiences introductory lessons in the history of Vietnamese resistance to foreign
colonizers and occupiers, the dynamics of U.S. foreign policy during the Cold
War, and the necessity of American withdrawal from Vietnam. Dan's style
was more poetic and philosophical—sometimes his words flew right over my
head—yet he was utterly clear in making the case that decent people needed
to join the resistance to this unjust and immoral war.

Our audiences were for the most part young people on college campuses.
To connect with my peers, I developed a style of speaking that was both
personal, in that I drew upon my own experience with the draft system,
and political in the way I presented the strategy of the Resistance. Thanks
to an offer from Julie Schulman, editor of the *New Patriot*, an Ithaca-based
antiwar periodical published by the Glad Day Press, I had an opportunity
to put my thoughts on the subject in print in an article titled "The Logic of
Resistance."

I would usually begin my speeches by criticizing both 2-S (student) and
1-O (conscientious objector) deferments as unfair, class based, and discriminatory. I explained that I became a noncooperator because all the other alternatives were wrong, and if this meant going to prison, so be it.

I made the point that one could not successfully persuade either college
students or nonstudents to resist the draft if the organizer was hiding behind

a deferment. That smacked of hypocrisy. By building a mass movement to resist the draft, I hoped we would eventually cut into the draft's supply of manpower for the armed forces, as well as flood the courts and fill the prisons. While our numbers were still small, they were growing all the time.

Finally, I argued that our actions as draft resisters would help build the antiwar movement. We had already seen increasing involvement by fellow students, professors, intellectuals, and ministers in support of our actions. I envisioned a time when our parents—those of the large American middle class—would support their draft resister sons in federal courts and federal prisons and demand an end to the war.

Federal Grand Juries and Selective Service Reprisals

Just as I began working on the Resistance's second action, the federal government and Selective Service reminded us that they had neither forgotten the April 15 draft card burning, nor would they ignore the October 16 draft card turn-in.

Although the FBI had visited some of the draft card burners shortly after April 15, in October some of us received phone calls from FBI agents and U.S. marshals seeking appointments. Their purpose: to deliver summonses for us to appear before a federal grand jury in New York City convened to investigate the April 15 action.

Calls from the FBI generated a variety of responses at Cornell throughout the draft resistance years. While some resisters had uneventful encounters with the agents and quietly accepted their subpoenas, others played a game we called "freak the feds." In these cases, appointments would be scheduled only to have the agents met by photographers and crowds of our supporters. In one case, the FBI contacted a Cornell resister, Joe Kelly, and requested to speak with him. Joe said he would meet the agents outside Cornell's main library. When the agents arrived, a bunch of us leaped out from where we were hiding, cameras in hand, and gleefully photographed the befuddled agents.

Our general attitude was that we would not let the FBI, U.S. marshals, or a federal grand jury intimidate us. We had conducted our draft resistance organizing openly, and we weren't about to change that now. Most of us felt we would be going to jail eventually anyway, so why worry about a grand jury?

Strangely, I was never served with a subpoena, apparently because the servers kept missing me. According to my FBI file, a report from the New York City office of the FBI stated that "on November 16, 1967, Assistant United States Attorney (AUSA) John R. Robinson, Southern District of New York, advised that the subject had been tentatively scheduled to appear before a Federal Grand Jury, Southern District of New York, on October 14, 1967 [just two days before the big draft card turn-in!], concerning the mass card burning in New York City, on April 15, 1967. However, to date the United States Marshal had been unsuccessful in serving a subpoena on the subject."

It seemed that whenever agents visited my parents' apartment in the Bronx looking for me, I was in Ithaca. Whenever they came to my apartment in Ithaca, I was either in New York City or on the road.

Eventually, on November 8, eight Cornellians, most of whom had burned their draft cards, and about an equal number of others from New York City, testified before the grand jury at the U.S. Courthouse in Manhattan's Foley Square. Although many of us were willing to testify openly about our own participation, we were not willing to name others who took the same action. Most, like Mike Rotkin, followed the advice of our attorneys to not say anything other than to give a name and address. According to grand jury procedures, once you answered even an innocuous additional question such as "Where were you born?" you had to answer all the DA's questions or else be subject to a contempt of court citation.

Burton Weiss had another idea, however. After consulting with the renowned Jewish scholar Rabbi Abraham Heschel, a supporter of the civil rights and antiwar movements, Burton decided he would admit he had burned his draft card on April 15 but would refuse to testify about any other individuals. His position was based on ancient Jewish laws that essentially said a Jewish man could not testify against another Jew in a Gentile court. Whether they were flummoxed or simply unsure of how to respond to Burton, the U.S. attorney allowed him to complete his testimony without citing him for contempt.

For reasons I have never understood, the FBI and the U.S. marshals continued to neglect serving me with a subpoena, even though I was standing outside the courthouse, handing out leaflets denouncing the grand jury hearings taking place inside. One FBI agent even noted: "Bruce Dancis was observed on the picket line at the above demonstration by Special Agents of the FBI."

Although we didn't know it at the time, the federal grand jury was considering charges against us for having taken part in a conspiracy aimed at "aiding, counseling and abetting" violation of the draft law as well as violating the 1965 law making the destruction of draft cards illegal. Several of the FBI reports on my activities at this time list the topic of their investigation as "Sedition."

But unlike the cases of the Oakland Seven, soon to be indicted for the Stop the Draft Week actions, and Dr. Spock, Rev. Coffin, and others who would also soon be indicted for aiding and abetting draft resisters, in our case the

U.S. attorney eventually decided not to pursue indictments for the April 15 draft card burning.

That decision was not made until more than a year later. According to my FBI file, "At this time [January 15, 1969] AUSA Robinson stated that he would authorize the discontinuance of any further investigation in this matter in the best interest of the Government. In rendering this opinion, Robinson stated that he took into consideration the lack of sufficient evidence leading to a successful prosecution in the SDNY."[1]

On the same day the grand jury convened, the *New York Times* revealed that shortly after the October 16 turn-in and the Pentagon confrontation, General Lewis Hershey, the director of Selective Service, had sent a letter to all local boards directing them to reclassify as 1-A or 1-A Delinquent all men who had violated the draft laws, as well as those who had taken part in demonstrations against the draft or military recruiting. It didn't matter if the resister or protester had a student deferment, a 4-F or 1-Y deferment for physical ailments, or even a ministerial deferment.

Hershey's position divided the Johnson administration, with the war hawks tending to favor it, and attorneys in both the Justice and Defense Departments, including Attorney General Ramsey Clark, opposing it on constitutional grounds.

We at Cornell felt the impact of Hershey's directive almost immediately. Within a month of the October 16 action, both of the ministers who had returned their draft cards, Father Dave Connor and Rev. Paul Gibbons, were reclassified 1-A. So were about a half dozen other Cornell resisters.

At the end of November I received a notice from my draft board in the Bronx ordering me to report for a preinduction physical. The order placed me in line for another confrontation with the legal system, this time over refusing induction into the armed forces. This seemed odd, since I should have been considered unfit for military service because I was already under indictment for violating a federal law.

More Actions at Cornell

Just as the fall 1967 term began, the *Sun* revealed that the Cornell Aeronautical Laboratory, the subject of earlier protests over its research in chemical and biological warfare, had received a contract from the Defense Department to

1. Usually, such language implied either that the government did not want to reveal the identities of undercover agents who were still working in the field or that the government knew it had obtained some information using illegal means, such as wiretapping phone lines without authorization.

develop counterinsurgency programs in Thailand. Campus activists immediately started to protest this.

The CAL contract proved too much for the Cornell administration, as
President Perkins and Provost Dale Corson, the chairman and vice chairman,
respectively, of the CAL board of directors, both resigned their positions.
With faculty and students in an uproar over the relationship of counterinsurgency to the purpose of the university, particularly over the impact such
a project might have on the university's international teaching and research,
the faculty soon voted to sever Cornell's ties with CAL. Within a few months,
the Cornell board of trustees agreed to sell CAL.

In mid-November it was announced that U.S. Marine recruiters would
be conducting interviews at Barton Hall, home of Cornell ROTC. Protesters
spent the first day of recruitment challenging the two Marines to discuss and
debate the war. On the second day, two hundred demonstrators surrounded
the Marines' table with a peaceful sit-in, the men taking part aware that their
participation could put them in the crosshairs of General Hershey and their
local draft boards. Father Connor, speaking at a rally, made the point that the
protest was not against the young men fighting in Vietnam. Rather, it was to
help the soldiers by bringing them home.

Although the protest brought the usual condemnations from pro-war
students and faculty, it produced, or coincided with, several developments
that showed growing support for the antiwar position at Cornell.

The Undergraduate Judiciary Board voted to drop all charges against the
students who had sat in. The Faculty Committee on Student Affairs, however,
issued reprimands to the graduate students who participated in the sit-in, and
decided to reconsider the UJB ruling.

In addition, President Perkins chose the day of the first demonstration
against the recruiters to announce his opposition to General Hershey's policy
of reclassifying and drafting demonstrators who obstructed on-campus
military recruiting. Although the timing of Perkins's statement struck many of
us as an attempt to deflect attention from the demand that military recruiters
leave the campus, there is no doubt Perkins influenced the Faculty Council's
vote a few weeks later to ban military recruiters on campus as long as General
Hershey's directive was in effect. Hershey's new policy, the council charged,
"endangers the intellectual freedom of the campus by posing a threat to
legitimate student protests."

Ignoring Hershey's threats, the Resistance went ahead with another round
of draft card turn-ins. Most took place on December 4, a Monday, but for
reasons I cannot recall we decided to hold the Ithaca turn-in three days later,
on December 7. This time around twelve men turned in their cards, including math professor Lenny Silver and two campus activists, Charles C. "Chip"

Marshall and Joe Kelly, with whom I would work closely during the next year and a half.

Nationwide, the number of cards turned in was around 375, about a third the number we had turned in on October 16. Although I was disappointed with the numbers, I thought one of the reasons for the decline was that we had moved too quickly, with only about six weeks between actions, to organize effectively. I remained optimistic we would do better on the next draft card turn-in day, April 3, 1968.

Cracks within the Johnson Administration

As 1967 came to a close, many of us were growing more frustrated over our inability to stop the Johnson administration's continued escalation of the war. By year's end, over 485,000 American troops were in South Vietnam, with their numbers mounting daily. The U.S. bombing campaign in North Vietnam, Operation Rolling Thunder, was expanding as well.

On the other hand, beginning in the summer of 1967, public opinion polls for the first time showed that the American people disagreed with Johnson's handling of the war and viewed American involvement in Vietnam as a mistake.

There were other cracks within the ranks of the administration that couldn't be kept from the public—most important, Defense Secretary McNamara's growing disenchantment with the U.S. war effort. In testimony before Congress, McNamara admitted that the bombing of North Vietnam had not produced the expected result of diminishing support for the rebels in South Vietnam. Short of the genocidal bombing of the North—which McNamara referred to in his testimony as "the virtual annihilation of North Vietnam, and its people"—U.S. bombing could not force the North to give up. In November, McNamara announced his resignation from Johnson's cabinet, though he did not publicly break with administration policy. (McNamara did not reveal his opposition to the war until years later, after the war had ended.) As an angry President Johnson put it privately, "That military genius, McNamara, has gone dovish on me."

Opposition to Johnson's policies were growing in Congress as well, and late in the year a relatively unknown junior Democratic senator from Minnesota, Eugene McCarthy, announced he would run against Johnson as an antiwar candidate in the 1968 Democratic primary elections. In his statement, McCarthy said he hoped his running would have particular impact on college campuses, where "it may counter the growing sense of alienation from politics."

Marching from the Cornell campus to the draft board in Ithaca,
New York, for the Resistance's December 7, 1967, draft card
turn-in, *left to right*: Lisa Johnson, Chip Marshall, Chris
Carroll, unidentified, Jeff Dowd, Bruce Dancis (with bullhorn),
Mike Rotkin, Jim Murray, and Jonathan Bishop. (From 1969
Cornellian, Division of Rare and Manuscript Collections,
Cornell University Library)

Liberals at Cornell who quickly endorsed McCarthy's campaign, including Cornell VPs Mark Barlow and Steven Muller, echoed McCarthy's belief
that his candidacy would undercut the New Left by bringing young people
back into the political system.

The student movement at Cornell ended the year facing a crisis. With
many of us who had been active in SDS now devoting most of our time to the
Resistance, SDS had become largely concerned with organizing study groups
on war and power. The leadership of the anti-recruiting drive came from
recently radicalized students who had not participated before in SDS. This
left a sense of fragmentation and an organizational void among activists at
Cornell.

Fortunately, shortly after the new year began we seized the opportunity to
build a larger and more powerful movement.

Chapter Nine

SDS, South Africa,

and the Security Index

It is believed that DANCIS should be placed on the Security Index.... His strong and
active opposition to Selective Service, U.S. policy in Vietnam, and legitimate authority
indicate that he has anarchist and revolutionary beliefs and is likely to seize upon the
opportunity presented by a national emergency to endanger the public safety.
—An FBI report in February 1968

What was left unstated, because everyone in the FBI already knew it, was
that individuals placed on the Security Index were targeted for arrest and
indefinite detention in the case of a "national emergency."

The FBI's Security Index dated back to World War II, when it began as a
list of possible enemy agents. It was revived during the McCarthy era to target
Communists and Trotskyists. But the growth of the antiwar movement and
the New Left, as well as the rise of black nationalism and urban rebellions
during the summer of 1967, led the FBI to create new ways of monitoring,
spying on, and, ultimately, attempting to disrupt these movements.

According to historian Robert Goldstein,

In August, 1967, the FBI began compiling a Rabble Rouser Index, later
renamed the Agitator Index. The list at first consisted of "racial agita-
tors and individuals who have demonstrated a potential for fomenting racial discord." The criteria was soon broadened to include persons
with a "propensity for fomenting" any disorders which affected the
"internal security," including "black nationalists, white supremacists,
Puerto Rican nationalists, anti-Vietnam demonstration leaders and
other extremists" as well as "any person who tries to arouse people to

violent actions by appealing to their emotions, prejudices, et cetera; a demagogue."

FBI agents and informers had been monitoring Cornell SDS since our first meeting in November 1965. By the time I was placed on the Rabble Rouser Index, probably in the latter part of 1967, I had become the subject of a bunch of FBI investigations and reports. Given that my activities were largely concerned with nonviolently protesting a war and a draft system that I and many others viewed as illegal and immoral, the FBI's contentions that I would "endanger the public safety," "arouse people to violent actions," and act like "a demagogue" were absurd and deceitful. They illustrated a paranoid worldview that led the FBI to abuse its power while trying to combat rising public opposition to the war and the draft.

Within a few months into 1968, two other developments apparently stoked the FBI's interest even more: I was among those who reenergized Cornell SDS, and I became the editor of a new radical magazine. These activities coincided with the FBI's updating of its Security Index to include New Leftists (classified as "Anarchists") like me, and black nationalists.

As an added bonus, being placed on the FBI's Security Index meant that my name and information about me would be shared with the U.S. Secret Service, which was in charge of protecting the president of the United States. Grounds for this, according to a February 21, 1967, letter from J. Edgar Hoover to the director of the Secret Service, were my "expressions of strong or violent anti-U.S. sentiment" and "prior acts (including arrests or convictions) or conduct or statements indicating a propensity for violence and antipathy toward good order and government."

Reviving Cornell SDS and Launching a Magazine

As the new year began, activists at Cornell held a series of meetings to discuss how to fix our organizational problems. I favored the creation of an umbrella organization, to be called something like the Movement at Cornell, which could unite campus radicals around specific issues, actions, and programs. Others wanted to revive the campus chapter of SDS.

I was committed to draft resistance as the most crucial activity the New Left could be engaged in, but I also saw the value of multi-issue organizations that offered a radical perspective on American society as a whole and not just the war in Vietnam and the draft. The members of such an organization could be engaged on many fronts, from draft resistance to student power to study groups. I also wanted to continue working against racism, despite the turn toward separatism on the part of many black activists. Despite my misgivings about the direction of national SDS, I was won over to the idea that SDS still offered the best chance of building the New Left in America and at Cornell.

We restructured Cornell SDS around regular biweekly (later weekly) meetings involving the entire membership and set up five program areas, each with an elected chair. I was elected chairman for draft resistance, which basically meant I would keep doing what I had been doing—organizing for the next draft card turn-in. Dave Burak was chosen national coordinator, with the charge of improving relations and communications with the National Office. Chip Marshall was elected campus coordinator, promising a big effort to organize in the undergraduate dorms. Joe Kelly became the Ithaca coordinator with the goal of organizing students at Ithaca High School and Ithaca College, as well as nonstudents in town. And two grad students were elected education chairmen, in charge of study groups.

Out of the meetings that led to reviving Cornell SDS came a desire to use the resources of the Office and the Glad Day Press, now in a new and larger space on Stewart Avenue, to publish an alternative magazine that would serve the Cornell movement. The Office was already putting out the *New Patriot*, an upstate New York periodical for antiwar news and information, and a town-oriented newsletter called *Dateline: Ithaca*. The new magazine, we hoped, would be livelier, flashier, and more reflective of our youthful spirit than its somewhat stodgy sister publications.

The problem was that no one wanted to take on the responsibility of running this new magazine. The consensus view was that the editor needed to be someone who was trusted by everyone on the left at Cornell, with journalistic talent and experience being secondary considerations. While I was seen by other Cornell radicals as fair-minded and reliable, I had no background as a writer or editor. I had never taken a journalism class and had written only a few published articles. I didn't know anything about assigning, writing, and editing stories, nor about assembling, producing, or distributing a magazine. Nevertheless, I was drafted for the (unpaid) job of editor.

I did have a vision, however, for what the contents and appearance of a new magazine should be. We would be unapologetically activist and partisan; no attempt would be made to pursue editorial objectivity or balance. Our magazine would be of, by, and for the movement, but also written in a style that would avoid lefty jargon—we wouldn't be railing against "imperialism" on every page—and be accessible to people who were starting to lean toward the left. Our articles would educate readers about the issues we cared about and, hopefully, inspire them to take action. To avoid becoming a dry political journal, our new magazine had to be fun to read, irreverent, exuberant, and oriented toward young people.

Putting out a magazine at the Office involved a different process from publishing almost anywhere else. We avoided the type of division of labor in which a few elite writers and editors (usually male) were the stars, and a larger, underappreciated body of "shit workers" (usually female) performed all of the more mundane tasks. Although I was responsible for making sure we had enough copy for each issue, most of the labor was shared by the fifteen to twenty-five volunteers who worked on each issue.

The production work was all done in-house: typing stories on IBM Selectrics; photographing the stories and laying them out on master boards, along with graphics and Letraset (rub-off) headlines; making plates of each page; printing the pages on the Office's offset printing press; collating and stapling pages together; and then selling each issue for fifteen cents ("if you have it"). Even the tasks that needed special skills, such as operating the printing press, were handled by members of the Office's paid staff and volunteer printers like Mike Rotkin. All of the paper, ink, and supplies were provided by the Office at no cost; any money we took in from sales went back to the Office.

But some problems remained, even after we had edited all the articles and selected the artwork for our debut issue. We had not yet chosen a name for this new magazine, because we couldn't come up with anything we liked. We finally settled on the *First Issue,* for reasons having more to do with creative exhaustion than genuine enthusiasm.

This being amateur hour, at least when it came to the editor's proficiency, we also didn't have a workable cover image until the very last minute. We decided to photograph the scruffiest person we could easily locate—which is why Jeff Grossman, already a volunteer, appeared on the premiere cover, looking...scruffy. In a parody of the famous U.S. Army recruiting poster featuring Uncle Sam, Jeff ordered those looking at him, "I Want You to Buy FIRST ISSUE."

The first issue of the *First Issue,* published in late January 1968, set the tone for future issues during the rest of the school term. It included a piece by Doug Dowd urging support for draft resisters and participation in an upcoming protest at Cornell over the appearance on campus of recruiters for the Dow Chemical Company, the manufacturer of napalm. Father Berrigan, well-known for his poetry, gave us three new poems. We also had articles about the draft resistance movement and legal developments affecting some of the Cornell resisters; a piece on the revival of Cornell SDS; a review of the new album by Country Joe and the Fish; a review of *Tashi,* a campus literary magazine published by African American students; a widely reprinted piece by Jerry Farber titled "The Student as Nigger"; the announcement of the formation of the Youth International Party (Yippie) and its plans for "an

Some covers of the *First Issue*, the Cornell SDS-affiliated magazine edited by Bruce Dancis in 1968 and 1969. (Bruce Dancis personal collection)

international festival of youth, music, and theatre" in August in Chicago, where the Democratic Party's national convention would be taking place; some artsy photographs of Ithaca nature scenes; several short news articles, including one on the repression of black students at Texas Southern University; a calendar of local movement events; and a list of contact numbers for movement groups.

We managed to publish six issues of the *First Issue* during the winter and spring of '68, each time using bolder and wilder-colored inks to give the magazine a vaguely psychedelic look. Each issue contained news about draft resistance, induction refusals, and a new column of draft counseling advice written by one Colonel Cauliflower (aka Mike Rotkin). Recently graduated Cornellians Marjorie Heins and Henry Balser contributed pieces from New York City and Chicago, including our first story about women's liberation. Dan Berrigan and Pat Griffith, who had both visited North Vietnam, took part in a joint interview about their experiences. From Liberation News Service (LNS), a New Left alternative to the Associated Press and United Press International, we obtained articles by radical scholar-activists Paul Goodman and Howard Zinn, as well as critical news articles about the peace candidacies of Eugene McCarthy and Robert Kennedy. We featured reviews of new albums by Bob Dylan, Simon and Garfunkel, Love, and jazz flutist Charles Lloyd, and made fun of narcs, district attorneys, and Cornell administrators for harassing young people who used psychedelics.

The Singer Case

Some of our best work was in reporting about the federal government's attempt to repress the draft resistance movement. We covered the January indictment of one draft resister (Michael Ferber, a Harvard grad student and activist in the New England Resistance) and four older supporters (Dr. Benjamin Spock, Rev. William Sloane Coffin of Yale, writer Mitchell Goodman, and Institute for Policy Studies cofounder Marcus Raskin) for aiding and abetting draft resistance. This marked the first time the government attempted to prosecute anyone on such charges.

Shortly after the indictment of Dr. Spock et al., Doug Dowd and I attended an inspiring meeting at New York City's Town Hall, chaired by Doug, in support of draft resisters and the new indictees. Ferber and Goodman, among others, spoke to the capacity crowd of fifteen hundred, with Ferber delivering the best line—about his never before seeing such a severe case of "subpoena envy."

The highlight of the evening took place when Doug called on those in attendance to sign a statement in solidarity with the defendants, which defiantly advocated exactly what they had been indicted for doing. A huge scroll contained this pledge: "To any young man who will not, because of conscience, serve as a soldier in this criminal war, I counsel draft refusal. I will aid and abet him, and make his welfare my concern until the war ends."

We hoped that perhaps fifty or seventy-five people would come forward to sign the scroll and put themselves in legal jeopardy. Instead, audience members began to pour into the aisles, creating a logjam onstage while waiting their turn to commit a felonious act. Over 550 people signed the scroll on the spot, including novelist Norman Mailer, poet Allen Ginsberg, writer Susan Sontag, social critic Jane Jacobs, and linguistics professor Noam Chomsky.

Closer to home, the Cornell administration again provided us with an issue and a cause célèbre when a member of the administration tried to get an antiwar student's college deferment rescinded and the student reclassified 1-A.

Mike Singer had been one of the Cornellians who burned his draft card on April 15, 1967. At the time, he also planned to decline his student deferment.

But, about seven months later, Mike admitted, he "got scared" and changed his mind. He decided he wanted to keep his student deferment until he graduated in June '68. So he went into the office of the registrar at Cornell, which acted as a liaison between Cornell and the Selective Service System, to request a new student deferment form. When assistant registrar Charles E. Maynard asked Mike for his Selective Service number, Mike told him he didn't know it because he had burned his draft card.

Maynard then took it upon himself to inform Mike's draft board in Mount Vernon, New York, about what Mike had said. Although Maynard verified Mike's continued enrollment at Cornell, he wrote Singer's board (on official Cornell stationery): "In accordance with selective service law and board policy I urge the board to consider Mr. Singer 'delinquent,' refuse him the priviledge [sic] of student deferment and reclassify him 1-A."

The draft board then informed Mike it was considering revoking his student deferment. In late January, Mike visited his local board to inspect what was in his file. There he found, and photographed, Maynard's letter.

When President Perkins found out about Maynard's action, he was understandably outraged—as were many students and faculty members—over this clear violation of university policy toward the Selective Service. Perkins wrote Mike's draft board to formally request that it disregard Maynard's letter, which Perkins said was "totally unauthorized." Maynard, no doubt under pressure, made a public apology to Mike and also wrote Mike's draft board to ask them to disregard his letter.

We published all these letters in the *First Issue* and even reprinted Maynard's original letter on a "Defend Mike Singer" leaflet. Eventually, the registrar's office revised its policies to specifically prohibit any communication with a student's draft board unless authorized by the student. This included the release of a student's grades or class standing. However, Mike's draft board persisted in reclassifying him 1-A. And Maynard was neither fired nor suspended.

The Tet Offensive Shakes America and American Policy

Critics of U.S. policy in Vietnam had long maintained that Americans knew little about the history of Vietnam and Indochina. In particular, our government failed to understand the history of Vietnamese resistance against foreign domination—whether the invader came from expansionist China, colonial France, or the United States.

In 1789, a Vietnamese hero named Nguyen Hue led a surprise attack against an occupying army from China. Hue chose the traditional Vietnamese holiday known as Tet, a celebration of the lunar new year, for his army's attack, which drove the Chinese out of Vietnam.

Early in the morning on January 31, 1968, on the second day of Tet, the National Liberation Front (NLF) and the North Vietnamese army began a series of coordinated attacks throughout South Vietnam. According to historian Marilyn Young, "For the first time, the war was brought directly to the cities. Five of the six largest cities in the country, thirty-six of forty-four district towns, Cholon, the sprawling Chinese section of Saigon, the heavily fortified American embassy, the imperial city of Hue, places that should have been absolutely secure, all were engulfed in battle."

The impact of the Tet Offensive, as the monthlong battle became known, has long been debated by historians of the U.S. military and American foreign policy. Supporters of the war point to the huge number of NLF casualties suffered during the offensive; afterward, the North Vietnamese army played a much larger role in the fighting. Rather than encouraging a massive outpouring of popular support for the NLF, the rebels killed many supporters of the South Vietnamese government, especially during their monthlong occupation of Hue. To backers of U.S. policy, the Tet Offensive was actually a military defeat for the NLF and North Vietnamese.

Critics, on the other hand, have argued that the thousands of civilian casualties in Hue and other areas were caused by indiscriminate U.S. artillery fire and aerial bombardment, rather than NLF assassinations. Indeed, the effort to recapture the cities and towns of South Vietnam led one U.S. military commander, upon retaking the provincial capital of Ben Tre, to tell reporters, "We had to destroy the town to save it"—a comment that became symbolic of the entire U.S. military campaign in Vietnam.

The Tet Offensive also gave us one of the most indelible images of the war. Nguyen Ngoc Loan, the head of the South Vietnamese National Police, was photographed shooting an unarmed and handcuffed NLF prisoner in the head. For many Americans watching this on TV or viewing still photographs of it in newspapers and magazines, the incident encapsulated much of what was wrong with the U.S. war effort. Our country had committed hundreds of thousands of troops and millions of dollars to prop up a corrupt South Vietnamese government that was represented by war criminals like Loan.

The impact of the Tet Offensive on American public opinion was unambiguous: the ability of the NLF and the North Vietnamese to expand the fighting throughout South Vietnam cast even further doubts on the rosy assessments the Johnson administration was trying to sell.

The uprising was still raging when Walter Cronkite, the widely respected anchor of CBS's nightly newscast, returned from a visit to South Vietnam and presented his personal commentary to the nation. During his February

27, 1968, broadcast, Cronkite said "we are mired in stalemate" in Vietnam, adding, "To say that we are closer to victory today is to believe, in the face of the evidence, the optimists who have been wrong in the past."

The "credibility gap" between what Americans were viewing on their TV screens every night and the statements of U.S. generals and administration representatives was captured by Art Buchwald, whose *Washington Post* column was syndicated through the United States. Datelining a February column "Little Big Horn, Dakota, June 27, 1876," Buchwald wrote: "Gen. George Armstrong Custer said today in an exclusive interview with this correspondent that the battle of Little Big Horn had just turned the corner and he could now see the light at the end of the tunnel. 'We have the Sioux on the run,' Gen. Custer told me. 'Of course, we still have some cleaning up to do, but the Redskins are hurting badly and it will only be a matter of time before they give in.'"

In the first Gallup poll taken after the Tet Offensive, only 33 percent of those polled believed the Unites States was making progress in Vietnam, and 49 percent stated that the United States should never have intervened in Vietnam.

Other events provided continued bad news for the Johnson administration. In March, the *New York Times* revealed that General Westmoreland, commander of U.S. forces in South Vietnam, had requested an additional 206,000 American troops—hardly an indication of American and South Vietnamese military success.

In New Hampshire, site of the year's first presidential primary on March 12, Eugene McCarthy captured 42.2 percent of the Democratic vote. After Republican crossover votes and write-in votes were counted, McCarthy had won only 230 fewer votes than the sitting president, who had not campaigned in New Hampshire. On March 16, Senator Robert Kennedy decided to enter the race against Johnson as well.

Plans for Chicago

Later in March, Doug Dowd and I drove to Chicago to attend a meeting of the National Mobilization Committee to discuss the pros and cons of calling for demonstrations at the Democratic National Convention, scheduled for late August in Chicago. (Although the meeting was not announced to the public, we found out later that it was teeming with agents from the FBI and the Chicago police.) Discussions about the convention protests had begun within the Mobe near the end of 1967, but nothing had yet been decided when 250 of us arrived on March 22 for the meeting at a YMCA camp in Lake Villa, just north of Chicago.

Tom Hayden and another SDS veteran, Rennie Davis, had been brought into the Mobe by Dave Dellinger to work on plans for the protest. They had already issued a call for "three days of sustained, organized protests...clogging the streets of Chicago with people demanding peace, justice and self-determination for all people." As to whether the protests would be nonviolent, Hayden and Davis hedged. While their report explicitly stated that the protests "should be nonviolent and legal," Hayden later wrote that "we expected violence, from the police and federal authorities, but we would not initiate it ourselves."

The Yippies, led by Abbie Hoffman and Jerry Rubin, were also at Lake Villa. When they weren't goofing around—Abbie called for "an end to pay toilets"—they pushed their previously announced plans for a countercultural youth festival, billed as a "Festival of Life," in contrast to the Democrats' "Convention of Death." Abbie was his usual cordial self, but Rubin, whom I barely knew, surprised me when he approached me with a big smile and an offer for me to become the upstate New York coordinator/organizer for the Yippies. I politely declined.

Doug was one of those who spoke against the Hayden-Davis proposal. Given the political climate in America and Chicago mayor Richard Daley's already apparent willingness to use his police force to attack peaceful protesters, Doug foresaw a bloodbath. Divided, the conference put off a final decision about Chicago.

By the end of March, President Johnson's overall approval rating had fallen to 36 percent, with only 26 percent approving his handling of the war. Perhaps we shouldn't have been surprised—though just about everyone I knew was—when on March 31 Johnson made the shocking announcement that he would not seek reelection. For the first time I felt that perhaps we could stop this war after all.

Cornell, Dow, and Five American Banks

Meanwhile, our recently reorganized Cornell SDS chapter had started to grow. For over a month, both radicals and moderate antiwar activists at Cornell had been planning a big protest over the upcoming February 19 appearance on campus of recruiters from the Dow Chemical Company. SDS sent organizers into the dorms to talk about Dow and its manufacture of napalm as an antipersonnel weapon.

For the *First Issue*, SDSer and Cornell graduate student Mark Sharefkin compiled some devastating data and information about Dow and its controversial product. Mark cited a report published in the *New England Journal of Medicine* that described the effect of napalm when dropped in 165-gallon canisters from low-flying planes: "Napalm burns are likely to be deep and extensive. The adhesiveness, prolonged burning time and high burning temperature...favor third-degree burns in all affected areas, with coagulation of muscle, fat and other deep tissues likely. Burns of this depth will probably result in severe scar contractures and deformities....Children will suffer a disproportionately high mortality."

This time we planned no civil disobedience actions. We succeeded in rallying between eight hundred and a thousand students and faculty to join a mass picket line outside Malott Hall, the home of the School of Business and Public Administration and the place where Dow recruiters were setting up shop.

Some of us in SDS also began to look for other examples of the university's complicity with the war in Vietnam and other harmful aspects of U.S. foreign policy. While we couldn't blame Cornell for what the Johnson administration was doing, we had previously identified and protested against programs and policies in which Cornell aided and abetted the war effort—including the presence of ROTC on campus, training future officers for war; allowing the Selective Service College Qualification Test to be held on campus, thus facilitating the ability of Selective Service to draft students; counterinsurgency research at CAL; and military recruitment on campus.

For several reasons, we turned our attention to the relationship between Cornell and the Republic of South Africa, where a white supremacist government representing less than one-fifth of the country's population denied political rights and civil liberties to blacks and mixed-race people (known as "coloreds"). These whites (Afrikaaners descended from Dutch settlers, as well as those of English ancestry) owned 87 percent of the land and enforced a policy of strict racial segregation known as apartheid. A knowledgeable law student and SDS member, Bruce Detwiler, had recently returned from South Africa, where he had learned firsthand about the brutalities being committed by the South African government. Together with the presence on campus of Rev. Gladstone Ntlabati, an exiled South African freedom fighter, we were exposed to antiapartheid thought by two articulate men.

Along with a few other SDS members, I began to investigate—on my first trips to the Cornell library in over a year—ties between Cornell and South Africa. Looking at standard business reference books, along with material provided by the American Committee on Africa, a liberal antiapartheid group, we discovered close links between Cornell and a consortium of American banks that had been propping up the South African regime with a $40 million revolving credit loan.

Cornell owned $3.5 million in stock in five of those banks—Chase Manhattan, Chemical Bank of New York, Continental Illinois Bank and Trust Company, First National City Bank of New York, and Manufacturers

Hanover Trust Company. In addition, President Perkins held a seat on the board of directors of Chase Manhattan, one of the leaders of the consortium. Arthur Dean, chairman of the Cornell board of trustees, sat on the board and was a former vice president of the American Metal Climax Company, one of the leading firms mining gold and uranium in South Africa.

In March, Cornell SDS began a program calling for the "economic disengagement of Cornell from the South African banks," and we started educating the campus community about apartheid. In less than a week we gathered over twelve hundred signatures on a petition demanding that Cornell immediately sell its investments and remove its deposits from the five banks that had loaned money to South Africa and that Perkins resign from the board of Chase Manhattan.

We found out later that Cornell had recently sold its stock in Chase Manhattan—for investment reasons rather than out of political or moral concerns. This didn't change our central points and demands, since Perkins remained on the Chase Manhattan board and Cornell retained its stock in the other banks in the consortium. It turned out that even Perkins didn't know about the Chase Manhattan stock sale.[1]

At the time we initiated our antiapartheid campaign at Cornell I was unaware that three years earlier, in March 1965—one month before SDS sponsored the first mass demonstration against the war in Vietnam—SDS led a protest against Chase Manhattan for its loans to South Africa. More than four hundred demonstrators took part in the protest, held outside the bank's headquarters in New York City, with forty-nine getting arrested for a sit-in on the sidewalk in front of the bank. The demonstration was endorsed by several civil rights organizations, including SNCC and CORE, as well as the Pan-African Student Organization in America.

A New Alliance

One important component of the new antiapartheid campaign was that the Cornell Afro-American Society agreed to cosponsor the demands with SDS. The AAS also drafted its own demands on another issue—the extremely tight housing market in Ithaca. The AAS believed that Cornell was contributing to the problem by not providing sufficient housing for its students, who then

---

1. The $3.5 million figure cited by SDS as Cornell's investment in banks that loaned money to the Republic of South Africa turned out to be low. According to an April 30, 1968, memo from Robert T. Horn, the university's associate treasurer, to the Cornell board of trustees' Commission on Investments and Public Policy, Cornell's shares in just four of the banks (excluding Chase Manhattan) were valued at $5 million.

had to seek housing in town, where they drove up rental prices for the city's poor. The AAS asked that Cornell donate a parcel of land to be used as a site for low-income housing.

The number of black undergraduates at Cornell had been increasing slowly but steadily since 1963, when Perkins initiated the COSEP (Committee on Special Education Projects) program to recruit minority students. (Doug Dowd was an active member of the committee from its inception.) Where there were only eight African American undergrads at Cornell in 1963, by the 1968–69 academic year their numbers were up to 250.

The Cornell Afro-American Society was formed in early 1966 but was just finding its collective political voice in 1968. Like black students around the country, AAS members were deeply affected by the civil rights movement's turn toward black power ideology and black nationalism. Although some black students from Cornell participated in the large antiwar rallies of 1967, and a few were on the periphery of SDS, most of the more political blacks had little desire to work with white student radicals. This began to change with our South Africa divestment campaign.

Despite the growing separatism of the black movement, many of us in SDS were still committed to fighting racism in America and around the world. But it was also the case that I, for one, had fewer and fewer black friends as the '60s progressed. Although the black movement's turn against integration obviously had something to do with this, I wasn't meeting people who were outside of my usual social sphere, which, in the case of Cornell SDS and the draft resistance movement, was almost entirely white. No longer was I a member of the track team or a student taking classes or a resident of the dorms—all places where in the past I had made black friends.

I was acquainted with some of the AAS leaders, but we seldom sat down to talk or get to know each other on more than a superficial level. Forging an alliance with radical black students was one of my goals when we began our antiapartheid work. That was one of the reasons I ran stories in the *First Issue* about student uprisings and police repression on the historically African American campuses of Howard University and South Carolina State.

As the antiapartheid campaign picked up steam, I was also working on the next draft card turn-in, scheduled for April 3. This was the period of my most extensive speaking tours for the Resistance, some with Doug Dowd and Dan Berrigan. One such event, at the University of Rochester, attracted more attention from the FBI.

In February, I was invited to speak at a forum sponsored by Rochester SDS titled "How to Avoid Military Service." The other speakers were a draft counselor from the Society of Friends, who offered advice about conscientious objection, and a Canadian working with the Toronto Anti-Draft Programme to help American exiles become landed immigrants in Canada. The forum was also broadcast live over the campus radio station.

The FBI report on the event, which included a transcript of the entire proceedings, summarized my participation (awkwardly) as, "Dancis, who currently is under indictment in Syracuse for draft violations, discussed illegal means of avoiding the draft implemented chiefly by the Resistance." I gave my standard talk about the unfairness of student deferments and CO status, and promoted the April draft card turn-in.

Based on this speech in Rochester, the FBI suggested to the regional U.S. attorney that I be indicted for advocating draft resistance. Fortunately, according to my FBI file, "On May 27, 1968, the facts of this case were presented to Assistant United States Attorney Stephen S. Joy, Rochester, New York, by [name deleted for security reasons]. Assistant United States Attorney Joy declined prosecution of the subject, as he felt the subject had not violated any Federal Statute."

Meanwhile, other Cornell resisters began feeling the wrath of General Hershey and his draft boards. About a dozen received notices that they were being reclassified 1-A. Lew Zipin and Steve Boldt were both called for induction and refused; both were awaiting indictment.

Having skipped my preinduction physical in early January, I also expected to be called for induction in the near future. And sure enough, just as had occurred immediately prior to our earlier draft resistance actions, I received notice a few days before April 3 that I had been ordered to appear in Syracuse on April 18 for induction into the armed forces. More surprisingly, Paul Gibbons, one of the two Cornell chaplains who had turned in their draft cards the previous fall, was also called for induction, on April 15 in New York City.

Just as we had in December, we planned to hold the Ithaca turn-in two days after the nationwide action on April 3. One of the reasons was that Joan Baez, a major supporter of the draft resistance movement—for better or worse, she was credited with popularizing the slogan "Girls say yes to boys who say no"—was coming to Cornell for an April 5 concert. Accompanying Baez on her trip to Ithaca were her husband of two weeks, David Harris, one of the founders of the Resistance, and Ira Sandperl, leader of the California-based Institute for the Study of Non-Violence and one of Baez's closest friends and advisers. The opportunity to have the three join us for our draft card turn-in seemed like a good reason to postpone the action for two days.

I had the chance to spend some time with Baez, Harris, and Sandperl over dinner in Collegetown the evening before her concert and the turn-in. It was great to talk to David, already under indictment for his own induction refusal, and share our experiences. He was eager to take part in our Resistance event, though Baez didn't want to on the same day she was performing. (In fairness to Baez, she expressed her ardent support for draft resistance in an interview with the *Sun* upon her arrival in Ithaca, and again in a public news conference the day after her concert.) Baez wasn't particularly friendly to me, in contrast to David and Ira, though I couldn't tell if it was because she was tired of all our dinner-table talk about the draft resistance movement or because she didn't like *not* being the center of attention.

A Cornell Confrontation and the Murder of Dr. King

On April 4, one day before our draft card turn-in, two events took place—one local, the other with national and international implications—that shook us all up.

Some of the African American students at Cornell had been upset over a class on economic development taught by Father Michael McPhelin, a Roman Catholic priest and visiting lecturer from the Philippines. Three AAS members in his class felt his teaching was racist and Eurocentric, and he was insensitive in his discussion of blacks, poverty, and welfare. In particular, the students were incensed by McPhelin's comment that poor children in urban areas played games that were "sickly and perverted."

After raising their objections directly and continually to McPhelin over several weeks and getting nowhere, they tried to meet with the vice president for student affairs, Mark Barlow, to express their grievances. But his office passed them along to the associate dean of students, Stanley Levy, who passed them along to the dean of the Arts College, Stuart Brown, who passed them along to the Economics Department chairman, Tom Davis, who said he could do nothing about it. Believing they had been given the runaround, the students rallied other members of the AAS to take action.

On the morning of April 4, after the students attempted to read a statement in McPhelin's class, to which McPhelin responded by canceling the class, sixty AAS members staged a sit-in in the Economics Department office in Goldwin Smith Hall. They demanded an apology, McPhelin's dismissal for incompetence, and equal time to express their opposing views. They also took over the office, unplugged the phones, and barricaded the doors, while letting three secretaries leave. They told Davis, the department chairman, he could not leave until he arranged a meeting with someone who had the power to meet their demands.

When word of the office takeover started to spread around the campus, a bunch of us from SDS rushed over to the Economics Department to see what was happening and, if possible, provide support for the black students. Proctor George and the campus cops also arrived to demand that the students open the office. Eventually, after more than six hours of negotiations between the AAS and top Cornell administrators led to a promise from Provost Corson that he would seriously examine their complaints, the students left the office. [2]

The conflict between the AAS and McPhelin led to a lengthy controversy on campus over the competing claims of academic freedom and fighting racism. According to Cleve Donald, a Cornell grad student and AAS member, "The McPhelin incident demonstrated the racist character of the university and impressed upon [black students] the necessity of establishing courses that would be relevant to their requirements. For some faculty members, the criticisms of McPhelin's teaching represented an attack on the right of a professor to determine his or her curriculum."

A few hours after the black students ended their occupation of the Economics Department office, Dr. Martin Luther King Jr. was assassinated outside his motel room in Memphis, Tennessee, where he had gone to support the city's striking sanitation workers. That evening, arson fires were set at Cornell, in Ithaca, and around the country.

The next day, April 5, CURW held a noon memorial service for Dr. King at Bailey Hall, filled with twenty-two hundred people, with another five hundred listening in at another building. Rev. Gibbons and Afro-American Society leader John Garner both received applause—Gibbons for reminding the audience that "the practice of nonviolence by whites has been dead for over three hundred years" and Garner for calling to keep Dr. King's dream alive. But for many in attendance, the most striking occurrences were the arrival, seating, and departure en masse of all the black students, and AAS member Larry Dickson's angry speech. "I don't believe [the] white man has any good in him," Dickson said. "When Martin Luther King died, nonviolence died." He then added, "I ain't preaching violence, brothers, I'm preaching self-defense."

Like most white radicals, I was saddened and dismayed by Dr. King's murder and troubled by its implications. I understood why so many black Americans, especially those my age, were filled with rage about living in a racist society and were lashing out at whites, but I did not believe that racial separatism constituted a viable solution. I had political differences with Dr. King— remembering his opposition to our draft card burning a year earlier—but he remained a hero and an inspiration to me. His antiwar stance, his efforts in Memphis in support of workers demanding economic justice, and his plans

---

2. The incident at the Economics Department also provided fodder for scenes in at least two novels—Alison Lurie's *The War between the Tates* (1974) and Joyce Thompson's *Hothouse* (1981).

for what became the Poor People's Campaign suggest that Dr. King was moving steadily to the left. His death deprived us of a leader and spokesman.

Another Turn-In and Two Induction Refusals

The rally for our draft card turn-in, which began as soon as the King service ended, packed over six hundred people into the Memorial Room at the Straight. But just before the start of the rally, which I was going to emcee, I learned that a particular guy—let's call him Sam—was planning to turn in his draft card. Sam often showed up for antiwar and draft resistance actions at Cornell, but I hardly knew him. He often talked aloud to himself and made strange faces for no apparent reason. It didn't take a psychotherapist to figure out that Sam had some kind of mental illness. He did not seem to me to be a good candidate for draft resistance, as I could not imagine him surviving in a prison environment.

Sam was on my mind as I began to speak. I started by reading an excerpt from an antiwar speech by Dr. King. I expressed my concern that the events of the previous day, which had aroused both the consciences and the emotions of many, might provoke someone to make a spur-of-the-moment decision to turn in his draft card. Such an action could result in severe consequences and should only be taken after considerable thought and soul-searching. I said I wasn't trying to keep the numbers down, but wanted to stress that a well-thought-out decision was more important than numbers. There would be other opportunities in the future to resist the draft.

I concluded my remarks by saying, "Our resistance will not end until all the killing ends, until every one of our brothers is back from Vietnam, until every resister is free from prison."

Two of the speakers, Jim Murray and Walt Edwards, explained why they were going to turn in their draft cards. Harriet Edwards (no relation to Walt), representing the local chapter of Women's Strike for Peace, urged women to sign a statement of complicity with draft resisters—"I have encouraged them, I honor them, and I am at one with them in this act"—which would be turned in along with draft cards. (About sixty women eventually signed.) Jay Schulman, representing faculty supporters, read a statement signed by twenty-four Cornell professors: "I pledge to support these young men with encouragement, counsel, and financial aid, and to offer them whatever other assistance I can."

David Harris spoke about the need to follow your conscience. He talked about his upcoming trial in San Francisco for refusing induction. He said that to be a criminal was a good thing in the context of the war. Finally,

Father Berrigan talked about the upcoming inductions of Rev. Gibbons and me, saying he wished he could bring the entire Cornell community to these events.

When the rally ended, we all marched to the Ithaca draft board. Eleven men—including English professor Dan Finlay, Jeff Dowd (Doug's son and an SDS member), and, despite my concerns, Sam—walked inside the building to turn in their cards. Harriet Edwards, Mimi Keck, and Laura Webber, representing the women, and English professor Doug Archibald, representing the faculty, followed to hand over their statements of complicity.

Nationally, about one thousand men turned in their cards in this third action sponsored by the Resistance, with more than five hundred of those coming from Boston and the San Francisco Bay Area. I was disappointed by those numbers—they were more than in December, but less than in October. It appeared that we had reached a plateau, instead of the hoped-for exponential expansion. Nevertheless, we weren't planning to stop. In a report in the *First Issue* about the results of the April action, I wrote, "The next national draft card turn-in is November 14, though anyone can turn in a card anytime, anyplace."

Paul Gibbons's induction refusal in New York City on April 15 was a major news event. TV cameras were out in force, and the *New York Times* devoted a long story and four photographs to it, as Paul was the first ordained minister in the United States to be called for induction. Over 150 Cornellians made the trip to New York, where a "service of commitment" at the historic St. Paul's Chapel (where George Washington once worshipped) was held to support Paul.

Before a crowd of about six hundred people in the packed church, Paul called on American society "to rid itself of the systemic violence that has become part of our lives." Father Berrigan, Doug Dowd, and I also spoke, and we were joined by Dr. John Bennett, president of the Union Theological Seminary, who said, "When anyone resists the draft these days, they have my admiration. It is the highest form of patriotism to call the country back to its true self."

Most of us then left St. Paul's to walk down Broadway to the Whitehall Street induction center, where Paul refused to take the traditional step forward to be inducted into the armed forces.

My turn came three days later.

SPOTLIGHT: REFUSING INDUCTION, APRIL 18, 1968

"What's going on?" asked one of the guys on the bus, speaking to no one in particular, as it pulled into the parking lot of the induction center in Syracuse. He had just seen the two hundred demonstrators who were standing outside the center, holding placards saying "Hell No, We Won't Go" and "Resist the Draft."

"I think they're here for me," I responded, "because I'm going to refuse to be inducted." He looked back at me blankly.

Ninety minutes earlier at the Ithaca bus station, sixteen of us had boarded a chartered bus for Syracuse, where we were all scheduled to be inducted into the U.S. Army. I didn't know any of the guys accompanying me, because I declined to attend a farewell breakfast for draftees hosted earlier in the morning by a local fraternal organization.

I also didn't get acquainted with the other men on the bus during the ride, despite my original intention to talk to my fellow draftees about the war and the draft. We all sat separately, alone in our thoughts. I imagined the others were thinking about their homes, the loved ones they were leaving behind, and the dangers they would be facing once they entered the armed forces. It seemed like a very private time, and I held back from breaking the silence and causing a stir.

I was in a pensive mood as well. There weren't any doubts as to what I would do when called to step forward and be inducted, but it all seemed unnecessary, a case of Selective Service and prosecutorial overkill. I had always viewed tearing up my draft card and returning it to my draft board with a letter declaring my noncooperation with the draft to be the single, sufficient act of draft resistance I needed to make. But with the U.S. Supreme Court still months away from deciding whether the law I was charged with breaking was constitutional, the feds might have thought they needed a more solid case against me. I interpreted my being called for induction, which the authorities must have known I would refuse, as a safeguard for the prosecution in the event the draft card destruction case was thrown out.

My introspection was also due to my concern about how many years in prison I would be facing. I had been expecting a maximum sentence of five years for tearing up my draft card. But the prospect of a second indictment and the possibility of two convictions meant that I could be facing ten years in prison—and even more if the grand jury in New York City brought charges for the April '67 draft card burning.

When we stopped outside the induction center, a man in uniform came out to lead the guys on the bus into the induction center. As the demonstrators shouted "Don't go!" to the inductees, I stayed outside to talk to the crowd. Joining me was a Cornell grad student in architecture, Gary Comstock, who had come to Syracuse to turn in his draft card. I explained why I would be refusing induction, even though, as someone already under federal indictment, I didn't think I would be allowed into the armed forces.

When I entered the center, the officer in charge was waiting for me. He pulled me aside and asked, "Are you refusing induction?" I said yes. He then told me I was free to go. I never got the chance to refuse to take the traditional step forward.

Afterward, we held a press conference at my attorney's office, with Doug Dowd and Dan Berrigan appearing with me to lend their support. Faith charged that my being called for induction while already under indictment was illegal on its face, and that prosecution for refusing induction alongside prosecution for draft card destruction and noncooperation was a case of double jeopardy. She said this was an obvious attempt to intimidate me.

When asked by a reporter why I was willing to face a possible ten years of imprisonment, I said, "It would be more of a crime to go into the armed forces and kill people."

A few weeks later, I was eating dinner at Father Dan's apartment when he said he had something important to talk about. Even though his brother Phil had just been convicted (though not yet sentenced) for destroying draft files in Baltimore, the brothers Berrigan were planning another, larger attack on poorly guarded Selective Service files. Dan offered me the opportunity to join them. But with at least two or three felonies already hanging over my head, I felt I was in enough legal trouble, and declined.

On May 18, Dan, Phil, and seven other Catholic activists walked into a Knights of Columbus Hall in the Baltimore suburb of Catonsville, a building that also housed the files of a Selective Service board. The nine gathered up all of the 1-A files they could find, brought them outside to the parking lot, and set them on fire. They were all arrested within minutes.

So I gave up my chance to be part of what became known as the Catonsville Nine. But I was in Baltimore for their trial the following October, which turned out to be just after my own encounter with the American legal system.

Debating South African Investment

On the same day Rev. Gibbons refused induction in New York City, President Perkins responded to Cornell SDS's South Africa demands in a letter to the *Sun*. Although he called apartheid "wicked" and "heinous," he wrote that neither selling the stocks nor his resigning from the Chase Manhattan board of directors would have any "substantial" impact on the policies of the South African regime, whereas American corporations operating in South Africa would have a beneficial effect. He challenged the idea that the university's investment policy should be based upon the community's judgment of social policy. He also described university policy with respect to investments as "the University does not try to tell these people how to run their business as long as they don't tell us how to run our business."

In response, Rev. Ntlabati, the South African freedom fighter who was studying at Cornell, wrote a letter to the *Sun* that critiqued Perkins's "hear-no-evil, see-no-evil, let's-make-money" philosophy of university investment. He cited the growing international pressure against the South African government, in particular the 1963 vote in which eighty-four members of the United Nations supported an oil embargo against South Africa (a vote that the United States opposed) and the American Methodist Church's decision to withdraw $10 million from one of the banks in the South Africa consortium. Rev. Ntlabati also demolished Perkins's view that U.S. businesses were having a positive influence on South Africa, pointing out that "American corporations take advantage of the cheap black labor, and thereby support and perpetuate all the viciousness that is implicit in apartheid. The American corporate record is, in fact, shameful."

SDS put out a leaflet in which Perkins's letter and Ntlabati's rejoinder were printed side by side. We also reprinted as a leaflet a devastating op-ed column in the *Sun* by SDS member Howard Rodman, "Why I Invest in the KKK," which satirized Perkins's rationale. We put out a ten-page position paper exploring the history of apartheid in South Africa and Cornell's complicity with it, and we presented our petition to the administration and the trustees.

With an upcoming board of trustees meeting scheduled on campus, in which the AAS's housing demands and the joint SDS-AAS South Africa demands would be discussed and, hopefully, decided upon, we held a contentious SDS meeting to decide what our response should be. In contrast to what would take place the following year, at this time the AAS acted as a restraining force on those in SDS who favored immediate militant action. Most of the SDS leadership opposed seizing a building, on the grounds that we had given our word to the AAS and the public that we would not take such disruptive actions before the administration had a chance to respond to our demands. We eventually decided to hold a peaceful "mill-in" outside the building where the trustees were meeting.

Revolt at Columbia

In the midst of all this, events at Columbia University in New York transfixed the nation and electrified the New Left. Beginning April 23, members of Columbia SDS and the Afro-American Society tore down construction fences and seized campus buildings, including President Grayson Kirk's office, in a joint protest over the university's construction of a new gym in nearby Morningside Park (one of the few city-owned parks easily accessible to the Harlem community) and the university's partnership with the Institute for Defense Analysis, a think tank doing weapons research for the Defense Department.

SDS chapters throughout the country were galvanized by the weeklong events at Columbia, which culminated with a student strike and New York City police coming onto the campus to arrest over six hundred protesters, brutalizing many. Within SDS, this led to the call for "Two, Three, Many Columbias"—a takeoff on Che Guevara's revolutionary call for "Two, Three, Many Vietnams." At Cornell, we devoted eleven pages of the final *First Issue* of the semester to a Liberation News Service story about the Columbia struggle.

The Cornell trustees, doing what in football is known as "running out the clock," avoided giving a clear answer to our demands before graduation and the end of the term. They agreed to donate some Cornell-owned land to the city of Ithaca for low-income housing. But with regard to South Africa, they offered only a few fellowships for South African exiles and a symposium on South Africa to be held the following February, while referring our demands to the Cornell faculty and a newly created joint student-faculty-administration commission.

The faculty surprised just about everyone by coming down on our side. A "sense of the faculty" statement declared that Cornell's investment policies "should reflect a serious concern with the possible moral implications of those policies" and that the racial policies of the government of South Africa were "flagrantly in violation of the ideals of the University." They recommended that the board of trustees "avoid making investments that significantly support...any such policies."

At the end of May, the commission appointed to investigate Cornell's investment policies delivered a majority report stating that the university should "avoid" any investments "supporting racial discrimination." The SDS representative on the commission, Bruce Detwiler, issued a minority report stating that the university needed to get rid of such investments. Still, both the faculty and the investment commission were clearly moving in our direction.

However, on June 1, the day of graduation, the trustees announced they would retain all the controversial investments. By then, Cornell was out of session, the student body dispersed. But for Cornell SDS, this was only the beginning of our South Africa campaign.

SPPOTLIGHT: SINK THE DRAFT WITH TITANIC, MAY 1968

The sweetness of the melody and the poignancy of the lyrics about love, peace, and brotherhood could be heard loud and clear on a late spring evening as the vocalist sang "Everybody get together, try to love one another right now." But it wasn't Jesse Colin Young and his band the Youngbloods who were performing their hit song "Get Together" at the block party in the Collegetown neighborhood of Ithaca. Instead, it was a local band, Titanic, and its singer was me.

I always liked to sing. Elementary-school talent shows, summer camp musicals, even family gatherings provided audiences for my crooning. But by 1968 I hadn't performed publicly for nearly three years, since I had sung folk songs with Happy Traum and played in a jug band.

During the winter of 1967–68, I was hanging out with Lenny Silver, a young Cornell math professor who was close to the student movement. Lenny was playing electric piano, mostly blues and rock, in his spare time with a band known as Titanic. The group—Jay Young and Kurt Lichtmann on guitar, Steve Lee on bass, and Barry the drummer on drums, plus Lenny—had been rehearsing for a couple of months but hadn't yet performed in public.[3]

One day at Lenny's house, he and Jay were fooling around and jamming when I said, "You know, I can sing." I knew the lyrics to one of the songs in their repertoire, Wilson Pickett's "In the Midnight Hour," and we agreed to try it, without a drummer and with Lenny playing the bass line on the piano with his left hand. I wasn't exactly Mr. Soul on my vocal, but I must have been better than Lenny and Jay expected. Over the next week or so, I took part in rehearsals with the entire group, and in short order, I was in and Kurt, who had previously been the lead vocalist, quit.

I wasn't a songwriter, and neither was anyone else in Titanic, but we all had a pretty clear sense of what types of music we liked and which songs we could cover. This was a wonderful era for rock, blues, and soul music, and we started to build our set list out of favorite songs. From the British Invasion bands, we learned the Stones' "Play with Fire" and "Under My Thumb," the Kinks' "Till the End of the

---

3. Lenny and I never knew our drummer's last name, and still don't. At one gig, we even listed him as "Barry T. Drummer."

Day" and "Rosie Won't You Please Come Home," and the Animals'
"We Gotta Get Out of This Place." Among American rock groups,
we played the Doors' "My Eyes Have Seen You," Country Joe and the
Fish's "Superbird," and the Youngbloods' "Get Together." The blues
and R&B artists we borrowed from included Howlin' Wolf ("Back-
door Man"), Junior Wells ("Messin' with the Kid"), the Blues Project
("I Can't Keep from Crying"), Cream ("Sunshine of Your Love"). and
Pickett ("Midnight Hour").

Maybe because I had experience speaking before crowds, I was
fairly uninhibited while performing. I'd dance around, banging a tam-
bourine and pumping my fist on our fast rockers, and I could emote
passionately on our slow dance tunes if the mood hit. Not that my
performing would have cost James Brown or Mick Jagger any sleep.

Cornell and Ithaca, with their fraternity and sorority parties and
local bars catering to students, provided many places for rock bands
to perform. One local group, Chrysalis, featuring SDS member and
my former East Harlem roommate Jon Sabin on lead guitar, even
signed a recording contract with MGM Records.[4]

Titanic wasn't as serious or as talented—as a "cover band" none of
us were quitting school or our day jobs—but we performed in off-
campus "associations" (independent houses that served as alternatives
to the fraternity/sorority system), in dorms, in the student union, and
in the CURW building. We did a few benefit concerts for the Resistance, billed as "Sink the Draft with Titanic." And we had a built-in
audience for every show from SDS members, resisters, and friends.

At one gig, the evening after Jane had persuaded me (OK, she
dragged me) to see the Merce Cunningham Dance Company perform
on campus, I noticed that a number of people dancing to our music
were a lot more graceful and inventive than our usual crowd. Sure
enough, many of the Cunningham company members had come to
our show following their performance.

Our material wasn't overtly political for the most part, with the
exception of "Get Together" and "Superbird," which I would introduce as a song about "that motherfucker in the White House." But I
would sometimes take the opportunity to add a little commentary,
dedicating "We Gotta Get Out of This Place" to "our friends living
in exile in Canada." (I didn't yet know that the song had also become
popular among American GIs stationed in Vietnam.)

---

4. Chrysalis's 1968 debut album, *Definition*, featured a photo of the band members with their fists
raised militantly in the air.

Curiosity about a band featuring two fairly well-known people on campus (Lenny and me) got us one quite large show, at the Straight. Several hundred people were in attendance, and the show was broadcast live on the campus radio station, WVBR-FM. Unfortunately for us, during our third song one of Lenny's electric piano strings broke, producing a weird and out-of-tune note whenever he hit that key. It wasn't possible to repair his piano on the spot, and our sound would have been pretty thin without Lenny.

But in a great stroke of luck, a musician friend in attendance had a small Farfisa organ in the trunk of his car, parked nearby. Within five minutes—an agonizingly slow five minutes, which I awkwardly tried to fill by talking to the crowd (and the radio audience)—we had the organ plugged in onstage and resumed our set. Even though he had never played an electric organ before, Lenny carried on like a pro, saving us from disaster.

Titanic's final gig took place around the end of the spring semester, at a block party on the Collegetown street where some friends lived. We had a large, friendly turnout, though one guy came up to me during a break between sets to ask, with hostility, if I was "that draft dodger Bruce Dancis." I replied that I was indeed that person, but I preferred the term "draft resister" to "draft dodger." He gave me a nasty look, but just walked away.

As a band, Titanic never formally broke up, but we all went our separate ways after June. My time in the band was a lot of fun while it lasted, and a great change of pace from my usual routine. Sadly, as far as I know there are no existing recordings of Titanic or photographs of the band.

Columbia and COINTELPRO

The Columbia protest and other student uprisings around the country provoked J. Edgar Hoover to issue a memorandum calling for the establishment of a new "Counter Intelligence Program" (known as COINTELPRO) aimed at the "Disruption of the New Left."

"The purpose of this program," Hoover wrote, "is to expose, disrupt, and otherwise neutralize the activities of the various new left organizations, their leadership and their adherents.... In every instance, consideration should be given to disrupting organized activity of these groups and no opportunity should be missed to capitalize on organizational or personal conflicts of their leadership."

Chapter Ten

From Resistance to Revolution

By 1968, like others in the New Left, I began to think of myself as a revolutionary. To be a young radical in the America of 1968 meant living in a personal state of rebellion over the war in Vietnam, the draft, racism, and a stultifying, avaricious culture. However, despite the serious fissures and disruptions taking place in American society, this country was not on the verge of a social revolution—no matter the pipe dreams and rhetorical excess coming from our side or the paranoid fantasies of J. Edgar Hoover.

The revolutionary posturing that many of us indulged in during the late '60s seems almost comical in hindsight, as the powers that be were not about to lose their grip, and we had yet to generate the kind of mass support needed to produce systemic change. While youthful enthusiasm had done much to build our movement, youthful impatience was now carrying many of us to unjustifiable and untenable positions. In addition to seriously misjudging the actual situation in America, revolutionary zeal led good people to take actions that hurt the movement and themselves, as well as others.

While we may have understood what we were revolting against, we seldom discussed what kind of society we hoped to build, or how to get there. If there was any consensus as to what it meant to be a revolutionary, it was a commitment to working full time for the cause.

I was a peculiar type of revolutionary in that I was anti-Leninist and a pacifist, though my commitment to nonviolence was beginning to waver. I opposed the key Leninist concept that a vanguard party must be built to lead the larger mass movement, which would generate a violent upheaval against the power of the state. To me, vanguard parties were inherently elitist and antidemocratic—despite the prattle about "democratic centralism," it seemed as if Leninist groups were far more interested in centralism than democracy. Instead, my goal was to build a popular, democratic, majoritarian socialist movement that would bring about revolutionary changes in American society and foreign policy because that was the will of the people.

To understand why so many young people, both black and white, came to see our goal as building a revolutionary movement in America, one has to place the United States of 1968 in the context of the revolutions, wars for national liberation, mass protests, and disruptions taking place around the world. As the Cold War between East and West continued, U.S. policy remained committed to supporting dictatorships and military juntas that proclaimed themselves anticommunist. Correspondingly, when popular movements—whether nationalist, communist, or nonaligned—sprang up against such U.S. allies, our country's aid and military might were used to crush them in the name of anticommunism.

The Specter of Revolutionary Students

Writing about the international events of 1968 shortly after they took place, New Left authors Barbara and John Ehrenreich paraphrased Marx and Engels's *Communist Manifesto:* "A new specter was haunting Europe, and America. It was no longer the specter of organized communism....In 1968 it was revolutionary students."

Consider these developments in 1968, not just in Europe and America, but worldwide (and I'm just scratching the surface):

In Asia, the war in Vietnam grew even hotter and deadlier, as it appeared that even the armed forces of the United States and South Vietnam could not defeat the National Liberation Front and the North Vietnamese; China was two years into its Cultural Revolution, apparently led by young people in the Red Guards,[1] to battle against "capitalist roaders" and to preserve the revolutionary nature of the regime; Japanese students led large and violent protests against the war in Vietnam and the presence of American troops in their country.

In Africa, the Portuguese colonies of Angola, Mozambique, and Guinea-Bissau were in various stages of national liberation revolt, while in South Africa, the African National Congress kept up its political and military assault against apartheid.

---

1. As more became known about the Cultural Revolution, it became clear that the movement was launched from the top down, by Mao and his supporters, in an internal fight for supremacy within the Chinese Communist Party.

In Latin America, students led demonstrations in Mexico against the corrupt, one-party rule of the Institutional Revolutionary Party (PRI), provoking brutal government repression on the eve of the Olympic Games in Mexico City; Cuba's Fidel Castro declared 1968 "the year of the heroic guerrilla fighter" in honor of the recently fallen Che Guevara and began a "revolutionary offensive" against the country's remaining privately owned businesses; in Nicaragua, young people led the Sandinista National Liberation Front (FSLN) in guerrilla raids against the Somoza dictatorship; urban guerrilla warfare against military juntas broke out in Brazil, Uruguay, and Argentina.

In Southern Europe, students led antigovernment demonstrations against the military dictators ruling Spain, Portugal, and Greece.

In Eastern Europe, dissenting students and others in Czechoslovakia brought about an opening to political pluralism and freedom of expression in opposition to authoritarian rule, which led to the invasion of Soviet troops to suppress what had been called "communism with a human face"; in Poland, university students demonstrated for freedom and human rights.

In Western Europe, strikes by French students against the war in Vietnam and in favor of greater freedom on college campuses were joined by workers (against the desires of the French Communist Party), leading to a general strike that nearly brought down the government of Charles de Gaulle; tens of thousands of students in Great Britain protested against the Vietnam War and seized buildings on college campuses in solidarity with the French; student-led struggles in West Germany opposed the war in Vietnam, rightwing control of the media, and new emergency laws passed by the government; and in Italy, tens of thousands of students demonstrated against the war and occupied universities in protests against campus authoritarianism.

Obviously, there were considerable differences among the struggles taking place in these countries, and wide disparities in ideology among the students in revolt. In Czechoslovakia, for instance, the struggle was for an increase in cultural freedom and individual liberty (and later, resistance against invading Soviet troops), while in the West students were protesting the war in Vietnam and domestic policies. Yet the similarity in spirit and style among young people internationally was hard to ignore.

The Beatles, the Stones, and the Revolution

Even the Beatles and the Rolling Stones, the two most popular and influential rock bands of the '60s, couldn't help getting involved in the 1968 discussions and debates about revolution. While both bands had been exerting considerable influence on the thoughts, appearance, and lifestyles of young people, in mid-1968, when the Beatles recorded "Revolution" and the Stones brought out "Street Fighting Man," they were reacting in response to what young rebels were doing.

Members of the Beatles, who had been publicly criticizing the war in Vietnam for several years, continued their vocal opposition. At the October 1967 London premiere of the film *How I Won the War,* John Lennon, who had a small role in the movie, said, "I hate war. If there is another war I won't fight and I'll try to tell all the youngsters not to fight either." When asked about the war in an April 1968 New York radio interview, Lennon replied, "It's just insane. It shouldn't be going on. There's no reason for it."

John began thinking about "Revolution," the song, early in 1968, when the Beatles went to India to study transcendental meditation with the Maharishi Mahesh Yogi. But by the time he finished the song and the Beatles began recording it, on May 30, 1968, he had been more immediately affected by an antiwar demonstration in March outside the American embassy in London that had turned violent, the assassination of Dr. Martin Luther King Jr. in April, and the May uprising of French students and workers.

In his song, John directly engaged and criticized young radicals. He sounded condescending and dismissive of revolutionary demands or requests for financial contributions to radical causes. He rejected violence and support for communist governments, taking aim at revolutionaries who supported Chairman Mao and China. He argued that seeking inner peace and freeing one's head needed to take place before anyone could contemplate changing society.

Not surprisingly, when "Revolution" was released in late August (as the B-side of a single, with "Hey Jude"), it generated considerable hostility from activists. Coming out while young radicals were still licking their wounds after getting beaten up by Chicago police at the Democratic National Convention, Lennon's commentary touched a raw nerve. *Ramparts* magazine, a leading New Left publication, called the song a "betrayal," while Britain's *New Left Review,* an independent Marxist journal, referred to "Revolution" as "a lamentable petty bourgeois cry of fear."

On the other hand, the music and rhythm of "Revolution" seemed to be telling a different story. The single version of "Revolution" featured some of the most blistering rock 'n' roll the Beatles ever recorded. Delivered at a rapid pace with distorted guitar sounds, "Revolution" had a hard, almost violent edge that could be seen to contradict, or at least amend, Lennon's pacific concerns.

When the Beatles released their *White Album* a few months later, "Revolution" appeared again (as "Revolution 1"), but this time in a much slower version. Yet in this version, which was actually recorded before the single,

Lennon seemed to be expressing greater ambivalence about his position. After telling young rebels that they should "count me out" when it came to revolutionary violence, he added the word "in."

I actually agreed with what Lennon had to say about Maoists in the West not connecting with the people they were trying to reach. Waving Mao's Little Red Book was a poor substitute for organizing or talking to people about the issues affecting their lives. Lennon's comments about violence and hatred were certainly worthy of discussion and debate. In the *First Issue* we ran a review of the *White Album* by rock musician Jon Sabin that defended the song. "[The Beatles] are contemptuous of certain revolutionaries hung up on violence," Jon wrote. "Is this really such a drag?...You can argue about the effectiveness of non-violence as a tactic, but it would be absurd to claim that it is a conservative notion."

But I also found the overall tone of Lennon's song very disappointing. As historian Jon Wiener wrote in his book *Come Together: John Lennon in His Time,* an astute assessment of Lennon and his changing political views and activities, Lennon took the "genuine problems of revolutionary morality and strategy as an excuse for abandoning politics altogether and substituting in its place a quest for personal liberation." While Lennon was still in India, searching for inner peace, Mick Jagger of the Rolling Stones was throwing rocks at mounted police in London who were bashing antiwar demonstrators. Jagger took part in a March 17 rally at Trafalgar Square against the war. After listening to an array of speakers, tens of thousands of protesters, Jagger among them, marched to the U.S. embassy, where they were met by a police riot squad and cops on horses. Jagger was then recognized by fans who wanted autographs and news reporters and photographers who wanted to interview him. This unwanted attention forced him to leave the demonstration.

Jagger's experience, along with his observation of radical students in France and America, was soon reflected in the song "Street Fighting Man" (cowritten with Stones guitarist Keith Richards). The Stones released it in the United States in late July as a single, packaged in a red sleeve featuring a photograph of Los Angeles cops beating a young demonstrator. The song also appeared on the band's *Beggars Banquet* album. (Conflicts between the Stones and their British and American record labels, Decca and London, over the artwork for that album delayed its release until early December.)

Set to a pounding beat by drummer Charlie Watts and the marching rhythms of Richards's guitar, Jagger's lyrics expressed the exuberance of activism as well as his resignation over a rock singer's lack of influence. "Street Fighting Man" captured Jagger's exhilaration over taking part in a street action with thousands of others and his simultaneous feeling that his fame had prevented him from fully participating. One can also read into it a sense of confusion and doubt as to whether revolutionary change could ever come to Britain.

But what certainly came through to those of us in the New Left was the Stones' solidarity with young radicals and revolutionaries. It was hardly a surprise when the song was banned from Chicago radio stations after the Democratic Convention, with other cities following suit.

Reflecting on the radio boycott of their song, Richards said, "They told me that 'Street Fighting Man' was subversive. 'Of course it's subversive,' we said."

SDS and the Coming Revolution

SDS chapters continued to grow throughout the first six months of 1968, and new chapters were springing up throughout the country. But at the same time, SDS nationally was in the midst of the most bitter and divisive internal struggle in the organization's history.

These clashes reached new heights and new heat, as well as some new lows, at the annual SDS convention, held in June on the Michigan State University campus in East Lansing. I had been elected one of Cornell SDS's delegates to the convention, which would be my first direct encounter with a national meeting of SDS in two years. Although I had problems with some of the policies and pronouncements put forth by the national organization, as part of a recently revived SDS chapter I felt a renewed sense of kinship with the organization.

Just before we left for Michigan, Robert Kennedy was shot in Los Angeles immediately after winning the California Democratic primary. He died a day later. I had not been a supporter of either Kennedy or Eugene McCarthy, the two antiwar candidates in the Democratic primary race. I viewed McCarthy as a not very serious candidate whose intent in running for president was in part to co-opt students who might have gone in a more radical direction.

As for Kennedy, I had doubts about his politics, as well as his reputation for ruthlessness. In the 1950s, he had been a staff member for the red-hunting senator Joseph McCarthy. As attorney general and chief adviser for his brother, President John F. Kennedy, he had continued the Democrats' practice of courting white segregationist politicians from the South, appointing pro-segregation judges to the federal courts, and refusing (for the most part) to use the power of the federal government to intervene in the South on the behalf of civil rights organizers and black citizens.

On the other hand, Kennedy had more recently shown greater sensitivity toward racism and poverty in America, and had supported Cesar Chavez and the United Farm Workers' struggle for union recognition. As for Vietnam,

Kennedy had come to his antiwar position belatedly. I remained dubious about his commitment to what he was now espousing.

Still, I hoped, especially after Johnson decided not to run for reelection, that McCarthy or Kennedy could win the Democratic nomination and the November election, and then bring peace to Vietnam. But now, with Kennedy dead and McCarthy running a lackluster campaign, it didn't seem as if Vice President Hubert Humphrey, the pro-war candidate of the Democratic establishment, could be stopped, even if he had fared poorly in the primaries. At the time, politicians and officeholders, rather than primary voters, still controlled a majority of delegates, and they weren't about to hand a victory to the party's antiwar wing.

It was apparent as soon as I arrived at the SDS convention that the long-simmering dispute between the National Office and its supporters and the cadres of the Progressive Labor Party was about to boil over. Those of us from Cornell had come to the convention unaligned—as were a majority of the delegates—but it soon proved impossible to avoid taking a side.

PL continued to push its brand of vulgar Marxism and its "Worker-Student Alliance." PL also opposed any form of draft resistance. On international matters, PL mirrored China's anti-Soviet line, opposing those nations that had taken Moscow's side in the Sino-Soviet dispute, including (for the most part) Cuba and North Vietnam. PL even had the hubris to attack the North Vietnamese and NLF for agreeing to enter into tentative peace negotiations with the United States and the South Vietnamese government, a move PL viewed as "counterrevolutionary."

I resented the manner in which PL, as a self-proclaimed vanguard party, was trying to use and manipulate SDS for its own ends. SDS, to PL, was a wonderful recruiting and training ground for its cadres. PL members caucused and voted as a disciplined block within SDS, and they never swayed from their previously agreed-upon line. With PL, open and honest debate had become meaningless.

Finally, I disliked PL's straitlaced style. PL assumed that American factory workers were turned off by every aspect of the contemporary youth culture, including rock music, marijuana, and blue jeans. It required its members to wear conservative clothing, with the men clean-shaven and sporting short-cropped hair. Like those college student supporters of Eugene McCarthy who went "clean for Gene" to reach older, more conservative voters, PL members went mundane for Mao.

At the SDS convention, PL was represented in greater proportion than its actual numbers deserved, making up perhaps one-fourth of the delegates. In part that was because PL members were often the only ones in local SDS chapters with the time and means to travel to East Lansing for a week.

But PL's large delegation did reflect genuine growth of support for it within SDS. With many SDS members searching for a revolutionary analysis or a theoretical system to understand what was going on in the world, PL provided an easy-to-comprehend set of answers.

In contrast, there was little agreement among the rest of the five hundred delegates, other than a vague feeling that we were all "revolutionaries." In the past, different points of view might have been debated openly in the convention, with people changing their minds when persuaded by a cogent argument. But in the climate of the 1968 SDS convention, this didn't happen.

A position paper was put forth at the convention by some of the anti-PL forces. Known as the Bell-Dohrn-Halliwell proposal, it was written in part by my friend Tom Bell, who was now trying to build a chapter of Movement for a Democratic Society (sort of a post-graduation SDS) in Springfield, Massachusetts. Tom was joined by Bernardine Dohrn, a young attorney with the National Lawyers Guild who had recently gotten involved in SDS, and Steve Halliwell of the New York Regional SDS office.

Their hastily put-together proposal was steeped in the revolutionary rhetoric of the day. But it also urged SDS to retain our traditional base on college campuses while also expanding our efforts to reach junior college and high school students, young people working in office jobs and as professionals as well as in factories, and movement veterans no longer in college. The proposal was one of the first attempts to apply programmatically some of the newer ideas on the left about the changing, expanding nature of the American working class and the transformation of the American economy from one that was production oriented to one that was consumption and service oriented.

But the Bell-Dohrn-Halliwell proposal was hard to understand; it was dealing with ideas that were both new and complex to many delegates, and it fell victim to attacks for not sufficiently recognizing the central nature of the industrial proletariat to the impending revolution. These attacks came, as expected, from PL, but they also arose from other SDS members who were adopting various types of Marxist-Leninist thought, even if they disliked PL's methods and style. At times, the debate seemed ludicrous—each side quoting Lenin or Mao (and less so Marx) to "prove" its points. Following a long and acrimonious debate, the proposal was defeated.

Who's a Communist?

But soon the anti-PL feelings of SDS veterans became more explicit and confrontational. After a long and ultimately futile debate over proposals to reorganize the SDS National Office, some delegates, including Tom, began to attack PL as an "external cadre" that was using SDS for its own ends. When Tom charged that PL was preventing open and honest debate, he was met with jeers from PL members and countercharges that he was "red baiting," a serious accusation in an organization that was proud of its nonexclusionary policies.

Tom responded with surprising fury. "Red baiting? Red baiting?" he shouted. "I'm the communist here, not you guys from PL!" Tom then started to chant, "PL out! PL out!" which was picked up by many delegates, including those of us from Cornell, and went on for four or five minutes.

Nothing of importance programmatically emerged from the convention, but the National Office crowd, now meeting as a caucus to counter PL, finally had some success when elections for new officers were held. National Office supporters won all eight regional positions on the National Interim Committee (a body charged with making important decisions between National Council meetings), including one for Chip Marshall of our Cornell chapter, representing the Niagara region of upstate New York. In the election of national officers, Bernardine Dohrn was chosen as the inter-organizational secretary, and Los Angeles's Mike Klonsky became national secretary. Fred Gordon, a relatively unknown graduate student who had studied with Herbert Marcuse and was not apparently allied with any faction, was elected education secretary. PL, in acknowledgment that it did not have the votes to win an election, declined to run any candidates.

James Weinstein, one of the most perceptive historians of the Left in America (and a friend, colleague, and mentor of mine in the 1970s and '80s), later summarized the National Office caucus's strategy as two-sided:

> To the majority of SDS members it presented itself as the only practical means to prevent capture by Progressive Labor. To the militants, it presented itself as more revolutionary than Progressive Labor—as the "real" communists. In its former role it could count on the support of almost all of SDS, but in gaining that support and in working to rid SDS of Progressive Labor, the national collective also laid the basis for the destruction of SDS as a whole and for the splintering of the new left.

In June 1968, we could not, and did not, predict this future. I ended up voting for all the candidates backed by the National Office, largely because I shared their antipathy toward PL. In doing so, I glossed over some significant political differences I had with the winners. I liked Klonsky personally (he was now married to Sue Eanet, a friend who had attended Cornell SDS meetings while briefly enrolled at nearby Ithaca College) and admired the organizing he had done at community colleges in the Los Angeles area. But he adhered to a brand of Marxism-Leninism that was nearly as doctrinaire and narrow as PL's—he, too, wanted SDS to organize the traditional working class, but with the emphasis on working-class youth.

As for Bernardine, I had supported the Bell-Dohrn-Halliwell proposal and thought she would make an effective representative of and recruiter for SDS. But I was taken aback by her reply, during a preelection question-and-answer session, to a query from a delegate:

"Do you consider yourself a socialist?" she was asked.

"I consider myself," Dohrn said, "a revolutionary communist."

Bernardine's statement was met with applause from many of the delegates in the room, but not from me. I recognized that she, and Tom earlier, were referring to communist with a small "c," and not the Communist Party of America, or the Soviet Union, or China. Labeling herself a revolutionary communist was intended to show her solidarity with the Vietnamese, the Cubans, and others who were fighting under the banner of communism against the imperialist forces of the United States.[2]

But communist was also a term and an ideology that the American public—presumably the people we in SDS were trying to reach—more likely associated with totalitarian dictatorships, the denial of civil liberties, the murder of political opponents, and a nuclear threat. Or to make this more personal, communism—wherever it existed in the world—was a political system that would have imprisoned and executed the likes of me, a democratic socialist with an independent streak who rebelled against ideological rigidity.

Despite my cringing over Bernardine's comment and my concerns about the growing reliance on various brands of Marxism-Leninism throughout SDS, I wasn't about to challenge either side in the debate. I had only recently returned to SDS, and I lacked the political sophistication or theoretical knowledge to take on the heavy hitters on each side. My dislike of PL and my friendship with those in the National Office caucus were enough for me to overlook my disagreements with them, at least for a while. In any event, what was happening on the national level within SDS had little relationship to what we were doing at Cornell.

2. "Imperialism" may have been an accurate term to describe a foreign policy that required the political and economic domination of other countries to further the profit-seeking of American corporations, but it was a term that turned off ordinary people. While I had previously eschewed the use of such words as unnecessarily rhetorical and doctrinaire, they had now entered my own lexicon.

Ithaca in the Summertime

The rest of the summer was an extraordinary time for those of us in Cornell SDS. In the midst of all the activities I had been involved in over the past three years, I had seldom taken the time to step back and seriously study the society we were rebelling against, reexamine the tactics and strategies we were using, and confront problems of organization and growth.

About twenty to twenty-five of the most active members of Cornell SDS decided to remain in Ithaca for the summer—some taking classes or finding jobs, others working full time for the movement—so we could meet regularly, work on committees, join study groups, and plan for the future. I was particularly interested in working on the newly constituted Research Committee, where we decided to produce a document about the Cornell board of trustees, their corporate ties and how their connections and ideological views affected university policies. Our model was a pamphlet distributed by Columbia SDS entitled *Who Rules Columbia?* written by Mike Locker, a veteran SDS member, and the North American Congress on Latin America (NACLA), a New Left think tank and research organization.

Some of the members of the Research Committee worked on the Ithaca housing crisis, the issue the Afro-American Society had raised the previous spring and won some concessions from the board of trustees. I resumed the research I had done earlier on the connections of trustees to corporations and banks doing business with South Africa. Soon, I was looking at all of the trustees' corporate affiliations, their interlocking directorates, and their links to U.S. foreign policy and defense interests.

Others in SDS worked on outreach programs aimed at the high school and college students taking summer classes at Cornell. We organized a lecture series, showed radical films, and held regular meetings to talk with students about SDS and the issues of the day.

Internally, our core group got to know each other much better. Friendships deepened throughout the summer. Even when we weren't in meetings, we partied together, played together (I organized a couple of SDS softball games), and generally hung out with each other. By now, virtually all my close friends were in the movement.

Perhaps most significantly for me, we held earnest discussions about the future of the draft resistance movement. Many of us in the Resistance had been disappointed with the number of draft cards turned in during our April action, and we were beginning to face the prospect that our grand strategy might not be working. The steady increase in the number of men turning in their draft cards had not materialized, and many who had already done so were facing reclassification of their draft status and calls for induction.

As Doug Dowd, as strong a supporter of draft resistance and draft resisters as you could find, put it to me, "You can't fall in love with a tactic." The tactic, of course, was the draft card turn-in. Doug stressed that we needed to make strategic decisions that were based on what would build the movement. A November date had already been selected for the next round of turn-ins. After much discussion and soul-searching, I finally concluded that organizing another draft card turn-in was not a good idea. But I remained steadfast in the belief that there was no legitimate alternative to resisting the draft by refusing induction.

Unity amid Factionalism

Cornell SDS's efforts during the summer did not escape the notice of the Cornell administration. In a memo to President Perkins near the beginning of the fall '68 semester, Vice President Barlow reported that

> SDS has been very active throughout the summer and one of the most interesting characteristics is that it has been very well organized with some emerging and identifiable leaders and committee structures. It has had large meetings and a rather impressive lecture series in which the attendance was high....SDS concentrated very heavily on "politicizing" or "radicalizing" the advance placement and other high school groups. Further, many summer school students were interested in the cultural and intellectual outlets in the evening that SDS provided, even though the presentations were very biased. They found the presentations exciting and interesting when compared to other summer school traditional fare.

Barlow's memo also pointed out, accurately, that "the leaders are not all united as to the direction in which SDS should go." Ideological factions, or tendencies, were forming within our chapter, although their impact would not be fully felt until the following April and May.

One of the main figures in developing Cornell SDS's housing campaign was Tony Fels, already a respected leader in our chapter, despite having just finished his freshman year. Tony's perspective had recently been influenced by two Columbia University SDS members, Tony Papert and Steve Fraser, and a Marxist-Trotskyist economist named Lyn Marcus,[3] who had formed

---

3. This was the same Lyn Marcus who within a few years changed his name to Lyndon Larouche and became a loony provocateur and conspiracy theorist of the Far Right.

the National Caucus of Labor Committees, a group that for a time operated openly within SDS in New York City, Philadelphia, and other areas. Although the Labor Committee, like PL, advocated organizing industrial workers, its adherents at Cornell remained on campus to organize students. They were committed to our South African divestment campaign and were activists and organizers, not just radical theorists.

Tony Fels brought Labor Committee ideas to Cornell SDS during the summer. While some of that was technical, neo-Marxist economics—I remember Tony and Doug Dowd arguing in one meeting about the falling rate of profit and whether or not the American working class was experiencing a decline in real wages—Tony's emphasis was on creating a housing campaign for Cornell SDS.

Tony's intellect and charisma helped draw some of our chapter's most active and intelligent members into a loose Labor Committee grouping within Cornell SDS. This group, which included my close friends Peter Agree, Larry Kramer, and Alan Snitow, didn't meet separately as a caucus and behaved very differently than PL members within SDS chapters.

Another faction also developed, also loosely, in Cornell SDS during the summer—one that followed the SDS National Office's anti-imperialist, pro–black liberation, and action-oriented policies. But it, too, did not turn into the kind of sectarian caucus that was disrupting and dividing SDS chapters throughout the country. This group, known as the "action faction" or anti-imperialists and led by Chip Marshall and Joe Kelly, tended to emphasize organization and confrontation tactics over ideology. But they didn't object to working on the housing campaign promoted by the Labor Committee, since it involved SDS with the black community of Ithaca—which had been hit hard by the city's housing shortage and high rents—and African American students at Cornell.

In the middle, making up a majority of Cornell SDS, were those of us—I was in this group—who were not aligned with either faction and tried to pursue an independent path that supported or rejected strategies and tactics case by case. Despite these differences, as the fall '68 semester began, Cornell SDS was far more united than divided. We all managed to remain friends during most of the school year, worked on the *First Issue* together, and continued to socialize with each other.

Unlike many other SDS chapters, Cornell SDS remained remarkably free of sectarian penetration and infighting. Alan Snitow later referred to this as "Cornell Exceptionalism," playing off the term "American Exceptionalism," which sought to explain why the United States followed a political and economic path different from that of the advanced industrial capitalist countries of Western Europe. Cornell and Ithaca's geographic isolation and the absence of a significant industrial base in Ithaca were among the factors that allowed Cornell to develop without needing to battle the small but disruptive Marxist-Leninist sects that undermined SDS chapters elsewhere.

Women in the Movement

By 1968, a renewed feminist movement was beginning to percolate throughout the United States and within the New Left. As historians Sara Evans and Ruth Rosen have shown, a vital presence within this movement for women's liberation had arisen among women in SNCC and SDS who complained about their second-class status and the sexist attitudes of men in the leadership and rank and file of each organization. Even when women's concerns were discussed (as opposed to being dismissed), women were often told that their issues were less serious and thus had to be relegated to a place beneath the *real* issues of the day—racism and black liberation, the war in Vietnam and American imperialism, the condition of workers in a capitalist society.

Much of Evans and Rosen's critiques of male leaders in SDS come from the earlier years of the organization (1962–66, roughly) and center on the arrogance and intellectual domination by the men who were leading local chapters and the national organization. By the late '60s, one could add as factors in putting women off or diminishing their influence such developments as the draft resistance movement, in which only men were threatened with prison, and the newly aggressive nature of street actions, which raised the testosterone level.

During the summer of '68 at Cornell, I became more aware that one of the problems with our draft resistance strategy was our failure to provide a worthwhile role for women. With women not eligible for the draft, and thus not in jeopardy of being drafted or jailed, they had been confined to a largely supportive role. That role wasn't as narrow as "girls who say yes to boys who say no," but it was limited nevertheless.

This gap between men and women was aptly expressed by Carolyn Craven, a West Coast SDS member. "No matter what we did," she said, "we were not going to get drafted, we were not going to go to Vietnam. And the men we were with—our lovers, brothers, sons—had to make decisions that we never had to make as women. I think one of the reasons the women's movement became important at that time was because there were issues, especially the issue of the draft, that so divided us."

At Cornell, women SDS members had been punished by the university for defying Proctor George in the draft-card-burning solicitation struggle of March 1967. In addition, some women assisted the men they were close to in burning draft cards, and many women signed statements declaring their complicity with draft resisters. But no women were prosecuted by the federal government for these actions, so the gap between men's and women's involvement in draft resistance remained wide.

However, as Michael Foley showed in his study of the New England Resistance, one of the largest Resistance groups in the country, women played active roles in the administration and day-to-day life of the organization. Yet many women also experienced the condescension of some male members who tried to relegate them to secondary and supportive roles.

At Cornell, the Resistance was barely an organization at all following the April '68 draft card turn-in. Most of us Cornell draft resisters who were organization oriented had transferred our allegiance to Cornell SDS, where I was chairman of the draft resistance committee.

Cornell SDS certainly had its own problems with sexism. I don't think the men in our chapter were worse than men in general, or worse than most male college students, but that's not really the point. As people committed to freedom and human liberation, we men should have welcomed and responded positively to the concerns of women in SDS for expanding the possibilities in our society for all people and in ending discrimination based on gender.

Our SDS chapter wasn't oblivious of women's liberation, which was beginning to gain more attention in 1968. A new women's liberation committee within Cornell SDS was formed at the end of the summer, with Ellie Dorsey elected as its first chair. In the *First Issue* we ran an article about feminist protests in Atlantic City, New Jersey, outside the Miss America Pageant, and a piece by Ellie on sexism at Cornell and in American society.

But our commitment to women's issues and the fight against sexism was shallow. Although by November 1968 we had elected three women to the SDS steering committee (out of a total of eight), we also had a group of powerful and active men who were among the chapter's de facto leaders. It's fair to say that Cornell SDS failed to locate, recognize, value, and support female leadership in our organization.

Some feminists also objected to the combative style of some of the men in Cornell SDS. Sheila Tobias, a feminist scholar who was an administrator at Cornell in the late '60s and on friendly terms with some of us in SDS, told political scientist Donald Downs of her "annoyance...with the radical student left leadership. *Macho* is the word, confrontational."

In later years, women in Cornell SDS have told me they felt their ideas were not valued by men in the chapter's leadership. Some were intimidated by the argumentative debating style of men during meetings. One friend recalls raising her hand repeatedly and not getting called upon by the men who were chairing the meetings.

Although women in our chapter weren't confronting men about sexism or pushing us to get involved in issues related to women's liberation, in retrospect it is apparent that we men had not provided an atmosphere or a culture in which female equality in all phases of the organization was valued and encouraged.

Chicago and the Democrats

I didn't go to Chicago in late August 1968 to join the protests outside the Democratic National Convention. Neither did many other antiwar activists, as the demonstrations called to protest the Democrats' war policy in Vietnam and the nomination of Hubert Humphrey for president drew fewer than ten thousand people. (In contrast, the demonstrations I had worked on during the previous year—April 15, 1967, in New York City and October 21, 1967, in Washington, D.C., and at the Pentagon—drew about four hundred thousand and one hundred thousand, respectively.)

This didn't mean that antiwar sentiment in the nation had diminished. The opposite was the case, based on national polls and the votes for the peace candidacies of Eugene McCarthy and Robert Kennedy. But the reason so many of us declined to participate in the Chicago demonstration was that we thought it would be a disaster.

Chicago's crusty mayor, Richard Daley, was refusing to authorize permits for rallies and protests, lest antiwar protesters ruin his celebration. Here lay the groundwork for violence on the streets of the Windy City. Daley put the entire twelve-thousand-member Chicago police force on twelve-hour shifts, along with six thousand National Guardsmen and seventy-five hundred U.S. Army troops.

While what eventually occurred may have been predictable, the scope and viciousness of the violence unleashed against demonstrators were staggering. As the convention week went on, the police became more and more violent—first in trying to remove demonstrators gathered in the city's Lincoln Park, and later in assaulting and teargassing demonstrators, reporters, and passersby on the city's streets and in Grant Park.

With live television cameras recording the violence, demonstrators chanted "The Whole World Is Watching" as helmeted police waded into unarmed and peaceful crowds with clubs and tear gas, causing hundreds of injuries. This led Senator Abraham Ribicoff of Connecticut to stand before the convention and a national TV audience to condemn "Gestapo tactics in the streets of Chicago." Mayor Daley's response, also recorded live on television, was also telling. His face curdled with rage, Daley shouted back at Ribicoff (according to lip readers), "Fuck you, you Jew son of a bitch! You lousy moth-erfucker! Go Home."

Months later, a presidential commission investigating the violence called the actions in Chicago a "police riot."

But our side was also acting in a provocative manner. The Yippies first tried stirring things up by bringing a live pig to Chicago and presenting the porker, named Pigasus, as their candidate for president. I also knew that some SDS members hoped to use the demonstrations to rally alienated young people into fighting back against the cops. A friend in the New York regional office of SDS who would in less than a year become a leader of the Weatherman fac-tion of SDS, told me beforehand that he was going to Chicago with the pur-pose of starting a "youth riot." His goal was to build a "fighting movement."

Despite the rhetoric flowing from our side, the violence committed by protesters was largely in self-defense. It was many times less than what was being dished out by the rabid Chicago police.

Given what took place, I'm glad I decided beforehand not to go to Chicago. I thought a movement strategy of fighting the cops was doomed to failure and would lead to nothing positive, other than our becoming more accomplished at administering first aid to our own people. But afterward I was furious over the Chicago police's sadistic treatment of my brothers and sisters. Although I disagreed with the tactics of some of my friends in SDS, the police actions challenged my belief in nonviolence as an alternative to violent resistance. The cops were indiscriminate in their targets. Anyone in the vicinity of the protests, including onlookers, residents, and protesters trying to engage in sit-ins and other acts of nonviolent civil disobedience, was assaulted as brutally as those who were fighting back.

At first, I thought the televised images of police violence would ben-efit the movement. Although it no doubt increased the sense of solidarity among young people across America, a majority of the American public sided with Daley and his police against the protesters. Richard Nixon, the Republican nominee for president, was able to successfully tie this back-lash over antiwar protests, student demonstrations, and black militancy to a subtle appeal to white racism and a hankering for the good old days when black people were quiet and college students were engaged in fraternity and sorority pranks.

But I had another reason for not attending the Chicago demonstration. A few weeks earlier, Dave Dellinger had invited me to take part in a meeting of American New Leftists, antiwar activists, and draft resisters with repre-sentatives of the National Liberation Front and the North Vietnamese. This conference, which would take place in Budapest, Hungary, was a follow-up to a similar meeting held a year earlier in Bratislava, Czechoslovakia.

Such gatherings were part of Dave's plan for Americans in the antiwar movement to meet and get to know the Vietnamese as people, not as enemies or faceless martyrs. The Vietnamese, of course, could not come to the United States to meet with us. It was the kind of "citizen diplomacy" the antiwar movement had been conducting since 1965, and had included visits to Hanoi by Cornellians Pat Griffith and Dan Berrigan, among others, and meetings with North Vietnamese representatives at the Paris Peace Talks by Doug Dowd and other antiwar professors.

I didn't have the money to fly to Budapest, but Dave was able to provide me with a scholarship to pay for my flight, my first trip outside the United States. En route we made a short stopover in Prague. This was itself educational, even though we weren't allowed to leave our airplane. As I looked out on the tarmac, I could see dozens of Soviet tanks and thousands of soldiers who had occupied the Prague airport. Soviet troops had invaded Czechoslovakia just two weeks earlier to crush the reformist communist government of Alexander Dubček and force Czechoslovakia to return to the repressive internal policies of other Soviet bloc countries.

During the Chicago demonstrations, some of the protesters had spoken out against the Soviet invasion and for democracy in Czechoslovakia. Dave Dellinger led a pro-Czechoslovakia picket line at Chicago's Polish tourism office—the only office in Chicago that represented a Warsaw Pact nation. Abbie Hoffman held a press conference in which he referred to Chicago as "Czechago" and compared the police state set up by Mayor Daley to the Soviet army's occupation of Prague and other major Czech cities.

Still, I wish that we, and I, had done more to demonstrate our support for the Czech freedom fighters. They were not only resisting Stalinist rule, but in calling for "communism with a human face," some were attempting to rebuild Czechoslovakia as a democratic socialist state that allowed and encouraged free expression in politics, religion, and the arts. The young people confronting Soviet tanks also looked an awful lot like those of us who were confronting the authorities on the streets of Chicago and throughout America.

Less than an hour after taking off from the Prague airport, we arrived in Budapest.

American Radicals Meet Vietnamese Revolutionaries

Why Budapest? As I wrote, tongue in cheek, in a report on our meeting for the *First Issue*, "Budapest was the site for the conference since the Hungarian government was willing to foot the bill, and the Vietnamese have not yet launched their fall offensive on San Francisco."

As enthusiastic as I was about meeting the Vietnamese representatives, I was concerned about our Hungarian hosts. The ruling Communist Party of Hungary was known as one of the most repressive parties in the Soviet bloc and a close follower of Moscow. I had studied enough of the history of communism and the Soviet Union to know how Western visitors to Russia in the 1930s had been taken to "Potemkin villages"—artificially affluent and picturesque towns that were used for propaganda purposes to demonstrate Soviet progress and modernization. I wanted neither to be duped nor used by our hosts.

When we arrived at our modern hotel, the Hotel Ifjusag (Hotel Youth), we learned that it was operated by the youth division of the Hungarian Communist Party. But when we were greeted by the head of the Communist Party youth organization, we found him to be a burly man in his late thirties or early forties. It appeared that Eastern European communists had a very liberal definition of "youth," in this case an apparatchik who was about twice my age and sported a crew cut that gave him the look of an American cop or a football linebacker.

We didn't spend much time with our Hungarian hosts, and I never discussed politics with any of them. But I did overhear a member of our delegation ask one of our liaisons, a Hungarian CP official who was fluent in English, what he thought about the current events in Czechoslovakia. The official said, coldly and without hesitation, "We had to deal with a similar problem in 1956," referring to the short-lived Hungarian uprising against Communist rule that was also crushed by the Soviet army.

I don't know how Dave Dellinger chose the twenty Americans in our delegation, but he gathered a cross-section of activists. We elected as our co-chairs Bernardine Dohrn, the new SDS inter-organizational secretary, and Vernon Grizzard, a former SDS national officer who was now working with the Boston Draft Resistance Group. My roommates during the six-day conference included Terry Cannon, one of the Oakland Seven defendants, and Ira Arlook of New England Resistance. Our delegation included SDS and Resistance members from around the country, activists who were organizing on college campuses, at high schools, and in working-class communities, and at least one progressive journalist, Elinor Langer. We were joined in Budapest by two U.S. Army deserters who were living in Sweden and were active in an antiwar group of soldiers called the American Deserters Committee.

The Vietnamese were represented by five men and women from the National Liberation Front and four from the Democratic Republic of Vietnam (North Vietnam). Although I no longer remember most of their names, as a group they made a profound impression on me and all the Americans.

The conference began with the Vietnamese delegates expressing their friendship toward us and the American people. It was a theme repeated throughout our meetings, that they felt no hostility toward the American people, only toward the American government. They continually talked about their admiration for us because of our opposition to our government, and expressed a particularly closeness to the draft resisters in our delegation who were risking jail because we refused to kill their people. We responded with statements of solidarity and promises that we would continue our fight for the withdrawal of all American troops from their country.

One of the main purposes of the conference was for us to gain a richer understanding of the Vietnamese struggle for self-determination and for them to learn about the antiwar movement in the United States. We held some sessions involving the entire delegations, while others were in small groups of seven Americans and two Vietnamese.

When we gave reports about the American draft resistance movement, organizing efforts on college campuses, in high schools, in the black community, and within the U.S. armed forces, the Vietnamese seemed quite knowledgeable about what we were talking about. (They did have a problem, however, understanding the meaning of a popular movement slogan that had emerged from New York's Lower East Side: "Up against the wall, mother-fucker!")

The Vietnamese discussed the origins of the National Liberation Front, their methods of organizing among youth and students and in the country-side and within cities, the role of women in the struggle, underground work from the time of the French colonial occupation through the present day, and much more. I was particularly interested in their descriptions of draft avoidance and draft resistance in South Vietnam, which took two forms. The first was similar to what we saw in the United States, including young people obtaining false certificates from doctors or taking medicines to cause fevers and other illnesses that would exempt them from being drafted into the South Vietnamese army. The second was more intriguing—villages hiding out or otherwise protecting potential draftees from army recruiting agents and police.

But for me and the other Americans, far more important, and lasting, was the impact the Vietnamese had on us as individuals. Some of the NLF representatives told us about their journeys to meet with us, which included hiking through the tunnels and NLF-controlled areas of South Vietnam on their way to Hanoi, then riding trains across the length of Asia to Moscow, followed by a flight to Budapest. They asked us about our families and loved ones, and spoke about their own. Virtually every one of them had lost family members in the war or had long been separated from their parents, husbands, wives, and children. Their lives and experiences made our own sacrifices look feeble.

Rockin' in Budapest

The conference was intense. Outside of breaks for lunch and dinner, and one free evening in which some of us were able to leave our hotel and roam around Budapest, we spent virtually every waking hour in meetings and discussions. But one lunch hour turned out differently from the others.

Hotel Ifjusag featured a house rock band—a quartet of electric guitar, bass, piano, and drums—that performed regularly in the hotel's nightclub. Unfortunately, the band's songs were just about the lamest form of rock 'n' roll one could imagine—tunes like "Hello Dolly" with a tepid rock backbeat. But I suspected that the band had the ability, if not the freedom, to play much edgier and harder-rocking material.

The band members were rehearsing in the nightclub when I approached them. Although they spoke no English, and my Hungarian began and ended with the word "goulash," I was able to get across that I sang in a rock band in America. I indicated that I would like to jam with them, if they were so inclined. The guitarist then handed me his guitar. Although I couldn't really play the guitar, I was able to pick out the melodies, if not the chords, for a couple of fairly easy songs; I also hummed or scatted a verse or two to establish the key and the rhythm. The band members quickly figured out what I was trying to play.

We then proceeded to run through, with me wailing into a microphone, what may have been the first Hungarian live performance of "Born in Chicago," a song recorded by the Paul Butterfield Blues Band. The Hungarians had no trouble handling this up-tempo blues-rock song, though they didn't understand the English lyrics.

Our loud sounds started to attract a small crowd, first among the American and Vietnamese delegates, then from hotel staffers and other guests. Seeing no party commissar approaching to get us to shut up or tone it down, I then taught the band how to play another simple tune, one that was about a subject not usually discussed in communist countries.

With both the band and me feeling looser, I started singing, "The best things in life are free / But you can keep 'em for the birds and bees," with the band swinging along behind me, not missing a beat. I always viewed the Beatles' version of "Money (That's What I Want)," originally an early Motown hit by Barrett Strong, as being intentionally ironic, and I hoped such irony would be understood in the current setting—or would at least not get the band in trouble for performing such a "capitalist" song.

When the song ended, I acknowledged the applause from my fellow delegates, shook the hands of the band members, and went back into a conference session on land distribution in the liberated zones of South Vietnam.

The Vietnamese and Nonviolence

As the conference went on and we began to get to know the Vietnamese on a more personal basis, some of them emerged as genuine characters. Nguyen Van Phong was the NLF's military expert at the conference. One evening, when we were all eating dinner together, a hotel waiter kept screwing up our orders. He delivered the wrong dishes, spilled others, and generally demonstrated a high degree of ineptitude. Those of us still waiting for our food were growing exasperated. Finally, Phong leaned over to a few of us Americans and said, "Next time, we attack."

Toward the end of the six-day conference, I received an urgent telegram from my lawyer. It appeared that Judge Port had heard I had left the country. Evidently, he felt I had violated the spirit of being released on my own recognizance and in the custody of my attorney, even though he had neglected to confine me to New York State, or the United States, as a condition for my release. As a result, he moved up my trial date to September 18, only ten days away. I had planned to follow the Budapest conference with a visit to West Germany along with Bernardine and some other SDS members, to meet with students in German SDS (Sozialistischer Deutscher Studentenbund, a radical student organization that was friendly toward but not affiliated with American SDS), but Port's decision made me alter my plans. My lawyer had to wire me $200 to change my airline ticket.

My flight back to the United States included an eighteen-hour stopover in Paris. I shared a hotel room with four other Budapest conference attendees, and we had the brief opportunity to walk around the streets of Paris. The events of the previous May were still raw and hard to forget—particularly since Parisian gendarmes and French army troops, rifles slung over their shoulders, were standing on just about every major street corner.

When I arrived back at JFK Airport in New York, I was surprised to make it through U.S. Customs with the stuff I had picked up at the conference—a record album of Vietnamese songs, posters, drawings, and printed material. But my travels were duly noted by the FBI, which shared its information with "appropriate Legal Attaches and interested U.S. Government agencies."

Meeting with the Vietnamese had a profound impact on me, particularly on my self-identification as a pacifist. I still admired the Buddhists in South Vietnam who had bravely challenged the Diem regime, and the military governments that came after it, through nonviolent street demonstrations and self-immolations. But I didn't think they represented a realistic nonviolent alternative to armed resistance against the oppressive South Vietnamese government and its U.S. allies.

I never had an "aha" moment in which, all of a sudden, I decided that nonviolent resistance no longer worked. My views on violence and pacifism were changing, in part, because the circumstances were changing. Many veterans of the civil rights movement in the South, the people I most admired in the movement, had decided they would no longer submit to police beatings during civil disobedience actions. My friends in SDS and the antiwar movement were increasingly getting their heads split open by police clubs. Although I wasn't about to join those seeking violent confrontations, I no longer viewed adherence to the principles of pacifism as a personal moral necessity.

Meanwhile, the trial over my own, initial act of civil disobedience against the draft was about to begin.

Chapter Eleven

Trials and Tribulations

Even before the beginning of my trial for tearing up my draft card, I knew I didn't stand a chance. I had the best possible legal counsel in my corner—lead attorney Faith Seidenberg of Syracuse, joined by Alan Levine and Burt Neuborne of the New York Civil Liberties Union—all working for free. But the evidence that I had mutilated my draft card was undeniable. Since I had mailed the four pieces of my card to my draft board in the Bronx, I assumed those pieces would be presented as evidence. So would the letter I sent to my draft board explaining why I would no longer cooperate with the Selective Service System. Even the *Cornell Daily Sun* story that ran on the day my trial began included a front-page photograph of me ripping up my draft card. It was an open and shut case.

I was experiencing a strange sense of detachment toward it all when I arrived at the U.S. District Court in Syracuse on September 18, 1968, a feeling that persisted throughout the one-day trial. It was as though I was an observer rather than a participant—the main participant. It wasn't that I couldn't believe I was actually on trial, after nearly two years of anticipation. Nor was my detachment a reflection of fear about going to prison—I expected to serve time, sooner or later, for either this charge or for refusing induction. Rather, I felt that it was all a fait accompli, that I didn't have the slightest chance of winning. I wanted to get it over and done with.

I even felt a little guilty in having so much attention placed on me for what I had done nearly two years earlier. I was still committed to resisting the draft, but I had also moved on from the place I was as an eighteen-year-old, when I stood alone, at least temporarily, in defying the draft. With the war still raging and the state (from the federal government to local cops) getting more repressive, the mood of the movement had hardened, and so had I. My little case of draft resistance didn't seem all that important anymore. Here I was, taking up the time of three valuable defense attorneys who could have been defending others in far more dire circumstances than I.

On the other hand, I was fully aware of my status as Cornell's first draft resister, and the first to stand trial. I knew my case had considerable importance for our community and the movement.

Faith and I had only a brief opportunity prior to the start of the trial to discuss our legal strategy. We first had to decide whether to ask for a trial by jury, or to waive that right and have Judge Port rule on my guilt or innocence. Port was known to Faith as a rigid but relatively fair-minded judge, one who had not yet presided over any draft resistance cases.

Faith didn't believe Port would allow us to present to a jury any witnesses discussing the immorality and illegality of the war in Vietnam, nor any detailed defense based on conscience or free speech. Nor did she think he would allow me to directly address a jury about my motivation in tearing up my draft card. But Faith hoped that Port might give us more leeway if a jury was not involved. She also had doubts about seating a sympathetic jury from the Syracuse area. Her counsel to me was that our best chance for securing either an acquittal (not likely) or a relatively short sentence was with Judge Port, rather than a jury trial. With some misgivings, I decided to follow my attorney's advice.

The prosecution, headed by U.S. District Attorney James P. Shanahan, first called an Ithaca radio station reporter, Michael Robinson of WTKO, to the stand. Robinson had been in attendance outside Cornell's Olin Hall when I took my action. Robinson testified—a bit too eagerly, I thought—as to what he had seen and heard. He also played a tape recording of the speech I made when I tore up my draft card.

Then the prosecution called James M. Herson, currently Ithaca's deputy chief of police but at the time I tore up my draft card in December 1966 the head of Cornell's Safety Division. (Readers may recall Herson's role as an anti-smut zealot who helped provoke the *Trojan Horse* incident of January 1967, a bungling that led to his resignation from Cornell.) Herson testified that he had been present outside Olin Hall when I ripped up my card, though he admitted under cross-examination that he was not close enough to be sure that what I tore up was in fact my draft card.

Finally, the executive secretary of my draft board testified that she had received my letter/statement of noncooperation and the four pieces of my draft card. DA Shanahan placed those four pieces of paper into evidence.

The prosecution then rested its case.

The Case for the Defense

Defense attorneys being defense attorneys, Alan Levine noticed a problem with the prosecution's evidence. It seems that I had so neatly ripped my draft card into four parts that it required only one or two pieces of strategically placed clear tape to put the card back together, fully legible and thus neither mutilated nor destroyed. I was wary of making such a technical defense, but my lawyers persuaded me to let them argue for a dismissal based on it. Judge Port quickly denied this motion.

Our defense strategy differed somewhat from the defenses offered by earlier draft card burners David Miller and David O'Brien, who had argued their actions constituted "symbolic speech," which should be protected by the freedom of speech clause in the First Amendment. In May, the Supreme Court had issued a 7–1 opinion ruling against Miller and O'Brien and upholding the law outlawing the mutilation or destruction of draft cards. In his majority opinion, Chief Justice Earl Warren wrote that such actions were not protected by the First Amendment. Furthermore, he rejected the contention that the law's enactment was intended to suppress antiwar protest. Justice William O. Douglas was the only dissenter.

In contrast, my attorneys argued that my action was an act of conscience protected by the freedom of religion clause of the First Amendment. Although I personally did not view my beliefs as "religious," nor did I ever use such terminology, I understood that my philosophical views about ethics, morality, and conscience could broadly be defined as such. We did not contest the fact that I had torn up my draft card and returned it to my draft board, or that I had submitted a statement declaring my unwillingness to cooperate any further with Selective Service.

We called as witnesses several Cornell clergymen to testify about my beliefs and activities against the war, as well as my parents and a few other "character witnesses." Both of Cornell's Catholic ministers, Father Dan Berrigan (a draft file destroyer) and Father Dave Connor (a draft resister), testified about my commitment to acting according to my conscience. So did Rev. Paul Gibbons, who said I was "an early voice speaking out for what needed to be spoken." Cornell law professor Harrop Freeman also testified about my act of conscience, though he erroneously stated that my beliefs were based on my deep and abiding Jewish faith—causing my atheist mother to shake her head with incredulity.

Doug Dowd also testified as a character witness, explaining that he and his wife, Kay, were such ardent supporters of my antiwar and draft resistance activities that they assisted me financially to continue such work. But Judge

Port stopped Doug from testifying about the history and legality of the war in Vietnam—ruling that it was immaterial to the case at hand.

Then my parents testified. My dad talked about my religious and philosophical upbringing in the freethinking Society for Ethical Culture and at home. My mother, always more of a firebrand than my dad, gave the most emotional testimony of the trial, telling the judge, "We're rather proud of our son, that he has the guts to stand up to do what he has done."

Finally, it was my turn to take the stand. Under Faith's questioning, I explained why I had, upon turning eighteen during my freshman year at Cornell, registered for the draft but rejected a student deferment and applied for conscientious objector status. I then discussed why I changed my mind about becoming a CO. I explained that tearing up my draft card was a statement of noncooperation with the draft system and my own way of protesting the war. I said it was both a personal act of conscience and an attempt to influence the antiwar movement to become more serious.

Once I finished testifying, the attorneys offered brief summations of the case, and it went before the judge. The entire trial lasted a little over six hours.

It didn't take Judge Port more than a few minutes to render his verdict. He found me guilty of "knowingly and with intent, mutilating and destroying" my draft card. He delayed sentencing pending an investigation by the U.S. Probation Office. As we had hoped, he agreed to release me on my own recognizance and the custody of my attorney until sentencing, which was expected to occur within two months.

I wasn't surprised by the verdict, as it was what I had expected. Nor were my friends and fellow resisters. We all took it rather stoically. Our view was that my sentencing and eventual imprisonment would only be the first of many.

My parents put on brave faces, though they were obviously shaken. What they had dreaded since I first started talking about noncooperation with the draft back in 1965 had now become a virtual certainty—their son was going to prison in the not too distant future.

I was too involved in my own thoughts to notice how my folks were doing, but Dan Berrigan wasn't. Father Dan immediately began talking to them, trying to console and comfort them. He didn't like the idea of their having to immediately begin a long drive back home to the Bronx. So Dan invited my parents and me to join him in a post-trial dinner at the Syracuse home of his brother Jerry and his sister-in-law Carol. There, three secular Jewish nonbelievers from New York concluded one of our family's worst days in a comforting, relaxing meal, thanks to the hospitality of two Roman Catholics from Syracuse and one renegade Catholic priest.

Cornell SDS Reaches Its Peak

In a survey of American college students, conducted in October 1968 by the Daniel Yankelovich Company for *Fortune* magazine, more than 20 percent identified with Che Guevara, outpolling presidential candidates Richard Nixon (19 percent), Hubert Humphrey (16 percent), and George Wallace (7 percent). About 750,000 students identified themselves as part of the New Left, and nearly 20 percent of the more than 7.39 million enrolled students surveyed either "strongly agreed" or "partially agreed" on the need for "a mass revolutionary party." A campus poll published in *Playboy* magazine in September 1970 (but conducted earlier) found 15 percent of the students agreeing on the need for revolution.

By the beginning of the fall term in 1968, SDS had grown to between eighty thousand and one hundred thousand members nationally. There were now 350 to 400 SDS chapters around the country, as the organization continued to expand from its initial base at large state universities and Ivy League campuses to regional state colleges, junior colleges, community colleges, and high schools.

Cornell SDS had finished the 1967–68 school year with an active membership of between 150 and 200. Given the organizing, research, and planning we had done during the summer, and the impact on young people of events such as the debacle at the Democratic National Convention and the continuing escalation of the war, we expected to attract even more students when the fall '68 term opened in September. And we did: the first SDS meeting in September drew between 200 and 250 students, and we believed those on campus who sympathized with SDS reached ten times that number.

"I suppose that SDS is slightly bigger this year," Vice President Mark Barlow grudgingly admitted to President Perkins in an October 17, 1968, internal memo titled "The Current Status of SDS." As the administrator most directly responsible for keeping an eye on us, Barlow noted that SDS was "better organized" than ever before. He also stated that the administration's "intelligence" about what we were up to was "more complete and more dependable" than in the past.

My federal conviction had the effect of making me even more serious about my political work, as it was clear I didn't have much time left before going to prison. I continued organizing and doing research for Cornell SDS and began working on a new edition of the *First Issue*, which we hadn't published since May.

Jane and I were doing well. Taking advantage of newly liberalized housing rules for women students at Cornell, she and two friends rented a three-bedroom apartment in Collegetown. I got my own place to live, sharing an apartment with Peter Orville, a friend from Buck's Rock Work Camp who was one of the leading activists at Ithaca College. But as the school year progressed, I spent more and more time at Jane's.

As our SDS chapter continued to grow, my ideas about democracy and organization became clearer. I remained a believer in "participatory democracy," as expressed in the founding document of SDS, the Port Huron Statement, which envisioned an America in which ordinary people could participate in making the decisions that affected their lives. Creating a truly democratic society, I believed, required building a democratic local organization that would itself be a part of national mass movement.

We never succeeded in making Cornell SDS such an organization, in part because we failed to reach equality between men and women in our chapter in terms of leadership, participation, and influence. But we made a genuine effort to operate democratically, to increase the involvement of new members, and to continually reach out to students.

Most of the members of Cornell SDS in the fall of '68 didn't just come to meetings to talk, as they paid their dues to the national organization and joined one or more of SDS's different committees. To get an idea of how much was going on within Cornell SDS, in just one week during the 1968–69 school year our chapter held committee and subcommittee meetings on the housing crisis (more on this later), militarism, labor organizing, draft resistance, cultural affairs, research, sorority and fraternity organizing, dorm organizing, South Africa divestment, and forming radical caucuses within academic disciplines.

I was again elected to the chapter's steering committee as chair for draft resistance. In contrast to eighteen months earlier, when, as Cornell SDS's president, I resigned my position because of my nonstudent status, this time there wasn't a peep of protest (at least publicly) over a nonstudent serving as an officer of a Cornell student organization. Although I thought it was important for there to be some turnover among our chapter's leadership, mainly to identify and create new, strong leaders and prevent the ossification of an old guard, I was against what was later called "term limits." I felt that our organization needed both new and old blood, the former to bring in fresh ideas and personalities, the latter to maintain and preserve the group's institutional memory and to provide some continuity in leadership. Evidently, members of our chapter felt the same way, as I was reelected to the steering committee a few months later in November, this time as national affairs chair.

While the steering committee, made up of the different cochairs of our chapter, had some administrative authority, it never functioned like an elite body within the wider organization. The weekly steering committee meetings were open to all SDS members, but important decisions regarding SDS programs, policies, and actions had to be decided upon by the entire membership. This sometimes resulted in long and difficult general meetings, but that was the price of democracy and growth.

Returning students in September 1968 were met with the announcement that the board of trustees had rejected SDS's demand from the previous spring that the university divest itself of stocks in banks that had lent money to buttress South Africa's apartheid regime. Despite our arguments for ending the university's complicity with South Africa, a position partly endorsed by the university faculty in May, the trustees restated their old position that university investment policies should not be affected by social concerns, only fiduciary ones. The trustees' decision made it certain that the South Africa issue would not be going away at Cornell.

Shortly after the fall term began, Cornell SDS presented students with a novel approach to radical education and organizing—the "America Game." The brainchild of Gary Comstock and a few other creative artsy types, the America Game was an audience-participation tour through the choices faced by young people in the United States. Reflecting the fact that only males could be drafted, the game was more oriented toward men than woman, though many women participated in it.

With the permission of the office of the dean of students, SDS members placed hundreds of posters on a large, grassy patch of the arts quad, setting out four distinctive life routes. The game offered participants the choice of following one of four paths—college, labor, "hippy," and military. Along the way, players learned some hard truths (and a few funny ones) about contemporary American society and their roles in each category. Not surprisingly, all players ended up in the same place regardless of the initial path they had chosen—they either had to enter the armed forces and go to Vietnam or resist the draft.

Hundreds, perhaps even thousands, of Cornell students played the America Game, which was generally well received on campus and demonstrated there was more to SDS than rallies, meetings, and leaflets—in this case, a sense of humor. Cultural critic and Cornell art history professor William C. Lipke described the America Game as a form of "open-air political theater" in which there was no audience, only "participant-actors." A few right-wing students attempted to tear down some of our posters, but they were quickly repelled by SDS members.

Gary Comstock's contribution to SDS was also reflected in a new look for the *First Issue*. Gary and Jerry Brown, another new SDS member with ability in art and design, brought to us exciting cover illustrations and collages, riotous displays of color, and striking page layouts. Our issue of September 27, 1968, emphasized the war in Vietnam and its history. It featured a lengthy article by Doug Dowd on his meetings with the peace delegation of the North Vietnamese in Paris and my report on the Budapest conference, as well as maps, graphics, and fiction from Vietnam.

Father Dan and the Catonsville Nine

The *First Issue* and SDS also tried to rally Cornell support for the upcoming trial of Dan Berrigan and the Catonsville Nine in Baltimore, calling on students to "Come to Agnew Country" for the trial and a mass march in support of the accused.[1] Dan and his codefendants had been out on bail since their arrest in May for burning about eight hundred 1-A draft files in Catonsville, Maryland. Their trial in federal court was expected to attract national attention, given the inclusion of Dan and his brother Phil among the defendants and the presence of William Kunstler, a celebrated radical defense attorney, as their lead counsel. Around two thousand students and faculty members attended a pretrial rally at Cornell.

Baltimore was already filled with local and state police and U.S. marshals when I arrived the night before the trial began. Over five hundred Cornellians made the trip to Baltimore to support the Catonsville Nine, and our presence swelled the crowd to somewhere between twenty-five hundred and five thousand demonstrators as we marched from the St. Ignatius Church hall (where many of us had crashed on the floor in sleeping bags) to the downtown Federal Courthouse. Tension was especially high because of the presence in Baltimore that day of third-party presidential candidate George Wallace, the segregationist former governor of Alabama. Wallace was holding his own campaign rally on the trial's opening day, and his speech attracted thousands of supporters, as well as some counterdemonstrators. But outside of a few scuffles, a direct confrontation between the antiwar folks and the Wallace supporters was averted.

I made it inside the courtroom on the trial's second day, securing one of the 250 seats available to spectators. Despite the efforts of Kunstler, who was assisted by Cornell's Harrop Freeman, Judge Roszel Thomsen ruled out the "justification" defense—whereby defendants would be allowed to speak to the jurors about their motivation and call witnesses to back up their statements

---

1. Spiro Agnew was the Republican governor of Maryland and Richard Nixon's vice-presidential running mate in 1968. Agnew was making a name for himself during the campaign through bellicose speeches attacking student radicals, black activists, liberals, intellectuals, and others. During one such speech at a college in Maryland, Agnew was being heckled by the student audience when he shouted back, "How many of you sick people are from Students for a Democratic Society?" According to news reports, nearly two-thirds of the audience of a thousand raised their hands.

about the war in Vietnam and its conduct. Thomsen did allow a bit of leeway in this regard when he let the defendants, under friendly questioning from their defense lawyers, talk about their personal histories.

That enabled Dan to make the eloquent statement that he had "burned some paper because I was trying to say that the burning of children was inhuman and unbearable. . . . I did not wish that the American flag be steeped in the blood of the innocent across the world." But Thomsen also ruled repeatedly that the case was solely about whether the accused had destroyed government property and harmed the Selective Service System.

I didn't get to stick around for the last days of the five-day trial, nor did I hear the jury's unanimous guilty verdict, as I had to leave Baltimore to drive quickly to the University of Colorado in Boulder for an SDS National Council meeting. But the conviction of Father Dan and the others, along with my own situation, was leading me to further ponder the issue of prison.

Shortly after my trial and conviction in September, a friendly interviewer, Dan Finlay, a Cornell English professor and fellow draft resister, asked me what I thought about going to prison. I said that the subject had been on my mind for over three years and I was prepared for prison. "Many of us will go to jail," I told Finlay. "In my opinion it's a better idea to replace yourself. There is no indispensable person. If I've been doing good work, it will be picked up by others."

But at a large post-Baltimore rally for Father Dan back at Cornell a few weeks after the Catonsville Nine trial, I told a crowd that the actions of the Catonsville Nine had taken the movement from the earlier paths of the personal, individualist "Hell No, I Won't Go" and the Resistance-led "Hell No, We Won't Go" to a new phase of "Hell No, Nobody Goes." We needed to continue to build our movement so that in the future "it will be massive enough so that when we say 'Hell No, Nobody Goes,' we also mean jail."

Little did I know that a year and a half later, when his appeals had run their course and Dan was supposed to begin his prison sentence, he would go underground and lead the FBI on a merry chase.

The Election of 1968

The Glenn Miller Ballroom at the University of Colorado was the unlikely setting for the fall SDS National Council meeting. As part of the Cornell SDS delegation, I had left Baltimore along with Chip Marshall, Joe Kelly, Walt Koken (a friend of Joe's who was a terrific bluegrass fiddler and banjo player), and Dave Matthews (a Cornell grad student, not the latter-day musician), all of us squeezing into Dave's big, old car. Our nonstop drive, pausing only for gas, food, and bathroom breaks, was my first trip west of Chicago.

With supporters of the SDS National Office outnumbering those from Progressive Labor about four to one among the 450 delegates, the attendees voted overwhelming in support of a proposal, "Boulder and Boulder," put forward by Bernardine Dohrn, former Columbia SDSer John Jacobs, and Jeff Jones from the New York regional office. Their plan called for SDS to "develop the seeds of revolution" by getting our ideas out to the public during the presidential election campaign. The proposal also had an activist component, calling for SDS chapters to embark upon a two-day national student strike that would include teach-ins and rallies as well as marches and demonstrations. The strike call was accompanied by militant slogans like "No Class Today, No Ruling Class Tomorrow" and "Vote with Your Feet, Vote in the Street."

I was dubious that many SDS chapters would be able to pull off such strikes and mass demonstrations. First of all, the plan was adopted only three weeks prior to the November elections, which was not enough time to organize effectively. But more important, the proposal failed to recognize that different SDS chapters were at different stages of development and organization. There was a wide disparity among chapters in terms of their size, the political experience and ideological sophistication of their members, and their status on particular campuses. While some chapters, like Cornell's, were large and active, others were still taking their first, risky stands against the war. The "Boulder and Boulder" resolution seemed far too ambitious.

Yet I also believed the presidential election involving Republican Richard Nixon, Democrat Hubert Humphrey, and independent George Wallace was attracting a lot of attention on campuses, and that we in SDS should not ignore it. This didn't mean we would support any of these candidates, as Nixon and Wallace were too far right for most moderate, liberal, and radical students, and Humphrey remained unpopular because of his continued backing of Johnson's policy in Vietnam and the lingering resentment many young people felt over what had taken place at the Democratic Convention.[2]

I shared the view of the "Boulder and Boulder" strategists that these elections gave SDS a prime opportunity to contrast our views with those of the three major candidates. I ended up voting for the proposal despite feeling that the action part of it would not be attainable.

2. In the waning days of the campaign, Humphrey belatedly suggested he would pursue a policy in Vietnam different from Johnson's. Humphrey's tentative move toward peace enabled him to narrow Nixon's edge in the polls and almost pull off a stunning election upset. But given Humphrey's vigorous support for Johnson's policy in the past, there was little enthusiasm for his candidacy by liberals and leftists—despite the prospect of a Nixon victory.

There was another electoral alternative in 1968, the Peace and Freedom Party, which had been formed two years earlier in California. A loose and unwieldy coalition of independent radicals, Old Left groups, and the Black Panther Party, Peace and Freedom had nominated Eldridge Cleaver, the Panther's minister of information and the author of the best-selling memoir *Soul on Ice*, as its presidential candidate. The choice of a vice presidential candidate was left up to each individual state party. According to Carl Oglesby, a former president of SDS and a member of SDS's National Interim Committee, Cleaver personally asked him to be his running mate, but other SDS leaders vetoed the idea.

Back in July, Doug Dowd and I were in New York City for a Mobe meeting when Doug said he had promised some Peace and Freedom organizers he would stop by their New York State convention. Doug had earlier lent his name to Peace and Freedom's organizing efforts, although he had not played an active role in the group. He was also dubious about the fledgling party's attempt to run a presidential campaign that year. I was even more hostile to the idea, believing that the effort to get a left-wing party on the New York State ballot would be both difficult (because of the state's onerous election laws) and a waste of the movement's relatively small financial resources.

As soon as we arrived at the Hotel Diplomat near Times Square, where the convention was taking place, Doug was met excitedly by some of its organizers, who said they needed to talk to him immediately. I wasn't interested in sticking around, so I told Doug I would meet him back there in a couple of hours. When I returned to hook up with Doug for our drive back to Ithaca, I was surprised to learn that my friend was now the vice presidential candidate of the Peace and Freedom Party of New York State.

Evidently, the convention had been deadlocked on a vice presidential choice. Yippie leader Jerry Rubin, who was already on the ticket with Cleaver in some states, had started to emerge as the most likely choice, even though many of the New Yorkers were opposed to him. Doug's arrival at the convention gave them an alternative. After several hours of discussion and persuasion—some of Doug's backers no doubt knew of his antipathy toward Rubin—Doug was persuaded to let his name be placed before the convention. A majority of the delegates then voted to nominate him. Doug's condition for filling the vacancy on the ticket was that he would not have to do any campaigning. And as far as I know, he fulfilled his promise.

But Doug did take part in Cornell SDS's Election Day program. It was almost entirely educational and aimed at both the SDS membership, which had been growing rapidly, and the wider community at Cornell and Ithaca. Our goal was to show why neither Nixon, Humphrey, nor Wallace was the answer to our country's problems and to present our broader critique of American society and U.S. foreign policy.

The availability of the Office and the Glad Day Press allowed us to churn out thousands of copies of leaflets for distribution on campus and in town. One of them, "Can't Get No Satisfaction," offered critiques of the candidates. Another leaflet laid out SDS's position on crucial national and international issues, while a third offered a critique of the university.

Finally, we put forward our recently adopted housing program. Based on research Tony Fels, Alan Snitow, and others had conducted over the summer, we charged that Cornell's failure to adequately house its students had resulted in overcrowding and high rents in Ithaca, an impact that was felt primarily by the town's most vulnerable, low-income residents. We proposed that Cornell finance, from funds obtained from the sale of the Cornell Aeronautical Laboratory and the liquidation of stocks held in banks supporting South Africa, the construction of over one thousand units of low- and middle-income housing downtown, which would be planned, controlled, and administered by a community housing group, and the construction of fifteen hundred to two thousand new housing units for students. In addition, we proposed that the jobs resulting from this construction should go to the Ithaca labor force, and that Cornell's nonacademic employees receive an across-the-board wage increase.

Unfortunately, our Election Day rally failed to attract the crowds we had expected. Only several hundred students, faculty, and university employees turned out for our noon rally in the student union. Doug moderated the event, while also offering his critique of Nixon, Humphrey, and Wallace, while Dave Burak spoke about Vietnam and U.S. foreign policy and Alan explained our housing proposal. In my own remarks, I discussed the role of universities like Cornell in producing the skilled technicians and white-collar workers needed for a modern capitalist economy. But I mostly talked about draft resistance and the necessity of making the antidraft slogan, "Hell No, We Won't Go," apply not only to Vietnam, but to other places where U.S. troops and National Guardsmen were being sent, such as Santo Domingo, Watts, and Chicago.

Nationally, not a single student strike was organized, as most SDS chapters ended up holding poorly attended rallies and teach-ins. Most of the city-wide marches planned by SDS fizzled as well, drawing numbers in the low thousands in Boston and Washington, D.C., and even fewer in New York, San Francisco, and Los Angeles.

"Boulder and Boulder" turned out to be more like a pair of pebbles.

So whom did I vote for in the 1968 presidential election? No one. I was still twenty years old, too young to vote in 1968 but old enough to be drafted and to drink alcohol (the drinking age in New York State was eighteen at the time). The Twenty-Sixth Amendment to the U.S. Constitution, which reduced the voting age to eighteen, was not adopted until 1971.

As troubling as the election of Richard Nixon was, I had more to worry about immediately than what a Nixon presidency would mean. Judge Port had set the date of my sentencing for November 12.

SPOTLIGHT: NO BAIL IN AUBURN, NOVEMBER 14, 1968

"Does the defendant have anything to say to this court before I pass sentence?" Judge Port asked.

"Yes, I do," I replied. I had been told by my attorney to expect such a question at my sentencing for tearing up my draft card. Faith didn't know what the judge's response would be, but whatever the sentence he handed out, she thought it likely that Port would allow me to remain out on bail while she and the NYCLU attorneys filed an appeal. Although the U.S. Supreme Court had already decided the constitutional issues raised by the draft card destruction law by ruling that such actions were not protected "symbolic" speech, my attorneys intended to file an appeal based on other issues raised in the trial. Little did we know that Judge Port's sentence would itself become grounds for appeal.

The sentencing was taking place two days later than originally scheduled, and in Auburn, New York, rather than in Syracuse, because an early pre-winter snowstorm had paralyzed upstate New York on November 12. My parents were already at the federal courthouse in Auburn when I arrived with Jane and about fifty supporters from Ithaca. My folks tried to smile when they saw me, not doing a very good job of concealing their true feelings about what was about to transpire. It didn't look like the day would be a happy birthday for my mother, who was turning fifty-five on November 14.

I had no plan to make a speech in response to Judge Port's query, but I did want to make one thing clear to him: "I would like to be sentenced as an adult, not under the Youth Corrections Act," I said.

The Federal Youth Corrections Act (YCA), enacted in 1950, was ostensibly a progressive piece of federal law governing the sentencing of defendants under the age of twenty-six. Known colloquially among inmates (I learned later) as a "Zip-6," it gave a federal judge the option of ordering an indeterminate sentence in which an inmate could be held for a maximum of four years before being granted a conditional parole and a maximum of six years before obtaining an unconditional release. After parole was completed or six years had elapsed, the recipient's felony conviction would be erased. There was no minimum amount of prison time that had to be served—though, as I found out later, there were unwritten rules about how much time a draft resister with a Zip-6 sentence might spend in prison. The law gave the federal board of parole the authority to grant a parole, should the board decide that an inmate had been rehabilitated, at any time during the first four years of the sentence.

From my perspective, receiving a YCA sentence was worse than getting the maximum sentence for the crime I had committed, which was five years in prison, with parole eligibility after serving the first third of the sentence. The whole matter of rehabilitation was problematic for a political prisoner, as it appeared that such rehabilitation could only be achieved by recanting one's beliefs.

Judge Port immediately rejected my request. "The major damage of conviction to a young man like yourself is not spending a few years in prison," Port said, adding condescendingly, "It will be part of your education." More important to him was that I would have a felony conviction on my record that could not be removed. "What if you would like to become a certified public accountant after serving your term in prison?" he asked rhetorically. (The judge must not have seen the grade I received in statistics class.) He said the provisions of the Youth Corrections Act would allow me to eventually pursue such a career because my felony conviction would have been wiped out.

Port granted that I was sincere in my beliefs but added that "society couldn't long exist in an atmosphere where the individual is given the choice of the laws to be obeyed and the laws to be violated." Then he got to his main point: "I am hopeful that your sentence will give pause to those who might follow your example."

Once Port issued his sentence, Faith immediately said she would be appealing both my conviction and the sentence. She asked for a continuance of my bail pending the outcome of such an appeal.

Port then surprised all of us by revoking my bail and ordering my immediate incarceration. He said that since the constitutional questions in the case had already been decided by the Supreme Court, "appeal could only be for the purpose of delay." But then he got angrier, charging that I had used my time on bail "to incite riot throughout the state of New York." He didn't offer any examples.

Two U.S. marshals immediately appeared at the defense table to escort me into a holding room. Faith and my parents followed, as did Jane. But when Jane reached the door, a court bailiff said that only immediate family members and my attorney could enter with me. Not having foreseen this development, I had to think quickly. I said, "She's my fiancée," and they let Jane in.

Jane and I never talked about the future, and I hadn't proposed marriage to her. Perhaps because of my looming prison sentence, it was too scary a subject to deal with. But we were living together, more or less, and I assumed we would be together as long as we could. In any event, she didn't object to my subterfuge.

Inside the Onondaga County Jail

Within a few minutes I was told I would be taken to the Onondaga County Jail in Syracuse. After saying goodbye to my parents and Jane, I was handcuffed and led out of the courthouse by two federal marshals. Despite the cuffs, as we walked past my supporters I raised my fist in defiance before I got into the car.

Even though I had not expected to start my prison sentence so soon, I was as prepared as I was going to be for it. I don't remember feeling particularly frightened; it was more a determination to face whatever was going happen. I had steeled myself as best I could.

I was placed in a maximum security cell block in the county jail with two other inmates who, like me, were under twenty-one years of age. Ted (not his real name), a young black man who had been convicted of manslaughter, was the more outgoing and lively of the two, as Phil (not his real name either), a white guy in for illegal possession of a shotgun, had the shakes from what appeared to be some kind of drug withdrawal.

As soon as I arrived, they asked me what I was in for. And when I told them, Ted's reaction was incredulous: "Man, they put you in for six years for tearing up a piece of paper?"

We must have been the only under-twenty-one inmates with felony convictions in the county jail, as the three of us had the entire twelve-bed cell block to ourselves. Both Ted and Phil told me they were against the war, and when I talked to them about the movement, they seemed interested, though they could just have been being polite. We got along really well, spending the hours talking, playing cards, and throwing around a rolled up ball of socks in a whirling game of catch. The friendship, laughter, and solidarity I shared with these two guys was, not surprisingly, in sharp contrast to the sullenness and hostility of the guards, who didn't appear to like the idea that we were enjoying ourselves in jail.

One of the hardest parts of my imprisonment in Syracuse was seeing the sadness and worry on the faces of my parents, Jane, Peter Agree, and Doug and Kay Dowd when they came to visit. I wasn't allowed to sit in the same room with them, as we had to confer by telephone while sitting in a booth and looking at each other through a thick glass window. Jane, struggling to hold back her tears and put on a brave face, told me that Cornell SDS had started a petition drive for my release on bail, which would be submitted to the appellate court judges hearing my case. Faith had already told me one of the grounds for appeal would be that my receiving a potential six-year sentence for a crime whose maximum penalty was five years constituted "cruel and unusual punishment." I didn't expect any positive results, however.

Having been jailed on a Thursday, I knew the bail hearing would probably take place sometime during the following week, but I wasn't sure when the appellate court would make its decision. So when it reached 5 p.m. on Tuesday, November 19, and I hadn't heard anything, I decided to take a shower when offered one by the guard. No sooner did I get wet when another guard interrupted me and said, "Dancis, get your clothes on. You're out."

My hair still dripping wet, I was picked up by Jane and Doug for a very happy drive back to Ithaca. It was only then that I found out what had been going on while I was in jail.

Petitions and Perkins

Cornell SDS and supporters of draft resisters began a campaign to get me released on bail as soon as they got back from the sentencing. The outpouring of support was both touching in its warmth and revealing in its size, in that it demonstrated how many people had been affected by my act of draft resistance nearly two years previously and by the resistance actions that followed.

It started with a rally within Professor Charles Ackerman's large sociology class in Bailey Hall. Ackerman, a faculty member not known for supporting draft resisters or SDS, turned his class over to a discussion of my situation by fellow resisters Tom Byers, James Matlack, and others.

The *Cornell Daily Sun* published three separate editorials calling for my release, along with op-ed pieces and letters of support by an English professor (Doug Archibald), a campus chaplain (Paul Gibbons), a fellow student (Fred Solowey), and an economics professor who happened to be my close friend and benefactor (Doug Dowd). Doug concluded his piece with a personal note that still makes me blush: "I have known many fine young people at Cornell and elsewhere. I have never known anyone of Bruce's character: warm, loving, joyous, serious, honest, committed, unselfish, and courageous. He will be missed; we must bring him back." (Damn, I thought later when I read Doug's letter, it sounded like he was nominating me for pope.)

Most of the energy went into circulating a petition, written by law student and SDS member Bruce Detwiler, urging my release on bail. The cover letter to the U.S. Court of Appeals in New York stated, "We present to you these petitions not because we presume to understand the law better than yourselves, but because we believe we know Bruce Dancis better than yourselves."

With Jane taking a leading role, SDS members and others gathered over fifty-five hundred signatures on the petition, copies of which were circulated at that weekend's Cornell-Dartmouth football game, at a campus concert by folksinger Judy Collins, in dorms, fraternities, sororities, and other living units, and in campus buildings. Surprisingly—to me, at least—two leading administrators at Cornell, Mark Barlow and Stuart Brown, vice presidents for student affairs and academic affairs, respectively, were among the signers.

An even bigger surprise came to light when the three-judge U.S. Court of Appeals panel in New York City unanimously overturned Judge Port's ruling and released me on bail. It was revealed that President Perkins had written a private letter to the appellate court on my behalf, even though he noted I was "a former student of Cornell University" and he was neither condoning my action nor contesting the duty of the court. Nevertheless, Perkins stated, "I am distressed that Mr. Dancis was not afforded the opportunity of being put free on bail pending his appeal. Surely no one can believe that Mr. Dancis could represent a public danger. He was certainly no public danger while he was at Cornell, nor would he be if he were released on bail."

The only reason anyone outside of the court became aware of Perkins's letter was that two of the appellate judges, while agreeing to release me on bail, publicly castigated Perkins and the petitioners for attempting to exert "shocking pressures" on the court. The judges' comments were cited in a news story on my case in the *New York Times*.[3] One of those judges was Irving R. Kaufman, who a decade and a half earlier had been the federal judge presiding over the Rosenberg espionage case and who sentenced both Julius and Ethel Rosenberg to death.

The day after my release, I spoke at a rally at the Straight. I described my five days in the Onondaga County Jail and thanked everyone who had circulated and signed the petition. After I finished my remarks, I took questions from the audience and the media. One person asked my reaction to Perkins's letter to the Court of Appeals. Rather than responding graciously, I dismissed Perkins's letter as a ploy to curry favor with the fifty-five hundred members of

3. One of my attorneys, Alan Levine of the NYCLU, later wrote a letter to *New York Times* reporter Edward Ranzal criticizing his story for not including Faith Seidenberg's defense of President Perkins and the petitioners. Alan pointed out that "community sentiments regarding the character and potential danger of a convicted felon are properly considered in a bail hearing."

"our resistance will not end until all the killing
ends, until everyone of our brothers is back from
vietnam, until every resister is free from prison"
bruce dancis april 68

6 years in prison—

while
america
burned the
children—
dancis burned
a draft card.
america is
still at large
dancis is in
jail——

join the
common
conspiracy
to end the
killing—
"when they
are jailed
we shall
take their
places"
Ω

for whose crimes?
rally at wsh mem. room
12:15

Cornell Resistance leaflet distributed after the imprisonment of
Bruce Dancis on November 14, 1968. Dancis received an indeter-
minate sentence of up to six years in federal prison from
U.S. District Court Judge Edmund Port in Auburn, New York, and
spent six days in the Onondaga County Jail in Syracuse before
a U.S. Appeals Court ordered him released on bail. (Lawrence
Felix Kramer Papers, Division of Rare and Manuscript
Collections, Cornell University Library)

the Cornell community who had signed the petition. After more than three years of clashing with Perkins and his administration over issues as serious and emotional as the draft and complicity with South Africa, I was not able to find a kind word to say about either him or his letter.

I don't have many lifelong regrets, but my reaction to Perkins's letter to the Court of Appeals is one of them. He took some heat for his statement, and not just from the two appeals court justices.[4] I should have thanked him for sticking his neck out to call for my release on bail. I should have recognized his letter as a sincere, humane reaction to a legal injustice. I'm sorry that I never took the opportunity to do so later.

Fissures in National SDS, Growth at Cornell

As SDS historian Kirk Sale has pointed out, the failure of the "Boulder and Boulder" program represented a deeper crisis within SDS. It was not just that an inadequate amount of time was given to plan and organize the Election Day actions, or that the vitriolic split between the National Office and PL was leading to a divisiveness that turned some formerly active chapters into dysfunctional debating societies. The failure showed that the gap that had always existed between the National Office and local chapters remained wider than ever.

Increasingly, SDS leaders aligned with the National Office took the view that American universities were so intertwined with a repressive American society that they must be destroyed. Three prominent SDSers—Mike Spiegel, Cathy Wilkerson, and Les Coleman—even put forth a strategy in October '68 calling for "an attack on the entire institution of the university, a challenge to its purpose and its right to exist. Wherever possible," they argued, "we must strive to shut it down—shut it down rather than 'reform' it." The National Office faction continued to view the SDS-led Columbia University revolt as the model for SDS organization and confrontation, but this was based on the flawed assumption that many campuses were on the verge of similar revolts.

Other splits were taking place within SDS nationally during the fall of 1968. New York City members of the SDS Labor Committee faction were supporting striking public school teachers in a racially charged conflict with community leaders in the largely African American Ocean Hill–Brownsville

4. I discovered in the James Perkins Papers housed in the Cornell University Library a letter from an outraged Cornell alumnus criticizing Perkins for writing to the Court of Appeals on my behalf. Perkins replied that his letter was intended to address "the injustice" of my being denied bail. He maintained that his letter to the court was intended to be private and that he had not expected it to be released. It would not be surprising if Perkins received other negative letters and telephone calls on this matter.

section of Brooklyn. This aroused the anger of the New York regional office of SDS, which supported the black parents and residents in their fight for community control of schools. The regional office voted to expel the Labor Committee members, an action unprecedented in SDS's history.

The internecine battles taking place in the SDS chapter at the University of Michigan, where SDS was born, were even more disturbing. Future Weathermen Bill Ayers, Terry Robbins, and Jim Mellen formed a caucus they called the Jesse James Gang. Their foes within the SDS chapter were not PL supporters, but veteran members of the chapter who favored base building and educational work among students before engaging in action. The James Gang leaders announced at the start of the fall term that their group believed in "aggressive confrontation politics," with one member saying, "If you think the only thing to do with war research is to burn it up, and the only thing to do with bad classes is to take them over, and the only thing to do about bullshit candidates is to run them out with your own lives, then let's talk." They pushed for a student strike on Election Day, confronting professors they disagreed with inside their classrooms and burning exams.

Within a month, the University of Michigan SDS chapter fractured, splitting into two competing and antagonistic groups. The Election Day student strike called by the James Gang was a failure. By the end of the fall term, "SDS in general had fallen into disrepute on the Michigan campus," Sale wrote.

One of the main problems with the James Gang, and most of those SDS members who would within a year become aligned with the Weatherman faction, was that they had divorced confrontation politics from the issues or wrongs they were confronting. On the one hand, they understood what many of us had learned from the civil rights movement and earlier antiwar and draft resistance struggles on campus—that action builds solidarity, commitment, and even a sense of liberation among those taking part. But spending the time to build the movement, which I viewed as a necessary step before mass action was possible, had fallen away as an option. Confrontation became almost an end in itself. In his book *The Sixties*, Todd Gitlin quotes Mark Rudd, the former Columbia SDS leader who was now working with the National Office faction and the James Gang, as saying, contemptuously, "Organizing is just another word for going slow."

In this regard, and in others, the action faction within Cornell SDS, though aligned with the National Office, operated more sensibly and in a less divisive manner. Chip Marshall deserves much of the credit for this. Before joining SDS, Chip had worked with SNCC, where he learned about the need for base building and recognized that direct action had to flow organically out of organizing. Although Chip favored confrontation as an important step in the radicalization of both participants and observers—a viewpoint

I shared—he saw that such confrontations would only be effective if they seemed like reasonable responses and reactions to the rejection of our legitimate demands.

That's one of the reasons why the action faction within Cornell SDS favored the housing campaign put forward by members of the Labor Committee and supported by a large majority of chapter members. Our research-based analysis of the housing crisis in Ithaca was accurate. Our basic demands were reasonable, and they were receiving support from black activists in Ithaca and reformers who had been working on the housing crisis. If the Cornell administration rejected, delayed, or tried to weasel its way out of meeting its social responsibilities, we would have just cause to take more-militant action.

While SDS was beginning to fall apart nationally, at Cornell we were growing larger and more influential. We were beginning to play a bigger role in the cultural life of the campus as well.

The annual "Fall Weekend" at Cornell had long been dominated by a Saturday afternoon football game, a Saturday evening concert, and lots of fraternity and sorority parties. But the power and the popularity of frats and sororities were weakening at Cornell and elsewhere, as many students were seeking something less defined, less traditional, and more countercultural. This group included SDS members and students in our orbit.

Our newly created Cultural Affairs Committee came up with the idea for an "Alternative Fall Weekend," which would be open to everyone—in contrast to the exclusivity and snobbishness of the fraternity/sorority system—and would combine culture, entertainment, and politics. "You don't need a date," we stated in all of the pre-event publicity. Spread over two days and nights, our program consisted of performances by radical theater groups, dances featuring local rock bands, radical movies by Newsreel and other left-wing film groups, a "Community Collage" of antiwar artwork, a performance by magician Ricky Jay (a Cornell student who later became a renowned magician and actor), an exhibit of revolutionary posters from Cuba presented by SDSers Larry Kramer and Jim Murray, who had just returned from a visit to the island, and more.

I missed all of the Alternative Fall Weekend while in jail in Syracuse, but by all accounts it was a rousing success.

The Impact of Revolutionary Cuba

The return of Larry and Jim from Cuba, where they had gone on a tour sponsored by SDS and the Cuban government, sparked new interest in the Cuban Revolution within our chapter. We devoted a special issue of the *First Issue* to their articles about their nine-week trip, which consisted of a two-and-a-half-week official tour and the rest devoted to travel on their own, including a week of voluntary labor in the sugarcane fields and visits with university students.

The Cuban Revolution had fascinated American radicals and left-liberals even before Fidel Castro and his guerrilla army overthrew the corrupt dictatorship of Fulgencio Batista and seized power on January 1, 1959. Although the U.S. government quickly turned against the Castro regime, particularly after it nationalized farmlands owned by the United Fruit Corporation and other foreign companies, Cuba's experiment in establishing a socialist economy only ninety miles from Florida attracted the support of many throughout the world. While the failed U.S.-backed invasion of Cuba at the Bay of Pigs in 1961, the Cuban Missile Crisis of 1962, and the assassination of President John F. Kennedy in 1963 by Lee Harvey Oswald, a loner who had apparently been a member of the Fair Play for Cuba Committee, all contributed to growing hostility toward the Cuban government on the part of many Americans, by the late '60s Cuba had achieved a special status among those critical of U.S. foreign policy and supporters of Third World revolutionary movements.

Like most SDSers visiting Cuba in 1967–68, Larry and Jim focused far more on Cuba's achievements—in education and literacy, health care, income equality, cultural expression in film and art, women's rights, and grassroots participation in revolutionary organizations—than problems with its authoritarian regime. They presented a picture of Cuba as an exciting place filled with enthusiastic students, workers, and Communist Party members who were taking active roles in building their new society and shaping their own futures, as distinct from the passivity of so many Americans. They also detailed the threat faced by Cuba from the United States in the form of invasions (the Bay of Pigs), sabotage, financing rebel groups of exiles, and a harmful trade blockade.

Larry and Jim didn't ignore the problems of Cuban society that were most frequently noted by critical observers—one-party rule and the outlawing of competing political parties, the cult of personality around Fidel Castro and the recently martyred Che Guevara, the scarcity of some goods and services, and the absence of a free and independent press. But on each of these issues, they defended the Cuban government's position. On the question of dissent, for example, they pointed out that while advocating a counterrevolution or a return to capitalism was illegal in Cuba, open and forthright debate was taking place throughout the society and within the party, neighborhood block committees, trade unions, and other associations and organizations.

At the time, we didn't realize—or didn't explore sufficiently—the extent of Cuba's jailing of dissidents, its harsh treatment of homosexuals, the

stultifying effects of Communist Party rule, and the country's growing economic reliance on the Soviet Union.

As 1968 and the fall semester at Cornell came to an end, our housing program was gathering momentum and gaining support. Organizations and
individuals in Ithaca who were already working on housing issues, including MOVE (a group formed the past April, following Martin Luther King's
assassination, to help alleviate problems of racism and divisiveness in Ithaca)
and the head of Tompkins County's Economic Opportunity Commission,
endorsed our proposal.

SDS, with Larry leading the way, was also involved in forming the Ithaca
Tenants Union. Though started by SDS members, this was an autonomous
group based largely in the student-filled Collegetown area of Ithaca that was
organized to challenge neglectful landlords, investigate and take action over
landlord discrimination, and generally represent the interests of renters.

But as well as we were doing locally, on the national level SDS continued to crumble. The infighting between the National Office group and Progressive Labor reached its highest intensity to date at the National Council
meeting held on the University of Michigan campus during Christmas week.
This was my last national SDS meeting, and my participation was mostly as
an observer, watching the various factions quoting Lenin and Mao at each
other and engaging in doctrinal debates about the black revolution, women's
liberation, and the role of youth in the movement. The National Office faction was able to pass (by only twelve votes) a proposal by national secretary
Mike Klonsky titled "Towards a Revolutionary Youth Movement," which
called for SDS to "organize young working people into our class-conscious
anti-capitalist movement."

To me, Klonsky's proposal wasn't all that different from what PL had repeatedly offered—subsuming student issues and concerns to organizing the
traditional working class—except that it placed greater emphasis on reaching youth and attacking racism. The closeness of the vote demonstrated PL's
strength at national meetings of SDS, a strength that would lead to the col-
lapse of SDS within six months.

Nevertheless, as I drove back from Ann Arbor to Ithaca with Larry, Chip,
and Joe, I didn't think the national turmoil would necessarily harm Cornell
SDS. We were all still getting along and working well together, despite some
ideological differences. Our discussions during the drive back from Michigan
to upstate New York through Ontario, Canada, were amiable and forward
looking.

Not even some mild harassment from the U.S. Customs when we reen-
tered the United States near Buffalo bothered us. We were delayed about five
hours at the border as the customs agents carefully inspected Joe's old car and

looked at all the literature we had brought back from the National Council meeting. The agents ended up illegally confiscating most of the printed material we had with us, but they eventually let us back in the country.

 I did not expect that my next confrontation with legal authorities would be over my dog.

SPOTLIGHT: DOG DAY EVENING, JANUARY 1969

"That's Dancis's dog!" yelled one of the Tompkins County animal control officers to the other. Their van was already parked on Eddy Street when they spied All Right.

It was just past 6 p.m. on a Saturday in January in the Collegetown section of Ithaca. All Right, a roughly six-year-old pooch of mixed parentage and a checkered past, was jauntily walking down the street, not a doggy care in the world. Judging from the time of day and his location, he was probably heading home for dinner. That's when the cops pounced.

All Right barked but was easily overcome by the two men, who hauled him into their waiting van. But before they could drive off and take All Right to the local jail, a passerby tried to intervene.

Jill Boskey, a former Cornell student activist and a participant in our Hiroshima Day protest in New York City back in August 1967, happened to be visiting Ithaca for the weekend. She was also walking on Eddy Street at the same time as All Right, and she witnessed his arrest and heard the cop's comments from across the street. She ran over to protest the bust. Jill was a dear friend of the accused, and she would not let his arrest go unprotested. The fur began to fly as she began arguing with the officers. She protested so loudly and vehemently and created such a ruckus that the animal control cops called the human control cops.

It turned out that a new county law prohibiting dogs from being on the streets without their masters after 6 p.m. had just gone into effect. Despite her efforts, Jill could not stop the cops from carting All Right off to the pound.

The political implications of the bust were obvious. All Right did not believe in the traditional master-pet relationship. As best I knew, he had been a street dog for the first several years of his life, before being adopted by Jill. When she left Ithaca in January 1968, she turned All Right's care and well-being over to me.

I gave All Right the option of doing more or less whatever he wanted, but he usually chose to hang out with me. This enabled him to become the Cornell SDS mascot and a staffer on the *First Issue*. He also set the canine record for attendance at antiwar demonstrations in Ithaca. All Right was also an excellent traveler, as he would sometimes accompany me on my various speaking trips around New York State; he even sat on my lap for a six-hour car ride to New York City in a friend's two-seater.

But, truth be told, the excitement of actively participating in the movement sometimes got All Right all tired out. As a result, one of his favorite activities was curling up in a comfy chair in the Office on Stewart Avenue, where the human adoration flowed freely along with the political discussions and debates.

It was in this very office that All Right had a revealing encounter with a man who turned out to be a police undercover agent and agent provocateur. A guy known as "Tommy the Traveler" (aka Tommy Tongyai) had befriended a couple of Cornell SDS members and become active in the Niagara region of SDS. As his nickname indicated, he went all over upstate New York claiming to be a militant SDSer and posing as a salesman of veterinary supplies. In 1970, it became known that he had met with radical students at Hobart College in nearby Geneva, New York, and had advocated the firebombing of the campus Air Force ROTC office. He also provided information to county police for a drug bust on the Hobart campus.

Tommy was visiting the Office in Ithaca when All Right started to complain about an itch in his hindquarters—or so I interpreted his scooting on the already deplorable office rug. Tommy suggested that perhaps All Right had a clogged anal gland. Sure enough, when I took All Right to the free clinic at the Cornell Veterinary School, the vet students confirmed that this was what ailed him. But All Right and I should have been suspicious when Tommy didn't offer us a free sample of the medication needed to speed All Right's recovery. Which just goes to show—All Right may have been a very intelligent dog, but he was unable to sniff out an informer in our midst.

I didn't have a lot of money in those days, but All Right always got fed. Once, I had to choose between either buying dog food or the Stones' new album, *Beggars Banquet*. All Right also was a Stones fan—he really liked their cover version of "Walking the Dog." But I decided that Alpo trumped "Stray Cat Blues."

As tight as All Right and I became, he vigorously guarded his freedom. Sometimes, instead of going to yet another long meeting with me, he would choose to hang out with the other street dogs in front of the Cornell Student Union. There he would chase the occasional car or join his pals in a raucous chorus of "woof, woof." Sometimes

he would even attend a class or two on an observer basis. He would go
off on his strolls, but would always show up for dinner.

It was this combination of his rebellious personal behavior and his
ties to me that led the animal control authorities to target All Right
for arrest. I realize this may sound far-fetched and even paranoid,
but I didn't suffer from a persecution complex. The evidence for this
claim may not be open and shut, but I believe it is beyond a reasonable doubt.

First of all, a day before he was busted, animal control cops had
come to the Office looking for All Right. Just as I had gained local
notoriety for my political activities, evidently so had All Right for his
flagrant defiance of the new off-the-leash law. Second, Jill heard those
animal control officers on Eddy Street identify All Right as my dog.
Finally, when I went to the dog pound to bail him out, I was recognized by the jailer despite my never having met him before. It sure
seemed like a political bust to me!

I was able to spring All Right from the pound by paying a ransom
of $17.25, which included $2.25 for a dog license. But whatever the
animal control authorities hoped to accomplish with their repressive
tactics, it didn't work.

Jail did not rehabilitate All Right. Nor did it have a deterrent
effect on his behavior. He continued to believe the new county law
constituted an abridgment of his freedom to travel. He refused to
wear the dog license around his neck. But he managed to avoid
any additional encounters with the Tompkins County animal control
police.

Chapter Twelve

Rebellion and Factionalism
in Black and White

The period from January to May 1969 was unparalleled in the history of Cornell University and in the lives of those of us who were involved in the protests that shook the campus community. Issues were coming to a head that had roiled the campus for the better part of a year—over Cornell's responsibility for Ithaca's housing shortage, over the university's complicity with the apartheid regime of South Africa, and over the presence of ROTC on campus.

But the programs, demands, and actions of Cornell SDS turned out to be far less significant than the dispute involving the Cornell Afro-American Society versus the university administration and faculty. As these disputes rushed toward confrontation, SDS found itself playing a supportive role to Cornell's black student activists.

During the fall, tensions between black students at Cornell and the administration and faculty had been escalating. At the heart of the disagreement were differences concerning the independence and mission of a proposed black studies program at the university. The AAS, which represented 100 to 150 of the 250 black students enrolled at Cornell, was pushing for an autonomous, black-controlled program within the university. The administration and faculty, though moving slowly toward the establishment of some kind of black studies division, refused to cede such control, in part because such an independent institution was illegal under Cornell's charter and New York State law. Other related issues remained unresolved, including the role, if any, of white faculty members and students in a black-run program.

Other problems stemmed from the cultural and social isolation of African American students in a largely white university located in a largely white town far away from the urban centers from which most of the black students came. The AAS had already persuaded the university to establish both men's and women's housing units for black undergraduates. Now it was making additional demands, some widely viewed on campus as reasonable, such as the hiring of a black psychiatrist at the university's health clinic in response to a case involving an African American female student, and others seen by many as unwarranted, such as the establishment of a blacks-only dining room in the Straight.

After meetings between the administration and AAS representatives not only failed to produce resolutions to the disagreements but actually increased the mistrust between both sides, the more militant members of the AAS began a series of aggressive, public actions on campus. Some of these activities were more like guerrilla theater than standard political action. They included the takeover of the building that had already been chosen as the future home of a black studies department; a series of demonstrations in which AAS members pointed toy guns at campus cops and other students, impeded traffic, overturned vending machines in several campus buildings, and staged a "faint-in" at the university health clinic; a sit-in of seventy-five students outside President Perkins's office; a demonstration in one of the Straight's dining rooms; disruptive gatherings in three university libraries in which students brought thousands of books to the circulation desk and proclaimed "these books have no relevance to me as a black student," and a march to Barton Hall that delayed a Cornell basketball game.

In addition, a member of the AAS assaulted a *Sun* reporter and seized the film of a *Sun* photographer while both were attempting to cover the building takeover. Although this action was neither planned by nor endorsed by the AAS, it contributed to growing tensions on campus.

The gulf separating blacks and whites at Cornell was certainly increased by the decision of black students to live together in black-only houses and to eat together in the Straight and other campus dining facilities. The separatist viewpoint of many AAS members, though no doubt arising out of negative experiences within white society and the need for self-defense, contributed to the isolation of black students at Cornell during this crucial period.

Despite these problems, by the beginning of 1969 the administration and the AAS were getting closer to an understanding of what a black studies program at Cornell might look like. The AAS was pleased that the university was apparently willing to offer the directorship of the new program to James Turner, a PhD candidate at Northwestern University who had been recommended by some AAS members.

Unfortunately, another development soon exacerbated the already tense situation: one of the campus judicial bodies long disparaged by radical students decided to prosecute six of the black students who had taken part in the

December demonstrations and disruptions. Within a month or two, the issue of punishment for a selected group of AAS members added another layer of strife to the acrimony.

Many of us in SDS were predisposed to supporting the AAS in its struggle with the administration. I thought the fight for self-determination was a valid response for African Americans living in a racist society. Although I still believed in integration as a goal, I rejected the notion that black separatism was the same thing as the kind of white separatism advocated by white supremacists like the KKK. The former was a defensive reaction to centuries of oppression at the hands of the white majority, while the latter was an attempt by whites to retain the privileges and advantages they had initially achieved through slavery and maintained after slavery's demise through the imposition of Jim Crow laws.

The Appeals Court Delivers Strike Two

The appeal of my conviction and sentence in Syracuse was held on January 9, 1969, at the U.S. Court of Appeals in New York City. I didn't go, as there was no role for the defendant in an appellate hearing.

My appellate attorneys, Alan Levine and Marvin Karpatkin of the NYCLU, argued that the indeterminate sentence I received under the Youth Corrections Act violated my First Amendment rights because it required me to recant my position on the war in Vietnam and the draft in order to demonstrate my "rehabilitation." They also argued that the sentence amounted to cruel and unusual punishment because it provided the possibility that I could be imprisoned longer (six years) than the maximum sentence (five years) proscribed by the law I was convicted of breaking. Finally, they again put forward the argument that ripping my draft card into four pieces did not constitute "mutilation."

On Jan. 21, the appeals court unanimously ruled against me on all counts. No surprises there, as I had not anticipated a favorable ruling. I just shrugged it off and waited for the U.S. Supreme Court to take up the case—or not—a decision that would probably be made in the next few months.

Housing Campaign Takes Off

Cornell SDS had been broadening the community coalition in support of our housing program. A Joint Housing Committee (JHC) was formed, with the participation of SDS, MOVE, the Tompkins County Economic Opportunity

Committee, the Ithaca Tenants Union, Ithaca Pride (an African American group), and an ever-increasing number of community organizations, to spearhead negotiations with the university.

The Cornell administration's first response to our housing demands was largely negative. Although President Perkins acknowledged the existence of a housing shortage in Ithaca (though not Cornell's role in creating it), he cited a number of obstacles that prevented him from replying positively to our proposals. Additional "careful study" was still needed. Furthermore, Perkins said that Ithaca's officials did not like Cornell to "tell them" how to solve their problems. As for financing the new housing, Perkins rejected our idea of selling stocks held in banks doing business in South Africa and using the proceeds from the sale of the Cornell Aeronautical Laboratory to pay for housing. He also claimed that the university's current budget crisis precluded any such spending.[1] But he offered an olive branch in the form of an invitation for us to choose an SDS representative to join a new administration, faculty, and student committee, to be headed by Cornell's vice president for planning, Thomas Mackesey, to examine the housing situation.

In reply, SDS's Tony Fels castigated the Cornell president for his "reluctance to face up to the magnitude and urgency of the problem," for ignoring "Cornell's responsibility for creating and intensifying Ithaca's housing problem," and for his delaying tactics. Tony reiterated our position that Cornell needed to supply funds to deal with the housing crisis, but he conceded that the source of such funds was not the key issue. Finally, Tony pointed out the disingenuous nature of Perkins's invitation for us to join a committee headed by Vice President Mackesey, as we had discovered that Mackesey was out of the country and would be away from Cornell for at least another month.

As a result, SDS refused to participate in any committee or commission on housing, or take part in any discussions, that did not include representatives of the Ithaca community. We repeated our desire to begin negotiations on our proposals on March 1, and waited for the administration's response.

This began a series of statements and counterstatements, negotiations and a boycott of negotiations, deadlines and the passing of deadlines, which continued for several months. As we held teach-ins on campus and in Ithaca neighborhoods to build community support, the administration attempted to divide the JHC by trying to persuade some of the coalition members, such as MOVE, to turn away from SDS. Such efforts failed.

---

1. In April 1973, a special faculty committee that had been formed to examine the university's financial condition found that over the previous ten years Cornell had made a "profit" of at least $200 million. The university had previously reported a $4 million deficit over the same period.

However, by putting our housing proposal in the hands of a coalition like the JHC, SDS, which had researched and developed the proposal, had now become just one of fifteen organizations working on the housing campaign. We were no longer in charge.

As often happens within coalitions, our initial demands were changed by the JHC. By the end of February, the proposal had been narrowed considerably. It now asked the university to provide land for the construction of 250 units of rental housing and up to 750 units of family-owned housing to be administered by Tompco Better Housing Inc., a local nonprofit group; give technical aid and credit support for a 250-unit tenant-managed rental project; make available funds for mortgage loans, estimated at $13 million, for one thousand units of housing under federally subsidized programs; and make an annual grant to subsidize rent and mortgage payments for families too poor to afford them otherwise. The JHC also dropped our demand that the monies for these efforts come from the sale of bank stocks involved in South Africa and the sale of the Cornell Aeronautical Laboratory.

SDS proved itself a good coalition partner by showing our flexibility and going along with the changed JHC demands. We remained the only group within the housing coalition possessing the political power to generate support for the plan on campus and to prod the university to take action.

On March 1, Perkins and his administration's commission agreed to meet with the JHC negotiating team for the first time. At the invitation of Perkins, Ithaca Mayor Jack Kiely was in attendance, as were the presidents of the Ithaca Gun Company (one of Ithaca's largest employers) and the First National Bank and Trust Company of Ithaca.

Such was the state of paranoia within the administration that the meeting, scheduled for 10 o'clock on a Saturday morning, was almost canceled when the JHC negotiators showed up at Day Hall with about one hundred supporters from SDS following a brief rally at the nearby student union. Evidently, the administration feared we were about to stage a sit-in at Day Hall, whereas the only purpose of the demonstrators' presence was to show support for the JHC prior to the start of discussions.

If the administration distrusted SDS and the JHC, the feeling was mutual. After the administration postponed a negotiating session on the grounds that one of its representatives was ill, we viewed this as just another stalling tactic. In response, on March 20 we held a rally and formed a peaceful picket line around Day Hall, which attracted more than eight hundred participants. The *Cornell Daily Sun* even endorsed our actions, editorializing that it was up to Cornell students to "keep the pressure of public opinion" on the university.

South Africa Debate Reemerges

The previous June, when the Cornell board of trustees had turned down SDS's demand that the university sell its stocks in banks that were aiding the South African regime, and President Perkins refused to resign his seat on the board of directors of Chase Manhattan Bank, the only concession (if you could call it that) the administration gave to us was the promise to hold a symposium during the next academic year on pertinent issues involving South Africa.

Before the symposium began in late February 1969, we put out a special edition of the *First Issue* devoted to liberation struggles in Africa. It included articles about South Africa, the national liberation revolts taking place in the Portuguese colonies of Angola, Mozambique, and what was then known as Portuguese Guinea (now Guinea-Bissau), and the ties of Cornell trustees to corporations doing business in those countries. The issue, which turned out to be the last one I edited, also featured articles about our housing campaign, sexism in American society and at Cornell, a critique of social realist art, a review of the Rolling Stones' *Beggars Banquet* album, and a brief story about the arrest of my dog All Right.

Most of us in Cornell SDS viewed the South Africa symposium as a smoke screen for inaction. It was a typical tactic of university administrations dealing with recalcitrant students: diffuse a provocative issue in a cloud of talk.

There was no doubt we could all learn much from knowledgeable speakers discussing the role of the U.S. government and American corporations in supporting apartheid, the state of the opposition movement led by the African National Congress, the long confinement in prison of ANC leaders such as Nelson Mandela, and different strategies to bring about apartheid's demise. But the idea of discussing and debating the rightness or wrongness of the South African regime seemed genuinely reactionary, akin to Cornell sponsoring a symposium in 1969 on the rightness or wrongness of Jim Crow laws and government-imposed racial segregation in the American South. That "debate" was over, as far as I was concerned. Apartheid was an evil system, and the time was long past where it could, or should, be the subject of detached discussion.

Shortly before the beginning of the South Africa symposium, I received a strange invitation via Dave Burak. It seemed that President Perkins wanted to meet personally with me, Burak, and Chip Marshall to discuss SDS's South Africa demands. It may be hard to believe, but I had never met Perkins face to face—despite my participation in a sit-in at his office in May 1966, his public criticism of me for allegedly provoking "the button incident" in November 1966, and his writing a letter in support of my being granted bail after my sentencing in November 1968. I was surprised he suggested a meeting with

Chip and me, as we were both no longer students at Cornell, but it showed the administration realized we were both quite influential within the SDS chapter. (I was still an elected cochairman of the chapter.) Unlike Burak, who enjoyed hanging out with Cornell administrators, neither Chip nor I welcomed a meeting with Perkins. But after consulting with other SDS members, we agreed to meet with him as our chapter's representatives. (Perkins held an additional meeting with other SDS leaders, including Alan Snitow, to discuss the South Africa issue.)

The meeting lasted no more than twenty minutes. It began with our reiterating the SDS demands. Perkins then turned to me and asked, "Do you really think I'm a racist?"

I replied, "No, I don't think you are personally a racist. But you are deeply involved in and are supporting institutionalized racism by serving on the board of a bank that does business with the apartheid government of South Africa and by Cornell retaining its stock holdings in banks that prop up that government."

Perkins gave the expected response—that fiduciary principles precluded Cornell from selling stock for social or political reasons, and that his seat on the board of Chase Manhattan gave him the opportunity to change corporate policies for the better. But when we asked Perkins if he had actually used his position on the Chase Manhattan board to criticize the bank's policies with respect to South Africa, he admitted that he had not.

Our meeting produced no agreement and served only to illustrate the gulf that existed between our respective positions.

A Provocative Symposium

The South Africa symposium was put together by Perkins and Cornell's Center for International Studies, headed by Government professor Douglas Ashford. When the speakers' list was announced, we were surprised that the symposium was loaded with businessmen who viewed American investment in South Africa as having a positive impact on race relations there and with U.S. State Department types who viewed the issue of apartheid through a Cold War lens. That is, since the African National Congress in South Africa and the liberation movements in the Portuguese colonies in Africa were receiving aid from the Soviet Union, and the repressive, whites-only South African government and the military junta that ruled Portugal were backing the United States' side in the Cold War, matters of justice, antiracism, and anticolonialism were viewed as secondary to geopolitical considerations. The symposium's speakers also included about a half dozen Cornell professors—mostly liberals and moderates but none an outspoken supporter of South African liberation—and at least one prominent South African defender of apartheid.

Cornell SDS was helped in our preparation for the symposium by the arrival of Danny Schecter in Ithaca. Danny, who would later become a popular radio "news dissector" in Boston, a TV producer for ABC News, a documentary filmmaker, and a well-known writer and blogger, had gone to Cornell in the early '60s, joined the New Left, and taken a special interest in South African liberation. (His younger brother Bill had also attended Cornell and was a participant in some of the earliest antiwar protests at the university.) I had known Danny years earlier when his family rented a house at Three Arrows for several summers, but this was the first time we had ever worked together in the movement.

Danny had recently returned from South Africa and helped form the Africa Research Group, a research organization dedicated to studying American policy in Africa and supporting antiapartheid and anticolonial struggles. Using the ARG's research, we were able to put out a guide to the speakers invited to the symposium, listing what was known about their attitudes toward apartheid and the fight against it.

Among the most prominent speakers were Otto Krause, editor of *News-Check,* a South African news magazine roughly akin to *Time* magazine, and an apologist for the apartheid system; Waldemar Campbell of the U.S. State Department; Erasmus Kloman, a former State Department adviser who worked for American Metal Climax, an international corporation with extensive holdings in Southern and Central African mines; and Allard Lowenstein, a liberal U.S. congressman and organizer in Eugene McCarthy's presidential campaign, but in the South African context a critic of apartheid who also opposed the ANC and the revolutionary movement.

SDS charged that in addition to presenting a symposium with an obvious bias against the revolutionary struggle in South Africa, Cornell had invited twenty white speakers and only three black speakers. And those black speakers had been relegated to a 9:30 Saturday morning time slot, rather than letting them debate or respond to the pro-apartheid or pro-going-slow speakers on other panels.

So when Otto Krause began the symposium with a lecture titled "The South African Perspective on Africa," we were already suspicious and angry. Though he was billed as a "moderate" white Afrikaaner, Krause not only argued that apartheid was a just system but claimed that black Africans benefited from it and supported it. "They're getting something out of it and for the moment they're buying it," Krause claimed.

The audience, filled with SDS and AAS members and other Cornell students, visiting black South African students, and Cornell professors, grew more hostile to Krause as he went along. During the question-and-answer session, as African students challenged Krause on his facts and opinions, I couldn't contain myself any longer. After Krause made the particularly odious remark that black South Africans backed the system of apartheid, I yelled out something like "That's a bunch of racist crap."

I'm not proud that I heckled Krause, but it wasn't as if I prevented him from expressing his noxious opinions. I had been heckled numerous times on the Cornell campus while speaking about the war in Vietnam and the draft, including when some chemical engineering students interrupted me when I tore up my draft card by yelling "Three cheers for Dow [Chemical]." In some democratic forums, such as the British Parliament, heckling—and responding cleverly to heckling—is an accepted political practice. Heckling a speaker may not be polite, but it is not the equivalent of stopping that person from speaking.

Unfortunately, another SDS member, Jeff Dowd, then interrupted Krause to ask the audience to vote if they wanted him to continue answering questions. This produced considerable consternation among the audience—and criticism afterward about SDS curtailing the right of free speech—until Bruce Detwiler, our SDS expert on South Africa, defused the situation by saying we needed to let Krause finish. "I think it's very important that we listen and listen carefully to this man," Detwiler said, because, in his own case, if he hadn't heard Krause speak, he "wouldn't have believed it could be this bad."

As the symposium continued during the next few days, sharp criticisms continued to be raised from the audience over the composition of panels. One panel, "The Origins of Racism in South Africa," featured not a single black speaker.

We succeeded in getting Ashford to agree to let two black South Africans speak following Lowenstein's lecture on the last day of the symposium. And we sponsored our own session, which packed the Straight's Memorial Room, featuring four black South African students studying in the United States. Their depiction of apartheid, based on their own personal experiences, was much harsher than what other symposium speakers were saying.

Audience members also increased their criticisms of the Cornell administration and board of trustees for the university's investment policies. At one session on the last day of the symposium, Perkins was challenged by black students about the trustees' decision not to sell the bank stocks. When Michael Thelwell, a former SNCC activist who was currently a fellow at Cornell's Society for the Humanities and an adviser to the AAS, insisted that

Perkins needed to publicly explain university policies, the audience voted overwhelmingly to raise this issue at Perkins's next public appearance. That same evening, the Cornell president was scheduled to introduce Congressman Lowenstein, the symposium's keynote speaker.

That event, to be held in the Statler Auditorium in Cornell's School of Hotel Administration, promised to be electrifying.

SPOTLIGHT: FACE TO FACE WITH PRESIDENT PERKINS, FEBRUARY 28, 1969

The tension inside Statler Auditorium was already palpable when I rose from my seat in the audience and addressed the president of Cornell University: "President Perkins, I want you to explain to the audience the university's investments in South Africa, and defend them." The capacity crowd of over eight hundred hushed. Even the bongo drums AAS members were playing just a few moments earlier had turned silent. The long-awaited public debate between antiapartheid activists with the Cornell administration over the university's financial complicity with the racist regime of South Africa had just begun.

Standing up to challenge Perkins wasn't a spontaneous decision on my part. Earlier that day, members of SDS and the AAS had met to discuss what to do. Although the two organizations had allied the previous spring over the South Africa issue, it took our shared frustration over the South Africa symposium to get us working together again. We worked out a plan to challenge Perkins to defend university policies at that evening's final symposium session.

The plan was to have the AAS's Eric Evans come onto the stage to interrupt Perkins before he introduced Lowenstein, and then call on me in the audience to state our case. As Perkins began moving toward the podium from his seat onstage, Evans quickly jumped onto the stage and walked over to the microphone, arriving just before Perkins. Evans then told the crowd, "The peculiar thing about this whole damn symposium is it's stacked." He then called on me to speak.

It was so quiet I didn't need a microphone to be heard in the large auditorium. I began by reminding Perkins and the audience what the controversy was all about: Cornell's ownership of stock in American banks that had organized a revolving line of credit for the South African regime and Perkins's refusal to give up his seat on the board of one of those banks, Chase Manhattan. I discussed how the loans were used to bolster the apartheid regime in the early 1960s after the Sharpeville Massacre left South Africa in the midst of an investment crisis due to its increasing isolation within the international economic community.

I also cited the research SDS had done documenting the institutional connections binding Cornell trustees and administrators to the South African regime, from Perkins's seat on the Chase Manhattan board to newly appointed board of trustees chairman Robert Purcell's directorship of the International Minerals and Chemical Corporation, which had a subsidiary in South Africa. In addition, I pointed out that eleven Cornell trustees were directors of firms with investments in South Africa, and five of these trustees served on the board's executive committee.

When I finished speaking, to cheers and applause from about half the audience, all eyes turned to Perkins on the stage.

"I doubt if I will satisfy you," Perkins began. "The trustees' policy with respect to investments—and I will, believe me, be as open as possible with you—has been that only in the last couple of years the question has ever been raised about whether there should be some considerations involved in investments other than what will maximize the return for the University's needs." This was a rambling way of saying that before you radicals came along, Cornell's investments had always been based on profits, not social concerns.

Perkins said that although stocks in two of the five banks were sold during the past summer, they were "not sold . . . on the grounds of the public policy to which you have addressed yourself, but rather a continuation of the view that the bank stocks were overpriced. I am not going to get any brownie points with parts of this audience," he continued, "by suggesting that either I or the board of trustees had this [the South Africa question] in mind in the sale of the two bank stocks." Referring to the bank holdings, Perkins added, "We're not pulling out right now, but don't worry, we're not putting more money in until we investigate."

The crowd groaned, and it wasn't just the SDS and AAS members who were shaking their heads and expressing their displeasure over Perkins's weak response. Here was Perkins, more than a year after receiving our demands and nine months after the board of trustees had rejected them, still claiming the need to "investigate." Ten minutes into his defense of university policy, Perkins's answers appeared to be satisfying few in the auditorium.

"We Blew It!"

Suddenly, and without the prior knowledge of either the AAS or
SDS, Gary Patton, an AAS member, quickly walked onto the stage,
grabbed Perkins from behind by his jacket collar and pulled him
away from the microphone. Perkins, appearing to be in shock, was
speechless and looked frightened. When Proctor George attempted to
climb onto the stage to defend Perkins, another AAS member, Larry
Dickson, brandished a wooden plank at him, apparently in an effort
to protect Patton. Patton then let go of Perkins, and the president
disappeared backstage, accompanied by George and several other
campus policemen. Patton and Dickson also left the auditorium.
As the audience's stunned silence started turning to boos, the AAS
drummers resumed their bongo playing.

I was, at first, as shocked as everyone else over what had just
occurred. But then I got bummed. It was obvious that what had taken
nearly a year for us to accomplish—to find a suitable public forum
where we could present the case against Cornell's complicity with
apartheid and force Perkins to defend university policy—had been
ruined by the angry, stupid, and self-defeating action of Patton.

Rev. Gladstone Ntlabati, the exiled South African freedom fighter
who had worked with SDS the previous spring and remained a grad
student at Cornell, then stepped up to the podium and told the
crowd, "I feel President Perkins should have finished his statement tonight." As the audience stood to give him a standing ovation, Ntlabati
continued, "What happened tonight is against all the principles of
what we black people in South Africa believe in." But Ntlabati also
restated his criticisms of Perkins and the board of trustees.

Douglas Ashford, the main man behind the symposium, then took
the microphone. Conflating the situation that had just occurred, bad
as it was, with the oppression of black South Africans, Ashford said,
"I am terribly humiliated to see the same kind of terror that goes on
in Africa take place on a stage at Cornell University."

The scheduled speaker, Allard Lowenstein, briefly took the
microphone to say that he could not deliver his prepared remarks
under the circumstances. As the crowd began to leave, Evans walked
back on stage to tell those remaining, "It is an understatement, to say
the least, that what happened this evening was unfortunate.... We
blew it."

Evans, and SDS's Chip Marshall after him, both attempted to
point out that it was also regrettable that the issue of Cornell's
complicity with South Africa would now most likely be obscured by

what happened to Perkins. But by then the damage was done. In a few seconds, the situation had completely turned. Perkins's ineffectual defense of an amoral university investment policy was immediately overwhelmed by the spectacle of a middle-aged man being physically attacked and prevented from speaking by a much younger man. That Perkins was white and Patton was black only made the situation worse.

SDS tried to keep the focus on apartheid. We organized emergency discussions in dorms over the weekend and put out a leaflet about the Statler fiasco that deplored Patton's action yet maintained it should not distract the community from the underlying issue. But not surprisingly, the topic of outraged newspaper editorials and op-ed pieces was on violence and free speech. We had held the moral high ground on this issue, but through the unfortunate action of an angry young man we lost it.

In the aftermath of the Statler incident, the AAS announced it would itself discipline Patton. He was expelled from the organization and quickly left Cornell and Ithaca. The AAS statement, signed by the group's chairman, Ed Whitfield, also lamented that Perkins did not have the opportunity to fully defend his and the administration's position. Furthermore, Whitfield wrote, "It is poor reasoning and poor moral arithmetic to equate the suffering, destruction and oppression of millions of our Black brothers with a moment's discomfiture on the part of a university president."

Nevertheless, the AAS and SDS were both blamed for what happened to Perkins, even though neither of our organizations had known about Patton's plans in advance or defended his actions afterward. Perhaps we should have been more vociferous in our condemnation of Patton. On the other hand, the hypocrisy of those like Ashford who equated the grabbing of Perkins with the day-to-day oppression of black people in South Africa was hard to take.

There was one strange coda to the incident: ten days later, it was revealed that Cornell treasurer Lewis Durland had actually sold all the stock Cornell owned in the objectionable banks—but he had not bothered to inform Perkins, others in the administration, or the public about it. Evidently, Durland had sold the remaining stock but then went on a honeymoon without mentioning to Perkins what he had done.

"I'm kicking myself," Perkins told the *Sun* after he was belatedly informed of the sale.

Meanwhile, another South Africa–related controversy was brew-
ing at Cornell. Recruiters from Chase Manhattan Bank were scheduled to appear on campus on March 10. SDS announced our plans to
"stop the recruiting."

Chasing Chase Manhattan

Does a private corporation have a "right" to recruit? Does corporate recruiting
constitute free speech and free expression? These were some of the issues we
were dealing with when Cornell SDS planned a confrontation with recruiters
from Chase Manhattan. To us, there were countervailing rights and issues
that needed to be considered. If a corporation such as Chase Manhattan or
Dow Chemical was engaged in policies that were viewed by the community as
being harmful to humanity or socially evil, stopping it from using university
space to recruit was justifiable. Society had accepted the necessity of regulations to prevent corporations from manufacturing and distributing harmful
products. Similarly, civil rights laws now made it illegal for prejudiced restaurant owners to refuse to serve black customers. So why couldn't a corporation
producing a harmful product—in this case, loans to support apartheid—be
prevented from using Cornell University as a place to find new employees?

That was the motivation of SDS and AAS members as we gathered at the
Straight to rally and then march over to Malott Hall, the home of the university's School of Business and Public Administration and the site of the Chase
Manhattan recruitment. The just-breaking news that Cornell had, in fact,
sold its stock in banks supporting South Africa did not alter our negative
view of the role of Chase Manhattan in that country.

I thought the university was acting stupidly, and not just immorally, in allowing the recruitment to take place. The timing was particularly bad, given
the tension that already existed on campus in the aftermath of the South
Africa symposium, in the AAS's continuing push for a black studies center,
and in the negotiations that were still dragging on between the administration and the Joint Housing Committee. Had the administration quietly postponed the Chase Manhattan recruitment, the entire South Africa issue might
have slowly disappeared, or at least gotten less heated. By obstinately keeping
Chase Manhattan recruiting on its schedule, and elevating such recruiting
into a constitutional right as important as free speech, the administration was
increasing the prospects for a dramatic, and possibly violent, confrontation.[2]

2. In an internal memo to President Perkins from Vice President Barlow written one month later,
Barlow noted that "some officers of [Chase Manhattan] had recommended that the recruiters not

When Cornell SDS made its decision to confront the recruiters, we never discussed exactly how that confrontation would proceed and what it might entail. It is illustrative of how far many of us had come from just a year or two previously, when our most militant actions would have involved some form of nonviolent civil disobedience, that the issue of nonviolence was never seriously discussed.

When we marched over to Malott Hall, I was with the main group of demonstrators, about three hundred strong, who walked to the front entrance of the building and found its doors locked and guarded by a few campus policemen. A smaller group of protesters was standing on the other side of the building. I noticed right away that some of the leaders of SDS's action faction were nowhere around, and I figured they were looking for an alternative way into Malott.

What to do? We had enough protesters willing to push aside the campus cops, but we would still be facing locked doors. As demonstrators milled around, I had some hasty talks with other SDS and AAS members. We decided that while we would try to avoid any physical confrontation with the cops, we would break the glass doors in order to gain entrance to the building. We began looking around for an object or objects large enough to smash the glass.

Just then, I saw some familiar faces already *inside* Malott Hall. Joe Kelly, Jeff Dowd, a new SDS member named Hugh Cregg,[3] and a few others were charging around a corner and heading for the front doors. According to Joe, while walking from the Straight, Jeff was handed a key to Malott Hall by a sympathetic student who worked there, and he and the others gained entrance to the building via a locked service door. Once they were "behind enemy lines," Jeff, Joe, and the others rushed to the front doors, unlocked them from the inside, and pushed them open. The cops didn't even try to keep us out after that, as dozens of demonstrators ran through the open doors on their way to the suite where the recruiting sessions were being held.

Within a few minutes Vice President Barlow canceled the recruiting and agreed not to return the next day. Barlow later stated that he made this decision "under duress"—that is, the presence of demonstrators demanding that recruitment be stopped and unwilling to obey Proctor George's order that we leave the premises.

Most of us were elated that we were able to stop the Chase Manhattan recruiting without having to push aside campus cops or break any windows

come, in light of the South African Symposium incident." Evidently, it was the Cornell administration that decided to proceed with the recruitment as scheduled.

3. Hugh Cregg later became known as the rock and blues singer Huey Lewis, whose band Huey Lewis and the News scored two number-one albums and eleven Top 10 singles in the '80s.

or glass doors—thanks to that key![4] Later on, however, we learned that a campus police detective suffered a cut on his hand during the action, though reports differed as to how he was injured. (The *Sun* reported that the detective was cut when he tried to put his hand over the door lock while SDSers were opening it, while Donald Downs's *Cornell '69* quoted him as saying he received a cut from broken glass inside the building.)

I was troubled to hear later than some SDS members, including Dave Burak, had demanded that a news photographer from the *Sun* turn over his film so that it could not be used by the administration or local police to identify and prosecute us. The photographer refused and was able to leave Malott Hall with his film. But this demand, which had not been discussed or approved by Cornell SDS, painted SDS in the minds of some observers as being hostile to a free press. In the past, our actions—even illegal ones such as our draft resistance activities—had been done with a "we have nothing to hide" attitude. That stance served us well in the battle for public opinion, and a rejection of it marked a departure, one that was in line with the declining support in the movement for civil disobedience.

I now view our repudiation of tactical nonviolence as one of my, and the New Left's, biggest mistakes. Our evolution on this question may be understandable, but by our willingness to engage in actions that could have violent consequences we again ceded the moral high ground that our struggle against apartheid had achieved. We made it far too easy for our detractors to turn the issue from Cornell complicity with South Africa to SDS and the AAS's rejection of widely accepted standards of political behavior. That little real violence occurred at either Statler Auditorium or Malott Hall was obscured by the outrage of some over our tactics.

How to "Handle the Rebels"

To some members of the Cornell administration and the university faculty, these incidents, along with the provocative actions of AAS members the previous December, constituted a breakdown of law and order at Cornell. No doubt they were watching the demonstrations and confrontations that were currently taking place on campuses throughout the United States, from Harvard and Columbia in the East to San Francisco State and the University of California–Berkeley on the West Coast, where city police were coming onto campuses and arresting students who had seized buildings.

---

4. The *Sun* mistakenly reported that I was one of the demonstrators who used the key to gain access to the building and open the doors from the inside. In fact, I was outside Malott Hall at the time.

What those who opposed us failed to understand was that Cornell SDS was acting with considerable restraint and self-control. After a year of meetings with the administration, submitting petitions, conducting peaceful marches, amassing support from our community, sitting through a symposium on apartheid, and facing an inflexible board of trustees and President Perkins, what did the university expect us to do about its invitation for Chase Manhattan recruiters to come onto the campus?

Two days after the Malott Hall action, the faculty held one of the largest meetings in its history, with over six hundred professors attending. Referring to the Chase Manhattan demonstration, university provost Dale Corson told the assembled faculty members, "I believe this is only the second time that a regularly scheduled Cornell University event has ever been completely disrupted and canceled." To Corson and those who supported his position, it was the challenge by SDS and AAS to Cornell operating as an "open" university that started this crisis—not the right or wrong of Cornell opening itself to recruiters for corporations that supported a brutally racist regime.

Using dramatic language, Corson urged the faculty to find new ways of responding to "the increasing frequency and intensity of demands, coupled with disruption and threats of disruption, specific acts of confrontation and harassment and the increasing frequency and intensity of attacks on the President, both with respect to his person and with respect to his position as the symbol of Cornell University." Here, Corson lumped together and failed to distinguish between the regrettable incident where Gary Patton grabbed Perkins and stopped him from speaking, on the one hand, with, on the other, our criticisms of Perkins's retaining a seat on the board of directors of Chase Manhattan, our demands for Cornell to take some responsibility in remedying the housing crisis the university had helped create, and the AAS's drive for the creation of a black studies center.

The administration and its faculty supporters also pushed for the faculty to endorse the oft-criticized Cornell judicial system, which had been under attack from both the AAS and SDS. The six black students who had been charged with violating university rules during their December actions had thus far refused to appear before any campus judicial body and were facing possible suspension. The AAS argued that the six were being unfairly singled out for punishment from the entire AAS membership and that they could not find a jury of their peers in such judicial proceedings, as no African American students were on the student-faculty judiciary board. They also repeated arguments SDS had been making for several years, that a judiciary formed to deal with petty campus crimes could not handle the kinds of political issues and cases raised by student protesters, and that when Cornell policies were the source of students' discontent and the target of our actions, it was wrong for Cornell to act as both judge and jury when trying to discipline students.

Indeed, in the Cornell SDS meeting held on the eve of the Chase Manhattan demonstration, our chapter had unanimously passed a resolution calling for the establishment of a student-faculty committee "to define the nature and limits of due process in the light of rapidly changing events on this and other campuses." Our resolution attacked the Student-Faculty Board on Student Conduct as "an anachronism which, originally designed to discipline frivolous, wayward students, becomes an instrument of political repression and disruption when set against today's deep-seated needs for social change."

The faculty meeting was long and contentious, as there were many professors who both supported the activists and shared our criticisms of the campus judiciary system. One of them, James Matlack, later described the mood of the faculty as "hard line, with law and order overtones" and the resolutions as "unyielding, stubborn and tough."

Eventually, however, the administration's position prevailed, and the resolution passed by a vote of 306–229. Given the much more dangerous crisis that engulfed Cornell a little more than a month later, the resolution's affirmation of the existing judiciary system—and its citations against six AAS members—proved to be both shortsighted and politically tone deaf. By failing to heed the warnings of Doug Dowd that "now was hardly the time to demand mechanistic implementation of the existing disciplinary machinery," the faculty vote played a key role in poisoning the already difficult relations between the AAS and the administration and faculty.

Privately, Perkins hoped that the newly involved faculty would buttress his administration's efforts to "handle the rebels." In a reply to a friendly letter from a Cornell faculty member, Perkins wrote that the faculty resolution and a petition then being circulated by "moderate" students calling for the restoration of "a rational and non-violent atmosphere at Cornell" represented the awakening of a "silent, middle majority of students and faculty" to oppose and isolate SDS and the AAS. Perkins also wrote that he shared his supporter's belief that arresting or expelling the "students who are making all the trouble" would backfire by generating much larger support for "the troublemakers."

Writing privately to Perkins about a month after the Malott Hall action, Vice President Barlow argued that while SDS's methods of protest were "unacceptable to an academic community," the "malaise and restlessness among students" were "real" and were felt among many students who did not participate in our actions. "There never has been a protest at Cornell," Barlow wrote, "in which the students were 'all wrong.' Frequently, their issue is more right than wrong; it is only their style that is often more wrong than right."

Barlow appeared to understand that many students on campus agreed with SDS on the issues in which we were engaged. It was commonplace for those who opposed us to claim that we only represented a small percentage of the student body; usually, these opponents waited wistfully for a "silent majority" of students to emerge. They failed to comprehend that Cornell SDS's membership of between three hundred and four hundred made us the largest political organization on campus, and that many more students, faculty members, and staffers at Cornell shared our view that fighting for justice was more important than obeying certain campus rules.

Another problem facing the administration was its failure to figure out how to handle those of us who were no longer matriculated at Cornell but were part of Cornell SDS. Although I had held no formal connection to the university since January 1967, I viewed myself as part of the Cornell community. This wasn't just my own self-serving perspective. My presence as a community member had been frequently acknowledged and affirmed by professors who supported Cornell's draft resisters, by *Sun* editorials, and by President Perkins himself.

In a hostile yet sometimes perceptive editorial in the *Cornell Alumni News* that ran shortly after the Statler and Malott events, editor John Marcham (a former member of the administration) tried to explain the impact of nonstudents on political disturbances at Cornell. "Young men who have left universities and do not appear to plan to return are tough customers to deal with," he wrote, citing our lack of fear of university reprisals or punishment. Although his editorial was quite critical of SDS, calling us a "mob" (among other things), he also praised SDS's effectiveness, skilled leadership, and "flexibility." Marcham noted that many of the Cornell SDS leaders had resisted the draft and were facing prison. "Their willingness to sacrifice for this stand has made them heroes to many on campus," Marcham wrote.

Marcham astutely saw one strategic advantage SDS obtained from its nonstudent members—our political experience and involvement in past struggles at Cornell enabled us to anticipate and react to administration strategies, such as its delaying tactics. But by attributing SDS members' lack of fear of university reprisals to the presence of nonstudents, Marcham missed the point that at least since 1965, student demonstrators at Cornell had been unafraid of campus disciplinary bodies. From the first anti-ROTC sit-in in the spring of 1965 (which took place before I arrived at Cornell) through our draft card burning solicitations in March 1967 through the Chase Manhattan action of March 1969, activist students had determined that fighting against the war in Vietnam, the draft, and complicity with apartheid trumped submission to campus rules and regulations. Like young people in revolt throughout America, we had learned a lot from the early '60s civil rights demonstrators in the South who refused to be intimidated by jailings and repression. The willingness of radical students to struggle and take risks on behalf of important causes was something those who opposed us never understood.

Ignoring Whites, Prosecuting Blacks

Given that the university's posture toward nonstudents had been, in Mark Barlow's words, "vague," both the university counsel and a special faculty committee formed to investigate the Malott Hall confrontation recommended to Perkins and the Faculty Council that no civil actions should be taken against either nonstudent or student demonstrators. In the future, however, "very serious breaches of the law" (again, per Barlow) would be brought to civil, or off-campus, authorities for prosecution.

The problem with this policy was that it appeared to the AAS a clear example of a racial double standard. A half dozen AAS members were still under the threat of suspension for failing to appear before the university's student-faculty conduct board for their December actions, while the predominantly white demonstrators against Chase Manhattan were not being similarly charged.

The crisis over punishment for the AAS members was temporarily averted in mid-March. The cited AAS members refused to attend the next conduct board meeting, their place taken by 150 AAS members instead. This led the conduct board to postpone action on the matter, pending a decision by the more powerful Faculty Committee on Student Affairs (FCSA).

But racial antagonisms at Cornell heightened after three white students were assaulted on campus in separate incidents, and two of the victims identified their assailants as being black. The *Sun* exacerbated the situation by publishing an editorial entitled "Blacks on Trial," which demanded that the AAS "immediately disavow" the attacks "that were believed to have been launched by blacks"—even though there was no evidence that the assailants had anything to do with the Afro-American Society or even Cornell. This was met with a stinging rebuke by the AAS and others for irresponsibly linking the attacks to the AAS and for fanning the flames of racial hysteria. In response, a second *Sun* editorial claimed that the original editorial had been misunderstood.

As we reached the end of March and the beginning of a weeklong spring break, the administration and the JHC remained far apart, but both sides professed some optimism. President Perkins also announced that the university was getting close to making a final, positive decision about a black studies center and the hiring of its first director. Both the housing and black studies issues would be coming before the university's board of trustees in April.

We in SDS contributed to the easing of tensions by deciding not to confront U.S. Marine recruiters who were slated to set up shop in Barton Hall. A new antiwar group in Ithaca, the Tompkins County Peace Association, was already planning a peaceful picket at the recruitment site. In a tense SDS meeting, Doug Dowd, among others, urged us to refrain from trying to take over the protest or attempting to stop the recruitment. Doug made the point that one of SDS's goals had long been to push liberals to become more active in opposition to the war, and the new Peace Association was an example of this happening. Some of our members thought we would be walking into a trap if, so soon after the Malott Hall action, we broke the law in any way, while others felt we needed to emphasize our housing campaign above everything else. Nevertheless, some members of the action faction pushed for SDS to take a more militant approach. Their position, which I opposed, was defeated by a solid majority vote.

The Barton Hall picket went ahead as planned, with SDS members taking part and no problems occurring. But the disagreement over tactics and strategy within our chapter that was revealed by the vote—with the action faction being outvoted by the Labor Committee faction and a majority of those of us in the middle—indicated a growing instability inside Cornell SDS. My main concern at the time was to ensure that whatever our chapter decided, it would be by a fair and democratic vote by the members.

Just before spring break began, the FCSA produced a report that reaffirmed the authority of the university's student conduct board—virtually guaranteeing more problems in the not too distant future. While the statement noted that the political nature of violations of the university code of conduct would be considered in any decision, it supported the principle that any individual or group that defied university regulations would be subject to punishment. The FCSA report also failed to explain or defend the justice of the university acting as judge and jury in a political case in which university policies were the target of demonstrations and disruptions.

Most seriously, at a time when more sensible and sensitive members of the administration and faculty were urging the FCSA to seek a compromise with the black students, the FCSA decided not to drop the charges. This occurred despite the FCSA being divided 6–6 over the AAS case. According to Donald Downs, "The six [members of the FCSA] who voted to not drop the charges voiced stronger convictions, and so the committee decided not to drop the charges."

National SDS and the New Vanguard

The next SDS National Council meeting was scheduled over the spring break, in Austin, Texas. I had no desire to go. Although I had taken part in a regional

SDS meeting in Albany, New York, a few months earlier, by now I was pretty much disgusted with what was happening within SDS on a national level.

The results of the Austin meeting were even worse than I had anticipated. Although PL was defeated on every issue by the National Office faction and its supporters, the passage of a new resolution on building a revolutionary youth movement called for SDS to abandon college campuses in favor of organizing a "working class youth movement." The resolution identified the black liberation struggle, particularly the Black Panther Party, as the "vanguard" of the revolutionary movement in this country. It also explicitly broke with the heritage of the New Left by referring to pacifism as "reactionary"—thus dismissing the legacy of the civil rights and draft resistance movements' use of creative nonviolence—and endorsed "the need for armed struggle as the only road to revolution."

There was another reason why I was happy I didn't join my fellow Cornell SDS members in driving to Texas for the National Council meeting. Following the meeting, Chip Marshall, Joe Kelly, Jeff Dowd, and a few others decided to visit Padre Island on the Gulf Coast of southern Texas. Finding a deserted section of remote beach, they went skinny dipping in the Gulf. Unfortunately, some onlooker tipped off the authorities about all these shaggy-haired folks swimming without clothes, and they were busted by local police. They ended up spending three harrowing nights in a Brownsville, Texas, jail before getting bailed out (by Doug Dowd) and returning to Ithaca.

The one unintentionally amusing thing to come out of the Texas bust for nude swimming was contained in an FBI report on the arrests. It may be recalled that the FBI's COINTELPRO campaign against the New Left, which began in May 1968, included plans to "expose, disrupt and otherwise neutralize" New Left groups and leaders. In a letter from the Albany FBI to J. Edgar Hoover, the agent in charge recounted the arrests of the Cornell SDSers in Texas but complained, "It was hoped that the dissemination of this arrest could possible [sic] result in the embarrassment of not only the subjects involved but also SDS itself. However, local newspapers all carried accounts of these arrests with no apparent consternation on the part of those involved."

"Manchild in the Corporate State"

I stayed in Ithaca to complete work on Cornell SDS's long-awaited investigative report on the corporate affiliations of the Cornell board of trustees and the Cornell administration, and the impact of those ties on university policy. Titled *Manchild in the Corporate State: Cornell's Ruling Elite and the National Economy,* our thirty-six-page report combined both hard data on the individuals involved and an analysis and indictment of what President Perkins had called "the public service university" in contemporary American society.[5]

Our report included sections such as "Cornell's Foreign Policy Establishment," "The Cornell Defense Nexus," "Cornell and Apartheid," "Cornell and Domestic Social Control," and "The Cornell Aeronautical Laboratory: A Case Study of Military Research and Corporate Enterprise at Cornell," and included a pull-out chart showing all the interlocking directorates among members of the board of trustees. We linked the corporations tied to Cornell with a critique of the social and economic harm such corporations, allied with the U.S. government, were responsible for both domestically and internationally.

Our goal in doing all this research was to show the many ways in which the people who ran Cornell and the financial holdings of the university were contributing to war, racism, and poverty, as well as the repression, domestically and internationally, of those who opposed them. We openly stated our hope that our publication would be another step in developing an analysis of "the system which oppresses us all."

Climax to the Housing Issue

As negotiations continued between the Joint Housing Committee and representatives of the board of trustees, the JHC further reduced its demands. Cornell was now being asked to sell, rather than donate, three hundred acres of university-owned land to Tompco Better Housing for the construction of low- and middle-income housing. There were indications the trustees might actually approve our proposals at their next meeting on April 10, as one trustee told the *Sun* the JHC proposals were "very thoughtful and well worked out."

Still, we felt it necessary to keep the pressure on the trustees and the administration. With only about six or seven weeks to go before the end of the semester, we were concerned about the administration running out the clock again, as they had done the previous year over our South Africa demands. Given that experience, SDS demanded that the trustees make a decision at their next meeting, scheduled to take place in New York City.

To indicate we were prepared to take action to back up the demands, SDS staged a torchlight parade on the eve of the trustee meeting in which nearly five hundred demonstrators marched around campus. We had originally

5. Our title (and I wish we had chosen a more gender-neutral term) was taken from Claude Brown's autobiographical novel, *Manchild in the Promised Land.*

planned to take our march to President Perkins's home in the affluent neighborhood of Cayuga Heights in order to present him with a petition signed by
supporters of the JHC demands. But we changed plans after being requested
to do so by a very nervous administration, which was guarding Perkins's
house with campus cops and New York State Police, and by the JHC negotiators, who feared that such an action could get out of control.

As we marched through the campus we remained peaceful at all times,
despite some provocations from small groups of hostile students who heckled us and set off firecrackers. We stopped occasionally outside dorms and
dining places to make brief speeches in support of the housing program.
Standing in front of a women's dormitory, I joked that Perkins's home
was "a lot nicer" than other Ithaca housing and called the JHC proposals
"a small price to pay for the hunger and misery that Cornell has caused" by
its policies.

An SDS steering committee meeting showed that our chapter was ready
to move in a more militant direction, if necessary, as a broad consensus had
emerged that viewed a rejection of the JHC proposals as grounds for taking some form of direct action. I shared that perspective, and was chosen to
chair what promised to be one of our most significant membership meetings ever.

The news about the trustees' decision quickly got back to the campus following the weekend meeting in New York City. Although the trustees issued a
statement saying they were "deeply impressed with the sincerity and interest"
shown by those of us working on the housing issue, they were unwilling to
do much more than sell fifty acres of Cornell-owned land for the development of low-income housing, establish for one year only a fund of $2 million
for investment in FHA-guaranteed mortgages to support home ownership by
low- and middle-income families, and conduct "feasibility studies" on a few
other projects.

The JHC's response indicated deep disappointment with the trustees'
counteroffers, calling them "far short of being acceptable in either the magnitude or the kind of commitment being made." Other objections concerned
the short-term nature of the trustees' offer (a fund available for only one year,
as opposed to the JHC's proposal of a five-year commitment), the university's failure to commit itself to housing 75 percent of Cornell's students or
allowing low-income people to make important planning decisions about the
housing they would live in.

When nearly four hundred SDS members gathered in a campus lecture
hall to decide on our response, there was considerable enthusiasm for immediately attempting to seize Day Hall. Some action faction members had been
gathering chains and locks to be used in a building takeover.

On the way to the meeting, I even received a surprise gift from Doug Dowd. A supporter of ours who worked inside the administration building had given Doug an envelope holding a key to Day Hall, and he passed it along to me.

But less than five minutes before the start of the SDS meeting, the JHC's lead negotiator, Gary Esolen, a Cornell graduate student, along with Jack Goldman of the Office and the JHC, came running up to me. "You've got to call off the building takeover," they said, because the trustees had changed their position.

In a memo to Esolen from board of trustees chairman Robert Purcell, the trustees "clarified" their position. Although they did not increase the amount of land they were willing to sell beyond fifty acres, the trustees promised to sell the land for $1,000 per acre or less. They also agreed to assist Tompco Better Housing in securing additional funding and FHA approval for the housing construction, accepted the "need" for Cornell to provide a reserve fund for mortgages, agreed that the program should continue beyond one year, and formally recognized Cornell's "need to house more of its students."

Although the trustees' "clarification" was not the acceptance of the JHC proposals we had hoped for, it was an advance for the JHC. A majority of the chapter accepted Gary and Jack's pleas that we cancel our plans to take over the administration building. Politically, there was no way for SDS to go ahead with our planned action when the JHC negotiators were claiming victory and asking us to stand down.

Still, some of the leaders of the action faction were seething after the SDS meeting. Their enthusiasm for our housing program kept diminishing in concert with the increasing moderation of the JHC's proposals. By now, their support for the entire campaign was based primarily on their expectation that it would lead to a major confrontation on campus. With that potential action now thwarted, the target of their anger shifted to the Labor Committee members—even though the Labor Committee SDSers had been as committed to taking militant action over housing as they were. These tensions within SDS remained through the rest of the tumultuous semester.

The JHC housing proposal had not been the only concern of the trustees' meeting. They had also formally voted to establish a black studies center at Cornell.

With crises over housing and black studies at least temporarily avoided, I decided this was the best time for me to leave Ithaca for a short visit with my parents. My attorney had alerted me that a Supreme Court decision on whether to hear my case was imminent. Should the court refuse to hear the case, as we expected, I would have to begin my prison sentence very soon. This might be my last chance to see my folks before starting my prison term.

I was in my parent's apartment in the Bronx when, on Saturday morning, April 19—Parents Weekend at Cornell—I learned that black students had seized the Straight and kicked out the parents who were staying in its hotel-like rooms.

Chapter Thirteen

Brinksmanship, or Cornell on the Brink

I had never seen the Cornell campus as tense as it was when I returned to Ithaca in the early afternoon of Sunday, April 20. About one hundred Afro-American Society members were occupying the Straight. SDS had organized a picket line outside the building to support and defend the black students inside. Campus cops, Cornell administrators, and curious students, faculty, and staff members were milling around, nervously watching and waiting to see what would happen next.

When I arrived at the Straight, my friends in SDS quickly filled me in on what had happened while I was away. On Thursday evening, April 17, the conduct board had gone ahead with its disciplinary hearing. The AAS defendants had refused to appear, but a group representing the defendants showed up to ask the board to take no action. When the board refused and decided to try the students in absentia, a larger group of about 150 AAS members arrived to protest. Shortly after midnight Friday morning, the board voted 4–1 to issue reprimands to three of the AAS members charged with harassment for their December actions; two of the students were given no penalties. (A sixth defendant, Gary Patton, had left Cornell and Ithaca by this time.)

In the early morning hours of Friday, April 18, eleven fire alarms were set off in campus dormitories; all turned out to be false alarms. But shortly before 3 a.m., a brick was thrown through the front window of Wari House, the on-campus residence for black women, and a cross was set afire on its doorstep. According to police reports on the incident, the women residents were "terrified."

The cross-burning outraged the Cornell community, as such actions had historically symbolized KKK terror against black people. The incident, which received national publicity, brought considerable sympathy to the black students. The failure of campus security forces to guard Wari House after the incident—the cops left the dormitory unguarded for a while to investigate the fire alarms—also contributed to a belief among the AAS that to protect their own people, especially women, they would have to take action.

(In his book *Cornell '69,* published in 1999, Donald Downs strongly suggests the cross-burning was staged by blacks, not by white racists. He quotes Cornell provost [and future Cornell president] Dale Corson as saying "I am 99.9 percent sure" that black people were responsible. Downs also cites one AAS member and several sympathizers admitting, twenty years later, that this was the case—though none of them were involved. On the other hand, there is no evidence that the residents of Wari House, or most members of the AAS, knew anything about this. To them, and to Cornell at large, the incident appeared to be a racist act of terror. The incident became one of the AAS's justifications for the action they were about to take. No one was ever charged with setting the cross on fire or throwing the brick through the window of Wari House.)

Leaders of the AAS and SDS had met earlier in the week to discuss possible actions and mutual support, and representatives of the two groups met again during the day on Friday. SDS called an emergency meeting for the unlikely time of 7 o'clock Saturday morning.

Seizure of the Straight

Shortly after 5:30 a.m. on Saturday, April 19, about one hundred AAS members quietly entered the Straight, awakened all the guests staying there for Parents Weekend, and told all the employees and visitors they had to leave the premises. Although accounts differ as to the treatment of the employees and guests by the AAS, no one was hurt during the takeover, which was conducted with minimal force.

Shortly thereafter, SDS members gathered in Anabel Taylor Hall, the CURW building near the Straight, and then set up a picket line outside the student union. SDS handed out leaflets supporting the AAS members inside and communicating the black students' demands for a revocation of the reprimands and amnesty for the Straight takeover.

By occupying the student union, the AAS undoubtedly surprised the Cornell administration. From the perspective of both the administration and campus radicals, Day Hall, the administration building, was always viewed as the most likely target for a building takeover. Day Hall represented the seat of power at Cornell. The Straight, on the other hand, was the focal point of student activities at Cornell and more relevant to the daily lives of students than almost any other building on campus. It was centrally located. It housed several dining facilities, game rooms, the university theater, a TV room, study rooms, meeting rooms, guest rooms, a library, the campus radio station WVBR-FM, and a hall for lectures and indoor rallies. The building's lobby was the place where SDS and other campus organizations set up information tables, and the front entrance was the site of many political rallies and the starting point for marches.

The Straight was also a massive edifice with many windows, built on a steep slope, with entrances on several levels. As such, it was difficult to defend, even by as many as five hundred SDS members and supporters gathered outside, along with campus cops.

In what proved to be a galvanizing and critical development, mid-morning on Saturday a group of twenty-five white fraternity men from Delta Upsilon (known as a "jock house") broke into the Straight from an unguarded side window. Accounts differ as to whether the DU attack was a vigilante action to forcefully retake the Straight or, as some DU members later claimed, simply an attempt to "discuss" the takeover with the black students.[1] (It became known later that other groups of fraternity men were also discussing a retaliative seizure of the AAS headquarters on campus, but the administration was able to talk them out of it.)

The DU members who managed to get inside the building were met by the AAS inside and SDSers outside and physically thrown out. Three of the DU guys received minor injuries, as did one AAS member. According to SDS's Chip Marshall, as the DU brothers retreated they promised to return with a much larger group of fraternity men.

It was particularly upsetting to the AAS that the campus cops, though limited in number, did nothing to prevent the frat boys from breaking into the Straight. To the more suspicious or conspiratorial occupiers, the fraternity action and the lack of an effective police response to it made it appear as if both had occurred with the administration's tacit support. This was not the case, however.

As the administration was attempting to negotiate an end of the Straight seizure with the AAS, rumors started circulating on campus, most of which were relayed to the occupiers, that fraternities were organizing a counterattack; that 250 armed white vigilantes were gathering to take back the Straight; that whites were planning to seize Wari House; that police and sheriff's

---

1. In its coverage of the Straight takeover and the DU effort to gain entrance to the building, the *Ithaca Journal* reported that some of the fraternity members said they entered the building hoping to throw open the doors and end the occupation.

deputies from the surrounding area, joined by National Guard troops, were massing in Ithaca to forcefully remove the black students. There were bomb threats all over the campus.

Later that day, the AAS began to arm itself, with members and supporters bringing in rifles, shotguns, and ammunition through a back window of the Straight. When word got out to the administration about the presence of arms in the Straight, the AAS assured them they would only be used in self-defense. The black students said they had neither the plan nor the desire to hurt anyone.

The AAS had first started accumulating weapons a year earlier, when their initial demands for a black studies program resulted in threatening phone calls. Similar anonymous threats continued throughout the year, and were even received inside the Straight during the occupation. Given the influence within the black movement of the late Malcolm X, the popularity of Robert Williams's book *Negroes with Guns,* and the ascendance of the Black Panther Party—all of whom emphasized the black community's right to defend itself—the decision by the AAS to obtain arms shouldn't have been a complete surprise. Still, the presence of guns inside the Straight was not yet widely known on campus.[2]

Saturday evening, SDS and the Inter-Fraternity Council (whose leaders tended to be more liberal than rank-and-file fraternity brothers) cosponsored a teach-in on racism in the university, attended by three thousand students and professors. Most of the speakers denounced Cornell's judicial system and the penalties imposed on the AAS members. The teach-in succeeded in building support for the black students by a substantial portion of the white student body.

Following the teach-in, over five hundred SDS members and supporters camped out in Anabel Taylor Hall in order to prevent further attempts by whites to retake the Straight. As it happened, the SDSers stayed in a large room next door to where the administration had set up a "rumor clinic" to amass information and dispel misinformation. SDS used this access to share information with the AAS in the Straight and to leaflet the campus about what was happening and caution against spreading unsubstantiated rumors.

I was proud of my brothers and sisters in SDS for physically placing themselves between the black students in the Straight and any parties attempting to forcibly eject them. This was a decision made by the entire chapter, not just those in the action faction.

---

2. Based on an interview with a Cornell SDS member who was directly involved but did not want his name used, Downs reported that several SDS leaders helped purchase guns for the AAS. Although I was not one of those involved, I believe this account is accurate.

By Sunday, the administration's main goals were to get the black students out of the Straight and to avoid violence. Although the threat of fraternity vigilantism had apparently subsided, the possibility that the mayor of Ithaca or other outside authorities could order a police action remained real. Provost Corson later said that during the occupation of the Straight there was "a big group of deputy sheriffs, one hundred, two hundred, downtown, itching to [cause harm]."

Consequently, the administration rejected the idea of calling in local authorities, the State Police, or the National Guard to remove the black students. They also decided against seeking a court injunction against the AAS, because the probable rejection of such an injunction by the AAS would have resulted in the use of the police or military to enforce it. As Vice President Steven Muller, one of the administration's negotiators with the AAS, later told a group of alumni, "Before you judge us, picture a nice big headline on Monday morning—SIX KILLED, 30 INJURED IN GUN BATTLE AT CORNELL."

Guns and Photographs

When I arrived at the front of the Straight I learned that a deal to end the occupation had been worked out between AAS and administration negotiators, and that the black students would soon be leaving the building. (The main provisions of the deal were amnesty for the students involved in the takeover and an administration promise to seek the "nullification" of the reprimands against the three AAS members.)

By this time many of us in SDS knew the AAS had armed itself during the past thirty-six hours. But we did not know the AAS was determined to leave the Straight carrying those arms, despite the efforts of the administration to avoid this.

Shortly after 4 p.m., about eighty AAS members, accompanied by some administrators, slowly walked out of the Straight. Raising their fists in black power salutes, the men in the group carried seventeen rifles and shotguns, a few handguns, and an assortment of clubs and homemade spears as they formed a protective perimeter around the women in their group. One of the AAS leaders, Eric Evans, wore a bandolier across his chest. A photographer from the Associated Press, Steven Starr, captured the dramatic scene in an image that appeared in newspapers and magazines around the country, including on the cover of *Newsweek* magazine, and later won a Pulitzer Prize.

An audible gasp could be heard from those standing on or near the Straight's front steps when the students first appeared with their guns. It was a stunning moment, as it graphically illustrated the precariousness of the situation and the ongoing potential for violence. At this point, of course, no one knew how widely Starr's photo and other images from the Straight take-over would be circulated.

But shock quickly gave way to cheers and shouts of support for the black students as they emerged from the Straight. I, too, was cheering, out of a sense of solidarity. Yet I was also taken aback by the spectacle. Despite my support for the AAS and my understanding of why the black students had armed themselves in self-defense, I could not help also feeling that their ac-tion was excessive. I believed that the university's disciplinary system was unfair and untenable, and that the continued prosecution of a small group of AAS members was shortsighted and politically obtuse. But the introduction of arms into the controversy seemed like a disproportionate response. Then again, I doubt AAS members would have resorted to arming themselves had the frat guys from Delta Upsilon not already attempted to violently retake the Straight or had the AAS not genuinely feared a response from well-armed vigilantes or police forces.

I did not follow the procession of AAS members, administrators, campus police, and onlookers as they walked through the campus to the AAS's head-quarters on Wait Avenue, where a final agreement to end the takeover was signed. Despite the physical exhaustion of many members of SDS who had remained on the picket line or in the CURW building throughout the thirty-six-hour siege, SDS held an emergency meeting to discuss what to do next.

We were heartened by the presence of AAS members at our meeting. One of the AAS leaders thanked SDS for our support during the Straight takeover: "In the beginning stages of the occupation, we felt very much alone in our cause," he said. "SDS not only gained for us campus-wide sympathy, but also helped to make known our grievances."

SDS decided to try to expand campus support for the black students and encourage the faculty to accept the deal worked out by the AAS and the ad-ministration. We planned a rally on Monday in front of the Straight, to be followed by a march to Bailey Hall, where the faculty would be meeting to approve or reject the agreement that ended the occupation.

Provocations from Faculty and Administration

The exhilaration we felt Sunday night quickly gave way on Monday morning to new challenges. With the *New York Times* (widely read at Cornell) running Starr's photograph on its front page along with the headline "Armed Negroes End Seizure; Cornell Yields," and reporter John Kifner referring to the agree-ment that ended the occupation as a "capitulation," it wasn't hard to predict there would be a counterreaction.

One of the problems with the massive news coverage of the event was that much of the reporting implied that the black students had armed themselves for their initial seizure of the Straight. For instance, Kifner's front page story in the *Times* never mentioned the attempt by Delta Upsilon fraternity men to forcibly retake the Straight, even though that was the action that precipitated the AAS's decision to bring in arms for self-defense. Nor did the *Times* story mention any of the other threats against the black students during their occupation of the Straight.

As a result, to some on campus it appeared as if the AAS was employing guns to coerce the administration and faculty to expunge the reprimands of the three AAS members. Lost in the coverage was the real reason why the black students armed themselves—self-defense.

Doug Dowd confirmed what had been reported in the morning's *Sun:* A large number of faculty members, probably a majority, were considering rejection of the agreement that would have nullified the disciplinary action. Unofficial faculty groups were forming to oppose or support the administration's handling of the crisis. The opposition was centered among well-known members of the Government and History Departments, such as Walter Berns, Alan Sindler, Donald Kagan, Walter LaFeber, Clinton Rossiter, and Allan Bloom. The supporters of the AAS and SDS, who came to be known as the Concerned Faculty, included, along with Doug Dowd, English professors James Matlack and Doug Archibald, Eldon Kenworthy from Government, and David Lyons from Philosophy.

President Perkins, undoubtedly feeling the heat from those who believed he and his administration had lost control of the campus, declared "a situation of emergency" at Cornell. It wasn't quite a declaration of martial law—although we in SDS did call it that in a leaflet—but it (1) prohibited any student from possessing a firearm "outside of their own rooms" and (2) banned any building takeovers or "disruptive demonstrations" on campus. Anyone disobeying these orders would be immediately suspended or, in the case of nonstudents, arrested. Any organization taking part in such activities would be disbanded. Perkins also ordered the campus cops to arm themselves.

Perkins also announced that a convocation would be held for the entire university community. With classes canceled, around ten thousand students and faculty members came to Barton Hall to hear what Perkins had to say about the Straight takeover and the agreement that ended it. Yet in his surprisingly unfocused and rambling speech, Perkins barely alluded to the recent events. Instead, he called for everyone to act like "humane men and women." Most people who attended, no matter what side they were on concerning the crisis, left disappointed and puzzled.

The hotly anticipated meeting of the Cornell faculty Monday afternoon produced the biggest turnout of professors in the history of the university, with over one thousand attending. After more than three hours of debate, the faculty voted 540–360 (with many abstentions) on a multipart resolution. Although administration and faculty supporters of the resolution later maintained it was intended to express empathy with the black students at Cornell while at the same time condemning their seizure of the Straight and their use of "coercion" to get the reprimands nullified, it didn't come across that way to those of us in SDS, AAS, or even in the wider student body.

"The Faculty expresses its sympathy for the problems of the black students in adjusting themselves to life at Cornell," the resolution began. Even though a later point condemned the cross-burning at Wari House, such a patronizing statement made it seem as if all the problems had been caused by the inability of the black students to adapt to their harmonious surroundings. The resolution's failure to recognize the existence of white racism and discrimination at Cornell and in Ithaca made many students feel that the faculty was simply—or willfully—out of touch and intransigent.

The hard-line, retaliative tone of other parts of the resolution—"The Faculty condemns the seizure of Willard Straight Hall"; "the Faculty condemns the carrying and use of weapons"; "the faculty supports, in principle, the President's action taken today to preserve law and order on campus"—similarly revealed that the faculty was stubbornly refusing to understand the issues involved. The matter of the students arming themselves for the purpose of self-defense was simply ignored.

Finally, the resolution's offer to "review the issues behind the Afro-American complaints" only under "secure and non-pressurized circumstances" suggested to us that the university was once more attempting to delay or put off dealing with those issues. From our perspective, it was only the use of such "pressurized circumstances"—direct action, or the threat of direct action—that compelled the administration to take seriously *any* student demands for change. It also appeared that the faculty had no problem breaking an agreement the administration had negotiated with the AAS. This was particularly insulting to the black students, who viewed the faculty vote as a betrayal.

The disgust that AAS, SDS, and others felt toward the faculty's vote was apparent when SDS began a mass meeting in Bailey Hall immediately after the faculty concluded its meeting. A crowd of twenty-five hundred students turned out, including a substantial group of AAS members. When Doug Dowd recounted what had just been voted upon by the faculty, boos engulfed the large lecture hall.[3]

---

3. The negative reaction to the faculty resolution was also shared by some influential members of the faculty and administration, and by the editor of the *Cornell Daily Sun*. Ernie Roberts, a law professor and secretary of the faculty, said later, "I knew of no dignified way of expressing what I felt the

Our meeting was filled with incendiary speeches, cheering for the AAS representatives, and raised fists. Skip Meade of the AAS declared that "we achieved a great revolutionary victory here. For the first time, students and blacks have not been dragged out of a building. They have come out walking and carrying guns." Father David Connor defended the black students' arming themselves for self-defense, recounting the many incidents of racial harassment, threatening phone calls, and verbal abuse they had suffered at Cornell even before the Straight takeover. Chip Marshall challenged President Perkins over his threat to suspend any student involved in a building takeover. My own participation included a condemnation of the faculty action as proving "they have no intention of solving this problem in any way that is just."

It was clear that both SDS and the AAS were ready to take further action if necessary, despite Perkins's "situation of emergency." In this day of resolutions, we passed our own, by an overwhelming vote, to support the demands of the AAS and to criticize "the failure of the administration and faculty to deal seriously with these demands." In addition, we gave the faculty "a vote of no confidence."

But we put off a final decision, as did the AAS, as to what actions we would take. Given the huge size of our meeting, a thorough discussion of tactics was impossible. So, as we had done earlier, we formed a new "tactical committee" to develop a plan of action for the next day. I was one of those elected to serve on the committee.

Tuesday loomed as a day of decision at Cornell.

The Road to the Barton Hall Takeover

Was a "revolution" about to begin at Cornell University? Two histories of the events at Cornell, both written from perspectives that were critical of the AAS and SDS, as well as of Perkins and his administration, suggest so. In their unpublished manuscript "Open Breeches: Guns at Cornell," George Fisher and Stephen Wallenstein describe "a revolutionary situation" existing at Cornell following Perkins's strange speech at Monday's convocation. Donald Downs, in his book *Cornell '69*, referred to "a potentially revolutionary situation" in which "authority was up for grabs" at Cornell. Downs also described the Tuesday night events at Barton Hall (which we'll get to shortly) as a "revolutionary moment" that was "almost Jacobin in inspiration."

---

faculty was really saying: 'The Cornell faculty has put itself on record as saying it is unwilling to give in to a bunch of armed niggers.'" *Sun* editor-in-chief Ed Zuckerman, who had previously editorialized against the AAS actions, criticized the faculty for "yielding itself up to the gut reactionaries and the insensitive rationalists."

But from my perspective as someone at the core of SDS, we were nowhere near a revolutionary situation or moment—despite Skip Meade's claim that the AAS had won "a great revolutionary victory." Our fight in support of the AAS had limited goals, and those goals were hardly revolutionary. To be sure, there were other issues at Cornell we in SDS were engaged in, such as housing and South Africa divestment, but the struggle in support of the black students was over nullification of the reprimands the AAS members had received and amnesty for the Straight takeover. At most, we were in the midst of a series of protests in which both black and white students were willing to take extralegal steps to achieve small and specific goals. Anything insurrectionary about our actions would have ended once the faculty and administration made some minor (to us) concessions.

The SDS tactical committee, along with representatives from the AAS, met for hours on Tuesday afternoon in Goldwin Smith Hall trying to decide what to do and how to proceed. Just by meeting, we managed to throw the administration into a panic. As it was later reported, key members of the administration somehow concluded that SDS members had already seized Goldwin Smith Hall and were on our way to occupy the administration building. Cornell's top brass, including President Perkins and Provost Corson, even evacuated Day Hall and alerted Ithaca mayor Jack Kiely that the situation on campus had "really deteriorated." Kiely then recalled hundreds of regional deputy sheriffs to Ithaca.

While the tactical committee was meeting, SDS sent members to talk to professors about changing their votes. We also passed out leaflets announcing an SDS meeting that evening in Bailey Hall.

Eventually, we decided on a plan of action. Based on the previous night's meeting, we estimated that a massive outpouring of students, perhaps two or three thousand, would be willing to join us in a major action as a way of pressuring the faculty to reconsider its vote. It was decided that I would chair this mass meeting, which would include representatives of SDS and the AAS making the case for another building takeover, and then marching from Bailey Hall to Day Hall. The plan was for the more militant students to seize Day Hall, while others who wanted to show their support for the black students but didn't want to risk arrest would set up a picket line outside the occupied building.

We knew that some members of the Concerned Faculty group were not only pushing for their colleagues to reverse Monday's faculty vote, but were also willing to either join us in occupying a building or forming a buffer between students and police massing outside the building to remove us. In this way, they hoped to reduce the possibility of violence and bloodshed.

What I didn't know was that while the tactical committee was immersed in a meeting that consumed the entire afternoon, many of the colleges at

Cornell were holding faculty meetings with the purpose of reversing the university faculty's Monday decision. Faculties in the Arts College, as well as in Architecture, Home Economics, and Business and Public Administration, each took that course—whether out of genuine support for the AAS demands or fear that a failure to nullify would lead to violence. However, the entire faculty needed to meet again in order to reverse its position, and for logistical or legal reasons (a requirement for advance notice), that couldn't take place until Wednesday at the earliest.

Our tactical committee concluded its meeting around 6 p.m., giving us little time before the mass meeting was scheduled to begin. By 6:30, the twenty-five-hundred-seat Bailey Hall was already overflowing, so we moved on to the cavernous Barton Hall. Fortunately, the sound equipment that had been set up for President Perkins's convocation on Monday was still operational.

At just this hectic time, the AAS's Tom Jones made some inflammatory remarks during a 6 p.m. interview on Ithaca radio station WHCU-AM. Jones was critical of Perkins's declaration of "martial law," noting that "the only violence that occurred over the weekend was when black students were attacked" by white fraternity members.

Toward the end of the interview, Jones was asked if there were any members of the Cornell administration or faculty the AAS had faith in. After saying that there were some faculty members who had supported the AAS (presumably referring to the Concerned Faculty group), Jones launched into an attack on key members of the administration and faculty: "James Perkins is a racist. [Vice President] Keith Kennedy is a racist. Dale Corson is a racist. Mark Barlow is a racist. And as racists they will be dealt with."

Turning his attention to some of the professors who had opposed the AAS's demands, Jones continued: "Allan Sindler is a racist. [Clinton] Rossiter is a racist. Walter Berns is a racist. And as racists they will be dealt with.... Before this is over James Perkins, Allan Sindler, and Clinton Rossiter are going to die in the gutter like dogs."

Asked by his interviewer if there was anything Cornell could do, Jones replied, "I would suggest that the faculty have an emergency meeting tonight and, if they can do so by nine o'clock, nullify the decision. After nine o'clock it's going to be too late.... Cornell University has three hours to live."[4]

Jones's interview was rebroadcast by the station at 7 p.m. But I never heard either broadcast, because by then, along with thousands of students, I had already walked through the cold night rain from Bailey Hall to Barton Hall.

---

4. Much of the later criticisms of the AAS and SDS were over Jones's apocalyptic tone, his threats of violence, and his and others' use of "racist" and "racism" as a epithet hurled against those who opposed them.

Bruce Dancis chairs the overflow Cornell SDS meeting in Barton
Hall on the evening of April 22, 1969. Later in the evening, the
assemblage voted to "seize" the building. (Richard L. Shulman,
Cornell Daily Sun; all rights reserved)

Later on, I regretted the inflated rhetoric that came from our side, in particular Jones's personal attacks on administrators and professors. I've often
thought how I might have better made the point that calling a person a "racist" was a form of verbal attack that had to be used judiciously, thoughtfully,
and, above all, accurately. We should have better articulated that we were opposing institutionalized racism at Cornell rather than individuals.

SPOTLIGHT: THE SEIZURE OF BARTON HALL, APRIL 22, 1969

"This crowd is a bit larger than our usual SDS meeting."

There were nine thousand people packed into Barton Hall when I
opened the meeting with that little joke. I was trying to cut through
the tension of the moment, but my remark generated only a mild
smattering of laughter.

Although Cornell SDS had already decided, with the AAS's support and encouragement, that we would attempt to move directly from the gathering in Barton Hall to an occupation of Day Hall, we had not spent much time figuring out how to accomplish this. The general plan was for me to call on different speakers from the AAS and SDS who would make the case for supporting the black students, pressuring the faculty to change its vote and defying Perkins's declaration of a "situation of emergency." We also decided to let other speakers address the crowd, even though this was officially an SDS meeting. We didn't fear dissent from our militant position.

But what we hadn't figured out in all our pre-meeting strategizing was how we would get the crowd—or at least a sizable portion of it—to decide to take over a building and then execute that action.

We had also not anticipated attracting such a large crowd. Based on our mass meeting the previous evening, in which support for the black students was overwhelming among the twenty-five hundred in Bailey Hall, we expected at least that number to be ready for some type of action on Tuesday night. It soon became apparent, based on the responses of the crowd in Barton to the various speakers, that while some who came were actually hostile to SDS and the AAS, and others were there largely out of curiosity, a considerable majority, perhaps 75 to 80 percent, were supportive of the black students. But many of these supporters were moderates who had not yet made up their minds as to what they were willing to do.

According to Fisher and Wallenstein's account, "the meeting was skillfully run. Tom Jones and Bruce Dancis whipped the students into a near frenzy, preparing them for militant action." I don't recall any "frenzy"; rather, it seemed as if the tone of the meeting ebbed and flowed with each speaker.

Jones's speech, delivered in a soft voice, did not reprise most of the threats he had made against individuals in his radio interview. He also stated that the AAS would not use its weapons or do anything else that would hurt anyone. But he did say "We are moving tonight. Cornell has until 9 to live. It is now three minutes after 8."

When Jones asked the crowd how many people were willing to take some action to support the AAS, about three-quarters of those in Barton raised their hands in affirmation. But it was hard to judge, at least from the speaker's platform, who was who in the large crowd. The SDS contingent was not together in one group; our members were scattered throughout the large structure.

Further support for militant action came from David Lyons, a young professor of philosophy and one of the Concerned Faculty. He criticized the faculty vote and announced that his group would not only refuse to teach until the faculty changed its vote, but would seize a building along with the students. When he said "At this moment I am ashamed to be a member of the faculty at Cornell University," Lyons received massive cheers from the audience.

Other speakers, however, asked for the crowd to "have compassion" for the faculty and give them time to change their minds. Eldon Kenworthy, a government professor who opposed the efforts of a majority of faculty members in his own department to maintain the punishment of the AAS members, told the audience that various colleges had decided to ask for a second faculty vote in order to nullify the previous vote. Another professor announced that the Faculty Council had called for a meeting of the university faculty to take place on Wednesday, at which time the nullification would be reexamined. The effect of these speeches was to dampen the enthusiasm for immediate action. Those of us in SDS who were on or near the speaker's platform were starting to feel that we were on the verge of losing momentum for a building takeover.

Another factor was SDS's commitment to internal democracy—a major concern for me. In this context, I wanted SDS members to decide as a group what we would do. Would we vote to take immediate action, as the tactical committee had planned, or would we decide to wait until the faculty had a chance to reverse its vote? Leaving that decision up to the crowd at Barton Hall negated SDS's need and right as an organization to take a stand based on the will of our members. But as an organization we were not adept at rapidly making critical strategic decisions.

A Personal Dilemma

I didn't know what to do. The situation was chaotic, and the mood of the crowd was going back and forth. At one point, when someone else had the microphone, I turned to Chip Marshall to talk about what we should do next. But the usually assured and forceful Chip was staring off into space. He looked paralyzed, even catatonic. Standing two feet away from him, I couldn't get his attention.

As I returned to the microphone and looked out at the crowd, I was torn. I considered saying something like, "We've heard lots of speakers and the time for talk is over. Let's support the black students by leaving this building and occupying Day Hall until the faculty reverses its vote." I'm certain that at least two or three thousand students would have followed my call and headed for the Barton Hall exits, but I was concerned that we would have to fight or push our way through hostile students who wanted to stop such a takeover. I was also aware that deputy sheriffs from the area were massing in Ithaca, but did not know how many. (It turned out that over four hundred law enforcement officials were ready to move against us.) I wasn't all that concerned about the potential for my getting busted for inciting to riot—I knew I was about to go to prison soon in any event. But given the potential for violence, I concluded that it wouldn't be right for me to order the building takeover without obtaining a vote of the SDS membership. Yet taking a vote of SDS members in the midst of this huge throng was clearly impossible. That's when I made a decision that has haunted me for years, one that Kenworthy later referred to as "one of the few instances of bad faith I've ever experienced in my dealings with SDS leaders."

I stood before the crowd and said, "Those of us who are really serious about doing something tonight, about moving tonight, let's go to Bailey Hall." Some in the crowd shouted their agreement, got up, and started moving toward to the doors. But others who didn't want to see a rupture in our ranks began yelling, "Don't go. Don't split the meeting!"

As we were starting to leave the building, Kenworthy returned to the microphone to implore us to stay. "If you're really serious about getting the change rather than playing out some psychodrama confrontation for confrontation's sake, then wait till tomorrow," he said. "Wait! Now is not the time to move.... A rational radical would not move now. The faculty meeting is tomorrow at noon; if they don't vote to nullify, then I'll be with you. But let's not move now."

For the majority of those in Barton Hall who wanted to support the black students but were reluctant or fearful of taking part in a dangerous action, Kenworthy gave them an alternative. After all, he promised that he—and presumably other liberal faculty members like him—would be with us the very next day to seize a building should the faculty refuse to nullify. Even some SDS members decided to remain in Barton instead of leaving for Bailey Hall.

I should have responded positively to Kenworthy's plea, but I didn't, and I've regretted that decision ever since. In this chaotic situation, only a few hundred SDSers, not the thousands I had expected, started walking over to Bailey Hall. It didn't take more than a few minutes for us to decide that leaving was a mistake, and we quickly returned to Barton.

We arrived just in time to see David Burak of SDS address the crowd, which had grown less tense since Kenworthy spoke but remained confused as to what to do next. Burak said he didn't agree with his fellow SDS members in leaving Barton Hall in order to occupy the administration building, because such a move was unnecessary.

"Look, Perkins has ordered us not to seize a building," Burak said. "You know what we're going to do? We're going to seize Barton Hall!"

As the crowd roared its approval, Burak added, "I think we have just taken Barton Hall. How many are prepared to stay until the demands are met?" By an overwhelming show of hands, Burak's suggestion was accepted.

Burak's speech was imaginative and clever. He kept the huge body together, making the crowd feel as if it had just taken a militant action on behalf of the black students, but one with less risk of violence at the hands of deputy sheriffs or disruption of work at Day Hall or, as it turned out, negative consequences for defying Perkins's edict against building seizures. He had effectively come up with a temporary solution to the crisis that simultaneously maintained support for the AAS and prodded undecided faculty to vote to nullify.

But Burak's individual action put him at odds with many of us in SDS. Acting as a lone wolf, he had violated the trust of the membership. Some of his closest friends in SDS, like Chip Marshall, viewed Burak's action as a betrayal that prevented SDS from taking the action we had planned and had been voted upon by the tactical committee.

What I did not know until Donald Downs interviewed me in the mid-1990s for his book was that Burak was on President Perkins's payroll throughout the 1968–69 academic year. In his own interview with Downs, Burak said, "I stayed in touch with [Perkins], even during the crisis. Once I used the phone in Barton Hall to call him." Burak maintained that his contacts with the administration enabled him to know how many deputy sheriffs were ready to come onto the Cornell campus and bust heads had SDS taken a building. He claimed that he made his speech in order to avoid unnecessary violence. He was probably right about what might have occurred had we gone ahead with an attempt to seize Day Hall.

In less than an hour, the administration released a statement sanctioning what it called the "teach-in" at Barton Hall. That action, taken quickly after Burak's speech, suggests how the administration and Burak were working together.

Seeing how things were going in Barton, the AAS leadership met to reconsider their strategy. With the time getting close to midnight, Tom Jones came back to address the more than seven thousand students who were still in Barton. He told the crowd the AAS had decided not to move against the administration and faculty, and would wait for the faculty meeting on Wednesday. He added, "Let me make it clear—this is the last time."

My viewpoint about Burak's action was complicated. I recognized right away that his speech had in some ways saved the day for SDS, as my suggestion that we leave Barton Hall had proved to be a lousy one. Keeping the massive Barton Hall body together and united was important, and, for a while, SDS speakers were able to reassert our leadership of the large group. As Fisher and Wallenstein wrote, "SDS handled the meeting skillfully after Kenworthy's intervention. There is little question that SDS did greatly increase its base of support."

David was a good public speaker, if somewhat long-winded. I never doubted the sincerity of his commitment to fighting racism and supporting the black students at Cornell. Yet I was also chagrined that he had become such a central figure in what became known as the "Barton Hall Community." I viewed him as unreliable and ego-maniacal. David seemed to constantly crave public attention, whether as a political orator or simply as a person who needed to be noticed. (It was difficult not to notice him when he walked around the Cornell campus carrying his large pet python on his shoulders.) He was not the person most of us in our organization, regardless of faction, would have chosen to be "the face of SDS."[5]

As many as three thousand students and fifty-five supportive faculty members remained in Barton Hall all night to talk about racism at Cornell and in America at large. These students were in a festive, celebrative mood, as they were feeling the same sense of exhilaration after taking a collective action that many of us in SDS had experienced in earlier demonstrations and sit-ins.

Some in SDS's action faction went home, disappointed in the turn of events and disgusted with Burak. But others in SDS stayed around to engage in the fervent discussions among students. Even though I was dispirited by what had happened, I remained in Barton

5. I hope this doesn't come across as my being jealous of Burak. But it has been particularly galling that over the years Burak has been referred to as "the president of Cornell SDS" in newspaper articles and commemorative discussions about these events, an error that Burak compounded in his own writings in which he claimed to have been SDS's "co-chairman" at the time. In reality, by April 1969 Burak had held no elective office in Cornell SDS for nearly a year and was not highly regarded by most SDS members.

throughout the night. I believed that those of us in SDS should not give up the opportunity to engage in discussions with so many liberal students who were, perhaps for the first time, open to a radical critique of American society.

Some of that organizing work was done for us by a particularly egregious display of media bias and inaccuracy. Shortly after the crowd agreed to "seize" Barton, a stringer for a major radio network ran into the press room that had been set up in a nearby building and told the network reporter that "four thousand armed blacks" had occupied Barton Hall and that five hundred of them were "copulating in the aisles." The network actually broadcast this story, despite its obvious hysteria, racial bias, and exaggeration. (The report was later retracted.) When word of this absurd news report got back to the students in Barton—it was announced from the speaker's platform—it helped outrage and unify the crowd.

For the rest of the evening and on into Wednesday and Thursday, the microphones at Barton Hall were thrown open for students and professors to talk, often in the most personal terms, about racism and race relations. Students and faculty met in small group discussions—some organized by college or department, others by interest groups—long into the night. Money was collected to buy food for the all-nighters.

It's easy to make fun of young people trying to come to terms, hesitantly and gropingly, with their own feelings about race. In the aftermath of the April events at Cornell, commentators who were hostile to the Barton Hall gathering referred to what went on there as "self-flagellation" (Marion O'Brien in the *Cornell Alumni News*), "mass catharsis" (Fisher and Wallenstein), and an expression of "liberal guilt" by white students who were "being exploited" by "demagoguery" (English professor Cushing Strout). For Downs, the Barton Hall community's focus on institutionalized and personal racism signified nothing less than "the beginning of the 'political correctness' that took off in the 1980s," a new form of McCarthyism in which a charge of racism could be used as a cudgel to suppress free thought and free speech.

What these critics failed to understand was that white Americans seldom chose to voluntarily examine the impact of racism on American society or the institutionalized racism that existed within organizations like Cornell University or even the depths of racial prejudice in their own hearts and minds. From my point of view, racism wasn't a black problem; it was something that concerned every

American who sought to create a more just society. How could it be a bad thing, something to be mocked and castigated, that young white people were finally engaged in discussions about the greatest stain on our culture and our collective history—the legacy of slavery and racism in America?

Barton Hall Community Meets Cornell Faculty

By Wednesday morning, most of the students who had remained all night inside Barton Hall fanned out on campus to lobby their professors to reverse the vote on nullification. Most classes had either been canceled or were devoted to discussions about the crisis on campus. From all reports, many faculty members were surprised, even shocked, that an overwhelming majority of their students were supporting the AAS and condemning the earlier faculty vote. After talking with their professors, thousands of students returned to Barton Hall to await the faculty's decision.

It was not a foregone conclusion that the faculty would vote for nullification. The Concerned Faculty remained pessimistic about the upcoming faculty meeting. They announced they would return to Barton Hall and take action alongside students should the faculty vote prove disappointing.

As the faculty got ready for its meeting, Government professor Allan Sindler, the creator of the embattled university judicial system and a critic of both the administration and the radical black and white students, announced his resignation from Cornell. Sindler was known as a liberal and a supporter of the civil rights movement during his years teaching at Duke University in North Carolina. But he had not been a political activist at Cornell. His exit from the university was followed within two days by another resignation, this time by conservative government professor Walter Berns, who said he was leaving to protest what he viewed as the demise of academic freedom at Cornell.

Despite the efforts of Berns, Sindler, and their allies, good sense and rationality prevailed among the university faculty, which by a ratio of approximately three to one nullified the punishment of the AAS members. The faculty also voted in support of the development of a judicial system "that all our students will consider fair" and to work with students in creating a "broadly based body" that would advise the university community on future matters.

The latter point came about because the discussions among students and faculty that were going on inside Barton Hall had begun to move away from racism and toward the idea of restructuring the university and making it more democratic. Key members of the administration and faculty, noting the continued presence of more than nine thousand students in Barton Hall awaiting the faculty's vote, realized that they were in danger of "losing" the student body to us radicals. To reingratiate themselves with their students, the faculty adopted a preamble written by mathematics professor Paul Olum, which was later read to the Barton Hall assemblage: "We hear you, we care, we are trying to understand you, and we would like to do something together with you."

SDS Abdicates

Most outsiders did not realize that we in SDS were inadvertently involved in our own effort to "lose" the support of students. Even though, as mentioned earlier, many SDSers remained in Barton Hall Tuesday night and all day Wednesday, others in SDS had become disenchanted with the Barton Hall community.

Several factors were at work here. The action faction, dismayed over its inability to produce its long-desired confrontation with the university, had abandoned Barton Hall shortly after Burak's speech. They wanted SDS to move on to other issues. Labor Committee members, as well as those who had come to believe that organizing the traditional working class was the main task of student radicals, wanted no part in university governance and restructuring. They, too, were ready to move on to issues that would directly appeal to working-class constituencies.

I shared part of the critique of the Barton Hall community's turn away from discussing racism to what seemed a more self-centered concern with how the university was run. As the efforts to restructure Cornell moved toward the formation of what was called a "Constituent Assembly"—in which students would elect their peers to serve on a body that only had the power to recommend changes—it looked like an attempt to co-opt the radical surge at Cornell. Deflecting newly radicalized students into an assembly of talk but no enforcement power seemed like a clever way to undercut the radicals and bring the campus back to normalcy.

On the other hand, having SDS members involved in an effort to make Cornell more democratic and give students more control over decisions that affected their lives, like grades, curriculum, and requirements, still made a good deal of sense, even to a nonstudent like me. Those members of SDS who were not aligned with any internal faction and were participating in the Barton Hall community were harking back to "old SDS" ideas about student power and antiauthoritarianism, and these ideas still had relevance. And they were not abandoning the thousands of students who were still looking to SDS for leadership and guidance.

With greater SDS participation in the Barton Hall community, we might have taken the opportunity to reraise our demands about university investment policy. Given the new consciousness about racism at Cornell, we might have successfully pushed the university to sell its holdings in banks supporting South African apartheid or persuaded Perkins to resign his seat on the Chase Manhattan board of directors.

Perhaps those demands would also have been co-opted and diverted had SDS, as a group, participated in the Constituent Assembly. But we'll never know, because we didn't try. The majority of SDS members distrusted the administration and the faculty too much to get sucked into a new, participatory role at Cornell. We were far more comfortable criticizing from outside.

What helped cement SDS's withdrawal from participation in the subsequent dealings of the Barton Hall community was the spectacle that took place at the moment of the Barton assemblage's triumph.

Shortly after the faculty vote was announced, to massive cheers by a Barton Hall crowd that had grown to nearly ten thousand, President Perkins arrived to address the crowd. Smiling shyly (or uncomfortably, depending on the viewpoint of the observer), Perkins stood on the speaker's platform next to a beaming David Burak and AAS leader Eric Evans. Burak remained popular with the Barton Hall crowd, even as he had become almost a pariah within SDS.

This unlikely triumvirate embraced and posed for the many TV news cameras and photographers recording the scene. Evans then gave a leisurely talk about the events leading up to this moment, making Perkins wait, awkwardly, next to him. When Perkins finally stood before the microphone, he began by saying "I came first to listen, then to talk.... [Barton Hall] is one of the most constructive, positive forces which have been set in motion in the history of Cornell."

Critics of Perkins among the faculty members who opposed the manner in which his administration had dealt with the Straight crisis and were incensed over the faculty's reversal maintained that this event was an abject "surrender" to "coercion," a humiliating "capitulation" made worse by Perkins's posing with Burak and Evans.

Yet for many of us in SDS, it was Burak and Evans's grandstanding and posturing while posing for the photographers with Perkins that was troublesome. Burak, we thought, was on a massive ego trip, which the crowd in Barton Hall was feeding with its applause. Yes, we had collectively won a significant victory in Barton Hall, but we were hardly in the mood to see an SDS member and an AAS member embrace and ham it up with the president of Cornell.

What came to pass was that both SDS and the AAS abandoned the Barton Hall community and its plans for a university-wide, but toothless, Constituent Assembly. This didn't happen immediately, as both organizations chose speakers to participate in a teach-in the next day on racism, which attracted five thousand students and faculty members. But as racism ebbed as the focus at Barton, so did SDS and AAS interest.

These developments didn't prevent anti-administration professors from complaining to a *New York Times* reporter that, as Allan Sindler put it, a "revolution" was under way in which "the effective authority at Cornell has shifted to the collective student masses" meeting as the Barton Hall community and dedicated to the restructuring of the university.

New Issues for SDS

Even as the crisis atmosphere at Cornell was ending, SDS continued to grow—our general meetings were now regularly attended by four hundred to five hundred people. Clearly, many students had been radicalized by recent events. Even though the spring semester was rapidly drawing to a close, we decided to pursue two new initiatives—a campaign for "open admissions" to bring more students from working-class backgrounds to Cornell, favored by the Labor Committee and others, and an effort to kick ROTC off campus, an antiwar, antimilitarism policy pushed by the action faction.

Initially, I supported both efforts, at least in principle. The open admissions campaign was an attempt to discuss the role of elite universities like Cornell in providing the future leaders and most highly trained personnel for our capitalist society. We contrasted the income levels and family backgrounds of Cornell students and the opportunities that lay before them with the more meager wealth of students who attended the underfunded and overcrowded public universities and colleges of America.

As for ROTC, its presence on the Cornell campus had been challenged throughout the Vietnam War era—as early as the spring of 1965, when antiwar students held a sit-in at a ROTC review. We argued that ROTC, which trained and provided the U.S. military with officers needed to fight the war in Vietnam, had no place in an educational institution. Its courses had little educational value and served only to support an aggressive military machine.

I was giving a lot of speeches at this time—as SDS's representative at the racism teach-in and at our own rallies for open admissions, an end to ROTC, and (cosponsored with the AAS) freedom for Black Panther leader Huey P. Newton, who was in prison in California but about to have a bail hearing.

Whatever the venue, I tried to keep the focus on the relationship between racism and the subject at hand: open admissions would benefit poor and working-class people, but especially black people; ROTC was being used to provide officers to fight a racist war in Vietnam; the Black Panther Party was being suppressed because it was fighting for the rights and self-defense of black people.

At the same time, the AAS decided that the continued existence of racism at Cornell prevented its members from joining the university community as represented by those who were still meeting in Barton Hall. The AAS cited the failure of the administration to properly investigate the earlier cross-burning outside Wari House, the Delta Upsilon effort to violently expel the black students when they were occupying the Straight, and the double standard that allowed the administration to call the occupation of the Straight by one hundred black students a "building seizure" and the occupation of Barton Hall by nine thousand predominantly white students a sanctioned "teach-in."

That the events of the past week had also radicalized many AAS members was evident by their changing the name of their organization to the Black Liberation Front. Now seeing themselves as part of an international struggle against racism and imperialism, the BLF adopted several issues SDS had been pushing, including our demand that Perkins resign from the Chase Manhattan board and that Cornell abolish ROTC, which, in the words of Tom Jones, was providing officer training for a military machine that was "suppressing black, yellow and brown people throughout the world."

Our open admissions and anti-ROTC campaigns failed to attract many students beyond our (still large and growing) core of SDS members. In the case of the former, our demands seemed to come out of nowhere—we had never raised any questions about admissions before—and had little connection to reality. We demanded that beginning with the class of 1974 (that is, by September 1970), Cornell should admit 50 percent of its incoming freshman class from the working class, with racial minorities making up half of that group, and that Cornell should provide adequate scholarship aid to all such students.

But by pushing for such a drastic change in a short period of time and not adequately considering the issues of funding, curriculum, and recruitment, we made it easy for those who opposed our plan to pick it apart instead of having to deal with the principle behind it. By introducing it with only a few weeks left before finals and the end of the spring term, we didn't give ourselves enough time to do sufficient organizing around it. Even under the most favorable conditions, it was not easy convincing middle-class and upper-middle-class students that Cornell's admission policies should be changed.

Internal Disputes and External Criticisms

Also playing into our lack of success were the internal disputes about ideology and tactics that were finally beginning to tear apart Cornell SDS. By early May, we were developing the kind of factional splits that had already paralyzed or destroyed SDS chapters around the country. Although differences between the action faction and Labor Committee had been apparent since the previous summer, it was only at this time that both groups began meeting separately, apart from SDS as a whole. Whereas in the recent past we all worked together on various projects, it was now the case that the Labor Committee was far more committed to open admissions than an anti-ROTC campaign, while the action faction viewed ROTC as the issue with the greatest potential for forcing a confrontation with the university.

This meant that our large general SDS meetings became arenas for increasingly bitter debates. As someone who was not aligned with either faction, I saw it as my responsibility to keep the organization together, if at all possible. Since I was viewed by most in the membership as both fair and militant, I was chosen to chair every SDS meeting for the remainder of the term—or until I had to begin my prison term.

Meanwhile, a counterreaction to the events of the past week, led by professors in the Government and History Departments, was developing. Government professor George McT. Kahin gave an impassioned speech in which he charged that academic freedom had been threatened at Cornell in ways it had never been before. Kahin was no activist, but he was revered by the antiwar movement for his academic work on Southeast Asia, which had early and effectively criticized U.S. policy in Vietnam. He drew a parallel between his own suffering during the McCarthy era and recent events at Cornell.

Sindler and Berns also spoke, explaining why they could no longer work at a university whose administration, they alleged, failed to defend academic freedom. In an op-ed piece for the *Sun* published the following week, Berns and Sindler cited the McPhelin case of April 1968—when black students protested glaringly uninformed and racially biased comments by a visiting professor—as the beginning of the end for them. They also raised a series of ludicrous fantasies about what the future would behold at Cornell, including SDS demanding courses taught by national SDS leaders, and militant blacks determining appropriate curriculum for the Government Department. They slammed an environment at Cornell where, they claimed, "an intransigent moralism promoting the cleansing of the campus of 'institutional racism' and of the 'military-industrial-complex' undercuts the freedom of inquiry and the profession of honest belief a faculty requires." In other words, for Sindler and Berns "honest belief" could not possibly include opposition to racism or to the university's complicity with counterinsurgency projects in Southeast Asia (the CAL project) or apartheid in South Africa. For them, even principled debate over political ideology and the role of the university was a manifestation of "intransigent moralism."

The counterreaction also was felt in Albany, where the New York State Assembly voted overwhelmingly in favor of a hastily drafted bill to ban guns from college campuses in New York State. The bill added a provision that made the unlawful occupation of a university building a felony punishable by a year in prison.

Nowhere was the negative response to what had occurred at Cornell more vehement than in the nation's press. Conservative columnist James J. Kilpatrick, a former segregationist and supporter of Sen. Joseph McCarthy's anticommunist crusade, had the nerve to charge Cornell with modern-day "McCarthyism." The conservative team of Rowland Evans and Robert Novak wrote of "anarchy" spreading far above Cayuga's waters.[6] Editorials in both the *New York Times* and the *Wall Street Journal* compared the events at Cornell to the onset of fascism—in the *Times*'s words, "the rise of jackbooted students in pre-Nazi Germany."

A series of articles by veteran *New York Times* reporter Homer Bigart did the most to undermine Perkins and his administration. Essentially, Bigart took the side of Sindler, Berns, and other members of the Government and History Departments in criticizing Perkins's leadership. His articles were filled with phrases such as "abject capitulation" and "surrender to intimidation."

On the other hand, the liberal *New York Times* columnist Tom Wicker wrote a defense of the Perkins administration's handling of the crisis. He also pointed out, implicitly contradicting Bigart's reportage, that the black students "were not armed" when they occupied the Straight—"the building was not seized at gunpoint"—and that they were responding to threats of violence against them. His column also reported on the nine thousand students who had massed in Barton Hall to support the black students in getting the judicial reprimands dropped.

ROTC Protests and Arrests

The split within SDS turned more acrimonious on May 1, when, following our "Free Huey" rally, SDS led a march to Barton Hall, where army ROTC

---

6. Evans and Novak got many of their facts wrong. They repeated the myth that "armed Negroes" had occupied the Straight, and added falsehoods about earlier events, such as their claim that the Chase Manhattan Bank recruiters had been "physically assaulted."

cadets were practicing for their annual Presidential Review. Although the action faction persuaded our chapter to support a peaceful protest—Perkins's edict against "disruptive demonstrations" was still in effect—only around 250 SDS members and supporters took part.

For a while, under the nervous gaze of fifteen campus policemen and Proctor George, SDS members stood outside a perimeter rope and chanted antiwar slogans, while supporters of the cadets booed and shouted back. But then, in what was apparently a preplanned move, about fifty action faction-ers led by Chip Marshall, Joe Kelly, and Jeff Dowd got into a fenced-off area containing an old naval destroyer deck gun used by navy ROTC for training. (Whether the door to the fence was left unlocked or the lock broken by SDS members later became a matter of dispute.) As they climbed on top of the large gun and Chip began speaking with a portable bullhorn, others spray-painted "End ROTC" on the gun.

Proctor George then ordered the demonstrators sitting and standing on the gun to leave or face arrest. Together with those of us who had remained behind the rope, they then marched out of the building.

Afterward, I was angry at Chip, Joe, and Jeff for intentionally taking the ROTC protest beyond what they had promised at the SDS meeting, where they said they would do nothing at Barton to provoke arrest. Despite our chapter's internal disputes, this was the first time I could recall such a breach of honesty by any faction.

The situation got a lot more complicated and troublesome over the next few days when Ithaca police, at the behest of the Cornell administration, arrested ten SDS members (including Chip, Joe, and Jeff) for second-degree criminal trespass, a misdemeanor punishable by three months in jail, for the incident involving the navy ROTC gun. The arrests were seen by many as a belated effort by the Perkins administration to get tough with campus radicals.

Support for those arrested, now out on bail and calling themselves the May Day Ten, came from a most unlikely source—Allan Sindler, whose res-ignation from Cornell was not yet in effect. Whether out of principle or con-tinued pique at Perkins (or a combination of both), Sindler charged that, at least in the case of the five SDSers arrested who were Cornell students, the administration had violated its own judicial procedures by calling in civil authorities in a case that did not amount to a serious breach of the law.

SDS demanded that all the charges against the May Day Ten be dropped, and we reiterated our demand for the abolition of ROTC at Cornell. But we put off any decision on further courses of action until yet another tactical committee could discuss and debate the matter.

The Supreme Court Says No

On Monday, May 5, while all this was going on, I got the bad news I knew was coming: the U.S. Supreme Court denied certiorari (refused to hear the case) in the appeal of my prison sentence. Within a few days my attorney informed me that I was scheduled to report to the U.S. marshal's office in Syracuse on May 20 to begin my sentence. At this point, Faith didn't know to which federal prison I would be sent.

I was determined to use whatever time I had left to try to keep Cornell SDS from splitting apart. We were in the midst of marathon meetings to decide what to do about the May Day Ten. The action faction saw the arrests as one final opportunity this semester for SDS to seize a building or lead some other form of confrontation with the authorities at Cornell. They also argued that SDS as a group must respond strongly to the arrest of its members. But many others were irritated at the action faction's disregard for what had been agreed on beforehand and for getting busted for as stupid a protest as sitting on the navy gun.

I was in this latter group, which wanted to support our arrested members despite our disagreements with them, but was not in favor of staging a major action in their defense. I was particularly angered when Chip and Joe, who favored seizing a building, threatened to lead such an action whether or not the chapter voted in support of it. I told them that I deplored such an undemocratic move, which would wreck Cornell SDS. And I promised that if they took such an action in SDS's name in defiance of the chapter's vote, I would publicly denounce them even if it was the last thing I did before going to prison.

Matters came to a head on May 8, when we held two contentious membership meetings—one in the morning and the other at night—to decide what we would do. After a meeting of over four hundred SDSers decided, narrowly, not to take a militant action, the action faction pushed for another vote that evening, when more than five hundred SDS members packed into a lecture room in Goldwin Smith Hall.

As chair of the meeting, I was determined to hold a fair debate and tried to alternate calling upon speakers of various persuasions. No members were more discomfited by the divergence of opinion than the Dowds—Jeff, one of the May Day Ten, was vehemently in favor of a building takeover, while Doug, the Cornell faculty member most closely involved with SDS, argued that such an action could mean the end of SDS at Cornell because of the reaction it would provoke from the administration and the schism it would bring to the membership.

According to our rules, as chair I had the right to call upon myself to speak, and I took the opportunity to argue against SDS taking any more militant actions this term. I felt that most students, including many in SDS, were emotionally and even physically exhausted from everything that had occurred during the past weeks and months. I argued that it would be difficult to generate significant student support for any action with so little time left in the semester. I concluded with an impassioned appeal for unity and internal democracy.

In the midst of the meeting, Chip made the gracious gesture—even though we were on opposite sides of an increasingly bitter and divisive argument—of mentioning my impending prison term and calling on the membership to show their support for me. I received a long standing ovation.

We eventually decided, again on a close vote, to oppose seizing any campus buildings.[7]

Shortly thereafter, Tompkins County DA Matthew McHugh brought charges against some of the black students involved in the Straight takeover. In mid-May, a Tompkins County grand jury released sixteen indictments for second-degree criminal trespass. In this case, unlike the case of the May Day Ten, the Cornell administration was not a party in pressing the charges.[8]

On May 14, my twenty-first birthday, the big news of the day was President Nixon calling for a major reorganization of the Selective Service System, which would be replaced by a draft lottery.

With little more than a week to go before the start of my prison term and political activity finally slowing down, I spent most of my time with Jane. Again, we avoided talking about the future, or our future together. I don't think our failure to discuss what would happen to us revealed ambivalence about our relationship on the part of either of us, but I can't be sure. We just promised we would write each other often and that she would visit me once we knew to which prison I would be assigned. Jane still had a year to go to finish her BA, so she assumed she would be back at Cornell in the fall.

I gave one final interview to the *Sun*. Asked to reflect on the growth I had seen in the movement at Cornell during my four years in Ithaca, I talked about "people moving away from just an anti-Vietnam stance. They're beginning to

---

7. The trial of the May Day Ten took place in September and October. Following the testimony of (now former) President Perkins, new Cornell president Dale Corson, and other administration bigwigs, the judge dismissed the trespassing charges against all the defendants, except for nonstudents Chip, Joe, and Jeff. They accepted a plea bargain in which they pleaded guilty to third-degree criminal trespass, paid fines of fifty dollars, and were given conditional discharges after agreeing not to participate in any unlawful activities in Tompkins County for one year.

8. Eventually, in September 1970, the court dismissed all charges against most of the black students, though three of the leaders—Tom Jones, Eric Evans, and Ed Whitfield—pleaded guilty to fourth-degree criminal trespass. They received unconditional discharges, paid no fines, and spent no time in jail.

see the source of their oppression in the capitalist system." As for my goals for SDS in the future, it was "to build a democratic, socialist movement in America."

On the morning of Tuesday, May 20, Doug Dowd, along with Mike Rotkin and Jane, drove me to my lawyer's office in Syracuse. It was a somber ride, to be sure, with occasional attempts at humor failing to lighten the mood for more than a moment or two. When I had to say goodbye, there were no tears, just sadness. I was already steeling myself for what lay ahead.

As Faith and I walked the few blocks to the U.S. marshal's office, I turned around once to look back at my friends as they walked in the opposite direction to Doug's car. The last thing I saw was Doug and Mike holding Jane by her arms to keep her from falling.

Part Three

FEDERAL PRISON

Chapter Fourteen

Safety and Survival in
My New Kentucky Home

I was not raped in prison. I didn't get into any fights. I suffered no physical abuse at the hands of fellow inmates or prison guards. But I had to disguise my fear during my stay in county jail and for the first few months of my time in federal prison. Although it would not be accurate to describe this fear as terror, I experienced a form of largely unabated tension. I was wound up tight, while trying to look cool, unafraid, and impervious to the danger around me. I learned to always be aware of my surroundings and avoided being isolated in any section of a jail or prison. I was prepared to fight if I had no other choice.[1]

When I first began my sentence in May 1969, I was placed in a crowded cell block with about nineteen other inmates, evenly divided between blacks and whites, in the Onondaga County Jail. Having turned twenty-one a week earlier, I was now in the adult section of the jail—unlike my five-day stay in November '68 when I shared a cell block with two other youthful offenders. Some of the guys were awaiting trial or sentencing, while others were serving sentences of less than a year.

One inmate, the resident Motor Mouth, said he recognized me from the TV news. He asked me who my lawyer was. When I told him I had been represented by Faith Seidenberg, he sneered, "She's a lesbian, ya know," as if that was relevant. (I never asked my feminist attorney about her sexual orientation, but she was married and had three children.)

---

1. I have changed the names of all the inmates, guards, teachers, and prison officials mentioned in this section, with the exception of fellow draft resisters and other close friends of mine among the inmates.

My individual cell was at the end of the block, and some of the inmates walked by to check me out. A few seemed friendly and said hello, while others just looked at me silently and walked away. I maintained a tight-lipped, stoic demeanor. Those who asked me what I was in for were mostly incredulous that I was doing time for tearing up a piece of paper. One very large guy, about six-foot-three and three hundred pounds, named Big Jackie, said he liked my boots. (We were all wearing prison clothes, but kept the footwear we had arrived in.) A few minutes later, Motor Mouth came by to tell me, "Big Jackie says he's going to turn you out."

At the time, I didn't know exactly what "turn you out" meant, but it didn't sound promising. I didn't do anything, nor did I talk to the guards about the threat, because I thought Motor Mouth could just have been trying to stir things up. Later that day I was moved to a smaller cell block with only three other guys, all in their thirties and experienced cons. Like me, they were awaiting transfers to other prisons. I found out the cell block I had been in was supposed to include only inmates doing short stretches, six months or less, in the county jail. Maybe I was originally placed there because there was no room in any other cell block; I never found out.

Among the three inmates in my new cell block, one of them, Leo, wore a Star of David around his neck, and he quickly figured out I was Jewish as well. He called me "lansman." The three needed me as a fourth hand in their endless card games of whist. I would have preferred to read and write, but what the hell. The rest of my nine days in the county jail were uneventful.

I didn't find out I was being sent to a federal youth prison in Ashland, Kentucky, until two U.S. marshals picked me up in Syracuse. I was handcuffed and placed in the backseat of their sedan, but not put in leg irons. We drove first to Buffalo, where we added another young guy also bound for Ashland. Then it was on to Cleveland, where our entourage added a third inmate, this one older and headed for the federal penitentiary in Atlanta. Our new addition was obviously considered a greater escape risk than me or the guy from Buffalo, as we were all placed in connected handcuffs and leg irons, and the marshals seemed a lot more uptight. After a quiet night in a county jail in Portsmouth, Ohio, we drove the rest of the way to Ashland.

The Numbers Game

Call me 18046. That was the prison number assigned to me when I arrived at the Federal Youth Center in Ashland, Kentucky. It's a number I had to memorize, as an inmate might be called upon to state his number at different times during the day. I learned that you could roughly estimate when an inmate began his sentence from his prison number—someone with a number in the sixteen thousands, for instance, had been in Ashland for several years when I arrived, or had already returned for a second stretch following a parole violation.

Ashland's population of five hundred inmates was small by modern prison standards, and most of the inmates were in their early twenties. According to official figures I saw at the end of 1969, Ashland's inmate population was about 80 percent white and 17 percent African American, with the rest made up of Puerto Ricans, Mexican Americans, and American Indians. (The relatively small percentage of minority inmates increased significantly in subsequent years.)

We all wore military surplus clothing—khaki shirts and pants, green belts and socks, and brown boots. When the weather got cold, we received green army jackets. The irony of draft resisters having to dress in military garb did not escape us. Athletic shoes were not provided, so if you wanted sneakers for sports, you had to get them sent from the outside. Fortunately, my parents kept me supplied with Converse All-Stars.

Most of us lived in one of three large structures, known as "units" or "dormitories," which housed around 100–120 inmates apiece. Picture a building a bit longer and narrower than a basketball court, divided into two sides with about fifty beds and lockers on each side against the walls and down the middle, and toilets, sinks, and showers at both ends. The beds were short and narrow, which affected larger guys a lot more than me. A friend and I once measured the space between beds, and it came to twenty-two inches. In between the two sides were a TV room with about twenty chairs, a card room, a guard's desk, and a guard's office. The windows, of course, had bars, and the building was locked after sundown.

Despite its euphemistic name, the Federal Youth Center was a medium-security prison. Ashland had gun towers manned by guards with rifles at various intervals surrounding the large compound. In place of a penitentiary wall were two fifteen-foot-high chicken-wire fences, about six feet apart, with razor wire curled around the tops of both. An electronic warning system that set off an alarm if anyone touched the fence provided an additional means to keep inmates in.

In the 1940s and '50s, before Ashland became a prison for younger inmates, its notable alumni included World War II draft resister and civil rights leader Bayard Rustin and blacklisted Hollywood screenwriters Dalton Trumbo and John Howard Lawson of the Hollywood Ten.

Despite its young and aggressive inmate population, Ashland was not a "gladiator school," as some prisons were known. There were fights almost every day—mostly over matters like cutting into line or what TV show to watch, though sometimes over racial slights. But fights usually involved fists, not improvised knives ("shanks"). As far as I know, no inmate was killed or seriously wounded by another inmate during my time in Ashland, though some were pressured into sexual submission.

In the womanless world of Ashland, homosexuality was defined differently than on the outside. The inmate playing the dominant-aggressive role would not consider himself a homosexual, nor would he be considered one by most inmates. Indeed, these inmates were usually the most assertive about their manliness and the first to call somebody else a "queer" or a "punk." On the other hand, the inmate with the submissive-passive role would be considered homosexual and might even be referred to as "she." These inmates often had effeminate mannerisms or were forced into such roles through physical intimidation. Once the sex act was over, they would usually be scorned by their partner.

New Arrivals

When a new inmate arrived at Ashland, he would usually be checked out by other inmates. They would talk to him to see if he was effeminate (which in this world would mean he was gay) or to ascertain if he could be pressured. In most cases, if the new arrival made it clear he wasn't interested and would fight if necessary, nothing else happened. But a small, uneasy guy who didn't make friends quickly, or made friends with the wrong group of people, could be in trouble.

When I first walked into K Unit, the living facility to which I was assigned, inmates came up to me to ask what I was in for. This surprised me, because I had thought—based on too many prison movies—this was not an appropriate introductory question. I had an image of prison as a place where inmates minded their own business and revealed the crimes they had been convicted of only after getting to know each other. Boy, was I wrong! At least in Ashland, the first questions I was asked by other inmates were where I was from, what was I in for, and how much "time" I had on my sentence.

But it was also a surprise that when I replied I was a draft resister and had been given an indeterminate sentence for tearing up my draft card, the response was usually, as it had been in the county jail, surprise that anyone could be sentenced to prison for destroying a piece of paper. I never received a hostile reaction—to my face, at least—from other inmates for being a draft resister, and this included inmates who had served in Vietnam before committing whatever crime that got them sent to federal prison.

I knew I would be tested in prison, so my first-night encounter with sexual pressure (described in Chapter 1) was not unexpected. Fortunately for me,

Bruce Dancis, aka 18046, on the visitors yard at the federal prison in Ashland, Kentucky, October 1969. (Lawrence Felix Kramer)

the would-be predator was not among the toughest or the most belligerent of Ashland's sexual aggressors, and my rejection of his demands ended his interest in me.

But it was a daunting first night in federal prison, to be sure. My immediate reaction upon arriving in Ashland was to write my attorney to ask her to request a transfer to a prison closer to home. It was the usual policy of the Federal Bureau of Prisons to send draft resisters to prisons relatively near to their hometowns. For me, that would have meant the federal prison in Danbury, Connecticut, or even more likely, the minimum-security federal prison farm in Allenwood, Pennsylvania, which held the largest number of East Coast draft resisters. If the authorities felt I would do better in a prison with a younger (under thirty) population, the youth prisons in Petersburg, Virginia, and Morgantown, West Virginia, were the closest to home.

Ashland, Kentucky, was an eleven-to-twelve-hour drive from New York. Being sent so far from my home seemed like an attempt by the authorities to make it even harder for me to communicate with relatives, friends, and supporters on the outside.

I also had the gnawing feeling that there was something wrong, or insignificant, with my doing time for tearing up a small piece of paper, rather than for refusing induction, for which I was never prosecuted. However, after a few days in Kentucky, having made some reliable friends and seeing that I could survive in such a place, I asked my attorney to withdraw the transfer request. I then settled in for my stretch.

All in the Family

Tension existed in Ashland between "hillbillies" and "hippies" and between hillbillies and blacks. Among the white population, the hillbillies were the largest group (about three-fourths), mainly working-class guys from the surrounding area—Kentucky, Ohio, West Virginia, Indiana, Tennessee, and North Carolina. Hippies were not only druggies, draft resisters, and college-educated inmates, but also any inmate who was middle class and/or came from Washington, D.C., or New York, Chicago, Boston, Cleveland, or other northern cities.

I belonged to an informal subgroup among the hippies—we called ourselves "the Family"—who banded together and shared our resources. Included in the ranks of the Family were three inmates who gave us the muscle we needed for self-protection and deterrence: Big Joe, an affable six-foot-two, 260-pound guy in for attempted murder of a federal narcotics officer; Charlie, a large, tough Irish kid from Boston; and Steve Jeffco, a University of

New Hampshire football player and wrestler who was doing time for bank robbery.

(A few months into my prison term, Steve and I were standing on the prison yard when the inmate who had pressured me during my first night in Ashland walked by. I pointed him out to Steve and mentioned that the guy hadn't bothered me since. Steve then revealed he had warned the guy to stay away from me.)

The Family's importance to my physical safety and mental health was crucial. Politically and socially, the Family provided a cooperative alternative to the usual isolation and antagonisms of prison life. We shared our resources, whether the (meager) wages we received for our prison jobs or from funds sent by friends and family. This provided all of us with cigarettes, cookies (the mainstay of the unofficial prison diet), coffee, and hot chocolate.

I'm not kidding about the importance of cookies, given how bad the regular food was. I even wrote Father Dan Berrigan about them, noting that "we still get excited over new events, like the commissary's getting in stock a new brand of cookies. (Dutch chocolate, if you're interested.)"

One time, one of the toughest hillbillies in Ashland walked near us while Family members were sharing some cookies. He came over and said, with a sheepish smile, "I'll be a hippie for a cookie." We gave him one, and didn't even require that he undergo a hippie transformation.

The black inmates, some of whom were allied with the Family, were about evenly divided between those from southern and border states and those from big northern cities. The few Latinos were almost entirely urban, and the Indians from reservations. Although some, though not most, of the black inmates were developing black power consciousness in 1969 and '70, such rising militancy did not extend to the few Latinos and Indians in Ashland. They tended to not make a fuss when guards or other inmates insultingly called them "Chico" or "Chief."

The distinctions among inmates may have reflected the parlance of the time and place, but they were absurd. Take the case of Louie Tagliatelli and Augie Benesi, Italian American inmates from New York. When Louie and Augie arrived in Ashland they were already members of a different "family" with a long history of organized crime. They disdained the counterculture and weren't especially sympathetic toward draft resistance. Yet in Ashland, Louie and Augie were called hippies.

In a largely successful effort to keep the inmate population divided, the guards often exacerbated these tensions by appealing to the hillbillies' racism toward the black inmates and their cultural and class antagonism toward the hippies. (They often called us "college boys.") It was also the case that many in our ranks were middle class and looked down on the hillbillies.

Fortunately, the incidents between the antagonistic groups never escalated into serious violence. Prison gangs, such as the Aryan Brotherhood
or the Black Guerrilla Family, did not exist in Ashland during the time I spent
there. Even though the black inmates were greatly outnumbered, they stuck
together, and most of the hillbillies were afraid to fight them alone.

When the civil rights leader Bayard Rustin was an inmate in Ashland during World War II, he led protests to challenge the racial segregation that then
existed in the prison dorms, at movies, and in the dining facilities. By the late
'60s legal segregation had ended, but de facto segregation continued to exist
in the prison mess hall, as white inmates ate on one side and black inmates
on the other.

Without having to organize a protest, members of the Family simply sat
down together, blacks and whites, at the same dining tables. Some white inmates and guards, and maybe a few blacks, may have grumbled about it, but
they did nothing to stop it.

Crimes and Punishments

Slightly more than two-thirds of the inmates were doing time for violating
the Dyer Act by transporting stolen motor vehicles across state lines. It was
(and undoubtedly still is) pretty easy to steal a car in Ohio, go for a joy-
ride, and cross a bridge or border into West Virginia or Kentucky. Ashland
is located in an area known as the "Tri-State," where the three states meet.
The rest of the inmates were largely in for bank robbery, mail theft, forgery,
drug smuggling and/or dealing, and draft resistance. Not counting the Jehovah's Witnesses, who were in prison for refusing the draft on purely religious
grounds, there were never more than a dozen of us resisters, usually around
six, and mostly white.

Virtually all the administrators, guards (we called them "hacks"), teachers, caseworkers, and secretaries were white men, except for two African
American men who worked in the recreation department and the kitchen,
and two white women, a teacher and a secretary.

K Unit, where I lived, was one of the three large dormitories housing most
of the inmates. There was also an honor dorm with individual rooms for
inmates on work release or study release, or in the special Newgate college
program. During my last two months in Ashland they converted two old cell
blocks into "preferred housing" units for inmates who were either due to be
released ("short timers") or had good conduct records.

There were also several detention cell blocks—although they had the
1984-ish name of the "Adjustment Center." One was for inmates in a "control"

status who were allowed out of their cells to work but were confined at all other times; the other, "Segregation," was for those who were locked up at all times for disciplinary purposes. I heard there was another cell block for incorrigible inmates who were uncontrollably violent or had assaulted a guard or another prison official, but I never saw it myself.

Most Ashland inmates had relatively short sentences. Many had received the same sentence as me—an indeterminate sentence of up to six years under the Youth Corrections Act. Under a "Zip-6" sentence you were technically eligible for immediate parole, but I knew of only one inmate with this sentence (not a draft resister) who was released in less than a year. Another popular sentence was called a "Minority," in which an inmate who was, say, eighteen, could be held for an indeterminate length of time until he reached twenty-one, when he had to be released.

These indeterminate sentences gave the institution and the U.S. Parole Board considerable leeway in deciding how long an inmate would remain in prison. As I will discuss shortly, parole usually depended upon achieving certain goals. But another effect of indeterminate sentences was to keep inmates agitated and nervous about how much time they would have to serve, and this added immeasurably to the tension in Ashland.

Work and Ye Shall Be Free

Every inmate had a job, except for those fortunate enough to become full-time students at a local community college. (Some inmates nearing the end of their sentences were able to get placed in a "work release" program wherein they could hold a job outside but return to prison at night.) The goal of the institution was to be relatively self-sufficient, and there was a surplus of inmate labor to see that most of the work was done by inmates, supervised by civilian employees.

Jobs broke down into four groups: (1) office-type jobs such as clerks, teachers, hospital workers, and medical lab technicians; (2) trade-oriented, blue-collar jobs, such as painting, cooking, masonry, plumbing, carpentry, auto repair, and gardening; (3) custodial jobs, usually given to new arrivals, such as food service and orderly; (4) minimum-security jobs such as driving trucks and other tasks that took an inmate outside the prison, which were allotted only to Jehovah's Witnesses. (Although most of the draft resisters had minimum custody, like the JWs, we were never given such jobs.)

Inmates with some college education were generally assigned to office-type work. I worked as a teacher in the education department during my entire stay in Ashland. In addition to the half-dozen inmates working in education, there were about a ten full-time civilian teachers, administrators, and secretaries.

Most inmates were given educational and vocational goals after their initial testing. Vocational goals usually involved the passing and completion of a trade course. Educational goals varied among inmates. Those who tested at a third-grade level might have the goal of reading at an eighth-grade level; illiterates might have the goal of reading at a third-grade level. But for most inmates who never finished high school, the goal was to get a GED.

Draft resisters, however, had no such goals. It was made clear to me by my caseworker, Mr. Jones, that I was in prison for punishment, not rehabilitation. Thus, the first staff evaluation of me, part of my initial classification study at Ashland, read: "Vocational Goals: None. Supportive Education Goals: None. Guide & Counseling Goals: None." My requests to attend community college classes were turned down without comment.

My primary job was to work with the GED students on math (fractions, decimals, percents) and English (usage, spelling, parts of speech). When I started, I was alarmed to see that nearly all teaching was done with programmed texts—a student read a page, took a test, and went on to the next page. But after observing how incompetent most of the hired staff was, I realized that this was probably the only workable solution, since the inmate teachers were not allowed to conduct our own classes.

Most of the hired teachers, from my perspective, either despised or looked down upon convicts but enjoyed receiving federal government salaries. Too many of these teachers spent perhaps three hours a day on instruction, and the rest of their time drinking coffee in their lounge and ordering expensive teaching machines that were seldom used by students but were shown off to the constant stream of visitors to the department. This modern equipment helped Ashland gain a reputation as a model prison for inmate educational training.

This is not to say that the civilian teachers I worked with most closely—Mr. Nell and Mrs. Rivers—were mean and incompetent. They were decent to me. Though I never got too friendly with them, I tried to respond to them with affability and politeness. I could easily talk about sports with Nell, and while Rivers wasn't exactly warm, I felt she did care about my welfare—up to a point. Nell and Rivers were probably the best civilian teachers in Ashland.

I did learn at least one thing from my civilian bosses: I had never heard the expression "Don't Jew me down" until Nell used the term when arguing with another inmate. To his credit, Nell apologized to me when he saw the shocked expression on my face.

My bosses were easily impressed by status and snobbery. They proudly let visitors to the department know that their staff included inmate instructors who had attended Ivy League universities—Harvard for Jim Wessner and Cornell for me.

Once, in a grandstanding move that still embarrasses me when I think about it, I persuaded Nell to let me make a long-distance call to City Hall in New York. One of my homeboys (inmate parlance for someone hailing from the same city) was about to be paroled, and he needed to find a job in New York City. An old friend from my Three Arrows summer community, Jeff Greenfield—the same Jeff Greenfield who became a prominent author and TV news broadcaster and commentator for ABC, CNN, and CBS—was then working as a speechwriter and aide for New York mayor John Lindsay. Nell let me call Jeff's office in City Hall so I could ask him if there were any city programs to help former offenders get a second chance and whether he could help my friend find a job. Jeff, who knew I was in prison, took my surprising call in stride and offered to help my friend when he was released from Ashland. Jeff also tried to inspire me by quoting something his former boss, the late Robert Kennedy, had told him about the need to stand up for one's convictions.

Needless to say, my instantly getting through to Jeff at City Hall duly impressed Nell and everyone else in the department. But I never found out whether my friend eventually got a job through my efforts.

The worst aspect of the vocational and educational programs at Ashland was the power the civilian teachers exercised over the lives of inmates. As I've mentioned, to be paroled an inmate usually had to complete both his educational and vocational training goals. At the pettiest whim, teachers could kick an inmate out of class for at least a month at a time. Without going to school, an inmate could not complete his goal. As a result, he would spend more time in prison.

All inmates received wages for our work, but they were minimal. Inmates who received good work reports and stayed out of trouble were given small monetary awards, perhaps five or ten dollars. As for me, for most of my term I received ten dollars a month in prison wages, which worked out to about six cents an hour for a forty-hour week.

I've dwelt on the education department since that's where I worked, but the same patterns appeared in other departments throughout the prison. We actually had a competent staff physician, Dr. Ponds, in the medical department during part of my time in Ashland. Facing the draft, Ponds had chosen to work in a federal prison rather than enter the armed forces.

But before Ponds arrived, we had a doctor who seemed to view his Hippocratic mission as the ferreting out of malingerers among the inmates. I once had to vomit all over the floor of the main medical office because the doctor didn't believe I was really sick. Later we learned that some inmate working in the kitchen had chopped up a dead rat and placed pieces of it in the beef stew served the previous evening, and that I was suffering from food poisoning.

Sometimes the medical staff ended up performing procedures for which they weren't adequately trained. The prison dentist, another youngish guy, might have been adequate at filling cavities or cleaning teeth, but he wasn't so good at oral surgery. Unfortunately, I discovered his limitations through personal experience. Without boring readers with my dental history, suffice it to say that I had a problem where some baby teeth had come out but their adult replacements were blocked by bone and tissue from taking their rightful place in my mouth. I needed surgery at the end of high school to remove one of these teeth. But I ignored the other until I started feeling a lot of pain. Unfortunately, I was in Ashland at the time.

The prison dentist decided to perform the oral surgery himself, despite his lack of training in this specialty. It was the most painful medical experience in my life, as the dentist failed to give me an adequate dose of novocaine. Not only that—his drill kept hitting bone, nerves, and everywhere else where it hurt like hell. When he was done, I had a big gap in my mouth and a shirt soaked with my blood.

Racial discrimination also existed within Ashland's vocational program. There was at least one segregated, all-white work detail—masonry. Although I had no direct observation of this practice, my fellow resister Dan Brustein did.

Dan, who started out working in the medical department, was different from most of us draft resisters in that he wanted to improve his craft and practical skills while in prison. He secured a transfer to the automobile repair shop, and later to the carpentry unit. Although the civilian employee teaching carpentry was a fair-minded guy, the supervisor for masonry was a crude racist who openly used bigoted language and prevented minorities from working on his detail. The man's racial attitude must have been known to his fellow civilian supervisors and to other prison officials, but nothing was done about it.

Another work detail—the prison laundry, which all inmates passed through twice a week to get clean clothes—seemed to be particularly popular with Ashland's few out-front gay inmates. These guys, called "sweet boys," wore makeup (when they could get away with it) and hung out together despite the crude remarks tossed their way by other inmates. They also liked to dress stylishly, at least by prison standards. So they chose to work in the laundry unit, where they could taper their own pants (we usually had to wear baggy and formless khakis) and locate tight-fitting shirts. The guards in charge of the laundry must have been tolerant or oblivious.

The Case of the Caseworker

The prison staff member who had the greatest impact on an inm___ ___ ___ was his caseworker. This was the official who decided where the inmate would work and what his educational or vocational goals might be. Most importantly, the caseworker was one of the key figures determining when an inmate would receive a parole. He would be present during an inmate's hearing before the parole board, and his recommendation had a major impact on the board's decision. Even after an inmate had secured a parole, the caseworker had to approve the parole plan before the inmate could be released.

I never trusted my caseworker, Mr. Jones. In part, this was due to my basic mistrust of prison authorities. Jones was a reasonably intelligent man, but he never came close to comprehending the motivations or needs of the draft resisters in his charge.

Here's one example, as told to me by my father: Early in my term in prison, my parents requested a meeting with Jones, for which they took time off from work on a weekday to see him. They wanted Jones to know they supported me emotionally and philosophically and would support me financially when I was paroled. Jones responded by calling me a "loser." According to my dad, my mother had to use all of her self-restraint in suppressing her anger while responding to Jones. She told him that he clearly did not know or understand her son, adding that she had no doubt about my intelligence, ability, and future prospects.

Despite Jones's attitude toward me, his initial "Caseworker's Analysis," written after I had been in Ashland for about a month or two, was occasionally accurate. "There is no question this small, dark, moody individual is of above average intelligence, considering he was in his second year at Cornell University," Jones wrote. "He is an interesting person with whom to converse, he is alert, hyper-tense, and cooperative....His major problem will be frustration at being confined and prohibited from pursuing further academic gains. Potentially, he should adjust well with peers, but will be selective in his acquaintances. He has already aligned himself with those of similar beliefs, and will perhaps receive some support and security among them."

A Fight That Didn't Happen

I mentioned earlier that I didn't get into any fights in prison. But about fourteen months into my sentence, I actually came close to being drawn into one.

It was on the prison yard's basketball court, where I spent many hours of my free time. Generally, the hillbillies weren't into basketball, preferring weight lifting, pool, and cards. So the courts were left to the blacks and the hippies. Basketball can be a rough sport, even when expertly officiated, so you can imagine how many fouls were committed in pickup games played by prison inmates with no referees. Yet I never had any problems playing basketball with the black guys.

But there was one white guy, Red, a car thief from Indiana, who mostly hung around with the hillbillies but loved basketball. He was a starter on the inmate basketball team that played against visiting civilian teams. He also had a nasty temper, which got him into frequent fights and arguments with other inmates.

One day we were playing a three-on-three game, with Red and me on opposite sides. He could usually light up anyone guarding him, including me, but this time I was beating him all over the court—contesting his shots while hitting my outside shots or driving by him on my way to the basket—despite his considerable height and weight advantage. So Red started playing dirty, shoving me under the boards and trying to trip me.

I ignored his provocations, and my team easily won the game. But Red was furious. He grabbed the basketball and threw it hard at my stomach from about six feet away. He was trying to start a fight. Yet even though I had friends at my back, I turned around and walked away. Red started cursing at me, but he soon found himself alone on the court and stopped.

Perhaps if this incident had taken place shortly after my arrival in Ashland I might have felt the necessity to fight, if only to prove that I was willing to stand up to bullies. But as a seasoned inmate with lots of friends, I didn't have to respond to Red's aggressive behavior. And I didn't lose any credibility among other inmates by refusing to fight him.

But not belonging to a group could be dangerous. There was an inmate in my dorm, Richards, who managed to antagonize just about everyone he encountered. He wasn't really a bad guy, just a jerk who was always running his mouth, grubbing cigarettes from other inmates, and being obnoxious. Richards was actually a large man, over 220 pounds, but he gave off the vibe that he wasn't a fighter. (Big guys like him who weren't tough were known as "lames.")

One night, after Richards had offended some inmates on his work detail, he was greeted with a "blanket party." He was asleep in his bed when another inmate threw a blanket over him and three inmates started beating him with their fists and with socks filled with hard items like padlocks. I'm ashamed to say that I looked on as all this happened, not wanting to get involved, and even persuaded Steve, who was ready to jump in, not to intervene. Partly this was because I didn't see the moral urgency of trying, at considerable risk, to come to the aid of an inmate I didn't like. But my behavior also showed that I had, consciously or not, begun to subscribe to traditional prison values like minding your own business and never being a rat.

Although the situation was often tense in Ashland, some real bonds of friendship managed to cut across the dividing lines between inmate groups. As an inmate-teacher, I often worked with hillbillies to help them get their GEDs. I treated each inmate-student with respect and solidarity, even those with swastikas, a popular jailhouse tattoo, on their arms. One time when it looked like a fight was about to break out between some hillbillies and hippies, a few of the hillbillies came over to me to say, "You're OK with us, man." We sometimes even had talks about how the guards were trying to divide us in order to keep the heat off them. Unfortunately, nothing substantial came from these discussions.

Elvis, the Inciter

Yet there was at least one time when inmate solidarity triumphed over separation. One evening, a guard who was universally despised by inmates was assigned to our unit. Lots of guards were grumpy, but this guy was just plain mean. And unlike some guards who didn't care for blacks and hippies but got along fine with hillbillies, this guard didn't like anyone.

Just after lights out, the loudspeaker was still on when the local radio station started playing "Hound Dog," Elvis Presley's early hit. As soon as Elvis and his band started to rock out with "You ain't nothin' but a hound dog," virtually everyone in the unit started—spontaneously and simultaneously—pounding on our lockers.

As the visceral rock 'n' roll beat of "Hound Dog" intensified, we then began throwing garbage, locks, and anything else we could get our hands on in the direction of the guard. It was dark, so he couldn't see who was doing the hurling. He had to climb under his desk for safety and used his walky-talky to call for help. Finally a squad of guards with clubs, known to inmates as the "goon squad," arrived to quiet us down.

It was one of the most enjoyable moments in my nineteen-month stay in Ashland.

Chapter Fifteen

A Typical Day in Prison, and a Few That Weren't

In prison, once you settled in and got your bearings, there was not much difference between one day and another.

Dalton Trumbo, the blacklisted, Oscar-winning screenwriter who spent around ten months in 1950–51 in Ashland for contempt of Congress, captured this feeling in a letter to his wife: "Things are so dry at the FCI [Federal Correctional Institution] that I'm ashamed to put pen to paper. There is absolutely no news. Today it rained. Yesterday it didn't. My cold persists. I rest. I work. I eat. Time passes more rapidly than it even should. I am not even too badly bored. But there is simply no news."

Here's a typical day during my nineteen-month stay in Ashland:

A horn came blasting over the loudspeaker at 6:45 a.m. and a voice shouted, "Wake up! Wake up!" You could skip breakfast if you wanted to, but since that was the only meal where milk was served (a half pint), I usually went. On the menu: cold cereal, runny scrambled eggs, grits, and coffee. After shaving (I preferred to shower in the evening), you had to make your bed, military fashion, with hospital corners and a four-inch collar. Then came inspection and one of the day's numerous "counts"—we had to sit at the foot of our beds while a guard walked down each aisle, counting inmates, to make sure no one was missing.

Work call was at 8 a.m. I straightened up the education department's classroom until 8:30, when the first class of the day began. After the civilian teachers determined what course of study each student-inmate would be assigned, I would set them up with their reading materials and tests and answer their questions and try to help them out. The first class ended at 10, and another one started immediately, continuing until 11:25. Then we ate lunch, the main meal of the day. It usually consisted of something the prison called "steak" but which we called "mystery meat." We had to return to our living units for another count at 12:30 p.m., and then another class started. There were additional classes at 2 and 3; at 4, we went back to the dorms.

Mail call, usually one of the best parts of the day for me, was next. I received a lot of mail: my parents wrote once a week, and I maintained a vigorous correspondence with Jane and my friends, both to hear how people were doing and to carry on political discussions about all the action I was missing.

The only time mail call was problematic was during the holiday season. Several antiwar and pacifist publications, like *The Peacemaker* or *News Notes* (the newsletter of the Central Committee for Conscientious Objectors), listed the names and addresses of draft resisters doing time in prisons throughout the United States and encouraged their readers to send us Christmas cards. A fine sentiment, but in practice this meant we resisters were receiving as many as twenty or thirty letters or cards a day, while most prisoners were getting very little mail or none at all. It led to resentment and cursing whenever the guard would read out our names and give us yet another letter or card.

After a 4:30 p.m. count came supper, usually cold cuts or pasty macaroni plus a canned vegetable. If it was warm and light out, the yard would remain open until 8:30 p.m. The large yard had room for a weight-lifting area, a baseball field, two basketball courts, and, believe it or not, a miniature golf course. Usually I would play basketball. At other times, I would jog around the ball field or just talk to friends.

Time went by much faster during the summer months when the yard was open longer. In the winter, there was an additional 6 p.m. count, and then the prison gym opened. As many as several hundred inmates had to squeeze into a gym built for fifty, with only one extremely overcrowded basketball court, a couple of weight boxes, and two ping-pong tables. We had to be back in the dorms by 9 p.m. for another count.

The lights were dimmed at 10, and the TV room closed. Lights went off at 11 p.m.

Weekends provided a departure from the Monday through Friday routine, as we didn't have to work, unless one was unlucky enough to be assigned to the kitchen. This meant we had hours to spend on the yard, in the gym, or back in our dorms.

National holidays also provided a few changes for the better, mostly in the area of food. Given our usual diet, it was a revelation to realize the prison kitchen staff could actually produce good-tasting meals if given decent ingredients. On the two Independence Days during my term in Ashland, we were served delicious fried chicken—much better than the Colonel's. National holidays also meant getting a can of soda and a dish of ice cream at dinner—I didn't know how much I missed such mundane items until I hadn't had them for months.

Prison Vices

Two things I didn't miss very much were alcohol and drugs. I had never been much of a drinker, and I disliked bars. (I grew up in an apartment building in the Bronx whose ground floor housed Daly's Bar & Grill; as a kid I hated the strangely sweet smells and loud voices that emanated from the bar, and the large bodies that sometimes staggered out of it, when I walked by its entrance.) So I never felt the urge to sample the various inmate-made moonshine drinks—"potato jack" was the most popular—that would occasionally appear.

While I missed smoking the occasional joint, I never suffered the cravings my druggie friends did. Among the druggies, those who were regular users of hallucinogens had it a lot easier than the heroin addicts among us who were sometimes still going through withdrawal. Every once in a while, I would get offered some weed or LSD that had been smuggled into the prison, but I never indulged. The thought of tripping while incarcerated was positively nightmarish. If there was any heroin, cocaine, or meth in Ashland, I never heard about it.

Among the hillbillies, "sniffing" was the abuse of choice. In this case it meant sniffing paint sealer. I was told that it produced a big rush, though at the cost of thousands of brain cells.

I was, however, a heavy cigarette smoker with a pack-and-a-half daily habit when I began my prison sentence. I had with me an almost full pack of Lucky Strikes when I arrived in Ashland. But I immediately discovered the problem of being the new guy in the dorm with cigarettes—inmates kept coming over to mooch smokes from me. I figured out right away that cigarettes were the units of black market currency among the inmates, and this was an area in which I did not want to get involved. The cost of purchasing a pack of smokes from another inmate was two for one—a pack now, for two later—a usurious rate that invariably got some new inmates into serious debt and trouble. So I immediately went cold turkey on my first day in federal prison. It wasn't as hard as one might expect, and I didn't smoke another cigarette for months.

In his study of imprisoned Vietnam-era draft resisters, psychoanalyst Willard Gaylin observed certain patterns of "deterioration" among the resisters: "low energy, diminished self-confidence, less capacity or desire to relate, less interest in people, more despair, a sense of impotence." While some of these conditions may have been caused by particularly fearful events or threats of violence, most arose from the simple fact of incarceration.

In prison, you controlled hardly anything affecting your life, as virtually all decisions were made for you. So much of your day was prescribed, and the days blurred together.

I decided early on that since I couldn't do anything to change the rigid structure of a typical day, I would try to make the most of it. Having always been a morning person, I had no trouble getting up early. I grew to almost like the regularity of the prison routine. My attitude was expressed in a letter I sent to Dan Berrigan, who began his own prison sentence in August 1970, after several months of tormenting the FBI by going underground. I wrote Father Dan in March 1970, after I had been in Ashland for more than nine months.

> In doing time, I find it easier to get myself into a routine in which I allot time for different things I want to do and try to stick to it. I never get bored that way, and in fact, I find I don't have enough time to do all the things I want.
>
> There are 2 schools of thought in doing time: one is to keep in close touch with the outside world, write a lot of letters, read the newspaper every day, get a lot of visits, etc. The other is to more or less cut yourself off from the streets. By temperament, I'm in the first group, but I can't knock the latter. A lot of people seem to do easier time that way.

In that same letter to Father Dan, I also had the chutzpah to advise him about what to expect in prison:

> I'm sure that you won't have much trouble doing time. Your seminary training will have prepared you well. I, as a confirmed extrovert, have had some trouble getting used to keeping my mouth shut at certain times. I've had to learn to become introspective. You poets have always been good at that, while we rock singers aren't. But I've learned.

While evenings and weekends provided the main opportunity to write letters and read newspapers and books, the conditions made it difficult to study or write. It was hard to concentrate in a dorm filled with a hundred or more young and noisy men, particularly when your only real "space" was the narrow bed you slept on and the small locker where you kept your books, correspondence, photos, and other stuff. Friends and acquaintances would constantly interrupt to talk. The lack of privacy was a constant. Indeed, the only time you were ever alone was on the toilet.

For most inmates, the toilet provided one of the only private places for masturbation. Given our population of young, horny men, beating off may have been the single most popular leisure-time activity in Ashland. As one of my friends put it, he had two girlfriends in Ashland—Raquel Lefty and Raquel Righty. As an alternative to the toilet, many inmates adopted the disgusting practice at night of masturbating in bed, ejaculating into a dirty sock and then throwing the used sock onto the dorm floor. That's another reason why having cleanup duty was so nasty.

Music and Movies for Inmates

A few pornographic books and copies of *Playboy* magazine somehow sneaked past the censors and became valued possessions as they were passed from inmate to inmate. But by far the most popular source of sexual stimulation was the television, and the most popular show, hands down, was *American Bandstand,* with its young and attractive female dancers.

Then there was the radio, which came in loud and clear over the loudspeaker virtually every hour we were awake in the dorm. Musically, this meant listening to the local Top 40 AM rock station, which, in 1969 and '70, maintained a racially integrated format in which DJs mixed in soul and R&B hits along with rock and pop. On the plus side, I was able to keep up with and enjoy the latest singles by the Rolling Stones ("Honky Tonk Women"), Elvis ("Suspicious Minds"), and Sly and the Family Stone ("Thank You [Falettinme Be Mice Elf Agin]"). And I will always be grateful to soul singer Edwin Starr for releasing "War" ("What is it good for / Absolutely nothing!") while I was in prison.

On the other hand, my friends and I weren't too thrilled with Merle Haggard's country crossover hit, "Okie from Muskogee," which made derogatory comments about hippies, marijuana smokers, and draft card burners. I also developed an inordinate amount of anger toward the Beatles' "Let It Be," the Paul McCartney song that, to my locked-up sensibilities, seemed like a paean to complacency and inactivity. The omnipresent radio also inflicted on us some of the worst pop hits of the era, like Zager and Evans's imbecilic "The Year 2525" or the Archies' insipid "Sugar, Sugar."

At times, a hit song played over the loudspeaker brought out the racial tensions simmering just beneath the surface. The Impressions' "Choice of Colors," a call for black pride that was a hit during the summer of '69, included the rhetorical question, "If you had a choice of colors / Which one would you choose, my brothers?" When Curtis Mayfield sang that line, it was usually met with some African American inmates shouting "Black!" and some whites yelling "White!"—leading to both groups glaring at each other.

The prison showed movies on Saturday nights in the gym, and we all piled in there, dorm by dorm in single file, with every guard on duty to prevent trouble. The fare was of fairly recent vintage, usually action films or war movies. To no one's surprise, the appearance onscreen of an attractive woman stirred up the most interest and shouting, while the characterization of any homosexual produced the most derision. *The Detective*, starring Frank Sinatra as a cop investigating the murder of a gay man, was particularly odious in its hateful portrayal of gays.

The biggest shocker occurred in 1970, when *Easy Rider* was screened for us—cocaine deals, pot smoking, casual sex, and all. The image of long-haired guys riding motorcycles and behaving like countercultural outlaws actually had the effect of temporarily breaking down the barriers between the hippies and the hillbillies, as the film's vision of sex, drugs, and rock 'n' roll looked pretty enticing to both groups of inmates. What were the prison authorities thinking when they booked that movie?

I also have a hazy memory of a night when a cartoon shown before a movie almost led to a riot. This cartoon, probably from the 1940s or '50s, featured a white explorer encountering black natives in the jungles of Africa. The Africans were drawn in a grossly stereotypical manner, as bloodthirsty cannibals with bones through their noses. Most of the black inmates and some of us whites immediately started shouting and stomping our feet in anger. The guards quickly turned off the projector, canceled the movie that was to follow, and marched us back to our dorm.

It was up to the guards to enforce institutional rules about grooming and personal cleanliness. Inmates were swiftly ushered into the prison barbershop shortly after their arrival in Ashland. When a new inmate with 1969-era long hair walked through the prison grounds on his way to the barbershop, it provided us with a visual reminder of the differences between the outside world and prison. Fortunately, the administration didn't require new inmates to get their heads shaved or buzz cuts—a Kennedyesque coif was acceptable for white inmates, though large Afros were not allowed for blacks.

Visits Pro and Con

For most inmates, weekends meant spending hours on the yard or in the gym. But for me, weekends often meant visitors.

I was fortunate in this regard. Visiting regulations were humane, as inmates were encouraged to maintain their contacts with friends, family, and loved ones. All visitors had to be approved in advance by one's caseworker. I was able to visit with just about everyone who made the long trip to Kentucky. My caseworker grumbled at times about all the "subversives" coming to see me, but he almost always approved them. With my SDS pals from Cornell spreading out their visits, a month didn't go by without a visit from some group of friends. Mike Rotkin even hitchhiked to Ashland from Santa Cruz,

California, where he had enrolled in graduate school at the local University of California campus, in order to visit me.

But one brief visit was unlike any other.

SPOTLIGHT: "WE'RE READY TO BREAK YOU OUT," JULY 1969

"Jesse is in the car, and we've got guns," my friend said calmly, with no emotion showing in his face or his voice. "We're ready to break you out."

I was at work in the prison education department on a weekday afternoon in July 1969. I had been in Ashland for only about two months at the time, when I was summoned to the prison visitors lounge to meet Mel Morris (not his real name). For reasons I have never understood, the prison officials let Mel visit me without his gaining prior approval, and on a weekday to boot.

Although I was already in prison when SDS split apart at its June 1969 national convention in Chicago, I knew Mel had become a leader in one of the Revolutionary Youth Movement factions that emerged from the convention, known as the Weathermen.[1] In the prison visiting room Mel told me he had been organizing in the area for an upcoming national action—which would become the disastrous Weatherman-sponsored "Days of Rage" in Chicago, scheduled for October. That's when he laid out his daring escape proposition to me. Jesse, an SDS acquaintance of mine, was waiting outside in their car, which was parked in a visitors parking space.

I couldn't believe what I was hearing. First of all, we were sitting in the prison visitors lounge, in full view of several guards and in an area that could easily have been bugged. But more important, as I explained to Mel, while I hadn't exactly volunteered to go to prison, had I decided to avoid incarceration I would have gone underground or left the country. I told him I was doing OK in prison and expected to get out in a couple of years, at which time I would rejoin the movement.

I also thought an escape attempt would have been suicidal. Although inmates periodically tried to escape from Ashland, they were

---

1. The Weatherman (aka Weathermen) faction of SDS took its name from a statement / position paper entitled "You Don't Need a Weatherman to Know Which Way the Wind Blows," based on a line in Bob Dylan's "Subterranean Homesick Blues."

usually caught before they even left the prison grounds. To get out—known as "hitting the fence"—one had to first climb over the two adjacent fences, each fifteen feet high, topped with razor wire, and wired electrically to a control panel. Then one had to avoid getting shot by a guard in one of the gun towers encircling the prison. During my time in Ashland, no inmate successfully escaped in this manner.

No matter how heavily armed Mel and Jesse were, they would have been no match for the prison guards with their gun towers and arsenal of firearms. And even if they had somehow gotten me outside of the prison grounds, how far could the three of us have driven?

So I told Mel "no thanks." He accepted my decision without rancor, and quickly left.

Over the years, I've thought often about Mel's visit and his offer to bust me out of prison. I keep coming back to two questions: Why did the Ashland authorities violate their established procedures and allow a person to see me on a weekday afternoon who was not on my visitors list and did not have preapproval from my caseworker? And how could Mel have believed that an unplanned prison breakout would succeed?

I've come up with some possible answers. Prison officials and guards are hardly infallible. Indeed, they may have been prone to screw-ups. So letting Mel in for a visit could be explained by the guard on gate duty deciding it was OK for me to have a visit from a friend. Mel, like other Weathermen, was both fearless and foolhardy, willing to take enormous risks on violent actions that he thought would inspire other young people to fight.[2]

Another explanation, which I think is dubious, is that the FBI was already tracking Mel's movements and activities in July '69. By this time, the Weathermen were most likely riddled with undercover agents. It's possible that the FBI had alerted Ashland officials as to who Mel was and, perhaps, what he was planning when he came to visit me. According to this theory, Mel was allowed into the prison to see me in order to trap us if we had gone ahead with an escape attempt.

I believe the first scenario to be true. But as crazy as Mel's proposed prison breakout might have been, I have always viewed his offer as courageous and a deep expression of friendship.

---

2. Several years later, after Mel and other members of Weatherman had disappeared from public view and formed the Weather Underground Organization, they planned and successfully pulled off Timothy Leary's escape from a minimum security state prison in California.

Minimum Custody

My parents were loyal and supportive throughout my time in prison. In his response to a questionnaire sent by my caseworker, my father wrote: "My wife and I respect our son's sincerity.... [We] deeply love our son, even though we disagree with some of his views. We are willing to give our son any assistance needed if he should have an opportunity to resume his collegiate studies."

Every five or six weeks, my folks made the long drive from New York to Ashland to visit me. It wasn't easy for them, as my dad had turned sixty shortly after my prison sentence began, my mother was in her mid-fifties, and they were both still working full time. But they essentially dropped everything they were doing in order to see me as often as they could.

Their visits were made a lot more comfortable, and considerably less expensive, by the kindness of a sympathetic family living in nearby Huntington, West Virginia. The Ritters, whom my family met through fellow resister Jim Wessner, opened their home and guest room to my folks whenever they made the trip from New York.

One Ashland policy benefited me greatly: inmates with "minimum" custody—such as us draft resisters, who were not viewed as escape risks—were routinely granted "town trips" once a month if accompanied by a parent. After I had been in Ashland for several months I was given minimum custody status, which meant that my parents could take me outside the prison for a few hours. This let me get a glimpse of the outside world, eat some good meals in local restaurants, and generally relax. Of course, these town trips made each return to prison hard to take, but they were certainly worth it.

My minimum custody also allowed me to meet my visiting friends on the prison's front lawn, away from the eavesdropping ears of prison guards and officials, during the warmer months. On visits like this, I tried to get caught up with the political debates taking place within the movement at Cornell and beyond.

In one particularly memorable visit from Cornell friends Larry Kramer, Jim Murray, Mimi Keck, and Epi Epton, they surprised me by bringing All Right with them. Epi had taken over as All Right's guardian when I began my prison sentence.

All Right was let out of their car in the visitors parking lot, several hundred feet away from me. We hadn't seen each other for about six months, but when I whistled he came charging across the lawn and greeted me with a torrent of wet licks. I'm sure there must have been a rule against visitors bringing pets with them to federal prisons—after all, there were rules governing just about everything—but I was thankful that in this case the prison authorities chose to look the other way.

The only time I resented Ashland's liberal visiting policy was when I felt I was losing control over it. About a year into my sentence, a friend from Cornell wanted to visit me, which was fine, except that she planned to bring three additional acquaintances I hardly knew. Rightly or wrongly, it seemed as if "visiting Bruce in prison" had become something of a status thing for Cornell radicals. I resented that this visit felt like it was being imposed upon me, taking away one of the only freedoms I had in prison—the ability to decide which visitors I would see. So I wrote my friend and told her not to come. Looking back, I think I was a jerk. I should have welcomed with open arms anyone willing to drive such a long way in order to see me.

As federal prison inmates, we weren't allowed any contact with members of the media. But that didn't stop an enterprising feature writer from the *Wall Street Journal* named Michael Drosnin from contacting me (through another visitor) and arranging to visit, posing as an old friend. Drosnin wanted to write a story on draft resisters in prison. Under the pseudonym of Michael Diamond, he spent two days on the visitor's lawn interviewing me while furtively taking notes. Unfortunately, Drosnin ran into obstacles from his *Journal* editors, who refused to run his story. I never discovered the reasons for this decision, but it might have been because Drosnin had used an assumed name and obtained our interview illegally.

There was one visit, however, that caused me the most stress of my entire prison term. In February 1970, a telegram arrived—the only telegram I received while at Ashland—from Jane: "I will be coming this weekend. Really want to talk with you."

During the first six months of my incarceration, Jane had written me often. I had her photograph pasted to the inside of my locker door. Although she had taken a trip to Europe with a girlfriend during the summer of '69, she visited me several times after she got back to the States.

For me, our relationship had taken on new dimensions and greater importance since I began my sentence. Having a girlfriend on the streets provided me with a lifeline to normalcy that the isolation of prison could not eradicate. Jane was the primary object of my sexual fantasies. I needed her more than ever before.

While a visit from Jane would normally have made me ecstatic, over the last several months I had sensed something was wrong. Her letters had come with diminishing frequency and were less romantic, more businesslike. When I met her in the prison visiting room, I could tell immediately from the pained expression on her face that she was about to deliver some very bad news. She had fallen in love with another man, an acquaintance of mine from Cornell. As much as she cared for me, she said she had to be with this person.

We spent the better part of her visit going over and over all of this, my endless "Why?" met by her tea   no change of her mind. Even as the visit was going on, I had the odd feeling that I, a draft resister, was in the middle of a not-very-original Hollywood movie set during World War II, playing the GI who receives a "Dear John" letter from his girl back home. I was incredulous and numb, not angry. The anger would come later.

When Jane and I said goodbye, I took what seemed to be an endless walk back to my unit. When I got to my bed, my friends could tell that something was wrong, and I told them that Jane had broken up with me. I then lay on my bed in stunned silence. I was left alone to sulk in my sad, sullen thoughts.

Fortunately, this day was the only one like it among the five-hundred-plus days I spent in prison.

Chapter Sixteen

Politics in Prison, or Keeping Up

with the Outside World

During my nineteen months in prison, I missed the Stonewall Riots in New York; the Manson cult's murder spree in Los Angeles; the Woodstock and Altamont rock festivals; the death of Ho Chi Minh; the demise of SDS nationally and the splintering of the Cornell chapter; the Chicago Eight and Seattle Seven conspiracy trials; the Weatherman-sponsored Days of Rage; the nationwide protests sponsored by the Vietnam Moratorium Committee and an even bigger protest in Washington, D.C., sponsored by the New Mobilization Committee; the introduction of the draft lottery; the breakup of the Beatles; the U.S. invasion of Cambodia; the Ohio National Guard killing four students at Kent State University; three Weathermen blowing themselves up in a Greenwich Village town house; Mississippi police killing two Jackson State students; the first Earth Day; the deaths of Jimi Hendrix and Janis Joplin; Chile electing socialist Salvador Allende as its president; and a lot more.

All of this was taking place "on the streets"—some of it good, some bad, some tragic, some inexplicable—and here I was in prison, unable to take part in or fight against any of it.

From a political standpoint, my first days in Ashland were both reassuring and alarming. I immediately met my fellow draft resisters—all five of them at the time—because, with sympathetic inmates working in the prison admissions department, word got around quickly that I was a new inmate. I was well known within draft resistance circles, and one of the resisters in Ashland had a well-read copy of the new issue of *Liberation* magazine, which contained a long article by Staughton Lynd about the draft resistance movement.

Meet the Resisters

Our little group of resisters was divided among three types when I arrived in Ashland. (There were also a half dozen or so Jehovah's Witnesses who were in prison for refusing induction on religious grounds but had no affiliation with the movement, nor any desire to associate with the resisters.)

The pacifists included Dan Bromley, a non-registrant from Ohio and the son of a prominent pacifist family that published the *Peacemaker* magazine, and Frank Femia, a member of the Committee for Non-Violent Action (CNVA), a group that was regularly committing acts of civil disobedience against the war. Frank was doing time both for refusing induction and for pouring paint on draft files in Boston. While Dan, a friendly, honest, socially awkward man of nineteen, didn't often express his political opinions, Frank took a dim view of student militants and SDS members, whom he regarded as mere spouters of revolutionary rhetoric.

Frank expressed his point of view in a letter published in the *New York Review of Books* in November 1969 in response to an article by author Francine du Plessix Gray on the "Ultra-Resistance"—her term for the Berrigan brothers and others who were destroying draft files. I couldn't help believing that what Frank wrote was in part a response to our political disagreements: "Love and joy and peace and all good things is what the revolution is about. SDS rhetoric is irrelevant. I'm not interested in closing down universities. I'm much more interested in closing down Selective Service. I distrust student militants. Romantic revolutionary rhetoric is what most spout but when the time comes for putting up or shutting up, most SDS kids (yes, kids) shut up."

There was another factor estranging Frank from me and the other draft resisters in Ashland: he was openly gay, effeminate, and sexually active in prison. (As far as I know, Frank chose his own sexual partners in Ashland and was never forced into having sex.) Frank usually sat in the mess hall with his fellow resisters and his medical department coworkers, but he spent a lot of his free time hanging out with the other gays in Ashland. Despite our differences, Frank was a loyal friend. After I got out of "the hole" for allegedly conspiring to riot (a story that will be told below), he surreptitiously typed at work—at considerable risk to himself—my handwritten diary, which I later smuggled out of prison.

I don't think I was bigoted against gays at the time. I had gay housemates at Cornell, and several gay men played crucial and prominent roles in Cornell's draft resistance contingent. I also admired the courage of the Cornell Student Homophile League, which had formed on campus in the spring of 1968. Its members were verbally abused every time they set up informational tables in the student union, even more than we in SDS had been in the early days of the antiwar movement. The bravery of these gay students was inspiring.

Yet I have to admit that while I supported civil rights for gays and an end to their legal repression, Frank's gayness made me uncomfortable inside an institution where being homosexual opened a person up to vilification and danger. Prison was not the place, for me at least, to confront any heterosexual fears of gayness and gay people I might have had.

Early in my prison term I received a letter from a journalist friend who worked for Liberation News Service in New York. We had become friends when I worked on the *First Issue* and LNS supplied us with much of our national and international reporting. His letter was chatty and filled with the latest political news. But he also took the opportunity to tell me that he had come out of the closet.

I didn't know how to react to this surprising news, especially in a response I assumed would be read by prison authorities before it was sent out. So I chose to write about everything else besides what was obviously a momentous personal decision on my friend's part. I didn't respond as a friend should have by congratulating and encouraging him.

If dealing with the gay liberation movement was difficult for a heterosexual in prison, so was the emerging women's liberation movement. Feminist activity had begun at Cornell, both inside and outside of SDS, around 1968, so I was already somewhat familiar with, and supportive of, women's demands for equality. Most of the radical inmates in Ashland shared this viewpoint, and we had developed some sensitivity toward the feminist demand that women not be objectified as sex objects.

So, when one of our guys, during a discussion of George Jackson and the Soledad Brothers' case in California, said that he would "sure like to fuck Angela Davis," it was easy to criticize him for being sexist. (Davis was a professor and Communist Party member who was involved in the prisoner's rights movement and Jackson's defense; she was accused of smuggling a gun into prison for Jackson.) But there were, of course, no women in Ashland for us to argue with and learn from, nor were writings from the women's movement available. So, at least for me, an understanding of the larger meaning of the women's movement and its critique of gender roles, hierarchies within organizations, and other aspects of a male-dominated society did not come about until after I left prison.

As for the other resisters, Dave Nickerson was not only the sole African American among us, but his decision to refuse induction was made as an individual who was not involved in the wider antidraft movement. Dave, a large, powerful, and inquisitive man from Columbus, Ohio, was particularly important to our group in forming good relationships with the more political black inmates. A minister's son, Dave always cracked me up when he would use the expression "Gee Christmas" instead of "Jesus Christ" or some curse word. With my encouragement and through the efforts of Doug Dowd, Dave was admitted to Cornell after he was paroled.

Jim Wessner was a former student at Harvard who had been part of the New England Resistance, and we had some mutual friends in the Boston-Cambridge area. At the time I arrived in Ashland, we were probably the most in sync, politically, among the resisters, though Jim and I never got particularly friendly.

In later months, some additional draft resisters entered our ranks and became among my closest friends in prison. These included Dan Brustein, an Antioch College student and non-registrant who had notified his Ohio draft board that he would not cooperate with Selective Service, and Ed Gargan, a University of Wisconsin student and a member of the Chicago Fifteen, a group of Catholic radicals influenced by the Berrigan brothers who destroyed thousands of draft files.

Like me, Dan and Ed had both been involved with the student New Left and desired to continue their political education while in prison. I had a special affinity with Dan since the two of us were among the few Jewish inmates in Ashland, even though we were both strictly secular.

Temperamentally, Dan and Ed were quite different. Dan could be talkative and opinionated with friends, but he knew how and when to be quiet—which, in prison, can be a lifesaving quality. He got along with a wide range of inmates and was one of the only college-educated resisters among us to seek out work assignments outside the usual "white collar" jobs in the education and medical departments.

Ed was louder and more effusive, not always to his own advantage in prison. But I enjoyed his willingness to do little things that caused consternation among the Ashland authorities. Ed's father was a professor of European intellectual history at the University of Wisconsin, and Ed was already a gifted multilinguist, fluent in several languages, including Chinese. I had to suppress my laughter one time when Mrs. Rivers watched Ed open a package he had received containing a new volume of Chairman Mao's works…in Chinese. The authorities let Ed keep the book—I guess they weren't too worried about other inmates reading that "political power grows out of the barrel of a gun" in Mandarin.

By 1970, our ranks of draft resisters in Ashland had increased to about a dozen. We now included some guys who didn't know how to do time—they didn't know when to keep their mouths shut and were oblivious of their effect on other inmates. I once had to intervene with one of the more militant black inmates, who had liked me ever since I helped him pass his GED exam, when he was about to beat the shit out of one of our new resisters over something the guy had said in their dorm. Another time, Dan and one of our burly

Family members had to escort the same resister back from the mess hall to his dorm to avoid another fight—again over his unwittingly irritating another hot-tempered inmate.

One other inmate was particularly close to us resisters—Steve Jeffco, who had attended the University of New Hampshire on a football and wrestling scholarship. A working-class guy from Altoona, Pennsylvania, Steve had robbed a bank, using a starter's pistol with blank cartridges, after his father was laid off from a railroad job and the shoe factory where his mother worked closed down. Steve, who was in K Unit with me, became my closest friend in Ashland.

Steve developed into a voracious reader in prison, using his time to further his education. He was a tough guy who didn't take any shit from anyone—inmates, guards, or prison officials. Although he never made any effort to ingratiate himself with the prison doctor and dentist in the medical department where he was assigned, it was widely known that the unit could barely function without his organizational skills and hard work. Steve's integrity and sense of justice sometimes got him into trouble, but few things seemed to faze him.

Lying Low

I was not a paranoid person when I entered Ashland, but I also learned from the start that I was being watched. On my second day in prison, an inmate stopped me near the mess hall. After introducing himself, he said, "Hey, I'm on study release. Do you want me to get in touch with the local SDS people for you?" Sensing that something was wrong with this offer from a complete stranger, I told him no. When I asked my new resister friends about him, I was told that the guy was a known snitch who should not be trusted. But I never found out who set him up to make contact with me, and for what purpose.

My strategy through my first eleven months in prison was to lie low and avoid confrontations or direct conflicts with the prison authorities unless I had no other choice. No matter how I now felt about the value of draft resistance as a political strategy, I knew I would be in prison for a while, and decided that I would try to do my time quietly and just let the days, weeks, and months roll by. I would use my time to further my education and make myself a better revolutionary by the time I got out.

I knew there might come a time when I had to take some action that would be guaranteed to get me into hot water, but I didn't go looking for trouble with guards or my civilian supervisors. Basically, I wanted to survive—without

Bruce Dancis in the visitors room in federal prison in Ashland, Kentucky, March 1970. (Lawrence Felix Kramer)

having to make too many compromises, and with my principles and self-esteem intact.

My friends and I, along with most of the African American inmates, didn't talk to guards unless we had to, unlike some of the young white guys who looked up to the guards as sort of father figures and vied for their attention. There were days when I would try to walk into my dorm and found myself being slowed to a stop by the crowd of inmates hanging out with the guard on duty.

The guards encouraged this behavior—it made them feel less like prison guards and more like counselors. It also put them in a good position to find out what the inmates were doing and thinking, and to influence impressionable inmates to act in certain ways.

Many of the guards feared the resisters, other Family members, and the black inmates because we wouldn't get involved in such friendly guard-inmate relationships. They thought we had "bad attitudes." They seemed especially paranoid that the more political inmates were "organizing" or "agitating." When I received my prison file years later, I found notations on my record that I had been "Anti-Administration" on January 17 and March 17, 1970. No explanation was given in either case as to what form my hostility took.

Late in the evening on April 21, 1970, I had my most serious collision with prison guards and the Ashland administration.

SPOTLIGHT: GOING TO THE HOLE, APRIL 21, 1970

"Everybody light up!"

With that modest request to the inmates in K Unit, the Ashland, Kentucky, federal prison conspiracy to riot began. Even though the episode was neither a conspiracy nor a riot nor a conspiracy to riot, it almost got me and a few friends indicted on new federal charges. And it did result in my only stretch in "the hole"—aka the D Block detention/segregation unit—for ten days.

The events leading up to April 21 began a few weeks earlier, when the guards in each dorm had their quarterly shift change. Coming on duty in my dorm from 4 to 12 p.m., the shift when most of the inmates were both in the dorm and awake, was Officer Dart, a guard with a reputation for disliking hippies and blacks. He seemed to have it in for Family members in particular, while at the same time enjoying palling around with "his boys"—immature white guys. From his first day on duty Dart began enforcing old rules that had long been forgotten and arbitrarily making up new ones. For one, he decided that no inmate could walk around the dorm between 10 and 11 p.m.

This was a new rule he enforced only against our group, while letting his pals do whatever they wished. When a bunch of us complained, he told us to shut up.

On April 20, Steve was walking to dinner along one of the two pathways used by inmates to go from our dorm to the prison mess hall. For no apparent reason, Dart told him to come back and use the other path. Steve refused, and kept walking. When Steve got back to the unit after dinner, Dart said he was giving Steve two hours of extra duty for insubordination, which usually meant pushing a broom or a mop. Steve complained to Captain Hopper, Ashland's chief correctional officer, but was told that the matter was between him and Dart.

The next evening, on April 21, just before the lights were turned off at 11, Steve and another friend, "Bunk" Ford, lit up cigarettes. A few minutes later, Dart came over to Steve and Bunk and told them to put the smokes out. Although a rule did exist prohibiting smoking after lights were out, it was never enforced in any of the dorms.

Steve replied, "Why should we?" Dart then told Steve and Bunk that their response would cost them one hour of extra duty.

I had no desire to get into a jam, but I felt I had to do something to support Steve and Bunk, whose beds were next to mine. So I asked Steve for one of his cigarettes and lit up in solidarity.

It was at this point that Steve yelled out "Everybody light up," and three more of our friends joined the smoke fest. By now, everyone on our side of the dorm was sitting up in their beds and watching. Dart called for help, and another guard arrived. He told us we were asking for trouble. Bunk complained that Dart was selectively enforcing rules against our group. According to the prison's official "Report of Misconduct," which described the incident as an "Attempted Conspiracy," we "rioters" then began disrupting the entire dorm by "talking and laughing."

Lieutenant Newell, the prison's second-ranked guard, then arrived on the scene. Newell was a tight-faced, mean-looking character— right out of central casting as a Nazi officer in a World War II movie. He told us to put out our cigarettes and promised to talk to us about the issue in the morning. We refused. We said we wanted to talk now. Newell then asked Steve, Bunk, and me to talk to him inside the guard's office in the unit.

After Steve complained that Dart was enforcing rules that were "petty bullshit," I joined in, charging Dart with discrimination against our group. Neither Newell nor the rest of the prison guards

listening to us were used to being spoken to in this manner by
inmates. Newell then called for the "goon squad" to hurry over to
K Unit.

By now about a dozen inmates were smoking cigarettes in defiance
of Dart and the guards. When the goon squad arrived, Newell told
six of us to get our jackets, and they marched us off to "the hole."

The hole at Ashland bore little resemblance to the horrific depri-
vation chambers we've all seen in prison movies like *The Shawshank
Redemption*. In Ashland, the detention/segregation unit was just an
old cell block in which inmates were placed in small individual cells
with solid metal doors instead of bars. The doors had small slits at eye
level for guards to look inside at inmates and enough space between
the floor and the door to pass through trays with food. My cell also
had a window with bars, giving me the lovely view of a brick wall.
Inside the cell, there was just enough room for a narrow bed, a locker,
a sink, and a commode with no toilet seat. Inmates in detention/seg-
regation were locked up twenty-four hours a day and not allowed out
of our cells for work details, meals, or recreation. But we were able to
keep our books and other personal items.

The next day I was called before the "Adjustment Committee,"
the court within the prison. The committee consisted of Captain
Hopper, the head of the education department, my caseworker, and
the associate warden. Together, the committee acted as prosecutor,
judge, and jury.

As soon as I sat down inside the committee room, I tried to ask
about my rights in this court: Was I presumed innocent before
proven guilty? Could I see written charges against me? Was I allowed
to question my accuser? Before I could finish, Captain Hopper, his
bull neck and buzz-cut scalp turning bright red, angrily interrupted
me, shouting, "Shut up! You're on trial here, not this court!"

I then said that in order to defend myself, I would need to recount
some of the incidents leading up to our confrontation with Dart.
Again the captain interrupted me. "My patience is wearing thin with
you, Dancis," he said. I replied that if the court was unwilling to hear
the facts of the case, I would say no more.

Captain Hopper then accused me of "mutiny" and said I could get
more prison time for what I did. In response, I said that what concerned me the most was that inmates had no one to go to if they felt a
guard was abusing his powers.

The associate warden, as thin as Captain Hopper was thick but
with a similar hairstyle, then spoke for the first time. "Abuse! Where

are your bruises?" he asked me rhetorically. Then, in something of a
non sequitur, he said, "There's no such thing as prison reform. You
better get that straight."

The captain then sentenced me to "indefinite segregation," as he
did Steve and Bunk. The other three inmates who had been sent to
detention along with us were allowed to return to K Unit.

The next day, a college student (not an inmate) who had been
working as an intern in the prison education department visited me
in the detention cell block. He had been friendly to me in our work
unit, but I viewed him with more than a little suspicion. I was always
aware of the possibility of the prison using informers to get to me
in some way. But I believed him when he told me he had found out
from a reliable source—an inmate I knew and trusted who worked as
a clerk for Captain Hopper—that prison authorities were preparing
"conspiracy to riot" indictments against Steve, Bunk, and me. The
proposed indictments were to be filed with a grand jury at a nearby
federal court in Catlettsburg, Kentucky.

Naturally, I was shaken. Or as the D Unit guard wrote on my
"Adjustment Record" report, I was "unhappy" and "quite" [sic].
I knew that my testimony in court as a convicted felon and prison
inmate wouldn't stand up against the testimony of a prison guard. It
would be my explaining why our action was, at most, a mild form of
insubordination, versus several guards claiming that we had started
a riot—as heard by a jury in semirural Kentucky. I wrote my parents and my lawyer; I found out later that my letters were held up by
prison officials and not sent out.

I spent most of my days in detention writing, reading, and exercis-
ing. After several unsuccessful efforts over the years, I finally managed to read all of volume one of Marx's *Capital*. The three volumes
of Marx's opus also proved to be passable substitutes for free weights,
and I did reps with them for hours, along with hundreds of push-ups
and sit-ups.

I also kept a diary while in detention, the only time I did so during
my time in prison. I realized that I might be facing prosecution and
wanted to maintain some sort of record or account of what was going
on. (A month or two later, after my fellow resister Frank Femia typed
it up on thin, onionskin paper, I smuggled the diary out of prison
during my next town trip with my parents. While it would have been
difficult to smuggle anything *into* prison, because inmates were strip-
searched by guards upon reentrance, no such screening took place
when you met visitors, other than a quick pat down. For smuggling

purposes, I employed the tie-the-folded-paper-to-my-penis-with-a-rubber-band method, and it worked.

Fortunately for me, during my first weekend in detention I had a visit from Doug and Kay Dowd. (Institutional rules allowed inmates in detention to have previously approved visits.) As we sat together in the visiting room, I told the Dowds what was happening. My visitors took copious notes during our conversation, and we made sure this was observed by the guards on duty.

Late Monday afternoon, I was visited again in the detention block by the intern. He had just heard from the same reliable source that federal charges were not going to be filed against us after all. Perhaps the Dowds' note taking had gotten back to the warden, and he decided to cool it. I'll never know what really happened.[1]

Later in the week, after ten days in D Block, Steve, Bunk, and I were let out of detention, sent back to our regular unit, and reassigned to our old prison jobs. No explanation was ever given, other than the D Block guard telling me, "You boys have been here long enough."

When we returned to our dorm, it was like nothing had happened. We ignored Dart, and he ignored us. Six months later, my "Parole Progress Report" incongruously stated that "there are no misconduct reports.... [Dancis] has impressed everyone with his ability to mind his own business, pursue his own interests, get along well with everyone, and be most helpful in his relations with peers."

Books behind Bars

Before the "conspiracy to riot," the only time I had gotten into trouble was when Mrs. Rivers, the head GED teacher and my boss, took me out of prison to help her purchase reading material for the prison library. In addition to going to a bookstore in Ashland, we went to the Marshall University bookstore in nearby Huntington, West Virginia. She felt, rightly, that I was more in tune than her about what books inmates might want to read, and she let me choose any book I wanted. I had a fine time selecting books off the shelves without the slightest care about how much they cost.

All went well until we got back to the prison. Mrs. Rivers was horrified when she realized that, because she had not been paying close attention to

---

1. The documents I later received under the Freedom of Information Act had many sections blacked out and shed no light on this matter.

the books I had chosen, the Federal Bureau of Prisons had purchased copies of Abbie Hoffman's *Woodstock Nation,* which included notes on how to make pipe bombs and other incendiary devices, and Frantz Fanon's *The Wretched of the Earth,* which in its paperback edition sported the subtitle *The Handbook for the Black Revolution That Is Changing the Face of the World.*

Mrs. Rivers was not happy with me, to say the least. But she didn't punish me, other than never again taking me out on a book-buying expedition. Needless to say, the inmates at Ashland never got a chance to read Abbie's and Fanon's books.

When Richard Nixon ordered the invasion of Cambodia in late April 1970, students and antiwar activists around the country reacted with renewed anger and vigor, spilling into the streets and organizing student strikes. At one of those demonstrations, at Kent State University in Ohio, the Ohio National Guard opened fire on a group of protesters, killing four and injuring nine. This led to even more student strikes and the temporary closing of over five hundred colleges around the country.

But what could we do about this in federal prison? I believed that refusing to work would only get us sent to detention and would have virtually no impact on the inmate population. A few of the resisters discussed making black armbands and wearing them to our work assignments, but we ultimately rejected such a symbolic act as being equally futile. So I went to work in the education department, mad as hell over the murders at Kent State but resigned that I couldn't do anything to protest them.

That morning, a half dozen students from Ohio State University were visiting Ashland's education department, and they came into the classroom where I was working. Seeing them just set me off.

"What are you doing here?" I yelled at the startled students. "Don't you know there's a nationwide student strike over the invasion of Cambodia and the shootings at Kent State!" But before I could say anything else, both Mrs. Rivers and Mr. Nell told me to be quiet and go to another classroom. I did. They could have called the guards to take me to detention, but they didn't. Instead, they let me seethe by myself, in silence.

I knew that generations of political prisoners and revolutionaries before me had used their time in prison to study and write. Before I began my prison term, I had always been more of an activist than a theorist or scholar. I read enough, in college and on my own, to buttress my gut feelings about war, poverty, and racism, and I had spent hours during 1968 and '69 doing economic research on the Cornell board of trustees and their corporate affiliations. But I wanted to gain a much richer understanding of history and economics.

Not being allowed to take college courses, I embarked upon a program of self-education. My friends from Cornell sent me any book I requested and threw in others they felt I would enjoy. My reading took me through the Russian Revolution and its legacy via Isaac Deutscher's critical biography of Stalin and his three-volume biography of Trotsky, and Rosa Luxemburg's *The Mass Strike.* These works reinforced my hostility toward Soviet-style communism and the Marxist-Leninist ideology that had become so popular within SDS. Doug Dowd, an economic historian, sent me Robert Heilbroner's *The Worldly Philosophers,* an ecumenical examination of leading economic theorists since Adam Smith, as well as major works by Marxist economists, beginning with Marx's *Capital* and continuing with Paul Baran and Paul Sweezy's *Monopoly Capital.* He also supplied books that offered critical perspectives on the history of American foreign policy by William Appleman Williams, Cornell's Walter LaFeber, and, prior to his right-wing conversion, David Horowitz. Other supporters, like Cornell English professor Jonathan Bishop, kept me going with fictional works. Thanks to Jonathan, I read Kurt Vonnegut, Joseph Heller, and Ken Kesey for the first time, along with Jack London and other writers.

I was usually able to get approval for the books I wanted. The prison education department, which determined which books were acceptable, was willing to let in radical books from another era or country. The works of Marx and Lenin, for example, were no problem. But requests for more timely material, particularly books on current events or anything pertaining to black liberation, were usually denied. The authorities rejected Jerry Rubin's *Do It!* Julius Lester's *Revolutionary Notes,* Eldridge Cleaver's *Soul on Ice* and *Post-Prison Writings,* and surprisingly, W. E. B. Du Bois's *The Souls of Black Folk.* After arguing with Nell about this, he said he would approve these books only if I read them at work and did not take them with me to the dorm. He didn't want me lending them to any other inmates, saying, "I won't aid your revolution." I refused the conditions.

Although our prison library was generally lousy, Ashland had been the recipient of a donation of books published by Pantheon, then a left-leaning imprint of Random House. This cache opened up the world of social history to me, through the works of British scholars like Eric Hobsbawn, Christopher Hill, and E. P. Thompson, and American historian Eugene Genovese.

What's Happening Outside?

Determined to stay involved in what was going on in the movement, I maintained an active correspondence, and had frequent visits, with my old comrades. They represented several of the political tendencies that had arisen within Cornell SDS before I went to prison. The movement at Cornell had become even more factionalized after the split of national SDS shortly after my term began.

In the climactic national convention of SDS in June 1969, the Revolutionary Youth Movement faction, led by the National Office group, walked out to hold its own convention and expelled Progressive Labor from SDS. Within a few months, the RYM faction itself split, largely between a group that would become the Weatherman faction (led by Bernardine Dohrn, Bill Ayers, and Jeff Jones) and a Marxist-Leninist faction (led by Mike Klonsky). Along with PL, this left three political groupings all claiming to be the rightful SDS—and this didn't even include my Labor Committee friends, who were opposed to the three other factions, and those who didn't support any faction, a position I would have shared.

There was one positive aspect of my incarceration during this turbulent time: I didn't have to choose sides among the splintering groups that emerged after the SDS debacle. In this way I was able to maintain many of my friendships at a time when years-old relationships were dissolving in acrimony.

I tried to keep up with events in the movement and beyond by reading whatever publications I could get my hands on. My parents gave me a subscription to the *New York Times,* which in those days arrived by mail, a few days late. But my folks refused to get me subscriptions to publications they disagreed with politically. So that meant no subscription, or no subscription paid by them, to the *National Guardian,* then the leading left-wing weekly newspaper in America, or even the *New York Review of Books.* Fortunately, my friends paid for subscriptions.

My incarceration did have some impact on my parents' political views. My mother had steadily become more and more antiwar as the war in Vietnam dragged on. In November 1969, she went to Washington, D.C., to participate in the large antiwar demonstration called by the Mobe. She made and carried a sign—"Free my draft resister son from prison"—and was teargassed when she got too close to the Justice Department, the site of a split-off protest by radical factions.

Among the more political inmates, we had frequent discussions about what was going on outside. A sympathetic staff member, Dr. Ponds, agreed to sponsor a biweekly "book club" in which about a half dozen of us would meet, without supervision, for a couple of hours during the evening in a medical department room.

One time, having just completed Deutscher's books on Stalin and Trotsky, I led a discussion on the Russian Revolution. On another occasion, I gave a detailed account of the student uprising at Cornell in the spring of '69. For the most part, we tried to make sense of developments like the fracturing of SDS, the emergence of the Weathermen and, later, the Weather Underground

Organization, and events such as the battle over People's Park in Berkeley and Jonathan Jackson's ill-fated attempt to free his imprisoned brother, George Jackson, from San Quentin by taking a judge and DA hostage in a Marin County courtroom.

Prison had the effect of making me more of a revolutionary than I was when I began my sentence. While I did not believe that revolution was at all imminent—and thus rejected the provocative, violent actions being undertaken by the Weather Underground and others—I thought that the tide of history was moving in our direction. Although the movement in America was fragmenting and becoming more and more absorbed in factional fighting, it seemed as if our overall ranks were growing.

So it was with a clear, if naïve, vision and purpose that I wrote in my application for admission to the University of California, whose Santa Cruz campus I hoped to attend when granted parole,

> When I came to prison I had the beginnings of a healthy socialist analysis of the United States. I have been able to do a good deal of studying during my [time] in jail and have added greatly to my understanding.... Yet I am quite far from achieving anything near the real understanding I need to have to be of service to the political movement I am a part of.... The problem of reconciling my school work with my political life will continue to be a difficult one. Yet there is one factor other than the conducive atmosphere of Santa Cruz that should help me to be a good student—I will be on parole and I do not want to go back to jail.

Chapter Seventeen

Getting Out

I first went up for parole during my fifth month of imprisonment in Ashland. I didn't expect to get paroled—none of the other draft resisters were paroled on their first attempt—and the proceedings seemed perfunctory. My parole was quickly denied, and the next parole hearing was scheduled for a year away, in October 1970. The FBI took note of this, as a memorandum from the Louisville, Kentucky, bureau of the FBI to Director J. Edgar Hoover stated that I would not be eligible for parole until October 1970 and that my address "will also be verified on an annual basis in view of [my] inclusion in the Agitator Index."

By the time a year had passed, I thought my chances for parole were good. Most of my fellow resisters were getting out after eighteen to twenty months in prison, and I hoped I would not be an exception. But I had to come up with a parole plan, which in my case meant returning to college.

Cornell had instituted a new policy, no doubt pushed through by faculty members who were sympathetic to our cause, to readmit to Cornell any student whose education had been interrupted by imprisonment for draft resistance. This aligned the university's policy toward resisters with its existing policy of readmitting students who left to do military service.

Although I had left Cornell in January 1967 with a mediocre academic record and a bad disciplinary record, and had caused a certain amount of trouble at Cornell while remaining in Ithaca as a nonstudent, friendly professors believed they could get me readmitted under the new policy. My parents were thrilled that I would be returning to college and generously offered to pay for my tuition, room, and board. Perhaps I could even get back my New York State Regents Scholarship.

But I was worried about returning to Cornell. During my time in prison, the movement at Cornell, SDS specifically, had split apart and was in disarray. Many of the most active SDSers in the action faction had left Ithaca and moved to Seattle, where they formed the Seattle Liberation Front. My friends in the Labor Committee had mostly moved to New York City. Dan Berrigan was serving his own prison term in Danbury, Connecticut. Doug Dowd was planning to take a position at the University of California in Berkeley, and many other sympathetic faculty members were being denied tenure or moving to other universities, or both. There were still groups in Ithaca I could have worked with, but they were small and somewhat dispirited.

The problem for me was not so much the difficulties that the movement at Cornell was facing, but what my role would be in it if I returned. Some friends were urging me to come back and help put the movement back together again. I was flattered by the requests and believed that I could make a difference. Yet even if I wasn't too concerned about meeting whatever expectations movement people at Cornell might have had of me upon my return, I was worried about academics. I had never done a good job of juggling study and activism. I did not know how I would react to the competing pressures I knew I would face if I went back to Cornell.

It was at this time that Mike Rotkin suggested I consider moving to California and enrolling at the Santa Cruz campus of the University of California. After graduating from Cornell, Mike had started graduate studies at UC Santa Cruz, and his wife, Karen, had taken a job on campus. One of the faculty members was sociologist Bill Friedland, who had been a Cornell SDS faculty adviser before getting a job at UCSC.

The newest campus in the University of California system, UC Santa Cruz had a reputation as a progressive institution. Instead of grades, a student could opt for professor evaluations. Individualized study was encouraged. There were many young and left-leaning faculty members, and the university—built upon a system of small colleges within one larger institution—encouraged close student-faculty relations.

I had Mike and Bill in my corner to persuade the admissions department to let me in as a probationary student despite my poor academic record at Cornell. It seemed like an ideal place for me, a motivated, largely self-educated, twenty-one-year-old parolee with radical politics and a hostility toward authority. Moving to California also looked like it would be a great adventure. I had never been farther west than Colorado. UC Santa Cruz appeared to be the ideal place to continue my education, renew my involvement in the movement, and make a fresh start in my personal life. Perhaps most important, gaining admission would satisfy my need to develop a parole plan that could be approved by prison authorities.

Unfortunately, the officials at Ashland didn't know much about the University of California and its many campuses, nor did they comprehend the geography of the state of California. To them, the University of California meant only one place—Berkeley—and they weren't about to let me enroll in a hotbed of radical student activism. As my caseworker put it, paroling me to Berkeley would be like "sending coal to Newcastle." It took me several months to convince Jones that Santa Cruz was actually a quiet beach town more than ninety miles from Berkeley and that UC Santa Cruz had no significant history of student unrest.

I found myself in the agonizing position of waiting for nearly six weeks to get the results of my parole hearing. The delay was apparently based on Jones and the parole board failing to agree upon a suitable college for me. At least Jones seemed to recognize, judging from his notes on the subject, that his problematic charge "had to go to [a] school which will accept him."

Finally, on December 3, 1970, I was told that I would be getting a "Christmas release"—a release date just before Christmas Day. I was thrilled to get a parole date, but it was also a bittersweet experience, particularly as my last days in Ashland wound down. I had seen some of my best friends leave prison before me—Steve Jeffco, Dave Nickerson, Big Joe, Dan Bromley—and even witnessed a pal who had been paroled come back to prison six months later for a parole violation. When they left, I felt happy for them but also a bit sad that their friendship would be gone as well. So when my time came, I was overjoyed yet also concerned about the buddies I would be leaving behind.

The FBI was monitoring my parole plans. A memorandum from the FBI office in Louisville to Hoover, dated November 30, 1970 (several days before I was even informed that my parole date had been determined), identified my contacts in Santa Cruz as "Michael Ratkin [sic] and Professor Friedland." Because of their friendship with me, the memorandum concluded, "San Francisco should check indices regarding MICHAEL RATKIN [sic] and if he can be identified concerning 'Professor Friedland.'"

I spent my last two months in Ashland in a preferred housing dorm, a routine move for inmates who were nearing the end of their sentences. The main advantage of this unit, one of the older ones in the prison, was that each inmate had an individual cell. After seventeen months of living in a large, noisy dorm, I finally had some occasional privacy. This made up for the cell block having no doors or enclosures for its toilets, leaving one to sit and shit in open view.

I was released from Ashland at 6:55 a.m. on December 23, 1970. The parole authorities had given me permission to visit my parents for four days in New York before I flew to California and reported to my parole officer. I dressed in the clothes I had arrived in, which felt loose, since I had lost a dozen pounds during my nineteen months in prison and was now down to 123. But my old boots, the ones that Big Jackie had so admired in the Onondaga County Jail, still fit. I was given a U.S. Navy surplus coat, as I had arrived in Ashland during warm weather. A guard drove me, without using handcuffs, to the local airport outside Huntington, where I caught a flight to Pittsburgh en route to New York City.

While waiting for my connecting flight in the Pittsburgh airport, I bought a newspaper and a soda with the money that had been in my pocket when I first arrived in Ashland. I went to the bathroom without having to get permission from Mr. Nell or Mrs. Rivers. I looked around at all the strange, unfamiliar faces of people walking past me, paying special attention to the young women rushing to and from planes, working behind counters, standing in lines, taking my ticket, and directing me to my plane seat. I noted that men my age appeared a lot shaggier than I did with my prison haircut.

I was subdued but happy as I thought about all the good things awaiting me—seeing my parents and friends again, moving to California, falling in love, going back to college, and getting laid (not necessarily in that order). But I was already concerned about how I could become part of the movement again without violating my parole while the Nixon administration expanded the air war in Vietnam and cracked down hard on dissent.

My "Certificate of Parole" listed, under "Conditions of Parole," all the things that were forbidden for parolees. Like the Ten Commandments, they were a bunch of "shalt nots" declaring that I was not allowed to

Leave the Northern District of California without permission;
Violate any laws;
Drink alcoholic beverages to excess;
Purchase, possess, use, or administer marihuana or narcotic [*sic*] or
    other habit-forming or dangerous drugs;
Associate with persons who have a criminal record or persons engaged
    in criminal activity;
Have firearms (or other dangerous weapons) in my possession.

According to the terms of my release, I could remain on parole until May 19, 1975, or for an additional 1,608 days.[1]

----

1. In October 1972, at the age of twenty-four and nearly two years after my release from prison, I received notice from the U.S. Board of Parole, which stated that because I had "received the maximum benefits from the Youth Corrections Act" and that my "discharge from this commitment would be compatible with the welfare of society," I was "unconditionally discharged." I also received a certificate noting that my felony conviction had been set aside. I couldn't have made it through parole unscathed without the support of parole officer Douglas Dilfer, the friendship of Mike Rotkin, Karen Rotkin, Bill Friedland, and Harry Chotiner, and the love of Lorna Hall, my companion and wife for nine years.

Part Four

EPILOGUE

Chapter Eighteen

Did We End the War?
Did Draft Resistance Matter?

It comes back to Vietnam.

In 1980, erstwhile Cornell SDS leader Chip Marshall was interviewed by *Time* magazine. The story was a snide piece about a former radical's exodus from the Left. Chip had become a businessman, and the story quoted him saying "America is in good shape." Most startling to those of us who knew Chip back in the '60s was his answer to a question about the Vietnamese "boat people" who were then fleeing Vietnam. He felt "terrible" about it, Chip told the *Time* reporter, giving a humane, nonpolitical response to a question about human suffering.

But then Chip continued: "Maybe we were completely wrong on Viet Nam."

Chip's remarks shocked a lot of his former friends in the antiwar movement, including me. Still, those of us who were part of the movement shouldn't duck the question Chip raised: Were we right in opposing the war?

Problems Facing a Unified Vietnam

By the time the war finally ended, in April 1975, 58,721 American troops had died in Vietnam. For the Vietnamese, the losses were far greater. In his powerful book *Kill Anything That Moves: The Real American War in Vietnam*, Nick Turse cites a 2008 study by researchers from Harvard University and the University of Washington that estimated 3.8 million violent war deaths of Vietnamese civilians and combatants from the North and the South. A much larger number of Vietnamese had been wounded and were suffering physically and emotionally.

The war-torn nation faced huge economic problems in 1975. According to historian Marilyn Young,

> In the South, 9,000 out of 15,000 hamlets, 25 million acres of farmland, 12 million acres of forest were destroyed, and 1.5 million farm animals had been killed; there were an estimated 200,000 prostitutes, 879,000 orphans, 181,000 disabled people, and 1 million widows; all six of the industrial cities in the North had been badly damaged, as were provincial and district towns, and 4,000 out of 5,800 agricultural communes. North and south the land was cratered and planted with tons of unexploded ordnance, so that long after the war farmers and their families suffered serious injuries as they attempted to bring the fields back into cultivation. Nineteen million gallons of herbicide had been sprayed on the South during the war, and while the long-term effects were unknown in 1975...severe birth defects and multiple miscarriages were apparent early on.

Massive foreign aid was needed to help Vietnam deal with these problems. However, the aid from the United States, a sum of $3.25 billion, which had been promised to the North Vietnamese "without any preconditions" during the Paris Peace Talks, was withheld by the Ford administration. The United States also enforced an economic embargo against the reunited country.

The scope of the political problems caused by reunification was huge. The war had ended so quickly that the United States was only able to evacuate about twenty thousand of its South Vietnamese allies. That left behind 1.2 million South Vietnamese soldiers and police, more than three hundred thousand civil servants who had worked in the South Vietnamese government, and many businessmen and merchants who had gotten rich under South Vietnamese and American capitalism. It wasn't difficult to imagine that there would be reprisals by the victors against those who had worked for or supported the U.S.-backed government in the South, and that this would lead to the attempt by many to flee. After all, following the American Revolution, tens of thousands of Tories who had supported Great Britain during the war left the former American colonies for Canada, England, and the West Indies.

In the face of this economic and humanitarian crisis, the new communist government of a united Vietnam made a number of bad decisions—forcing the rapid collectivization of agriculture and industry; imposing the one-party state and state-controlled media that had existed in the North; banning "reactionary" books and journals, along with Western music and movies. Many former military officers and government officials in the South were sent to "reeducation" camps.

Exacerbating the situation was Vietnam's deteriorating relationship with its neighbors to the west (Cambodia) and north (China). Border skirmishes between Vietnam and the Chinese-backed Khmer Rouge in Cambodia led to a December 1977 Vietnamese invasion of Cambodia and the overthrow of Pol Pot's homicidal regime. In February 1979, after more than 250,000 ethnic Chinese who lived in Vietnam fled the country following the Vietnamese government's adoption of repressive policies against them, the Chinese army invaded Vietnam. About twenty thousand soldiers were killed on each side, though Vietnamese civilians bore the brunt of the fighting.

Chip Marshall's remarks about Vietnam were made shortly after these events took place, while Vietnam was reeling from severe economic problems and the effects of the war with China. Yet projecting backward from 1980 to the civil war and the fight against the United States is unfair, illusory, and ahistorical.

While the war was going on, I was not particularly interested in what type of society the North Vietnamese and the NLF would set up in a unified Vietnam should they be victorious. For me, that was an issue that should be left up to the Vietnamese people. At the least, a united Vietnam would be no more repressive than the military dictatorships running South Vietnam. Many of us in the antiwar movement developed tunnel vision that caused us to look ahead only at ending the war and not at what would come next.

At the time I was working to end the war, I never adequately came to grips with the failure of communist nations to address the human desire for freedom and democracy. Although I knew that communist countries represented a perverted and distorted form of the kind of socialism I believed in, I rarely expressed such feelings while the war was still raging.

In the case of the North Vietnamese and NLF, especially after meeting representatives of both in Budapest in 1968, I was humbled by their heroism and commitment. When they told us how they survived massive American bombing raids by living underground in makeshift shelters and tunnels or described the loss of life and separation from their own families over the many years of war, raising a matter such as the lack of press freedom in Hanoi seemed inappropriate.

It wasn't as if the Vietnamese were propagandizing us Americans with stories about the wonders of life under communism. They tried to inspire us to put more pressure on *our* government to end the war; none of the Vietnamese I met suggested that we build a new society in America based on theirs. Nor did I look at North Vietnam as a society worth replicating in the United

States. As historian Michael Kazin has pointed out, even though many in the American New Left admired the revolutionary societies of North Vietnam, Cuba, and China, "few regarded any of these peasant nations as models for an overdeveloped America."

Nevertheless, we in the antiwar movement should have more forcefully and publicly made clear our commitment to certain universal standards of freedom and human rights. Such a position would not only have been morally right, but would most likely have been to our tactical benefit as well in building the movement and reaching out to people who had previously been uninvolved. It might even have had a positive effect on the Vietnamese government after the country was unified.

Since the mid-1980s, the government in Vietnam has initiated economic and political reforms, including the reintroduction of private markets and private companies, the decentralization of agricultural decision making, and allowing greater freedom in literature, filmmaking, and the arts. Vietnam now has normal diplomatic and trade relations with the United States. In 2010, following several visits to the country, the United Nations special reporter on human rights issued a generally positive report on developments in Vietnam. On the other hand, in Amnesty International's 2012 report on the state of human rights around the world, the government of Vietnam was strongly criticized: "Harsh repression of dissidents continued, with severe restrictions on freedom of expression, association and peaceful assembly. Critics of government policies were targeted, including social and political activists." Similar criticisms of Vietnam were made by Human Rights Watch in its *World Report 2012*.

But I still believe that American involvement in Vietnam was unwarranted, immoral, and a blot on our national honor. The sorrow among those who lost loved ones in the war, on all sides, will never go away. The war brought untold misery to the Vietnamese people and damaged many of the soldiers who fought in it.

The antiwar movement was right in opposing the war in Vietnam. But how successful was the movement?

The Antiwar Movement's Role in Ending the War in Vietnam

Back in 1975, I believed there were two main causes for the war's ending: the North Vietnamese and NLF had, despite suffering unfathomable casualties for many years, won a military victory on the ground, and the U.S. Congress was finally able to cut off funding to the military dictatorship of South Vietnam. Other important factors were the problems war spending was inflicting on the American economy and the urban unrest that forced the Johnson administration to keep the National Guard and Reserves back home to put down domestic rebellions, rather than having them available to fight in Vietnam.

It was only later, when scholars gained access to the notes, memos, and other internal documents written by members the Johnson and Nixon administrations, and when participants in those administrations began writing about their involvement, that the antiwar movement's effectiveness became clearer. As Tom Wells wrote in *The War Within,* his history of the antiwar movement, "As the cutting edge of domestic antiwar sentiment as a whole, it played a major role in restricting, deescalating, and ending the war." Wells's book is filled with examples of Johnson, Nixon, and their advisers worrying about the movement's potential reaction to military actions that were under consideration. To mention just two: Wells, citing David Halberstam's *The Best and the Brightest,* quotes President Johnson's response, in late 1966, to his top military officials' advice that he order the obliteration of Hanoi and Haiphong through massive U.S. bombing: "How long [will] it take [for] five hundred thousand angry Americans to climb that White House wall and lynch their President," Johnson said, "if he does something like that." And in a postwar interview, retired admiral Thomas Moorer, chairman of the Joint Chiefs of Staff under Nixon, claimed that "the reaction of the noisy radical groups was considered all the time. And it served to inhibit and restrain the decision makers." The antiwar movement, Moorer said, "had a major impact...both in the executive and legislative branches of the government."

Crucial to that impact was the emergence, particularly in 1971 and after, of Vietnam veterans as antiwar protesters. Opposition to the war among GIs first received widespread attention in February 1966, when Donald Duncan, a retired master sergeant in the Special Forces who had served eighteen months in Vietnam, published a devastating article in *Ramparts* magazine titled "The Whole Thing Was a Lie."

In April 1971, protests led by Vietnam Veterans against the War drew the attention of the nation. About a thousand Vietnam vets, accompanied by the mothers of deceased soldiers, placed wreaths at Arlington National Cemetery, met with members of Congress, and, most powerfully, gathered behind a fence outside the U.S. Capitol and threw away the medals and ribbons they had won for their service in Vietnam. The latter action, which was shown on TV newscasts nationwide, was perhaps the most dramatic, gut-wrenching protest I had ever seen in the history of the war in Vietnam.

Sociologist Paul Joseph made a strong case that even though polling suggested the antiwar movement was not popular with the American public, its impact on how ordinary Americans looked at the war, on the opinions of political elites, and on the attitudes of the media, scholars, and policy advisers was very important. Joseph wrote: "Opposition to the war undermined the virtual consensus that then existed toward U.S. armed intervention and the efficacy of military force." Joseph, like Wells, also demonstrated how the antiwar movement continually constrained both Johnson and Nixon from taking measures that would have escalated the war and drastically increased casualties.

Historian Eric Foner's assessment of the abolitionist movement before the Civil War could apply to the antiwar movement as well: "By changing public discourse, by redefining the politically 'possible,' the abolitionist movement affected far more Americans than actually joined its ranks."

Finally, it must be noted that Nixon's involvement in the Watergate scandal and his subsequent resignation emerged out of his desire to have the escalation of the war into Cambodia kept secret from the American public, and from his authorization of a break-in into the office of Daniel Ellsberg's psychiatrist in order to find damaging information about the man who released the "Pentagon Papers."

For these reasons, Wells concluded that "the American movement against the Vietnam War was perhaps the most successful antiwar movement in history."

The Impact of Draft Resistance on the War and the Movement

I've always been proud to have been a draft resister during the Vietnam War. Having gone to prison for refusing to fight in a war I viewed as unjust and resisting a draft system that was unfair and coercive remains a badge of honor.

When our group at Cornell organized the first mass draft card burning in April 1967, and later, when the Resistance sponsored a series of draft card turn-ins, we hoped the number of participants would be large to start with and would increase exponentially with every national action. The theory was that each action would inspire more and more men of draft age to make a decisive break with Selective Service. As the number of resisters grew, we anticipated a vast increase in induction refusals, followed by mass indictments, trials in federal courts, and, finally, tens of thousands of resisters filling federal prisons. Our ultimate goal was to organize so many men to resist the draft, coupled with increased resistance within the U.S. armed forces, that the military would have trouble finding enough soldiers to fight in Vietnam.

However, by mid-1968 I had come to the view that we had failed to organize enough men willing to risk prison by committing an act of draft resistance. Maybe we underestimated the difficulty of organizing enough people to place themselves in such danger, especially when there were so many alternatives to going to jail. Perhaps we were lousy organizers.

There also was attrition within our ranks, as some who turned in their draft cards later had second thoughts about their actions and the prospect of prison. They reapplied for draft cards, moved to Canada, or successfully challenged the punitive actions of draft boards that took away their student deferments. Some flunked their physical exams and received 4-Fs. Others acted so aggressively at their draft physicals that the military decided not to bother with them.

This all led me to believe our efforts weren't successful, and that's what I told Tom Wells when he interviewed me in the mid-1990s for his book on the antiwar movement.

However, I now think I was wrong about our lack of effectiveness. One factor in my change of mind was a study of the Vietnam-era draft conducted in the late 1970s—of which I was unaware until twenty years after it was published. The authors of the study, Lawrence M. Baskir and William A. Strauss, found that while the movement did not reach our numerical goals in getting men to destroy or turn in their draft cards, and we did not stop the war machine from functioning, we were successful in other ways. By our bringing public attention to draft resistance, Baskir and Strauss wrote, "heavy media exposure contributed to the grass-roots, unorganized movement by more than a half million young men who broke the law and defied their draft boards."

Yet if so many men broke the law, why didn't this have more serious repercussions on the criminal justice system? One reason was that the federal government chose to prosecute only a small percentage of draft resisters for induction refusal, draft card destruction, noncooperation, or non-registration.

For example, there were perhaps fifty "public" draft resisters from Cornell—men who had returned their draft cards to either their local boards or the draft board in Ithaca, destroyed their draft cards while identifying themselves (as I did), or openly announced their noncooperation with the draft. A small portion of these resisters, about a dozen, were reclassified 1-A and called for induction, which all of us refused. But among our entire group, only two of us ever went to prison—me, the first local resister, and Joe Gilchrist, who had initially been sentenced to five years in prison for refusing induction in his native Oklahoma but ended up serving time for ransacking draft files stored in a federal office building in Rochester, New York.

Ramsey Clark, U.S. attorney general in the Johnson administration, but a closet dove on Vietnam, later explained the policy of selective prosecution: "We tried to cull it down to people who were what you could call 'ringleaders,' in speaking for, creating, organizing and moving toward dissolution of the Selective Service System."

This was a smart move by the Justice Department. But there was another factor as well. It turned out that draft resistance cases really were overwhelming the American legal system. Massive case backlogs were occurring throughout the country, and lawyers representing draft resisters became adept at finding holes in the cases against their clients. Eventually, according to Baskir and Strauss, "the criminal justice system became swamped to the point where Selective Service prosecutions became almost impossible. By 1971, the enforcement of the draft law was in shambles."

The San Francisco Bay Area was both a hotbed for draft resistance and for federal judges willing to either dismiss charges against resisters or sentence them to probation instead of prison. In addition, the top U.S. attorney in San Francisco, Cecil Poole, was himself reluctant to prosecute draft cases. As early as 1967 and 1968, more than 90 percent of all cases referred to the U.S. attorney's office in San Francisco were dropped before indictment.

Soon, a similar pattern was evident elsewhere. According to Baskir and Strauss, in the District of Columbia, between 1967 and 1970, 99 percent of draft cases were never prosecuted. Prosecutors in New York City, San Diego, El Paso, New Orleans, and Miami dropped 95 percent of their cases, and the national average was 89 percent. Even in cases where resisters were prosecuted, more than half saw their cases dropped because of defective procedures at local draft boards, unenforceable induction orders, or successful legal defenses.

This policy undercut the Resistance's strategy of filling the nation's prisons with young, largely middle-class men. We may have successfully clogged the court system, but this never became common knowledge among either the general public or the movement.

Still, the draft resistance movement played a significant role in changing national draft policy—specifically in influencing Nixon's introduction of a lottery system and later in his ending of conscription. According to historian Michael S. Foley, "the Nixon administration decided to reform and ultimately end the draft in reaction to the draft resistance movement and its success in publicizing the conscription system's inequities."

Furthermore, the combined strength of the draft resistance movement and the larger antiwar movement made it virtually impossible for future American presidents to rely on conscription to fight wars that were unpopular or aroused serious opposition. These movements did not, in the long run, impede American hubris, an attitude held by various administrations that has sanctioned our military intervention all over the globe. But if presidents following Nixon learned anything from the experience of Vietnam, it was that drafting or even the threat of drafting unwilling combatants would vastly increase the size and vehemence of domestic dissent.

I eventually came to accept Wells's assessment of the draft resistance movement: "The Resistance was a conspicuous component of that cutting edge of active opposition to the war that played such a crucial role in turning U.S. policy around. It promoted official and public perceptions that the war-as-usual had unacceptable domestic costs. Resisters' personal courage increased the peace movement's credibility among some Americans. Their sheer numbers nourished public questioning of the war as well. Perhaps most important, *the Resistance inspired greater dedication and resolve among other antiwar activists*" (italics in original).

How Draft Resistance Affected the Rest of My Life

As for my personal role as a resister, it's not for me to say whether or not my actions were courageous. I don't compare what I did in going to prison with the courage it takes to be in combat. I've never experienced warfare, so I cannot imagine how I would have reacted to a life-or-death situation. The only violence inflicted on my body came from a sucker punch to my ear from a counterdemonstrator in Brooklyn and a few whacks to my ribs by a U.S. marshal outside the Pentagon. Prison was scary at times, but Ashland was probably less violent than most of the institutions in the federal prison system. While my resistance to the draft may have placed me in physical danger, I never thought I was risking my life.

As I write this, it's now more than forty-six years since I resisted the draft. Yet in 2011 I received an e-mail out of the blue from a Cornell contemporary, Judith Fuchs Jacobson. We had never met or communicated before. Judith wrote that she had recently come across a letter she had sent her father in December 1966 after watching me tear up my draft card. Her letter, Judith said, "shows what your effect was on one sensitive freshman. It seemed only right to track you down and share it with you."

Judith wrote her father:

Bruce Dancis, a sophomore and 18 years old, ripped up his draft card today. He is the president of SDS and a cool and laughing and human person. Today he just screwed [up] his life. And now every boy who's against the war is wondering why he's not doing the same....

Down to my level—I was wearing my expensive new winter coat and here was this crowd of people and Bruce speaking seriously over a loudspeaker and reading from his beautiful letter to the draft board about how he couldn't do otherwise and when the U.S. bombed near Hanoi he couldn't wait any longer.... And there I was, totally immersed in triviality. And there he was, a year older than me, making a big decision—and scared, kind of, and proud, and very serious.

I was twenty-two years old when I was paroled from federal prison. By most accounts of friends and relatives who knew me both before and after my nineteen-plus months of incarceration, I became less gregarious after prison, and more serious and scholarly. The combination of changing times and a desire not to return to prison, especially when I was on parole, made me less confrontational, though I remained just as outspoken. Thankfully, my experiences did not screw up my life, as Judith Fuchs Jacobson had worried.

But prison did have some lasting repercussions. One of these was the way in which my sleep patterns changed. For more than a decade after I was released from Ashland, I was awakened by nightmares in which I found myself back in prison. It was usually the case of my parole being unjustly revoked after I was framed by the FBI or the local police, and being sent back to Ashland. These nightmares ended in my thirties, yet returned when I began work on this book. Ever since my first night in Ashland, I have slept on my back, straight as a rail, my arms at my sides. Those who have shared a bed with me have all commented upon how little room I take up, even as my body has, ahem, expanded over the years. I still wake up at the slightest sound.

In the years since prison I've deposited the ashes of my parents in the lake of the cooperative community they helped build. Although I always expressed my gratitude for their love and support, I'm sorry that I never took the opportunity to ask them how they dealt with their son's imprisonment. As a father myself, I cannot imagine enduring what I put my folks through.

Since my release from prison, it has been my personal policy to never duck the question "What did you do during the war in Vietnam?" even though my response often raises eyebrows. I've brought up my felonious past during interviews for graduate schools and graduate fellowships, and later when applying for jobs at newspapers and magazines.

Although my activism slowly diminished over the ensuing forty-plus years, the result of both changing political circumstances and the demands of work and family life, I still view democratic socialism as America's best hope to eliminate the ravages of capitalism and war and to create a society in which human needs take precedence over profits.

American capitalism has failed to produce an egalitarian, fair, and just social order; indeed, the gaps between rich and poor, and between the rich and the middle class, have grown much wider in the twenty-first century. We live in a country that practices socialism for the wealthy, where unscrupulous banks are too big to fail, the government protects giant corporations from foundering as a result of their own misguided policies, and tax policies favor the wealthiest.

I still use the term "socialism" to describe the type of society in which I wish to live. Yet I realize how much that word has been tarnished, besmirched, and distorted by those on the left who have used it in connection with autocratic communist societies, and those on the right who accuse a moderate-to-liberal defender of capitalism like Barack Obama of being a socialist.

Yet no matter what one calls the society I envision, it must be a free society that expands the rights of all, including but going beyond the rights of freedom of expression, assembly, and religion guaranteed by the U.S. Constitution. These rights include, but are certainly not confined to, the right to live in comfort, peace, and security; the right to have a decent job and sufficient wages to support oneself and one's family; the right to have free access to health care and education; the right to live without suffering discrimination on the basis of race, class, gender, sexual orientation, physical impairment, or age; the right of women to control their own bodies; the right of all people to marry the person they love; and the right of everyone to live in a healthy and sustainable world that is no longer poisoning itself.

But a decent society has to address human needs that go beyond all this. A century ago, in 1914, a socialist-feminist named Mary White Ovington wrote that socialist women had learned that "the coming of Socialism is not purely material. It does not mean simply a full stomach—that was often attained under chattel slavery—but a full life."

Only by building a movement that will resist the forces that oppress us, organize the millions of Americans we have not yet reached, and create structures and institutions that are life affirming rather than life destructive will we have a chance to move toward a decent society. In the second decade of the twenty-first century, such a society seems very far away, almost out of reach. The political goals of my life remain unmet, as was the case with my parents and my grandparents before them.

Yet I continue to believe that someday these goals will be attained. I may be a dreamer, but, as John Lennon once said, I'm not the only one.

Acknowledgments

Working on this book gave me the chance to deepen and, in some cases, renew my friendships with fellow '60s activists at Cornell University and beyond. Peter Agree, Joe Kelly, Lawrence Felix Kramer, and Alan Snitow always responded promptly and thoughtfully to my many and continual questions about our activities and lives back in the day. I have also benefited from e-mail, telephone, and in-person interviews and conversations with Ellen (Solomon) Chandler, Harry Chotiner, Doug Dowd, Sarah Elbert, Tony Fels, Abby Ginzberg, Gregory Heins, Marjorie (Holt) Heins, Lisa Johnson, Jeff Jones, Mimi Keck, Rochelle Lefkowitz, Susan (Mokotoff) Reverby, Howard Rodman, Michael Rotkin, Susan Rutberg, and Lenny Silver. I was fortunate to interview Burton Weiss before his death in 2011. In addition to Burton, I remember with fondness and gratitude other friends appearing in these pages who passed away over the years, including Eqbal Ahmad, Norma Becker, Jill Boskey, Bruce Cohen, Dave Dellinger, Ellie Dorsey, Kay Dowd, Matty Goodman, Paul Goodman, Abbie Hoffman, Jim Murray, Karen Frost Rotkin, Jon Sabin, Jay Schulman, Mike Shaffer, and James Weinstein.

Friends from my summer community, the Three Arrows Cooperative Society, who responded to my queries include Carol Bier, Charney Bromberg, Sharon Fromowitz Bromberg, Helen Brown, Jerry Cooper, Nina Drooker, Deborah Gorman, Susan Gorman, Carol Gruber, Carol Marsh, Robert Melnick, and Susan Vladeck.

Stephen Wallenstein graciously shared with me his unpublished 1972 manuscript, "Open Breeches: Guns at Cornell," which he coauthored with George Fisher.

Getting back in touch with my prison buddies Dan Brustein, Ed Gargan, and Steve Jeffco, folksinger/camp counselor Happy Traum, and summer camp bunkmate David Fine enabled me to refresh my own memories and gain their insights about some important issues.

Director Elaine Engst and her staff at the Division of Rare and Manuscript Collections in the Kroch Library within the Cornell University Library made my first visit to a Cornell library in nearly forty years a pleasant and successful one.

John Schroeder, the *Cornell Daily Sun*'s archivist, worked beyond the call of duty to locate, clean up, and provide several of the photographs used in this book, including the image on the cover.

The entire manuscript was read chapter by chapter, as I wrote it, by my wife, Karen Dean-Dancis, and longtime friends Peter Agree, Harry Chotiner, Doug Dowd, and Lawrence Felix Kramer. Their feedback improved my work and sustained me whenever I had doubts about the project. Once I finished the first draft, Naomi Adler Dancis, Paul Joseph, and Susan Reverby read the entire manuscript, and I have benefited greatly from their suggestions. Comments on particular chapters by Robby Adler Peckerer, Charney Bromberg, Dan Brustein, David Fine, Ed Gargan, Lorna Hall, Joe Kelly, Carol Marsh, Robert Melnick, Derk Richardson, Mike Rotkin, and Alan Snitow also assisted my research and editing.

At Cornell University Press, director John Ackerman was the first to read my manuscript, and his encouragement and support have been indispensable. My editor, Frances Benson, has been a pleasure to work with, as she patiently assisted me on matters both major and minor concerning the manuscript, photographs, permissions, and more. I am grateful for the guidance and friendship she has shown me throughout the publishing process. Helpful and timely suggestions about the structure of this book and where to trim it were provided by Fred Solowey and Winthrop "Pete" Wetherbee. Managing editor Ange Romeo-Hall, copy editor Glenn Novak, and acquisitions assistant Katherine Liu offered gracious and valuable assistance in the process of turning a manuscript into a book. Thanks to my children—Chloe Taylor, Lily Dancis Vistica, Alexis Dean, and Nick Dean—for their continued and unequivocal love and support.

This book is dedicated to my late parents, Winston Dancis and Ethel Schachner Dancis, for showing me the way, and to my wife, Karen Dean-Dancis, for sharing it with me.

Notes

Introduction

On statistical information about the Vietnam-era draft, see Lawrence M. Baskir and William A. Strauss, *Chance and Circumstance: The Draft, the War and the Vietnam Generation* (Vintage Books, 1978).

On prominent pro-war individuals who avoided going to Vietnam, see Al Franken, *Rush Limbaugh Is a Big Fat Idiot and Other Observations* (Delacorte Press, 1996), 54–68; Nicholas Kristof, "The 2000 Campaign: Close to Home; Bush's Choice in War: Devoid of Passion and Anxiety," *New York Times*, July 11, 2000; Katherine Q. Seelye, "Cheney's Five Draft Deferments during the Vietnam Era Emerge as Campaign Issues," *New York Times*, May 1, 2004; Michael Wines, "Dissecting Romney's Vietnam Stance at Stanford," *New York Times*, Sept. 11, 2012; Peter J. Boyer, "Good Newt, Bad Newt," *Vanity Fair*, July 1989; Clyde Haberman, "Leaving a War out of Politics and in Hearts," *New York Times*, Nov. 12, 1996; Jodi Wilgoren, "Kerry Attacks Bush Officials Who Received Draft Deferments," *New York Times*, April 17, 2004; Tim Mak, "10 Little-Known Rush Limbaugh Facts," www.Politico.com, March 6, 2012; Bob Geiger, "Malkin: Just Another Chickenhawk Smearing Democratic Veterans," *Huffington Post*, April 25, 2007; *New Hampshire Gazette*, "Chickenhawk Hall of Shame," www.nhgazette.com/chickenhawks/.

On the myth of the "spat-upon Vietnam veteran," see Jerry Lembcke, *The Spitting Image: Myth, Memory, and the Legacy of Vietnam* (NYU Press, 1998).

On the author's early 1970s reflections on the '60s, see Bruce Dancis, "Notes from an Ex-con," *Cornell Alumni News*, July 1971; Bruce Dancis, "Learning from Past Mistakes, Part Two: SDS, Collectives and the Future," *Loaded* (Santa Cruz, CA), Feb. 22, 1972; Bruce Dancis, "SDS: Hope and Failure of the 60's" (a review essay on Kirkpatrick Sale's *SDS*); *New American Movement*, Oct. 1974, and sections on SDS and the New Left in William Friedland with Amy Barton, Bruce Dancis, Michael Rotkin, and Michael Spiro, *Revolutionary Theory* (Allenheld, Osmun Publishers, 1982; written in 1971–72).

On the 1960s draft resistance movement, see Alice Lynd, ed., *We Won't Go: Personal Accounts of War Objectors* (Beacon Press, 1968); Michael Ferber and Staughton Lynd, *The Resistance* (Beacon Press, 1971); Sherry Gershon Gottlieb, ed., *Hell No We Won't Go: Resisting the Draft during the Vietnam War* (Viking, 1991); James W. Tollefson, ed., *The Strength Not to Fight: Conscientious Objectors of the Vietnam War in Their Own Words* (Brassey's, 2000); and Michael S. Foley, *Confronting the War Machine: Draft Resistance during the Vietnam War* (University of North Carolina Press), 2003.

On the prison experiences of Vietnam-era draft resisters, see Dr. Willard Gaylin, *In the Service of Their Country: War Resisters in Prison* (Viking, 1970); Baskir and Strauss, *Chance and Circumstance*, 88–108; Todd Illig's and Norman Lewis's essays in Gottlieb, *Hell No We Won't Go*, 198–210.

On David Miller's experiences in federal prison, see David Miller, *I Didn't Know God Made Honky Tonk Communists* (Regent Press, 2002), 85–109.

On David Harris's writings on the war in Vietnam, draft resistance, and prison, see David Harris, *I Shoulda Been Home Yesterday: 20 Months in Jail for Not Killing Anybody* (Delacorte Press / Seymour Lawrence, 1976); Davis Harris, *Dreams Die Hard: Three Men's Journey through the Sixties* (St. Martin's / Marek, 1982), and David Harris, *Our War: What We Did in Vietnam and What It Did to Us* (Times Books, 1996).

On the 1960s in general, see Todd Gitlin, *The Sixties: Years of Hope, Days of Rage* (Bantam Books, 1987), and Maurice Isserman and Michael Kazin, *America Divided: The Civil War of the 1960s* (Oxford University Press, 2000).

On the antiwar movement and the New Left, see Tom Wells, *The War Within: America's Battle over Vietnam* (University of California Press, 1994); Nancy Zaroulis and Gerald Sullivan, *Who Spoke Up? American Protest against the War in Vietnam, 1963–1975* (Holt, Rinehart and Winston, 1984); Kirkpatrick Sale, *SDS* (Random House, 1973); Todd Gitlin, *The Whole World Is Watching: Mass Media in the Making and Unmaking of the New Left* (University of California Press, 1980); Gitlin, *Sixties;* Helen Garvy, *Rebels with a Cause: A Collective Memoir of the Hopes, Rebellions and Repression of the 1960s* (Shire Press, 2007); James Miller, *Democracy Is in the Streets: From Port Huron to the Siege of Chicago* (Harvard University Press, 1994; originally published in 1987); Marian Mollin, *Radical Pacifism in Modern America: Egalitarianism and Protest* (University of Pennsylvania Press, 2006); James Tracy, *Direct Action: Radical Pacifism from the Union Eight to the Chicago Seven* (University of Chicago Press, 1996); Charles DeBenedetti, *An American Ordeal: The Antiwar Movement of the Vietnam Era* (Syracuse University Press, 1990); Thomas Powers, *Vietnam: The War at Home* (G. K. Hall, 1984); David Barber, *A Hard Rain Fell: SDS and Why It Failed* (University Press of Mississippi, 2008); Simon Hall, *Rethinking the American Anti-War Movement* (Routledge, 2012); Michael Kazin, *American Dreamers: How the Left Changed a Nation* (Alfred A. Knopf, 2011), 209–51; Maurice Isserman, *If I Had a Hammer… the Death of the Old Left and the Birth of the New Left* (Basic Books, 1987), 171–219; Isserman and Kazin, *America Divided*, 165–86, 228–300.

1. Boy from the Bronx

On Parkchester, see Linda Greenhouse, "Parkchester: Trouble in Paradise," *New York* magazine, Feb. 17, 1969; Martha Biondi, *To Stand and Fight: The Struggle for Civil Rights in Postwar New York City* (Harvard University Press, 2003), 121–36, 228–31; Josh Barbanel, "Still a Beacon, Parkchester Climbs Back," *New York Times,* Real Estate, March 14, 2004; Elizabeth Lent, "A Successful Experiment in Living: The Evolution of Parkchester," *Cooperator,* July 2006.

On the discriminatory racial policies of Parkchester and other Metropolitan Life properties, see "Housing Bias Alleged," *New York Times,* Jan. 11, 1953; "Women in Chains Protest Eviction," *New York Times,* May 20, 1953; "Bronx Family of 4 Evicted by Force," *New York Times,* May 21, 1953; "N.Y. Deputies Batter Down Door to Evict Family," *Jet* magazine, June 4, 1953; "Along the N.A.A.C.P. Battlefront: Metropolitan Life," *Crisis,* October 1963; Joseph P. Fried, "City Charges Bias at Three Projects," *New York Times,* May 28, 1968; "Metropolitan Life Denies Racial Bias," *New York Times,* May 29, 1968; Joseph P. Fried, "3 Projects Move to Admit Negroes," *New York Times,* July 19, 1968; Greenhouse, "Parkchester"; Frederick M. Binder and David M. Reimers, *All the Nations under Heaven: An Ethnic and Racial History of New York City* (Columbia University Press, 1996), 195–96; Evelyn Gonzales, *The Bronx* (Columbia University Press, 2004), 115; Cheryl Lynn Greenberg, *Troubling the Waters: Black-Jewish Relations in the American Century* (Princeton University Press, 2006), 195. Also based on e-mails to the author from Helen Pasik Brown, Nina Drooker, Deborah Gorman, Judy Gorman, and Susan Gorman, October 2009.

On conflicts between socialists and communists in the United States, see James Weinstein, *Ambiguous Legacy: The Left in American Politics* (New Viewpoints, 1975), 19–86, 93–113; James Weinstein, *The Decline of Socialism in America: 1912–1925* (Vintage Books, 1969), 162–339; Irving Howe and Lewis Coser, *The American Communist Party* (Praeger, 1962); Theodore Draper, *The Roots of American Communism* (Viking Press, 1963), 92–383; Theodore Draper, *American Communism and Soviet Russia* (Viking Press, 1963); Harvey Klehr, John Earl Haynes, and Kyrill M. Anderson, *The Soviet World of American Communism* (Yale University Press, 1998), 272–90; and Frank A. Warren, *An Alternative Vision: The Socialist Party in the 1930s* (Indiana University Press, 1974), 134–57.

On the socialist pacifism of Winston Dancis, see Warren, *Alternative Vision*, 112, 158–75, and Scott Bennett, "Socialist Pacifism and Nonviolent Social Revolution: The War Resisters League and the Spanish Civil War, 1936–1939," *Peace & Change,* January 2000.

On Winston Dancis being heckled by communists, see "Reds Start Fights at Anti-War Rally: Police Eject Communists Who Heckle Socialists at Union Square Peace Meeting," *New York Times,* April 9, 1933.

On the 1963 March on Washington, see Clayborne Carson, *In Struggle: SNCC and the Black Awakening of the 1960s* (Harvard University Press, 1981), 83–95; Taylor Branch, *Parting the Waters: America in the King Years, 1954–63* (Simon & Schuster, 1988), 846–87.

On SNCC and Freedom Summer (1964), see Howard Zinn, *SNCC: The New Abolitionists* (Beacon Press, 1964), 242–50; Elizabeth Sutherland, ed., *Letters from Mississippi* (McGraw-Hill, 1965); James Forman, *The Making of Black Revolutionaries* (Macmillan, 1972), 354–61, 371–86; Cleveland Sellers with Robert Terrell, *The River of No Return: The Autobiography of a Black Militant and the Life and Death of SNCC* (William Morrow, 1973), 94–110; Carson, *In Struggle,* 96–129.

On the attacks on civil rights demonstrators in Selma, Alabama, see Taylor Branch, *Pillar of Fire: America in the King Years, 1963–1965* (Simon & Schuster, 1998), 390–92, 552–97; Taylor Branch, *At Canaan's Edge: America in the King Years, 1965–68* (Simon & Schuster, 2006), xi–xiii, 5–202; Adam Fairclough, *To Redeem the Soul of America: The Southern Christian Leadership Conference and Martin Luther King, Jr.* (University of Georgia Press, 1987), 224–51; David J. Garrow, *Protest at Selma: Martin Luther King, Jr., and the Voting Rights Act of 1965* (Yale University Press, 1978).

On the Freedom Run from New York to Washington, see Philip Benjamin, "15,000 March through Harlem to Protest the Racial Strife in Selma," *New York Times,* March 15, 1965; "Runners Complete Trip to Washington as Selma Protest," *New York Times,* March 17, 1965; statement by Rep. William Fitts Ryan (D-NY), *Congressional Record,* House of Representatives, March 17, 1965.

On the Pulaski Skyway, see David Plowden, *Bridges: The Spans of North America* (W. W. Norton, 2002), 286–87; www.nycroads.com/crossings/pulaski.

2. Socialism in Two Summer Communities

On the history of the Three Arrows Cooperative Society, see the anniversary celebration journals published by the society for the twenty-fifth, fortieth, fiftieth, and seventieth anniversaries, all in the Three Arrows archive housed in New York University's Tamiment Library, dlib.nyu.edu/findingaids/html/tamwag/3arrows.html (as well as in my possession). Also see "The Story of a Cooperative Colony" (Camp Three Arrows prospectus, January 1937), in the Tamiment collection; Baila Round Shargel, "Leftist Summer Colonies of Northern Westchester County, New York," *American Jewish History,* 1995, and Winston Dancis, "And Ye Shall Prosper...Three Arrows—a Successful Cooperative," in the twenty-fifth-anniversary journal, 1962. Thanks to fellow Three Arrowsite Jerry Cooper, a retired history professor at Johns Hopkins University, for sharing his research on the origins of the Three Arrows insignia, in an e-mail to the author, Sept. 12, 2009.

On Norman Thomas's annual visit to Three Arrows, see Tom Koppel, "Norman Thomas Slept Here," *Progressive,* June 1984.

On city kids spending summers at Three Arrows, see Robert Z. Melnick, "Are We There Yet? Travels and Tribulations in the Cultural Landscape," in *Cultural Landscapes: Balancing Nature and Heritage in Preservation Practice,* ed. Richard Longstreth (University of Minnesota Press, 2008), 197–210.

On the origins of U.S. involvement in Vietnam, see George McT. Kahin, *Intervention: How America Became Involved in Vietnam* (Anchor Books, 1987), 3–331; Dwight D. Eisenhower, *Mandate for Change, 1953–56* (Doubleday, 1963), 372; Marilyn Young, *The Vietnam Wars: 1945–1990* (HarperCollins, 1991), 20–171; Neil L. Jamieson, *Understanding Vietnam* (University of California Press, 1995), 191–306.

On the June 8, 1965, rally against the war in Vietnam, see Raymond Daniell, "U.S. Assailed on Vietnam Policy before 17,000 at a Garden Rally," *New York Times,* June 9, 1965; Jack Newfield, "Respectables Fill Garden to Protest Viet War," *Village Voice,* June 17, 1965; Wells, *War Within,* 50.

On civilian casualties in South Vietnam in June 1965, see Jack Langguth, "Drive by Viet Cong Wiping Out Gains of Saigon Troops," *New York Times,* June 6, 1965.

On Buck's Rock Work Camp, see Douglas Martin, "Ernst Bulova, 98, Founder of Camp with a Free Spirit," *New York Times,* Jan. 28, 2001; Martin Tolchin, "Camps Shed a New Light on Working," *New York Times,* March 15, 1962; and www.en.wikipedia.org/wiki/Buck's_Rock. Also, e-mails to the author from David Fine, March and April 2010.

On the songs of the civil rights movement, see Guy and Candie Carawan, eds., *Freedom Is a Constant Struggle: Songs of the Freedom Movement* (Oak Publications, 1968); T. V. Reed, *The Art of*

Protest: Culture and Activism from the Civil Rights Movement to the Streets of Seattle (University of Minnesota Press, 2005), 1–39.

On Happy Traum's career in folk music, see www.happytraum.com and www.bobdylanroots.com/happy.html; also based on telephone interview with Traum by the author, April 13, 2010, and e-mail from Traum to the author, April 14, 2010.

On Phil Ochs, see Michael Schumacher, *There but for Fortune: The Life of Phil Ochs* (Hyperion, 1996), 76–92; Mark Kemp, "Song of a Soldier: The Life and Times of Phil Ochs," and Ben Edmonds, "Track by Track," both essays included in the CD box set *Phil Ochs: Farewells & Fantasies,* Elektra Records, 1997.

On David McReynolds, see Martin Duberman, *A Saving Remnant: The Radical Lives of Barbara Deming and David McReynolds* (New Press, 2011); Ferber and Lynd, *Resistance,* 21–27; Zaroulis and Sullivan, *Who Spoke Up?* 61–62; Paul Buhle, "David McReynolds: Socialist Peacemaker," and David McReynolds, "Thinking about Retirement," both in *Nonviolent Activist: The Magazine of the War Resisters League,* March/April 1999.

3. First Year at Cornell

On Cornell SDS's activities during 1965–66, see "Five Years of Confrontation at Cornell," in Irving Louis Horowitz and William H. Friedland, *The Knowledge Factory: Student Power and Academic Politics in America* (Arcturus Books / Southern Illinois University Press, 1972), 220–43.

On Bob Dylan's transition from topical folksinger to poetic rock 'n' roller, see Sean Wilentz, *Bob Dylan in America* (Doubleday, 2010), 87–104.

On the Fugs, see www.thefugs.com; Vladimir Bogdanov, Chris Woodstra, and Stephen Erlewine, eds., *All Music Guide to Rock* (AMG / Backbeat Books, 2002), 437–38; and Richie Unterberger, *Eight Miles High: Folk-Rock's Flight from Haight-Ashbury to Woodstock* (Backbeat Books, 2003), xix, 29–30.

On the Beatles' opposition to the war in Vietnam, see Philip Norman, *Shout! The Beatles in Their Generation* (Fireside, 2005; originally published in 1981), 300; and Jon Wiener, *Come Together: John Lennon and His Time* (Random House, 1984), 11–21.

On Cornell's pre-1965 reputation as a relatively apolitical college, see Horowitz and Friedland, *Knowledge Factory,* 220–26; Susan Brownmiller, "Up from Silence: Cornell Then and Now—Pantie [*sic*] Raids to Guerilla Theatre," *Esquire,* March 1969; Richard Farina, *Been Down So Long It Looks Like Up to Me* (Random House, 1966); "Students Protest University Relations," *Cornell Alumni News,* June 15, 1958, and Robert S. Pearlman, "Birth of the New Left," *Cornell Alumni News,* May 1969.

On the formation of Cornell SDS, see Richard M. Samson, "Revived SDS Plans Viet Nam Involvement," *Cornell Daily Sun,* Nov. 22, 1965.

On national SDS activities regarding the draft during 1965–66, see Sale, *SDS,* 222–78, and Ferber and Lynd, *Resistance,* 41–46.

On the FBI's investigation and infiltration of SDS chapters in 1965 and 1966, see Richard Powers, *Secrecy and Power: The Life of J. Edgar Hoover* (Free Press, 1987), 427–33; James Kirkpatrick Davis, *Assault on the Left: The FBI and the Sixties Antiwar Movement* (Praeger, 1997), 21–38, and Sale, *SDS,* 275–76.

On the Cornell SDS campaign for humanitarian aid to Vietnam, see Marvin Marshak, "SDS Sends Aid to Cong," *Cornell Daily Sun,* Dec. 2, 1965; A. Richard Mangiot, "From Right Field: Treason," *Cornell Daily Sun,* Dec. 7, 1965; "SDS Makes Blood Drive Statement," *Cornell Daily Sun,* Dec. 9, 1965; Mark S. Kashen, "Executive Board Vote Overrules Straight Ban on SDS Fund Drive," *Cornell Daily Sun,* Jan. 5, 1966; Stan Chess, "SCARB Grants Permission for SDS Fund Solicitation," *Cornell Daily Sun,* Jan. 6, 1966.

On Congress's passage of a law making it illegal to destroy draft cards, see "Stiff Penalties Voted in House for Burning Draft Registrations," *New York Times,* Aug. 11, 1965; Zaroulis and Sullivan, *Who Spoke Up?* 53–54; Ferber and Lynd, *Resistance,* 21–22; Powers, *Vietnam,* 86.

On draft board reprisals against antiwar and antidraft demonstrators, see Sale, *SDS,* 231; Wells, *War Within,* 57–58; DeBenedetti, *American Ordeal,* 128.

On conscientious objection and the draft, see Baskir and Strauss, *Chance and Circumstance,* 68–71, and Peter Brock and Nigel Young, *Pacifism in the Twentieth Century* (University of Toronto Press, 1999), 264–66.

On General Hershey, the Selective Service Qualifying Test, and national SDS opposition to it, see Baskir and Strauss, *Chance and Circumstance,* 3; Wells, *War Within,* 82–84; Sale, *SDS,* 253–63.

On Cornell SDS's opposition to the Selective Service test, see Richard M. Samson, "SDS Decides to Boycott Service Test," *Cornell Daily Sun,* April 13, 1966, and "Perkins Justifies Draft Exams Here," *Cornell Daily Sun,* May 11, 1966.

On the sit-in at President Perkins's office, see Sam Roberts, "Pledge to Review Test Policy Ends Lengthy Day Hall Sit-In," *Cornell Daily Sun,* May 18, 1966; Sam Roberts, "Protesters End Sit-In," *Cornell Daily Sun,* May 19, 1966. First draft of statement by seven students occupying President Perkins's office and undated letter (probably late May or June 1966) from the author to Alan H. Levine of the New York Civil Liberties Union describing the sit-in are both in the author's possession.

On the aftermath of the sit-in, see David Maisel, "UJB Dismisses All Charges against Day Hall Protesters," *Cornell Daily Sun,* May 23, 1966; Kathleen Frankovic, "Students Vote Yes on Four Sections of Poll," *Cornell Daily Sun,* May 26, 1966; "Perspective '65–'66: The Draft Furor," *Cornell Daily Sun,* June 1, 1966.

On the SDS National Council Meeting in June 1966, see Sale, *SDS,* 277–78.

Author's application for conscientious objector status draws on partial copy of the author's statement, in the author's possession.

4. Tenant Organizing in East Harlem

On SNCC's expulsion of whites and turn toward "black power," see Carson, *In Struggle,* 191–228; Simon Hall, *Peace and Freedom: The Civil Rights and Antiwar Movements in the 1960s* (University of Pennsylvania Press, 2005), 39–71; Sale, *SDS,* 276.

On the Cornell project in Fayette County, Tennessee, see Douglas Dowd and Mary Nichols, eds., *Step by Step* (W. W. Norton, 1965); Douglas Dowd, *Blues for America: A Critique, a Lament, and Some Memories* (Monthly Review Press, 1997), 143–46; Charles Atkinson Haynie, *A Memoir of the New Left: The Political Autobiography of Charles A. Haynie,* ed. Aeron Haynie and Timothy S. Miller (University of Tennessee Press, 2009), 51–78, and esp. foreword by Douglas Dowd, ix–xv1. Also, e-mail from Douglas Dowd to the author, Feb. 13, 2010, and Pearlman, "Birth of the New Left."

On the organizing styles of SNCC and Saul Alinsky, see Charles M. Payne, *I've Got the Light of Freedom: The Organizing Tradition and the Mississippi Freedom Struggle* (University of California Press, 1995), and Sanford D. Horwitt, *Let Them Call Me Rebel: Saul Alinsky—His Life and Legacy* (Alfred A. Knopf, 1989), 174–76.

On the East Harlem Project, see the project's files, #39/1/1268, in the Kroch Library, Cornell University, especially box 3, folder marked "Final E. H. Evaluations," Jonathan Sabin, "110 St. Student Project"; folder marked "Cornell University East Harlem Project 1966," Paul Gibbons, diary and reports; folder marked "East Harlem Project 1966 Report," probably written by Paul Gibbons; and unlabeled folder including two typewritten reports by the author, one dated July 20, 1966, the other undated; box 5, folder marked "1966 Cornell East Harlem Project—Report and Evaluation," probably written by Paul Gibbons; David M. Brandt, "CURW Civil Rights Committee Pledges $1,000 to East Harlem Tenants Council," *Cornell Daily Sun,* Dec. 10, 1964.

On the East Harlem Tenants Council, see Charles G. Bennett, "Harlem Sit-In at City Hall Wins Promise of Heat for Tenements," *New York Times,* Jan. 22, 1965, and Michael Stern, "Lindsay's Office Has First Sit-In: East Harlem Tenants See Action on Apartments," *New York Times,* Jan. 16, 1966.

On the Aug. 6, 1966, antiwar rally, see Douglas Robinson, "5,000 in Times Square: Thousands March to Protest War," *New York Times,* Aug. 7, 1966; Zaroulis and Sullivan, *Who Spoke Up?* 87, 91.

5. From Protest to Resistance

On the Cornell draft resistance union, see Tom Bell, "Organizing Draft Resistance," in Alice Lynd, *We Won't Go,* 206–19, and Tom Bell, "We Won't Go—a Case Study of a Draft Resistance Union," *New Left Notes,* March 27, 1967, a longer and earlier version.

On draft resistance unions nationally, see Ferber and Lynd, *Resistance,* 47–67; Sale, *SDS,* 311–16; and Dee Jacobsen, "From Frustration to Affirmation: Developing Draft Resistance Unions in America," and Jeff Segal, "SDS Draft Unions—a Report," both in *New Left Notes,* March 27, 1967.

On the Office and the Glad Day Press, see "'The Office' Services the Peace Movement," *New Patriot* (Ithaca), Sept. 11, 1967; Horowitz and Friedland, *Knowledge Factory,* 243–45, 253–54; Dowd, *Blues for America,* 135–36; Pearlman, "Birth of the New Left."

On the formation of the Spring Mobilization Committee, see Wells, *War Within,* 91–95, 112–14.

On Cornell SDS's fall 1966 protests, see Sam Roberts, "The Draft Debate: University Inaction Affects Cornellians," *Cornell Daily Sun*, Sept. 21, 1966; and letter from Cornell SDS to Cornell president James Perkins, Oct. 6, 1966, in the Perkins Papers, box 21, #3/10/1022. Also, Cornell SDS leaflet, cowritten by the author, "The University in Transition...from What? To What?" from late October 1966, in the author's possession; and Research Committee of Cornell SDS (of which the author was a member and cowriter), *Manchild in the Corporate State: Cornell's Ruling Elite and the National Economy* (Glad Day Press, April 1969).

On the Cornell administration and "the button incident," see unreleased investigative report by Vice President for Student Affairs Mark Barlow Jr., associate dean of the College of Architecture A. Henry Detweiler, and Physics Department chairman Lyman G. Parratt; President Perkins's statement of Nov. 30, 1966; unsigned memo (probably from Mark Barlow) to President Perkins revealing Proctor George's behind-the-scenes lobbying; and "Cornell University—University Proctor" (undated pamphlet), all in box 13, folder 24, "Proctor Travis, Richard M., Dancis, Bruce D.," in the James Perkins Papers, #3/10/1022, Division of Rare and Manuscript Collections, Cornell University Library; and Dowd, *Blues for America*, 137–38.

On the *Cornell Daily Sun*'s coverage of the button incident, see Sam Roberts, "Travis, Sophomore Engage in Scuffle"; Phyllis E. Kaye, "'Tasteless' Buttons Precipitate Student Briefing Cancellation"; and "Contemptible" (editorial), all Nov. 18, 1966; also, Sam Roberts, "Committee of Three to Begin Investigating Travis Incident," Nov. 21, 1966; Sam Roberts, "Travis Censured in Button Brawl," Nov. 30, 1966; and Stan Chess, "Dining Considered at Briefing," Dec. 1, 1966.

On Burton Weiss disrupting a university-sponsored symposium on drugs, see Horowitz and Friedland, *Knowledge Factory*, 245. Also Burton Weiss, interview by author, May 20, 2010, Berkeley, CA.

On the author's response to the button incident: Bruce Dancis, "Concerning the Incident of November 17, 1966," along with a list of witnesses and the FBI's summary of the incident, in the author's possession.

On the state of the war in Vietnam at the end of 1966, see Stanley Karnow, *Vietnam: A History* (Penguin Books, 1984), 511–16, 696, and Young, *Vietnam Wars*, 172–91.

On the author tearing up his draft card: letters from the author to his parents and to his draft board, in the author's possession (the latter conveniently reprinted in the author's FBI file); also, see James R. Michaels, "Dancis Rips Up Draft Card to Protest Selective Service," *Cornell Daily Sun*, Dec. 15, 1966; Jon Levy, "Cornell Soph Tears Draft Card—FBI Investigating," *Syracuse Post-Standard*, Dec. 15, 1966; Sale, *SDS*, 313. Also, e-mails from Peter Agree to the author, Oct. 19 and 20, 2010.

On "Universal Soldier" see Buffy Sainte-Marie, *It's My Way*, Vanguard Records, 1964; also see www.creative-native.com/universal-soldier.php.

On Mario Savio's "Bodies upon the Gears" speech, see Robert Cohen, *Freedom's Orator: Mario Savio and the Radical Legacy of the 1960s* (Oxford University Press, 2009), 178–79, 326–28.

On the ratio of male-female undergraduates at Cornell, see "The Dating Game: Socializing Set by Ratio," *Cornell Daily Sun*, Sept. 6, 1967.

On Cornell's changing regulations for female undergraduates, see Mary Ann Landmesser, "Freedom: Women Discuss Curfew Reform," *Cornell Daily Sun*, Dec. 14, 1967; "Junior Women Freed to Live out of Dorms," *Cornell Daily Sun*, Feb. 28, 1968; "FCSA Approves Demise of Sophomore Curfews," *Cornell Daily Sun*, April 15, 1968; "Frosh Coed Begins Drive to End Required Curfew," *Cornell Daily Sun*, Oct. 4, 1968; Marsha E. Ackermann, "What Now?" *Cornell Daily Sun*, March 4, 1970.

On the *Trojan Horse* incident: e-mail from Greg Heins to the author, Oct. 21, 2010, and e-mail from Marjorie (Holt) Heins to the author, Nov. 21, 2010; also, see Horowitz and Friedland, *Knowledge Factory*, 246–47, and Donald Alexander Downs, *Cornell '69: Liberalism and the Crisis of the American University* (Cornell University Press, 1999), 37–38.

6. Draft Cards Are for Burning

On national SDS's changing position on the draft, see Sale, *SDS*, 312–22, and Bob Randolph, "Berkeley Conference: SDS Plans to Mobilize Draft Defiers," *Guardian*, Jan. 7, 1967.

On the Selective Service System's "Channeling" document, see Peter Henig, "On the Manpower Channelers," *New Left Notes*, Jan. 20, 1967; "Channeling," *Ramparts*, December 1967; Ferber and Lynd, *Resistance*, 132–33.

On the critical stance of Tom Bell and some national SDS leaders toward going to jail for draft resistance, see Bell, "We Won't Go"; Carl Davidson, "Praxis Makes Perfect," *New Left Notes*, March 27, 1967.

On the "call to burn draft cards," see Alice Lynd, *We Won't Go,* 216–17; Ferber and Lynd, *Resistance,* 72–73.

On the support for draft resisters by older antiwar activists, see Paul Goodman's "Appeal," *New York Review of Books,* April 6, 1967; Staughton Lynd and Dave Dellinger, "A Call to Burn Draft Cards," statement distributed at the April 6 National Council meeting of SDS (copy in the author's possession); Nat Hentoff, "The Unpleasant Ones," *Village Voice,* March 16, 1967.

On the confrontation at Cornell over the solicitation of the "call to burn draft cards," see the *Cornell Daily Sun,* March 7–24, 1967; Burton Weiss, "Just Because a Million Civilians Have Been Killed in Vietnam," a letter to the editor of the *Sun,* reprinted as an SDS leaflet, ca. end of March 1967, in the Felix Kramer Collection, #37/7/2151, box 3, Rare and Manuscript Collections, Kroch Library, Cornell University; Horowitz and Friedland, *Knowledge Factory,* 248–51. Also, Cornell SDS, "Sgt. Perkins?" (leaflet distributed during the confrontation), in the author's possession.

On the author's indictment and arraignment, see "Innocent Plea Filed in Draft Card Case," *Syracuse Herald-Journal,* April 11, 1967.

On the U.S. Court of Appeals in Boston ruling in the David O'Brien case, see "Appeals Court Upsets Ban on Draft-Card Burning," *New York Times,* April 11, 1967.

On the disagreements between the Spring Mobilization and the draft card burners, see David Dellinger, *From Yale to Jail: The Life Story of a Moral Dissenter* (Pantheon Books, 1993), 293–95; Andrew E. Hunt, *David Dellinger: The Life and Times of a Nonviolent Revolutionary* (NYU Press, 2006), 163–64; Wells, *War Within,* 124–35; Zaroulis and Sullivan, *Who Spoke Up?* 112–14.

On the April 15, 1967, draft card burning, see Douglas Robinson, "100,000 Rally at U.N. against Vietnam War—Many Draft Cards Burned—Eggs Tossed at Parade," *New York Times,* April 16, 1967; Martin Jezer, "The Bread Has Risen—Apr 15" (special issue on the Spring Mobilization and the draft card burning), *WIN,* April 28, 1967; Martin Jezer, "Sheep Meadow Graduation" (a longer version of his *WIN* article), in Alice Lynd, *We Won't Go,* 220–25; Paul Goodman, "We Won't Go," *New York Review of Books,* May 18, 1967; Bruce Dancis and Tom Bell, "Dear Friends" (mimeographed letter to those who burned their draft cards), April 21, 1967, in the author's possession; Wells, *War Within,* 132–35; Ferber and Lynd, *Resistance,* 68–77; Mike Rotkin, interview by the author, Santa Cruz, CA, May 14, 2010; Burton Weiss, interview by the author, Berkeley, CA, May 20, 2010.

On Gary Rader and his involvement in the draft card burning, see "Suspect, 23, Held as Card Burner," *New York Times,* April 20, 1967, and Gary Rader, "Draft Resistance," *New York Review of Books,* Sept. 14, 1967.

On the formation of the Resistance in Northern California, see Ferber and Lynd, *Resistance,* 78–91.

On Cornell VP Mark Barlow's concern about Cornell chaplains, see memo from Barlow to James Perkins, April 26, 1967, James Perkins Papers, box 12, folder 34, Student Demonstrations, U.S. Selective Service, Rare and Manuscript Collections, Kroch Library, Cornell University.

On the impact of the antiwar and draft resistance movements on the Johnson administration in May 1967, see James Reston, "Washington: Compromise on the Military Draft," *New York Times,* May 5, 1967, and Wells, *War Within,* 143–58.

On Muhammad Ali's draft resistance, see David Remnick, *King of the World: Muhammad Ali and the Rise of an American Hero* (Random House, 1998), 287–91; Tom Wicker, "In the Nation: Muhammad Ali and Dissent," *New York Times,* May 2, 1967.

7. The Summer of Love and Disobedience

On the creation of the Mobilization Direct Action Project (MDAP), see Robert Greenblatt, "Some Possible Directions for the Mobilization" (working paper prepared for a Spring Mobilization conference in Washington, DC), May 20–21, 1967; Robert Greenblatt, "Mobilization Direct Action Project" (proposal for the Spring Mobilization Committee), ca. May 1967; and Robert Greenblatt, "The Peace Force: A Program for Direct Action and Radical Education" (submitted to the Spring Mobilization Committee), ca. June 1, 1967, all in the Alan Snitow Collection.

On the attack on MDAP members in Brooklyn, see Robert Greenblatt, "Letter Sent to Recruitment Centers," July 3, 1967; Matthew Clark, two MDAP press releases, July 11 and 12, 1967; "To Recruit for Peace" and "What Is Happening to America?!" / "Attacked on the Streets of Flatbush!" (MDAP leaflets), July 11 and 13, 1967, all in the Alan Snitow Collection. Also, Alan Snitow and Felix Kramer, interview by the author, Berkeley, CA, June 6, 2010; e-mail from Alan Snitow to the author, Jan. 20, 2011.

On the Beatles' *Sgt. Pepper's Lonely Hearts Club Band* album, see Bruce Dancis, "Sgt. Pepper at 40, from A to Z," *Sacramento Bee,* June 1, 2007.

On the Aug. 6, 1967, demonstration at the USS *Newman K. Perry,* see Matthew Clark, "The Paradox of Power: A Report from the Mobilization Direct Action Project," undated mimeographed report (probably Aug. 7, 1967); Alan Snitow, "Memorandum on the Hiroshima Day demonstration and witness," Aug. 12, 1967; and "Why We Are Here" (leaflet handed out at the demonstration), all in the Alan Snitow Collection; John Kifner, "War Protesters Barred at Destroyer," *New York Times,* Aug. 7, 1967, and Leticia Kent, "The Day of Hiroshima: A Visit to a Destroyer," *Village Voice,* Aug. 10, 1967. Also, e-mail from Alan Snitow to the author, Feb. 18, 2013.

On the New York State law banning masks, see Colin Moynihan, "Law Banning Masks at Protests Is to Be Challenged," *New York Times,* Oct. 21, 2012.

On the Bread and Puppet Theater and its involvement in the antiwar movement, see Zaroulis and Sullivan, *Who Spoke Up?* 56, 64, 80, 379; Nora M. Alter, *Vietnam Protest Theatre: The Television War on Stage* (Indiana University Press, 1996), 6–8; John Bell, "Beyond the Cold War: Bread and Puppet Theater and the New World Order," in Jeanne Colleran and Jenny S. Spencer, *Staging Resistance: Essays on Political Theater* (University of Michigan Press, 1998), 31–53; John Bell, "Bread and Puppet and the Possibilities of Puppet Theater," in *Restaging the Sixties: Radical Theaters and Their Legacies,* ed. James M. Harding and Cindy Rosenthal (University of Michigan Press, 2006), 377–83, and Fred W. McDarrah, *Anarchy, Protest and Rebellion and the Counterculture That Changed America: A Photographic Memoir of the 60s in Black and White* (Thunder's Mouth Press, 2003), 17–19.

On Abbie Hoffman's journey from civil rights organizer to countercultural Digger, see Jonah Raskin, *For the Hell of It: The Life and Times of Abbie Hoffman* (University of California Press, 1996), 90–108; Marty Jezer, *Abbie Hoffman: American Rebel* (Rutgers University Press, 1993), 92–114; Abbie Hoffman (as Free), *Revolution for the Hell of It* (Dial Press, 1968), 23–38; and Tom Hayden, *Reunion: A Memoir* (Random House, 1988), 150–57.

On Abbie Hoffman and the New York Stock Exchange demonstration, see Bruce Dancis, "The Day the Money Fell from the Sky" (an earlier version of this chapter), *Sacramento Bee,* Aug. 24, 2007; Raskin, *For the Hell of It,* 111–17; Hoffman, *Revolution,* 32–33; Abbie Hoffman, *Soon to Be a Major Motion Picture* (Perigee Books, 1980), 100–102; Jezer, *Abbie Hoffman,* 111–12; John Kifner, "Hippies Shower $1 Bills on Stock Exchange Floor," *New York Times,* April 25, 1967; Walter Bowart, "Casting the Money Throwers from the Temple," *East Village Other,* September 1967; and Barry Cunningham, "Hippies Raid Wall St.," *New York Post,* April 24, 1967.

On the New York Stock Exchange's response to the demonstration, see photo caption on the installation of a bulletproof glass barrier, accompanying John J. Abele, "Market Active; Gains Moderate," *New York Times,* Nov. 23, 1967.

On the urban riots of July 1967, see *Report of the Advisory Commission on Civil Disorders* (aka the Kerner Report) (Bantam Books, 1968); Mark Hamilton Lytle, *America's Uncivil Wars: The Sixties Era from Elvis to the Fall of Richard Nixon* (Oxford University Press, 2006), 230–39; Terry H. Anderson, *The Movement and the Sixties: Protest in America from Greensboro to Wounded Knee* (Oxford University Press, 1995), 168–70; Vincent Harding, Robin D. G. Kelley, and Earl Lewis, "We Changed the World," in *To Make Our World Anew: A History of African Americans,* ed. Robin D. G. Kelley and Earl Lewis (Oxford University Press, 2000), 530; Kwame Anthony Appiah and Henry Louis Gates Jr., eds., *Africana—Civil Rights: An A–Z Reference of the Movement That Changed America* (Running Press, 2003), 233.

On the origins of the Black Panther Party for Self-Defense, see Gene Marine, *The Black Panthers* (Signet Books, 1969), 24–76; Hugh Pearson, *The Shadow of the Panther: Huey Newton and the Price of Black Power in America* (Addison-Wesley, 1994), 107–35.

On the speeches and activities of H. Rap Brown during the summer of 1967, see Carson, *In Struggle,* 252–57; Sellers, *River of No Return,* 197–201; Homer Bigart, "Rap Brown Calls Riots 'Rehearsal for Revolution,'" *New York Times,* Aug. 7, 1967; "Brown Bids Whites Join Negroes' Fight," *New York Times,* Aug. 30, 1967.

On the National Conference for New Politics (NCNP), see Gitlin, *Sixties,* 244–48; Branch, *At Canaan's Edge,* 637–40; Andrew Kopkind, "They'd Rather Be Left," *New York Review of Books,* Sept. 28, 1967; and James Forman, *The Making of Black Revolutionaries: A Personal Account* (Macmillan, 1972), 497–504.

On the announcement of the Oct. 21–22 demonstration at the Pentagon, see Earl Caldwell, "War Foes to Try to Shut Pentagon," *New York Times,* Aug. 29, 1967; Norman Mailer, *The Armies of the Night: History as a Novel, the Novel as History* (Plume, 1994; originally published in 1968), 233–35; Wells, *War Within,* 174–75; Raskin, *For the Hell of It,* 117–20.

On the national leadership of SDS during the spring and summer of 1967, see Sale, *SDS,* 317–68; Greg Calvert, "In White America: Radical Consciousness and Social Change," *National Guardian,*

March 25, 1967, reprinted in *The New Left: A Documentary History,* ed. Massimo Teodori (Bobbs-Merrill, 1969), 412–18.

On SDS's membership policy of "non-exclusion," see Sale, *SDS,* 56–57, 210–13, 237–39, 463, 571–74; Paul Berman, *A Tale of Two Utopias: The Political Journey of the Generation of 1968* (W. W. Norton, 1996), 66–88.

8. The Resistance

On the postponement of the author's trial, see James R. Michaels, "Judge Stays Dancis Trial," *Cornell Daily Sun,* Sept. 13, 1967.

On Father Daniel Berrigan's hiring at Cornell, see Murray Polner and Jim O'Grady, *Disarmed and Dangerous: The Radical Lives of Daniel and Philip Berrigan* (Basic Books, 1997), 149–53; Kathleen A. Frankovic, "Berrigan: An Anti-War Priest," *Cornell Daily Sun,* Sept. 15, 1967; Joseph A. Palermo, "Father Daniel J. Berrigan: The FBI's Most Wanted Peace Activist," in *The Human Tradition in America since 1945,* ed. David Anderson (Scholarly Resources Books, 2003), 71–93.

On "A Call to Resist Illegitimate Authority," see Ferber and Lynd, *Resistance,* 121–24; the call was reprinted in the *New York Review of Books,* Oct. 12, 1967, and the *New Republic,* Oct. 7, 1967.

On the Oct. 16 draft card turn-in in Ithaca, see Peter Agree, "Aim and Effect—at Issue: The Resistance," *Cornell Daily Sun,* Oct. 16, 1967; Stan Chess, "Fourteen Resist, 300 March in Selective Service Protest," *Cornell Daily Sun,* Oct. 17, 1967; "Oct. 16—the Resistance" (leaflet distributed by Cornell Resistance, ca. Oct. 1967), in the Lawrence Kramer Collection, #37/7/2151, box 3, Rare and Manuscript Collections, Cornell University Library.

On the Oct. 16 draft card turn-in nationally, see Ferber and Lynd, *Resistance,* 104–14; Zaroulis and Sullivan, *Who Spoke Up?* 133–35; Wallace Turner, "Anti-War Demonstrations Held outside Draft Boards across U.S.," *New York Times,* Oct. 17, 1967; "Protesters Rebuffed Here," *New York Times,* Oct. 17, 1967; Lawrence Kramer and the Ithaca Resistance, untitled leaflet / press release dated Nov. 29, 1967, giving a city-by-city tally of draft cards turned in on Oct. 16, in the Lawrence Kramer Collection, #37/7/2151, box 3, Rare and Manuscript Collections, Cornell University Library.

On the October 21–22 demonstration at the Pentagon, see Wells, *War Within,* 181–203; Zaroulis and Sullivan, *Who Spoke Up?* 135–42; Dowd, *Blues for America,* 150–53; Cathy Wilkerson, *Flying Close to the Sun: My Life and Times as a Weatherman* (Seven Stories Press, 2007), 145–51; Mailer, *Armies of the Night,* 89–211; George Dennison, "Talking with the Troops," *Liberation,* November 1967, reprinted in Mitchell Goodman (assembler), *The Movement toward a New America* (Alfred A. Knopf, 1970), 471–75; Joseph A. Loftus, "Guards Repulse War Protesters at the Pentagon," *New York Times,* Oct. 22, 1967; "Scene at Pentagon: Beards, Bayonets and Bonfires," *New York Times,* Oct. 22, 1967; Stan Chess, "Cornellians Nabbed at Pentagon," *Cornell Daily Sun,* Oct. 23, 1967; Ben A. Franklin, "War Protesters Defying Deadline Seized in Capital," *New York Times,* Oct. 23, 1967; Thai Jones, *A Radical Line: From the Labor Movement to the Weather Underground, One Family's Century of Conscience* (Free Press, 2004), 137–42.

On the debates within the antiwar movement and SDS about tactics and violence, see Wells, *War Within,* 170–217; Ferber and Lynd, *Resistance,* 126–35, 141–48; Frank Bardacke, "Stop-the-Draft Week," *Steps* (a publication of the Free University of Berkeley), December 1967, reprinted in Mitchell Goodman, *Movement toward a New America,* 476–79.

On Rev. Phil Berrigan and the Baltimore Four, see Polner and O'Grady, *Disarmed and Dangerous,* 176–92; Wells, *War Within,* 213.

On the Nov. 14, 1967, demonstration against Secretary of State Dean Rusk, see Wells, *War Within,* 213–14; Zaroulis and Sullivan, *Who Spoke Up?* 142–43; Homer Bigart, "War Foes Clash with Police Here as Rusk Speaks," *New York Times,* Nov. 15, 1967; Homer Bigart, "Leaders of Rusk Demonstration Cite New Techniques of Protest," *New York Times,* Nov. 16, 1967; Barnard L. Collier, "War Foes Charge Police Brutality," *New York Times,* Nov. 17, 1967; Edward C. Burks, "A Draft Resister Defends Tactics of 'Disruption,'" *New York Times,* Nov. 22, 1967; "City Police Accused of Abuse in Protest," *New York Times,* Nov. 24, 1967.

On Larry Kramer's campaign to write antiwar messages on corporate business reply mail, see Lawrence Kramer, "You and the Post Office: A New Coalition to End the War," *First Issue,* Feb. 26, 1968.

On the speaking tours of Doug Dowd, Father Dan Berrigan, and the author, see Dowd, *Blues,* 136–41; Polner and O'Grady, *Disarmed and Dangerous,* 153–56.

On the author's explanation of the Resistance's strategy, see Bruce Dancis, "The Logic of Resistance," *New Patriot,* Nov. 29, 1967.

On draft resisters playing "freak the feds" with the FBI: Mike Rotkin, interview by the author, Santa Cruz, CA, May 14, 2010; e-mail from Joe Kelly to the author, Oct. 7, 2011. Also, Horowitz and Friedland, *Knowledge Factory,* 256.

On the federal grand jury investigation of the April 15 draft card burning: Mike Rotkin, interview by the author, May 14, 2010; Burton Weiss, interview by the author, Berkeley, CA, May 20, 2010. Also see Horowitz and Friedland, *Knowledge Factory,* 256; "Eight Subpoenaed to Attend Draft Law Violation Inquest," *Cornell Daily Sun,* Nov. 6, 1967; "4 Burn Draft Cards Here as 5 Face Grand Jurors," *New York Times,* Nov. 9, 1967.

On General Hershey's effort to reclassify draft resisters and antidraft demonstrators, see B. Drummond Ayres Jr., "Hershey Pledges Draft Crackdown," *New York Times,* Nov. 8, 1967; "Texts of Letter and Memo on the Draft," *New York Times,* Nov. 9, 1967; Neil Sheehan, "Hershey Talked with White House," *New York Times,* Nov. 9, 1967; Neil Sheehan, "Hershey Opposed by U.S. Lawyers," *New York Times,* Nov. 10, 1967; Wells, *War Within,* 229–30.

On the reclassification of Cornell draft resisters following General Hershey's directive, see "Priest Loses 4-D," *Cornell Daily Sun,* Nov. 17, 1967; "Two More Protesters Given Reclassified Draft Status," *Cornell Daily Sun,* Nov. 20, 1967; "Gibbons Given 1-A Reclassification," *Cornell Daily Sun,* Nov. 28, 1967; "7 Are Reclassified after Draft Protest," *New York Times,* Nov. 30, 1967.

On the author being called for a preinduction physical, see "Draft Challenged," *Cornell Daily Sun,* Dec. 1, 1967.

On the Cornell Aeronautical Laboratory's Defense Department contract to develop counterinsurgency programs in Thailand, see Horowitz and Friedland, *Knowledge Factory,* 252–54; Sam Roberts, "CAL, 'Rural Security' Thaied: Link Thai Counterinsurgency and Cornell Lab Project," *Cornell Daily Sun,* Sept. 9, 1967; Sam Roberts, "Perkins Quits CAL Post," *Cornell Daily Sun,* Sept. 14, 1967; Deborah Huffman, "Faculty Calls CAL Tie Untenable," *Cornell Daily Sun,* Oct. 12, 1967; Sam Roberts, "Trustees to Slash CAL Ties," *Cornell Daily Sun,* Jan. 22, 1968; George Fisher and Stephen Wallenstein, "Open Breeches: Guns at Cornell," unpublished manuscript (made available to me by coauthor Stephen Wallenstein), 1972, 25–30.

On protests at Cornell against U.S. Marine recruiters, see Gary Goodman, "Protesters Face Marines," *Cornell Daily Sun,* Nov. 17, 1967; Gary Goodman, "Demonstrators Block Recruiters," *Cornell Daily Sun,* Nov. 20, 1967; Sam Roberts, "The Sundial: Ruckus over Recruiting," *Cornell Daily Sun,* Nov. 20, 1967; Deborah Huffman, "Faculty Council Votes to Ban Military Recruiters on Campus," *Cornell Daily Sun,* Dec. 6, 1967.

On Cornell president Perkins's criticisms of General Hershey, see statement of James Perkins, Nov. 16, 1967; joint statement by Attorney General Ramsey Clark and Director of Selective Service Lewis B. Hershey, Dec. 9, 1967, and letter from Yale President Kingman Brewster (signed by Perkins) to President Lyndon Johnson, Dec. 21, 1967, all in box 32, folder 14, Student Demonstrations, James Perkins Papers, #3/10/1022, Cornell University Library, Division of Rare and Manuscript Collections; "Perkins Bid: Don't Draft Obstructors," *Cornell Daily Sun,* Nov. 17, 1967; Neil Sheehan, "Hershey Upholds Induction Policy: Says He and Clark Differ on Drafting Protesters," *New York Times,* Dec. 12, 1967.

On the Dec. 4–7 draft card turn-ins nationally and in Ithaca, see Ferber and Lynd, *Resistance,* 222; Wells, *War Within,* 217–19, and E. J. Stevenson, "12 Said to Return Draft Cards," *Cornell Daily Sun,* Dec. 8, 1967.

On the state of the war in Vietnam and growing opposition to Johnson's policies at the end of 1967, see Wells, *War Within,* 219–22; Paul Joseph, *Cracks in the Empire: State Politics in the Vietnam War* (South End Press, 1981), 163–79, 213–32; Karnow, *Vietnam,* 516–27, 697.

On Senator Eugene McCarthy's candidacy, see Warren Weaver Jr., "McCarthy to Fight Johnson Polices in 5 or 6 Primaries," *New York Times,* Dec. 1, 1967; "McCarthy Statement on Entering the 1968 Primaries," *New York Times,* Dec. 1, 1967; Dominick Sandbrook, *Eugene McCarthy: The Rise and Fall of Postwar American Liberalism* (Alfred A. Knopf, 2004), 173; and Sam Roberts, "Cornellians Back Antiwar Hopeful," *Cornell Daily Sun,* Dec. 8, 1967.

9. SDS, South Africa, and the Security Index

On the FBI and its Security Index, Rabble Rouser Index, and Agitator Index, see Robert Justin Goldstein, *Political Repression in America: From 1870–1976* (University of Illinois Press, 2001), 451–53; Athan G. Theoharis, "A Brief History of the FBI's Role and Powers," in *The FBI: A Comprehensive Reference Guide,* ed. Athan G. Theoharis (Oryx Books, 1999), 28–48; James Kirkpatrick Davis, *Assault on the*

Left: The FBI and the Sixties Antiwar Movement (Praeger, 1997), 30–36; Richard Gid Powers, *Secrecy and Power: The Life of J. Edgar Hoover* (Free Press, 1987), 428–33.

On the reorganization of Cornell SDS and the founding of the *First Issue,* see Laura Webber, "SDS Restructures," *First Issue,* Jan. 29, 1968; Downs, *Cornell '69,* 32–33; Daniel M. Taubman, "Underground Press Publishes 'First Issue,' New Magazine," *Cornell Daily Sun,* Jan. 29, 1968.

On the Town Hall rally in support of draft resisters, see Sally Kempton, "Viet Critics: They Put Themselves on the Line," *Village Voice,* Jan. 18, 1968; "Rally Supports 5 Held in Draft Case," *New York Times,* Jan. 15, 1968; Bruce Dancis (unsigned), "Resistance News," *First Issue,* Jan. 29, 1968.

On the Mike Singer case, see "Collected Letters on the Singer Case" and "Collected Demands of Cornell Students on the Singer Case," both in *First Issue,* Feb. 12, 1968; "Defend Mike Singer" (Cornell SDS leaflet), Feb. 9, 1968, in the Alan Snitow Collection; Gary Goodman, "Official Urges 1-A for Student," *Cornell Daily Sun,* Feb. 9, 1968; Gary Goodman, "Maynard Apologizes for Sending Letter," *Cornell Daily Sun,* Feb. 12, 1968; "Registrar Makes Changes in Selective Service Rule," *Cornell Daily Sun,* Feb. 19, 1968; Gary Goodman, "Singer Reclassified; Draft Board Rules after Cornell Note," *Cornell Daily Sun,* Feb. 27, 1968; Michael Rosenbaum, "Cornell Withholds Students' Grades," *Cornell Daily Sun,* April 18, 1968; "Singer Told to Report," *Cornell Daily Sun,* April 22, 1968.

On the Tet Offensive and its political impact, see Young, *Vietnam Wars,* 216–31; Joseph, *Cracks in the Empire,* 232–83; Wells, *War Within,* 240–62; Karnow, *Vietnam,* 528–81.

On the Cornell demonstration against Dow Chemical, see Douglas Dowd, "Dowd on Dow, Resistance, Etc.," *First Issue,* Jan. 29, 1968; Mark Sharefkin (compiler), "Better Things for Better Living thru Chemistry," and Howard Zinn, "Dow Shalt Not Kill," both in *First Issue,* Feb. 12, 1968; Kal Lindenberg, "800 Protesters Greet Dow," *Cornell Daily Sun,* Feb. 20, 1968.

On the Mobilization Committee's Illinois meeting to plan demonstrations at the Democratic National Convention, see Wells, *War Within,* 237–40; Zaroulis and Sullivan, *Who Spoke Up?* 176–77; Hunt, *David Dellinger,* 185–87; Hayden, *Reunion,* 254–63; Dave Dellinger, *More Power Than We Know: The People's Movement toward Democracy* (Anchor Press, 1975), 120–23; Dowd, *Blues,* 154; Gitlin, *Sixties,* 320–21, and Raskin, *For the Hell of It,* 131–38.

On the beginnings of Cornell SDS's antiapartheid campaign, see Alan Snitow, "Cornell South African Investments Scored," *Dateline: Ithaca,* no date (probably March or April 1968); internal SDS document (written by Alan Snitow) and Alan Snitow, "A Brief History of the SDS South Africa Campaign," all in the Alan Snitow Collection; Horowitz and Friedland, *Knowledge Factory,* 257–58; Cornell Associate Treasurer Robert T. Horn, "Bank Loan to the Republic of South Africa" (memorandum to the board of trustees' Commission on Investments and Public Policy), April 30, 1968, and SDS position paper (written primarily by Bruce Detwiler), "Racism in Southern Africa and the Cornell Responsibility" (submitted to the Commission on Investments and Public Policy), both in the Perkins Papers, #3/10/1022, box 32, Rare and Manuscript Collections, Cornell University Library; Peter Agree and Sam Pizzigati, "Cornell and South Africa: A Study in Black and White," *Cornell Daily Sun,* April 12, 1968; Edward Zuckerman, "Perkins Defends Cornell Policy on Banks against SDS Demands," *Cornell Daily Sun,* April 16, 1968; Sam Pizzigati, "Rev. Ntlabati Warns U.S.," *Cornell Daily Sun,* April 17, 1968; Howard Rodman, "Why I Invest in the KKK," *Cornell Daily Sun,* April 23, 1968; Edward Zuckerman, "Trustee Unit Hears AAS, SDS Demands," *Cornell Daily Sun,* April 19, 1968; Edward Zuckerman, "Trustees Discuss Housing, Investments: Study Group Picked on Investments," *Cornell Daily Sun,* April 22, 1968; "Grants for Africans Set," *Cornell Daily Sun,* May 10, 1968; Lawrence Litvak, Robert DeGrasse, and Kathleen McTigue, *South Africa: Foreign Investment and Apartheid* (Institute for Policy Studies, 1979), 58.

On the March 1965 SDS demonstration in New York City against Chase Manhattan Bank, see Gitlin, *Sixties,* 296, 317, and Theodore Jones, "49 Arrested at Chase Building in Protest on South Africa Loans," *New York Times,* March 20, 1965.

On the increased number of black students at Cornell and the formation of the Afro-American Society, see Downs, *Cornell '69,* 3–4, 46–49, 60–68.

On the McPhelin case and the takeover of the Economics Department office, see Michael Rosenbaum, "60 Afro-Americans Obstruct Eco Office," *Cornell Daily Sun,* April 5, 1968; Downs, *Cornell '69,* 68–78; Cleveland Donald Jr., "Cornell: Confrontation in Black and White," in *Divided We Stand: Reflections on the Crisis at Cornell,* ed. Cushing Strout and David I. Grossvogel (Doubleday, 1970), 170–71; Horowitz and Friedland, *Knowledge Factory,* 257.

On the memorial service for Dr. Martin Luther King Jr., see Daniel M. Taubman, "Memorial Service Spurs Discussion," *Cornell Daily Sun,* April 8, 1968; Downs, *Cornell '69,* 78–81.

On the April 1968 draft card turn-in, see "Dear Colleague" (letter from Douglas Archibald and eight other Cornell faculty members in support of draft resisters), March 5, 1968, and "Fellow Students" (leaflet from Cornell Resistance), March 6, 1968, both in the Lawrence Kramer Collection, #37/7/2151, box 3, Rare and Manuscript Collections, Cornell University Library; Lance Davidow and Kal Lindenberg, "500 March to City Draft Board in Protest of Selective Service," *Cornell Daily Sun,* April 8, 1968; Bruce Dancis (unsigned), "Resistance News," *First Issue,* May 8, 1968; Ferber and Lynd, *Resistance,* 279.

On Rev. Paul Gibbons's refusing induction, see John Leo, "Cleric, Classified 1-A after Protest, Refuses Draft," *New York Times,* April 16, 1968; Fred J. Solowey and Donna B. Greenberg, "Gibbons Refuses to Take Oath at New York Draft Center," *Cornell Daily Sun,* April 16, 1968; "Monday, April 15: Gibbons to Refuse Induction" (Cornell Resistance leaflet, ca. early April 1968), Lawrence Kramer Collection, #37/7/2151, box 3, Rare and Manuscript Collections, Cornell University Library.

On the author refusing induction, see Lance S. Davidow, "Dancis Refuses Induction in Syracuse," *Cornell Daily Sun,* April 19, 1968; "A Call to Brotherhood: Bruce Dancis Has Often Acted for the Sake of Others. Let Us, Then, Not Forsake Him" (Cornell Resistance leaflet), April 18, 1968, in the Alan Snitow collection.

On the Catonsville Nine, see Polner and O'Grady, *Disarmed and Dangerous,* 193–201.

On the Columbia University student strike of April 1968, see Liberation News Service, "Berkeley East—Columbia: The Revolution Is Now," *First Issue,* May 8, 1968; Mark Rudd, *Underground: My Life with SDS and the Weathermen* (William Morrow, 2009), 53–116; Gitlin, *Sixties,* 306–9; Sale, *SDS,* 429–41; Hayden, *Reunion,* 272–84; Jerry Avorn and the Columbia Spectator staff, *Up against the Ivy Wall: A History of the Columbia Crisis* (Atheneum, 1968); Dale R. Corson, "Memorandum for the Record" (a report on a Seven Universities Group meeting in New York on May 24, 1968), May 27, 1968, James Perkins Papers, #3/10/1022, box 23, Rare and Manuscript Collections, Cornell University Library; Mark Kurlansky, *1968: The Year That Rocked the World* (Random House, 2005), 192–208.

On the FBI's establishment of a new Counter Intelligence Program aimed at disrupting the New Left, see Seth Rosenfeld, *Subversives: The FBI's War on Student Radicals, and Reagan's Rise to Power* (Farrar, Straus and Giroux, 2012), 414–15; Goldstein, *Political Repression in America,* 451–53; Davis, *Assault on the Left,* 39–61; Hayden, *Reunion,* 283–84.

10. From Resistance to Revolution

On the international student rebellions of 1968, see Kurlansky, *Year That Rocked the World;* Barbara and John Ehrenreich, *Long March, Short Spring: The Student Uprising at Home and Abroad* (Monthly Review Press, 1969); Charles Posner, ed., *Reflections on the Revolution in France: 1968* (Penguin Books, 1970); Angelo Quattrocchi and Tom Nairn, *The Beginning of the End: France, May 1968* (Verso, 1998; originally published in 1968); Young, *Vietnam Wars,* 216–31; Joseph, *Cracks in the Empire,* 232–83; Wells, *War Within,* 240–62; Karnow, *Vietnam,* 528–81.

On John Lennon's statements against the war in Vietnam in 1967 and 1968, see Wiener, *Come Together,* 53, 73–74.

On the Beatles' "Revolution" and the reaction to it by the New Left, see Wiener, *Come Together,* 58–63, 81–84; Jann Wenner, *Lennon Remembers: The Rolling Stone Interviews* (Popular Library, 1971), 131–32; the Beatles, *The Beatles Anthology* (Chronicle Books, 2000), 297–99; Ian MacDonald, *Revolution in the Head: The Beatles' Records and the Sixties* (Henry Holt, 1994), 223–29; Mark Lewisohn, *The Beatles Recording Sessions: The Official Abbey Road Studio Session Notes, 1962–1970* (Harmony Books, 1988), 135–36, 138–39; 142–43, 152, 163; Bob Spitz, *The Beatles: The Biography* (Little, Brown, 2005), 775–77; Jon Sabin, "Back in the U.S.A.," *First Issue,* December 1968.

On the Rolling Stones' "Street Fighting Man," see Wiener, *Come Together,* 65–69; Stephen Davis, *Old Gods Almost Dead: The 40-Year Odyssey of the Rolling Stones* (Broadway Books, 2001), 231–32, 256–57; Jann Wenner, "Jagger Remembers," *Rolling Stone,* Dec. 14, 1995.

On Robert Kennedy, see Nick Bryant, *The Bystander: John F. Kennedy and the Struggle for Black Equality* (Basic Books, 2006); Ronald Steel, *In Love with Night: The American Romance with Robert Kennedy* (Touchstone, 2001); David Talbot, *Brothers: The Hidden History of the Kennedy Years* (Free Press, 2007).

On the SDS national convention of June 1968, see Sale, *SDS,* 440–41, 455–72; Greg Calvert and Carol Neiman, *A Disrupted History: The New Left and the New Capitalism* (Random House, 1971), 87–88, 140–41; Weinstein, *Ambiguous Legacy,* 147–51.

On Cornell vice president Mark Barlow's assessment of Cornell SDS following the summer of 1968, see memorandum from Mark Barlow Jr. to the President (James Perkins) re "The Current Status of SDS," Oct. 17, 1968, in the James Perkins Papers, #3/10/1022, box 24, folder 25, Rare and Manuscript Collections, Cornell University Library.

On the formation of the Labor Committee and the action faction within Cornell SDS: e-mails from Felix Kramer, Peter Agree, Tony Fels, and Joe Kelly, to the author, April and May 2011 (in the author's possession); also, Sale, *SDS*, 482n, 514.

On the role of women in the draft resistance movement, see Marian Mollin, *Radical Pacifism in Modern America: Egalitarianism and Protest* (University of Pennsylvania Press, 2006), 151–81; Garvy, *Rebels*, 86; Sara Evans, *Personal Politics: The Roots of Women's Liberation in the Civil Rights Movement and the New Left* (Alfred A. Knopf, 1979), 179–85; Foley, *Confronting the War Machine*, 180–91.

On the rise of the women's liberation movement and the critique of male sexism within SDS and SNCC, see Evans, *Personal Politics*, and Ruth Rosen, *The World Split Open: How the Modern Women's Movement Changed America* (Penguin Books, 2001), 95–140; also, e-mails from Mimi Keck, Susan Rutberg, and Ellen Solomon Chandler, to the author, April and May 2011 (in the author's possession).

On the August 1968 demonstrations at the Democratic National Convention, see Wells, *War Within*, 276–85; Isserman and Kazin, *America Divided*, 230–35; Kurlansky, *Year That Rocked the World*, 269–86; Sale, *SDS*, 473–77; James Miller, *Democracy Is in the Streets*, 295–313; Gitlin, *Sixties*, 320–36; Carl Oglesby, *Ravens in the Storm: A Personal History of the 1960s Antiwar Movement* (Scribner, 2008), 187–98; Jules Witcover, *The Year the Dream Died: Revisiting 1968 in America* (Warner Books, 1997), 308–45.

On the reaction of American antiwar leaders to the Soviet invasion of Czechoslovakia, see Kurlansky, *Year That Rocked the World*, 276–77; Gitlin, *Sixties*, 280–81, 325, 331.

On the 1968 meeting between members of the American antiwar movement with representatives from the NLF and North Vietnam, see Bruce Dancis, "American Radicals Meet Vietnamese Revolutionaries," *First Issue*, Sept. 27, 1968; Elinor Langer, "Notes for Next Time: A Memoir of the 1960s," in R. David Myers, *Toward a History of the New Left: Essays from within the Movement* (Carlson Publishing, 1989), 91–93 (originally published in *Working Papers for a New Society*, Fall 1973); Garvy, *Rebels*, 198–201.

11. Trials and Tribulations

On the U.S. Supreme Court's ruling on the law banning the destruction of draft cards, see Fred Graham, "High Court Backs Ban on Burning of Draft Cards," *New York Times*, May 28, 1968.

On the author's trial for tearing up his draft card, see Michael Rosenbaum, "Dancis Trial to Begin Tomorrow," *Cornell Daily Sun*, Sept. 17, 1968; Daniel M. Taubman, "Dancis Found Guilty," *Cornell Daily Sun*, Sept. 19, 1968; Dan Finlay, "Two Resisters," *Dateline: Ithaca*, Sept. 26, 1968 (reprinted in *Year One*, no. 3, December 1969 / January 1970, 48–52); Polner and O'Grady, *Disarmed and Dangerous*, 155.

On surveys about the political attitudes of American youth in 1968, see Sale, *SDS*, 457, 478–81, 713–15n; Gitlin, *Sixties*, 344–45; Daniel Yankelovich Inc., *The Changing Values on Campus: Political and Personal Attitudes of Today's College Students* (an expanded version of Yankelovich's survey for *Fortune*) (Washington Square Press / Pocket Books), 1972.

On Mark Barlow's assessment of Cornell SDS following the summer of 1968, see memorandum from Mark Barlow Jr. to the President (James Perkins) on "The Current Status of SDS," Oct. 17, 1968, in the James Perkins Papers, #3/10/1022, box 24, folder 25, Rare and Manuscript Collections, Cornell University Library.

On the Cornell board of trustees' announcement that they would not change university investment policies, see Edward Zuckerman, "Trustees Turn Down Demands to Sell S. Africa Bank Stock," *Cornell Daily Sun*, Sept. 12, 1968.

On the multifaceted activities of Cornell SDS during 1968–69, see "SDS Meeting Agenda" (ca. March 1969), in Lawrence F. Kramer Papers, 1966–80, 37-7-2151, folder 39, Cornell SDS—Internal Documents 1969, Rare and Manuscript Collections, Kroch Library, Cornell University Library.

On Cornell SDS's "America Game," see Lance Davidow, "SDS Presents 'America' Game," *Cornell Daily Sun*, Sept. 25, 1968; W. C. Lipke, "Art and Politics: Some Reflections," *First Issue*, Nov. 11, 1968.

On the *First Issue*'s special section on the war in Vietnam, see Douglas Dowd, "A Drop of Blood for a Grain of Rice: Report on Meetings with the Parisian Delegation of North Vietnam," and Dancis, "American Radicals," both in *First Issue*, Sept. 27, 1968.

On the 1968 campaign speeches of Spiro Agnew, see Rick Perlstein, *Nixonland: The Rise of a President and the Fracturing of America* (Scribner, 2008), 343–45, 349, and Sale, *SDS*, 499.

On the trial of the Catonsville Nine, see "Support Father Berrigan: A National Call: Free the Catonsville Nine," *First Issue*, Sept. 27, 1968; Harvey G. Cox Jr., "Tongues of Flame: The Trial of the Catonsville 9," in *Witness of the Berrigans*, ed. Stephen Halpert and Tom Murray (Doubleday, 1972),

19–23; Dowd, *Blues,* 138–41; Polner and O'Grady, *Disarmed and Dangerous,* 202–8; Lance Davidow, "2000 Hear Berrigan at Pre-Trial Rally," *Cornell Daily Sun,* Oct. 4, 1968; Barton Reppert and A. J. Mayer, "2,500 March for Berrigan as Wallace Harangues Crowd," *Cornell Daily Sun,* Oct. 8, 1968; Barton Reppert, "Berrigan Attorneys Plan Court Strategy," *Cornell Daily Sun,* Oct. 8, 1968; A. J. Mayer, "Marches Mark Berrigan Trial: Protest Moves Continue," *Cornell Daily Sun,* Oct. 9, 1968; Barton Reppert, "Defendant Darst Tells Court of Motives for Action," *Cornell Daily Sun,* Oct. 9, 1968; "Fr. Berrigan Guilty," *Cornell Daily Sun,* Oct. 11, 1968; Ellen Kirk, "Catonsville Nine Trial Re-appraised by Panel," *Cornell Daily Sun,* Oct. 25, 1968.

On the October 1968 SDS National Council meeting, see Sale, *SDS,* 483–86; also, e-mails from Joe Kelly to the author, Aug. 22, 2011.

On Doug Dowd's nomination for vice president on the Peace and Freedom Party ticket, see John Kifner, "Freedom Party Endorses Candidates," *New York Times,* July 22, 1968; Dowd, *Blues,* 156–58; Wells, *War Within,* 264; Oglesby, *Ravens,* 204–8; "Dowd Stands-In as V.P. Candidate," *Cornell Daily Sun,* Sept. 17, 1968.

On SDS's Election Day 1968 activities, see Bruce Dancis, "On the Stump with the Hump, a Proposal for an Election Program for Cornell SDS" (internal SDS position paper), and Cornell SDS leaflets, "Columbia…and Cornell," "Can't Get No Satisfaction," "Where Do We Stand?" and "Ithaca's Housing Crisis," all in Lawrence F. Kramer Papers, 1966–80, 37–7-2151, folder 39, Cornell SDS—Internal Documents 1969, Rare and Manuscript Collections, Kroch Library, Cornell University Library; partial transcript of Cornell SDS Election Day rally, Nov. 5, 1968, in the Sarah Elbert Papers, 1968–76, Collection #2914, no. 38, Rare and Manuscript Collections, Kroch Library, Cornell University Library; Lance S. Davidow, "Cornell SDS Discusses Election; Protests Staged across Country," *Cornell Daily Sun,* Nov. 6, 1968; Sale, *SDS,* 487–88.

On the introduction of Cornell SDS's housing proposal, see Lance S. Davidow, "Housing Looms as SDS Issue," *Cornell Daily Sun,* Oct. 24, 1968; Tony Fels, "SDS Housing Proposal," *First Issue,* Nov. 11, 1968; Barton Reppert, "SDS Opens Housing Drive," *Cornell Daily Sun,* Nov. 12, 1968; Horowitz and Friedland, *Knowledge Factory,* 265–66.

On the author's sentencing and incarceration, see Finlay, "Two Resisters"; Edward Zuckerman, "Judge Sentences Dancis, Denies Bail," *Cornell Daily Sun,* Nov. 15, 1968; "Student Gets Indefinite Term for Tearing Up Draft Card," *New York Times,* Nov. 15, 1968; "SDSer Gets 6 Years," *New Left Notes,* ca. November 1968, reprinted in Garvy, *Rebels,* 83.

On the author's time in the Onondaga County Jail, see "Release Takes Dancis by Surprise," *Cornell Daily Sun,* Nov. 20, 1968; David M. Stolow, "Dancis Tells of Jail Experience," *Cornell Daily Sun,* Nov. 21, 1968.

On the campaign at Cornell to get the author released on bail, see Fred J. Solowey, "Bruce's Education"; Douglas F. Dowd, "The Fight Continues"; and "After the Trial" (editorial), all in *Cornell Daily Sun,* Nov. 15, 1968; also, Lance S. Davidow, "Petition, Rally Mark Dancis Trial Protest"; Rev. Paul E. Gibbons, "Offender or Defender?"; and "5000 and One" (editorial), all in *Cornell Daily Sun,* Nov. 18; also, Douglas Archibald, "Bruce's Punishment," and "The Wrong Rectal Kick" (editorial), both in *Cornell Daily Sun,* Nov. 20, 1968.

On James Perkins's letter to the U.S. Court of Appeals, see a copy of the letter in "Dancis, Bruce D. Draft card destruction," #3/10/1022, box 28, file 44, James Perkins Papers, Rare and Manuscript Collections, Kroch Library, Cornell University Library; letter from James Perkins to alumnus Oscar M. Fuller of Gaffney, SC, Dec. 20, 1968, in same file.

On the U.S. Court of Appeals' decision to release the author on bail, see Edward Ranzal, "Cornell Rebuked for Court Tactic: 2 Judges Assail President and Students for Pressure," *New York Times,* Nov. 20, 1968; "Appeal Court Releases Dancis, Blasts Perkins, C.U. Students," *Cornell Daily Sun,* Nov. 20, 1968; "Youth Is Released in Draft Card Case," *New York Times,* Nov. 21, 1968; letter from Alan H. Levine (NYCLU staff counsel) to *New York Times* reporter Edward Ranzal, Nov. 26, 1968, in "Dancis, Bruce D. Draft card destruction," #3/10/1022, box 28, file 44, James Perkins Papers, Rare and Manuscript Collections, Kroch Library, Cornell University Library.

On factionalism in SDS nationally during the fall of 1968, see Sale, *SDS,* 487–510; Barber, *Hard Rain Fell,* 148–49; Wilkerson, *Flying Close to the Sun,* 222–27; Gitlin, *Sixties,* 336–40; Wells, *War Within,* 284–86.

On Cornell SDS's "Alternative Fall Weekend," see SDS poster, "Fall Weekend—an Alternative," in Lawrence F. Kramer Papers, 1966–80, 37–7-2151, folder 39, Cornell SDS—Internal Documents 1969, Rare and Manuscript Collections, Kroch Library, Cornell University Library; "Fall Weekend Alternative, Nov. 15, 16—Issues & Celebration," *First Issue,* Nov. 11, 1968.

On the New Left and Cuba, see Larry Kramer and Jim Murray, various articles in special issue of the *First Issue* on Cuba, December 1968; Gitlin, *Sixties,* 274–82; Kurlansky, *Year That Rocked the World,* 158–77.

On the formation of the Ithaca Tenants Union, see Lance Davidow, "SDS Plans Housing, Forms Tenant Union," *Cornell Daily Sun,* Dec. 19, 1968.

On the December 1968 SDS National Council meeting, see Sale, *SDS,* 506–10.

On All Right's arrest, see Bruce Dancis (unsigned), "SDS Member Busted!" *First Issue,* February 1969.

On "Tommy the Traveler," see Ron Rosenbaum, "Run, Tommy, Run! Many Had Him for a Friend, and He Had Them," *Esquire,* July 1971; Gary T. Marx, "Thoughts on a Neglected Category of Social Movement Participant: The Agent Provocateur and the Informant," *American Journal of Sociology* 80, no. 2 (1974); "Hobart College Upset by Police Agent," *New York Times,* June 7, 1970; Anthony Ripley, "Big Man on the Campus: Police Undercover Agent," *New York Times,* March 29, 1971; and "Nation: Police: Tales of Three Cities," *Time,* June 22, 1970.

12. Rebellion and Factionalism in Black and White

On the Afro-American Society and its effort to establish a black studies program at Cornell, see Downs, *Cornell '69,* 46–67, 101–29; Donald, "Cornell: Confrontation," 151–204; Horowitz and Friedland, *Knowledge Factory,* 267–69.

On the Cornell administration's initial responses to SDS's housing proposals, see letter from James A. Perkins to Cornell SDS, Jan. 15, 1969; SDS's reply to Perkins, Jan. 23, 1969; and Tony Fels, "Progress on the Housing Issue," all in the *First Issue,* February 1969.

On the belated discovery that Cornell had made a profit from 1963 to 1973, see Daniel Margulis, "Study Cites Cornell 'Profit': University Made $200 Million in 10 Years, Report Says," *Cornell Daily Sun,* April 26, 1973.

On the negotiations between the Joint Housing Committee and the Cornell administration in February and March 1969, see Barton Reppert, "Ithaca Group Asks Cornell Housing Aids," *Cornell Daily Sun,* Feb. 19, 1969; Lance S. Davidow, "Housing Talks Set; SDS Deadline Nears," *Cornell Daily Sun,* Feb. 25, 1969; Kal Lindenberg, "Perkins to Meet Unit on Housing," "Panel Discusses Community Role in Housing Plan," and "Seznec Committee, CURW Support Housing Proposal," all in *Cornell Daily Sun,* Feb. 27, 1969; Kal Lindenberg, "Perkins Meets JHC on Housing," *Cornell Daily Sun,* March 3, 1969; Lance S. Davidow, "Housing Drive Builds Committees, Plans," *Cornell Daily Sun,* March 17, 1969; "Time to Put Up" (editorial), *Cornell Daily Sun,* March 19, 1969; Ronni L. Mann, "700 Persons Stage Protest for Day Hall Housing Action," and Michael Horowitz, "University Meets with JHC; Progress Made on Issues," both in *Cornell Daily Sun,* March 21, 1969.

On President Perkins meeting privately with Cornell SDS members about the South Africa issue: e-mail from Alan Snitow to the author, Feb. 2, 2013, in the author's possession.

On the South African symposium, see Cornell SDS pamphlet, *South Africa Symposium: Directory of Participants and Visitors,* ca. Feb. 1969, in the Alan Snitow Collection; "Symposium to Investigate Problems of South Africa," *Cornell Daily Sun,* Dec. 20, 1968; Ellen Kirk, "Krause Defends Apartheid," and "Not a Bad Start" (editorial), both in *Cornell Daily Sun,* Feb. 27, 1968; Lance S. Davidow, "Africans Criticize S. African Violence, American Interests," Andrew Kreig, "South African Revolution Urged," and E. J. Stevenson, "Panel Says South African Whites Carry Blame for Race Problems," all in *Cornell Daily Sun,* Feb. 28, 1968.

On Danny Schecter and the Africa Research Group, see Danny Schecter, *The More You Watch the Less You Know* (Seven Stories Press, 1997), 255, 271–72.

On the confrontation with President Perkins on the final evening of the South Africa symposium, see "Perkins Pulled from Podium after Outlining Stock Policy," *Ithaca Journal,* March 1, 1969; Mark Katz and Richard Neubauer, "Perkins Harassed on Stage during Lowenstein Lecture," "Friday Night…Ugly and Stupid" (editorial), Paul A. Rahe Jr., "Southern Africa Symposium," and Edward Whitfield and the Afro-American Society, "AAS Statement," all in *Cornell Daily Sun,* March 3, 1969; John Marcham (unsigned), "An Unhappy Month on the Hill," *Cornell Alumni News,* May 1969; Downs, *Cornell '69,* 131–35; Cornell SDS leaflet, "Were You at Statler Friday Nite?" in the Alan Snitow collection.

On the belated discovery that Cornell had sold its stock in banks that lent money to South Africa, see Stan Chess, "Cornell's Bank Stocks Already Sold, a Red-Faced Administration Learns," and Ed Zuckerman, "Perkins Learns of Sale: 'I'm Kicking Myself,'" both in *Cornell Daily Sun,* March 10, 1969.

On the Cornell SDS and AAS confrontation with recruiters from Chase Manhattan Bank, see Cornell SDS leaflet, "Cornell Has a Friend at Chase Manhattan... No Recruiting for Racism!" March 10, 1969, in Alan Snitow Collection; Paul A. Rahe Jr. and Richard M. Warshauer, "Bank Recruiters Chased," and "Holier Than Thou" (editorial), both in *Cornell Daily Sun,* March 11, 1969; Downs, *Cornell '69,* 135–37; memorandum from Mark Barlow Jr. to the President (Perkins), no title, April 8, 1969, in the James Perkins Papers, #3/10/1022, box 33, Rare and Manuscript Collections, Cornell University Library; also, e-mail from Joe Kelly to the author, Oct. 18, 2011.

On the reaction of the Cornell administration and faculty following the Statler and Malott Hall incidents, see Barton Reppert, "Faculty Backs Judiciary," *Cornell Daily Sun,* March 13, 1969; John Marcham, "SDS Tests the University," *Cornell Alumni News,* May 1969; letter from Professor William F. Whyte to President James Perkins, March 10, 1969, and letter from James A. Perkins to Professor Whyte, March 17, 1969, both in the James Perkins Papers, #3/10/1022, box 32, Rare and Manuscript Collections, Cornell University Library; Barlow memo, April 8, 1969; Downs, *Cornell '69,* 135–40; Fisher and Wallenstein, "Open Breeches," 153–55.

On the continuing dispute over punishing six AAS members, see Michael Rosenbaum, "Board Postpones Action," Afro-American Society, "Text of AAS Statement to Board," and "Last Night's Victory" (editorial), all in *Cornell Daily Sun,* March 14, 1969; Downs, *Cornell '69,* 145–55.

On the attack of three students at Cornell, see Richard M. Warshauer, "3 Students Injured in Weekend Attacks," and "Blacks on Trial" (editorial), both in *Cornell Daily Sun,* March 17, 1969; Ed Whitfield, "Black Response," and "Yesterday's Editorial... an Elaboration," both in *Cornell Daily Sun,* March 18, 1969; Downs, *Cornell '69,* 154–55.

On Cornell SDS's decision not to confront military recruiters, see Richard L. Neubauer, "SDS Decides Not to Block Marine Recruiting Officers," *Cornell Daily Sun,* March 25, 1969; Richard L. Neubauer, "TCPA Protests Army Recruiters," *Cornell Daily Sun,* March 26, 1969.

On the FCSA upholding the university's judiciary system, see Michael Rosenbaum, "FCSA Backs Judicial System Power to Judge Afro Case" and "FCSA Report on the Judiciary," both in *Cornell Daily Sun,* March 26, 1969; Chandler Morse, "Judging Political Action," *Cornell Daily Sun,* April 15, 1969; Richard M. Warshauer, "AAS Blasts FCSA Statement; Judiciary Contradiction Shown," and "AAS Statement," both in *Cornell Daily Sun,* April 16, 1969; Downs, *Cornell '69,* 155–59.

On the SDS National Council meeting in Austin, see Sale, *SDS,* 513–17.

On the FBI's response to the arrest of Cornell SDSers in Texas, see William Ringle, "1967 FBI Surveillance at CU Revealed," *Ithaca Journal,* Nov. 26, 1977; also, e-mails from Joe Kelly to the author, Oct. 28 and 29, 2011.

On SDS's investigative report on the Cornell board of trustees, see Research Committee of Cornell Students for a Democratic Society, *Manchild in the Corporate State: Cornell's Ruling Elite and the National Economy* (Ithaca, NY: Glad Day Press, April 1969); James G. Condon, "Cornell Trustees' Power Studied in SDS Booklet," *Cornell Daily Sun,* April 7, 1969; "Wayward Masters" (editorial), *Cornell Daily Sun,* April 8, 1969.

On the negotiations between the JHC and the board of trustees in April 1969, see Barton Reppert, "Trustees Meet in New York to Discuss JHC, Afro Center," *Cornell Daily Sun,* April 10, 1969; Richard M. Warshauer, "Trustees Meet Some JHC Demands: JHC Dubs Loan-Land Offer 'Far Short of Acceptable,'" "Statement on Housing by Board of Trustees," "Joint Housing Committee Reply," and "Not Enough" (editorial), all in *Cornell Daily Sun,* April 14, 1969.

On SDS demonstrations in support of the JHC proposals, see Richard M. Warshauer, "Torchlighters Support JHC," *Cornell Daily Sun,* April 10, 1969; Fisher and Wallenstein, "Open Breeches," 172–73.

On the tentative agreement between the board of trustees and the JHC, see Aric J. Press, "Trustees' Statement 'Clarified' in Memo," "Housing Memorandum" from Robert W. Purcell, Chairman, Board of Trustees to Joint Housing Committee," and "Belated Pledge" (editorial), all in *Cornell Daily Sun,* April 15, 1969; Kal Lindenberg, "JHC States Satisfaction with Cornell 'Good Faith,'" *Cornell Daily Sun,* April 16, 1969; Fisher and Wallenstein, "Open Breeches," 173–75.

13. Brinksmanship, or Cornell on the Brink

On the events that immediately preceded the seizure of the Straight, see Richard M. Warshauer and Mark D. Goldman, "Board Reprimands 3 Blacks, Gives No Penalties to Two," *Cornell Daily Sun,* April 18, 1969; Downs, *Cornell '69,* 145–70; Fisher and Wallenstein, "Open Breeches," 175–87, 198–223.

On the occupation of the Straight by the AAS, see extra edition of the *Cornell Daily Sun*, April 20, 1969, and regular edition of April 21, 1969; Downs, *Cornell '69*, 165–204; Fisher and Wallenstein, "Open Breeches," 224–308.

On SDS support for the AAS, see Aric Press, "SDS Readies Rally, Still Guarding WSH," *Cornell Daily Sun* extra edition, April 20, 1969; Roberta Gordon, "SDS Rally to Support Black Move," *Cornell Daily Sun*, April 21, 1969; Downs, *Cornell '69*, 166–67, 173–91, 202–8; Fisher and Wallenstein, "Open Breeches," 249–50, 260, 265–65A, 276–78, 284–88, 307–8; Cornell SDS leaflet, "There Have Been Lots of Rumors Floating around Campus—Here Are the Facts," undated (probably April 21, 1969), in the Alan Snitow collection.

On members of Delta Upsilon attempting to retake the Straight, see Dale Lashnits, "The Scene, Dialogue Outside 'Occupied' Willard Straight" and "Chronology of Events," both in *Ithaca Journal*, April 21, 1969; Richard Warshauer, "White Attempt to Break in Sparks Dispute over Cops," *Cornell Daily Sun* extra edition, April 20, 1969; Downs, *Cornell '69*, 177–81; Fisher and Wallenstein, "Open Breeches," 260–76.

On the agreement that ended the Straight occupation and the famous photograph of armed black students leaving the building, see Richard Warshauer, "Black Students Leave Straight as C.U. Accedes to Demands," *Cornell Daily Sun*, April 21, 1969; Downs, *Cornell '69*, 192–210; Fisher and Wallenstein, "Open Breeches," 291–300, 308–57.

On negative press coverage of the agreement ending the Straight occupation, see John Kifner, "Armed Negroes End Seizure; Cornell Yields," *New York Times*, April 21, 1969; Downs, *Cornell '69*, 211; Fisher and Wallenstein, "Open Breeches," 403–4.

On President Perkins's decree outlawing "disruptive demonstrations" at Cornell, see Barton Reppert, "Perkins Takes Action for Campus Security," *Cornell Daily Sun*, April 22, 1969; Downs, *Cornell '69*, 212–14; Fisher and Wallenstein, "Open Breeches," 364–65.

On the schism among Cornell faculty members and between the faculty and Perkins's administration, see Eric Weiss and Aric Press, "Faculty Meeting Set for Bailey; Members Split" and "Text of the Agreement," both in *Cornell Daily Sun*, April 21, 1969; Downs, *Cornell '69*, 208–9, 214–20, 231–38; Fisher and Wallenstein, "Open Breeches," 6–14, 353–97.

On President Perkins's "convocation," see Barton Reppert, "Perkins Takes Action for Campus Security," *Cornell Daily Sun*, April 22, 1969; Downs, *Cornell '69*, 220–22; Fisher and Wallenstein, "Open Breeches," 369–74.

On the Cornell faculty's vote to maintain judicial punishments against AAS members, see Betty Mills and Richard Warshauer, "Faculty Takes Controversial Stand," and Ed Zuckerman, "Wrong Road," both in *Cornell Daily Sun*, April 22, 1969; Downs, *Cornell '69*, 222–27; Fisher and Wallenstein, "Open Breeches," 376–97.

On SDS and the AAS's reaction to the faculty vote, see Richard Neubauer, "SDS Scores Profs, Gives AAS Support," *Cornell Daily Sun*, April 22, 1969; Downs, *Cornell '69*, 227–30, 234–35; Fisher and Wallenstein, "Open Breeches," 397–401, 413–14.

On AAS leader Tom Jones's inflammatory radio interview, see Downs, *Cornell '69*, 238–42; Fisher and Wallenstein, "Open Breeches," 418–24.

On the student takeover of Barton Hall, see Aric Press and Richard Neubauer, "2,000 Stay All Night in Barton," *Cornell Daily Sun*, April 23, 1969; Downs, *Cornell '69*, 242–54, 260–63; Fisher and Wallenstein, "Open Breeches," 430–46; Horowitz and Friedland, *Knowledge Factory*, 276–77.

On the origins of the Barton Hall community, see Eric Weiss, "Discussion Planned for Today," and Daniel M. Taubman, "The Barton Experience: Students Find Life Different," both in *Cornell Daily Sun*, April 24, 1969; Downs, *Cornell '69*, 249–53; Fisher and Wallenstein, "Open Breeches," 446–53.

On the critics of the Barton Hall community, see Marion O'Brien, "'The Body' Comes into Being," *Cornell Alumni News*, June 1969; Fisher and Wallenstein, "Open Breeches," 447–48; Cushing Strout, "A Personal Narrative of a Rude Awakening," in Strout and Grossvogel, *Divided We Stand*, 45–74; Downs, *Cornell '69*, 260–66.

On the alleged existence of a "revolutionary situation" at Cornell, see Downs, *Cornell '69*, 214, 244–45, Fisher and Wallenstein, "Open Breeches," 373.

On the stance of the Concerned Faculty before the crucial faculty meeting, see Fisher and Wallenstein, "Open Breeches," 450.

On the Cornell faculty meeting that nullified the earlier punishments against AAS members, see Betty Mills, "Faculty Drops Judicial Actions; Sindler Resigns from University," *Cornell Daily Sun*, April 24, 1969; Downs, *Cornell '69*, 255–60; Fisher and Wallenstein, "Open Breeches," 455–61, 466–77; Horowitz and Friedland, *Knowledge Factory*, 277–79.

On the Barton Hall "victory" celebration following the faculty reversal, see Richard Neubauer, "Perkins Cheered by Barton Throng after Faculty Drops Penalties," *Cornell Daily Sun,* April 24, 1969; Downs, *Cornell '69,* 260–63; Fisher and Wallenstein, "Open Breeches," 462–66.

On the Barton Hall community's turn toward "restructuring the university" and the creation of a Constituent Assembly, see Gene Resnick, "Council Urges Cornell Reforms," and Ronni Mann and Richard Neubauer, "5,000 Attend Barton Teach-In on Racism," both in *Cornell Daily Sun,* April 25, 1969; Richard Neubauer, "Convocations Offer University Reforms," and Betty Mills, "Faculty Debate Assembly Idea," both in *Cornell Daily Sun,* April 28, 1969; Betty Mills, "Profs View Proposals for Provisional Body," *Cornell Daily Sun,* April 29, 1969; Betty Mills, "Faculty Proposes New Assembly, Suggests Self-Study Committee," *Cornell Daily Sun,* May 5, 1969; Downs, *Cornell '69,* 269–72; Fisher and Wallenstein, "Open Breeches," 471–75, 492–501, 522–24, 554–59.

On faculty criticism of the Barton Hall community, see Betty Mills, Pat Samuels, and Daniel Taubman, "Berns Announces Resignation from Cornell; 15 Profs Halt Instruction, Petition President," *Cornell Daily Sun,* April 25, 1969; Ronni Mann, "5,000 Hear Professors Score 'Loss of Freedom,'" *Cornell Daily Sun,* April 28, 1969; Homer Bigart, "Cornell Stance and Future Are Debated Bitterly," *New York Times,* April 29, 1969; Walter Berns and Allan Sindler, "Academic Freedom Abridged," *Cornell Daily Sun,* May 2, 1969; Downs, *Cornell '69,* 263–75, 284–87, 289–96; Fisher and Wallenstein, "Open Breeches," 466d–71, 475–76, 483–88, 502–3, 527–34.

On the New York State Legislature's passage of legislation following the events at Cornell, see "Assembly Votes Gun Ban for N.Y. State Campuses," *Cornell Daily Sun,* April 29, 1969; Fisher and Wallenstein, "Open Breeches," 519.

On Homer Bigart's coverage of the Cornell events for the *New York Times,* see Downs, *Cornell '69,* 281–84; Fisher and Wallenstein, "Open Breeches," 466b–66c, 628. The most pertinent *Times* articles by Bigart were "Peaceful Sit-In at Cornell Ends New Seizure Threat," April 23; "Faculty Revolt Upsets Cornell—Charges of Sellout Made," April 25; "Perkins Denounces Black Separatism—Concedes," April 28; "Cornell Stance and Future Are Debated Bitterly," April 29; "Cornell Outlaws 'Terror' Tactics," May 2; and "R.O.T.C. Taunted by Cornell S.D.S.," May 3, 1969.

On Tom Wicker's column on the Cornell crisis, see Tom Wicker, "Humanity vs. Principle at Cornell," *New York Times,* April 27, 1969.

On other negative media coverage of the April and May '69 events at Cornell, see Downs, *Cornell '69,* 281; Fisher and Wallenstein, "Open Breeches," 565–69, which reprints Evans and Novak's two columns about Cornell.

On Cornell SDS's open admissions campaign: SDS Research Committee position paper, "The University in Context," ca. May 1969, in the author's possession; also see Fisher and Wallenstein, "Open Breeches," 490–91; Aric Press, "SDS Holds Rally Today, Asks Open Admissions," *Cornell Daily Sun,* April 29, 1969; Michael Horowitz, "SDS Rallies for Open Admissions," and "Class Hoax" (editorial), both in *Cornell Daily Sun,* April 30, 1969.

On Cornell SDS's "Free Huey" rally, see Michael Horowitz, "200 Rally for Huey's Bail; BLF, SDS Laud Panther," *Cornell Daily Sun,* May 2, 1969.

On Cornell SDS's anti-ROTC demonstrations and the arrest of the May Day Ten, see Richard Warshauer, "SDS Protest ROTC; Paint Barton Gun," *Cornell Daily Sun,* May 2, 1969; Richard Warshauer, "Barton Demonstrators Booked for Trespass," and "Lots of Laughs" (editorial), both in *Cornell Daily Sun,* May 5, 1969; Richard Warshauer, "May Day Protesters Arraigned," *Cornell Daily Sun,* May 6, 1969; Aric Press, "Perkins Rejects ROTC Abolition," *Cornell Daily Sun,* May 8, 1969; Mark Goldman and Richard Neubauer, "No Action Vote Taken by SDS," *Cornell Daily Sun,* May 9, 1969.

On the trial of the May Day Ten, see Eric Weiss, "Three Face Hearing on Trespass Charge," *Cornell Daily Sun,* Sept. 23, 1969; Phil Benedict, "Corson Takes Stand in May Day 10 Trial," *Cornell Daily Sun,* Sept. 29, 1969; E. J. Stevenson and Phil Benedict, "Perkins Testifies in Trial of May Day 10," *Cornell Daily Sun,* Sept. 30, 1969; Richard Neubauer, "Hearings End in May Day Trial," *Cornell Daily Sun,* Oct. 1, 1969; Richard Neubauer, "Case of May Day 3 Dropped; Court Cites Lack of Evidence," *Cornell Daily Sun,* Dec. 12, 1969; "Clynes Dismisses Charges against 3 of 'May Day 10,'" *Cornell Daily Sun,* Dec. 19, 1969; Fisher and Wallenstein, "Open Breeches," 535–48c.

On the indictment of sixteen black students for the Straight takeover, see Richard Warshauer, "Blacks Charged with Trespass; 16 Arraigned," *Cornell Daily Sun,* May 16, 1969; "Three Plead Guilty in Straight Takeover," *Cornell Daily Sun,* Sept. 9, 1970; Downs, *Cornell '69,* 296.

On President Nixon's call for a draft lottery, see Robert B. Semple Jr., "Nixon Asks Draft Lottery with 19-Year-Olds First; Orders Deferment Study," *New York Times,* May 14, 1969; "Nixon Asks Draft Lottery System," *Cornell Daily Sun,* May 14, 1969.

On the denial of the author's appeal and his last interview before starting prison term, see "High Court Denies Appeal," *Cornell Daily Sun*, May 7, 1969; Michael Rosenbaum, "Dancis in Ky. Prison," *Cornell Daily Sun*, June 2, 1969.

14. Safety and Survival in My New Kentucky Home

General Sources for the Prison Chapters

Some of the material in the chapters about my prison term in Ashland, Kentucky, has been adapted from "Notes from an Ex-con," an article I wrote for the *Cornell Alumni News* magazine (July 1971) several months after my release from prison. The statistics cited in that article came from a fact sheet on Ashland I obtained from a fellow inmate who worked as a clerk in the prison's administrative office. I smuggled it out of prison, along with a diary I wrote during my stay in detention. I was able to refer to both these documents while writing the *Alumni News* article. Unfortunately, they are no longer in my possession forty years later.

In the mid-1970s I obtained more than five hundred pages from my Federal Bureau of Prisons file through the Freedom of Information Act. Among the useful documents are my caseworker's "Analysis" and "Parole Progress" reports; statements by prison guards about my alleged involvement in a "conspiracy to riot"; a list of all my visitors during nineteen months in Ashland; and my application to attend the University of California at Santa Cruz once I was released on parole.

On the Bureau of Prisons' policy of assigning East Coast draft resisters to prisons nearest their hometowns, see Foley, *Confronting the War Machine*, 331–32.

On sexual violence against draft resisters in federal prisons, see Gaylin, *In the Service of Their Country*, and Foley, *Confronting the War Machine*, 331–34.

On Bayard Rustin's imprisonment in Ashland during World War II, see John D'Emilio, *Lost Prophet: The Life and Times of Bayard Rustin* (Free Press, 2003), 73–160, and Daniel Levine, *Bayard Rustin and the Civil Rights Movement* (Rutgers University Press, 2000), 41–43.

On Dalton Trumbo's imprisonment in Ashland in 1950–51, see Trumbo's collection of letters, *Additional Dialogue: Letters of Dalton Trumbo, 1942–1962*, ed. Helen Manfull (Bantam Books, 1972), 141–204, and Bruce Cook, *Dalton Trumbo* (Charles Scribner's Sons, 1977), 208–21.

On John Howard Lawson's imprisonment in Ashland, see Gerald Horne, *The Final Victim of the Blacklist: John Howard Lawson, Dean of the Hollywood Ten* (University of California Press, 2006), 202–21.

On the discrepancy between judges' wishes and Bureau of Prisons policy regarding draft resisters, and on the unwritten BOP policy barring resisters from obtaining study releases, see Gaylin, *In the Service of Their Country*, 332–42.

15. A Typical Day in Prison, and a Few That Weren't

Although I carried on an active correspondence with friends and my parents during my imprisonment, few of my letters were saved. Two exceptions were letters I wrote to Father Daniel Berrigan, who began his own prison term fifteen months after mine. The letters, dated Nov. 15, 1969, and March 8, 1970, are in the Berrigan Collection—4602, box 121 Outgoing Correspondence / Other Authors / D-Dd, Division of Rare and Manuscript Collections, Kroch Library, Cornell University Library.

On Dalton Trumbo's description of life in Ashland, see Trumbo, *Additional Dialogue*, 169.

On the deleterious effect of prison on draft resisters, see Gaylin, *In the Service of Their Country*, 84; Baskir and Strauss, *Chance and Circumstance*, 102–8.

On "You Don't Need a Weatherman to Know Which Way the Wind Blows," see Harold Jacobs, ed., *Weatherman* (Ramparts Press, 1970), 51–90.

16. Politics in Prison, or Keeping Up with the Outside World

On Staughton Lynd's history of the draft resistance movement, see Staughton Lynd, "The Movement: A New Beginning," *Liberation*, May 1969, reprinted in Goodman, *Movement toward a New America*, 488–97.

On Frank Femia's political views, see a letter he wrote to author Francine du Plessix Gray in response to her article "The Ultra-Resistance," in the *New York Review of Books*, Sept. 25, 1969; Gray then shared Frank's letter, "Dear Francine," with *NYRB*'s readers, Nov. 20, 1969; both reprinted in *Trials of the Resistance* (New York Review Books / Vintage Books, 1970), 125–67.

On the invasion of Cambodia and the student strikes that erupted in its wake, see Wells, *War Within*, 417–37.

On the SDS split at the June 1969 national convention, see Sale, *SDS*, 557–99; also, Andrew Kopkind, "The Real SDS Stands Up"; Karen Ashley, Bill Ayers, Bernardine Dohrn, John Jacobs, Jeff Jones, Gerry Long, Howie Machtinger, Jim Mellen, Terry Robbins, Mark Rudd, and Steve Tappis, "You Don't Need a Weatherman to Know Which Way the Wind Blows"; James Weinstein, "Weatherman: A Lot of Thunder but a Short Reign"; and Todd Gitlin, "New Left: Old Traps," all reprinted in Jacobs, *Weatherman;* Carl Oglesby, "Notes on a Decade Ready for the Dustbin," *Liberation,* Aug.–Sept. 1969, reprinted in Myers, *Toward a History of the New Left,* 21–48.

18. Did We End the War? Did Draft Resistance Matter?

On Chip Marshall's 1980 quote about Vietnam, see David Aikman, "In Seattle: Up from Revolution," *Time,* April 14, 1980.

On the total number of American and Vietnamese casualties during the war, see Nick Turse, *Kill Anything That Moves: The Real American War in Vietnam* (Metropolitan Books, 2013), 12–13.

On the economic and political conditions facing Vietnam upon its reunification in 1975, see Young, *Vietnam Wars,* 279–315; Dave Dellinger, *Vietnam Revisited: Covert Action to Invasion to Reconstruction* (South End Press, 1986), 85–220; and Neil L. Jamieson, *Understanding Vietnam* (University of California Press, 1995), 357–71.

On the conflict in the late 1970s between Vietnam and Cambodia's Khmer Rouge, and between Vietnam and China, see Young, *Vietnam Wars,* 305–13; Dellinger, *Vietnam Revisited,* 162–64.

On changes in Vietnam since the mid-1980s, see Jamieson, *Understanding Vietnam,* 371–74; Amnesty International, *Annual Report 2012,* "Viet Nam," www.amnesty.org/en/region/viet-nam/report-2012; Human Rights Watch, *World Report 2012,* "Vietnam," www.hrw.org/world-report-2012/world-report-2012-vietnam.

On the antiwar stance of former Green Beret and Vietnam veteran Donald Duncan, see Duncan, "The Whole Thing Was a Lie," *Ramparts,* February 1966.

On the increased antiwar activity of Vietnam veterans beginning in 1971, see Young, *Vietnam Wars,* 255–59; Gerald Nicosia, *Home to War: A History of the Vietnam Veterans' Movement* (Three Rivers Press, 2001), 84–154; David Cortright, *Soldiers in Revolt: GI Resistance during the Vietnam War* (Haymarket Books, 2005; originally published in 1975), 80–91.

On the effectiveness of the American antiwar movement, see Wells, *War Within,* 579–82; Paul Joseph, "Direct and Indirect Effects of the Movement against the Vietnam War," in *The Vietnam War: Vietnamese and American Perspectives,* ed. Jayne Werner and Luu Doan Huynh (M. E. Sharpe, 1993), 165–84; Joseph, *Cracks in the Empire,* 153–79; Todd Gitlin, "The Achievement of the Anti-War Movement," in Myers, *Toward a History of the New Left,* 183–94; and Hall, *Rethinking,* 137–50.

On Eric Foner's assessment of the American abolitionist movement, see Foner, *The Fiery Trial: Abraham Lincoln and American Slavery* (W. W. Norton, 2010), 20.

On former secretary of defense Robert McNamara's turn against the war, see Harris, *Our War,* 124–29.

On New Leftists not viewing North Vietnam, Cuba, or China as models for American society, see Kazin, *American Dreamers,* 212.

On the selective prosecution of draft resisters by local attorney generals, see Wells, *War Within,* 131–32, 234–37, 268–70.

On the draft resistance movement's impact on the U.S. legal system, see Baskir and Strauss, *Chance and Circumstance,* 62–90.

On the draft resistance movement's impact on national draft policy, see Foley, *Confronting the War Machine,* 344–48.

On Tom Wells's assessment of the draft resistance movement, see his *War Within,* 265–70.

On the impact of the author's act of draft resistance on others: Judith Fuchs Jacobson, e-mail to the author, June 6, 2011, in the author's possession.

On the early twentieth-century socialist-feminism of Mary White Ovington, see Mary White Ovington, "Socialism and the Feminist Movement," *New Review,* March 1914, 145, quoted in Bruce Dancis, "Socialism and Women in the United States, 1900–1917," *Socialist Revolution,* January–March 1976.

Index